The Battle
and the Backlash
The Child Sexual Abuse War

The Battle
and the Backlash
The Child Sexual Abuse War

by

DAVID HECHLER

Lexington Books

D.C. Heath and Company • Lexington, Massachusetts • Toronto

Library of Congress Cataloging-in-Publication Data

Hechler, David.
The battle and the backlash.

Includes bibliographical references and index.
1. Child molesting—United States.   2. Sexually
abused children—United States.   I. Title.
HQ72.U53H38   1988   362.7′044   86–45633
ISBN 0–669–14097–X (alk. paper)

Published simultaneously in Canada
Printed in the United States of America
International Standard Book Number: 0–669–14097–X
Library of Congress Catalog Card Number: 86–45633

The paper used in this publication meets
the minimum requirements of American National Standard
for Information Sciences—Permanence of Paper
for Printed Library Materials, ANSI Z39.48-1984.
♾️™

ISBN 0-669-14097-X

88 89 90 91 8 7 6 5 4 3 2 1

To my family, related and not, for their support.
Would that every child were so blessed.

Contents

II
The Backlash

III
Conclusions, Solutions, and Future Directions

Acknowledgments

T HANKS to all those who took time out of their lives to be interviewed—whether once or many times, for a few minutes or many hours. Some provided seemingly insignificant information; others spoke about the most painful experiences of their lives. Some will see the results of their contributions; others will never even know what theirs were. I am indebted to them all.

I am also grateful to teachers who gave me support, encouragement, and knowledge over the years: Morris Parslow, Frances Tidey, Roland Miller, and Melvin Mencher.

Introduction

I N RECENT years there have been a number of highly publicized child sexual abuse cases that have drawn national attention and increasing controversy. The most discussed have been those involving many young children allegedly abused by groups of adults for long periods—sometimes years. The twists and turns of these cases have, alternately, startled, shocked, and angered observers, though for different reasons. Some thought that the defendants charged were permitted to manipulate the criminal justice system to their advantage, abusing the process as they had once (allegedly) abused the children. Others claimed that an atmosphere of hysteria had led police and child protective investigators to collect suspects about as selectively as Joe McCarthy uncloaked "Communists."

The most notorious of these cases, those alleging mass molestation in Jordan, Minnesota, and at the McMartin Preschool (in California), are even now so disturbing and puzzling that they tend to obscure the issues that arise in the more "typical" cases. And they have utterly polarized observers. As one professional in this field put it, "People outside of the field use these cases as examples of what didn't happen. People in the field use them as examples of what did."[1] Amid all the shouting, one tends to forget that the vast majority of sexual abuse in this country does not involve sex rings and large groups of children. The problems these larger cases present to investigators, prosecutors, and defendants may have little in common with those involving a single child and perpetrator.

This is not to say that the high-profile cases are unimportant or uninteresting. Far from it. They merit books of their own—and will no doubt get them, as one mass molestation case already has.[2] But this book, while periodically referring to some of those cases (and examining Jordan at some length in chapter 6), will focus primarily on issues that affect the majority of cases. What are some of these issues? The denial and minimization of child sexual abuse. The difficulty of prosecuting abusers. The legitimate rights of defendants. The debate between those who argue that children never lie and those who claim that children have been "brainwashed" by investigators. The proper role of experts. False accusations in divorce and custody proceedings. The potential of civil lawsuits to deter abuse and bring those responsible to account. Therapy for offenders and victims. The role of the media.

Clearly, all of these issues are relevant to the headline cases. But they also apply to many more. In an effort to report on the issues from the front lines, where the battles are being waged, literally hundreds of interviews were conducted with sources that included convicted child molesters, judges, social workers, cops, therapists, victims, parents of victims, prosecutors, defense attorneys, physicians, and assorted critics of the system.

In addition to the chapters that focus on various aspects of the controversy, at the end of the book are excerpts from interviews with five individuals who have strong and divergent opinions on the issues. They range from an incest survivor to a spokesman for the North American Man/Boy Love Association. There are also chapters that consist of case studies in which individual cases were investigated. They were chosen because they illustrate with particular clarity— and poignancy—some of the myriad problems one finds in this area. These were not the headline-makers, though. Some of these stories never even made the newspapers. They were cases that "fell between the cracks."

By the time you finish this book, you will understand why.

I
The Battle

1

The Battle for Acceptance

N OT much in the world of child sexual abuse is clear-cut. One expert says "X." Many more can be found (some would say "paid") to say just the opposite. Some argue that child molesters are sick; others say they are evil. They battle over whether the criminal justice system favors victims or defendants. And they war over how children who were allegedly abused should be interviewed.

But even the very battle lines are not clear-cut. Some "child advocates" think prosecution of an offender does more damage to a child victim than good; some think it empowers the child and demonstrates society's support. Some critics of the system would like to see children testify in open court; others would prefer to see them testify in a less intimidating setting from which their testimony is transmitted via closed circuit television. "Child advocates" frequently criticize the system, and most critics of the system claim they are "child advocates."

But one thing is clear: there *is* a war. There are those who feel that the country is suffering from an epidemic of child sexual abuse and those who feel that there is an epidemic all right, but not of sex abuse—of "sex accuse," as some have disparagingly called it. The pendulum has swung too far, they say, and what we see now is a blizzard of false accusations. In response they are trying to winch the pendulum back. (See the advertisement on page 4 for an example of the salvos that have been fired.)

From Battered to Molested

Debates about child sexual abuse are nothing new. In the past, however, they were not nearly so public. The increased publicity

Note: This advertisement was published in various southern California newspapers in the summer of 1985.

undoubtedly owes a large debt to the growth during the 1970s and early 1980s of two forerunners of what might be called the "child advocacy movement." They were the women's and the victims' rights movements, and many of today's child advocates were active in one or both.

The clearest connection among the three movements centers on the way rape cases are investigated and prosecuted. Feminists and victim advocates raised concerns in the 1970s that rape victims often felt themselves "on trial" when interrogated by police and when questioned in courts by defense attorneys seeking to impugn their morals and character in order to undermine their credibility as witnesses. Their largely successful efforts to educate the public and change the way to the criminal justice system handles rape cases led them ultimately to focus on how the same system treats the most defenseless sex crimes victims of all: children.

That movement dovetailed with the effort, championed by C. Henry Kempe and his colleagues in the early 1960s, to better identify and protect children who were physically maltreated. The acceptance by the medical profession and courts alike of the "battered child syndrome" went a long way toward protecting children from abuse, as did laws passed in the 1970s in virtually all states requiring a variety of professionals, including teachers, doctors, and social workers, to report any suspicion of child abuse—including sexual abuse—to state authorities.

Once physical abuse was recognized as a serious problem, it was probably inevitable that sexual abuse would also receive attention. For years child sexual abuse was believed to be rare in this country. And for years the subject was rarely discussed in the media—and little understood by the public. Many believed sexual abuse allegations were the product of children's fantasies. Some still do.

But the sexual revolution brought a new candor. Ancient taboos were questioned. Articles were written defending the practice of incest. The North American Man/Boy Love Association (NAMBLA) was founded in 1978 on the belief that children should be sexually liberated and that age of consent laws should be abolished (see appendix). NAMBLA's monthly newsletter (still published regularly) contains letters, articles, poems, and cartoons proclaiming the joys of man/boy love. The media coverage of the group made it harder for skeptics to maintain that such practices do not exist.

The increasing public awareness of child abuse and the increasingly open discussions of sex helped to create the climate for the media's "discovery" of sexual abuse. But nothing could have prepared the public for the onslaught of both cases and coverage. And some were cases the like of which had never been seen before. Day care workers were charged with abusing children in their care—in some instances for years. Cases were uncovered, one by one, around the country. Then, it seemed, "all hell broke loose." Suddenly there were cases everywhere. Teachers, principals, clergymen, camp counselors, choir leaders, and scout masters were charged. In Jordan, Minnesota, twenty-four adults were accused of running a sex ring in which they shared in abusing their own and each other's children. And on and on. Every day in the papers, every night on television, another arrest was made. Or so it seemed.

While some of the coverage was superficial and sensational, there were also articles that examined the issues more carefully. Authorities in the field explained that yes, it does exist and is much more widespread than many would like to believe. And any child may be a target, they said. Victims and offenders come from all racial, ethnic, and socioeconomic groups. And the effect of victimization on a child may be devastating.

Experts—both long-standing and recently dubbed—were regularly interviewed by the media. When they said the country was besieged by a sexual abuse epidemic, they were not contradicted. At long last, they felt, the country was waking up. The pendulum had begun to swing.

But what the media giveth, the media taketh away. And it was not long before the media were covering the backlash as enthusiastically as they had covered the epidemic. Some wondered aloud whether the media were immoral or just amoral. In general, they are neither.

Most journalists working in the mass media will acknowledge, when pressed, that their stories often lack context. Frequently this is a result of space constraints. But the most important reason is that reporters, who usually cover isolated events, do not always understand the context themselves. Although this may sound like criticism, it is not necessarily. A newspaper is not a book. Reporters do not have time to learn all there is to know about the tobacco industry and the consumer rights movement before covering an antismoking rally. Nor should they be criticized for that. But their lack of perspective makes reporters and particularly their editors nervous. Is the story balanced? Have they missed some interest group that is going to be up in arms when the story appears? Despite what some may believe, most journalists would rather include in a story a quote from an organization with a strong view on an issue than have the organization call or write angry letters to the editor later, demanding to know why they were not contacted before the story appeared.

Controversy? What Controversy?

Child sexual abuse seemed safe, though. After all, who was for it? Suddenly, prominent citizens were stepping forward, disclosing that they had been sexually abused when young. And nothing had been done to their abusers. Politicians came out against it. Legislation was introduced and passed in some states to allow a child's statements to be videotaped and, in some instances, admitted into evidence. Funding for services, including treatment and prevention programs, was increased. The public was exhorted to "believe the children" and was assured that "children don't lie about sexual abuse." Cases were being prosecuted—and won. Prosecutors found that even so-called one-on-one cases—cases in which the only evidence was the word of a child against the word of the adult defendant—could bring convictions.

The media hung on the story. And *what* a story: crime, sex, innocent victims, heinous criminals, outraged parents. Some of the more responsible publications added a sidebar on how to protect children from this apparently ubiquitous danger. And that was the way the coverage went—for a while.

But then the charges turned bizarre. Allegedly abused children were talking about strange rituals, possibly satanic, involving the killing (and eating, in some cases) of animals. They told of eating excrement, drinking urine, and observing the murder (and cannibalizing, in some instances) of babies.

The Jordan, Minnesota, case garnered the most publicity, and it was there that the backlash was born. The national media descended on the small town as it rarely does anywhere short of a summit conference, a political primary, or a Super Bowl. In front of all those watchful eyes and cameras, the case fell apart. The first two (and the last) defendants to stand trial were acquitted. Then, suddenly, charges against all but one of the remaining defendants were dropped in order to allow authorities to investigate stories that babies had been murdered and dumped in the river—or so the prosecutor said.

What really happened in Jordan? All the questions may never be answered. It will take a book or two to begin the process (and there will certainly be more than one). We will examine the case briefly in chapter 6, but suffice it to say that in Jordan the backlash gained a beachhead. It was in nearby Minneapolis, in the wake of the debacle, that VOCAL (Victims of Child Abuse Laws) was founded by, among others, the couple acquitted in the lone trial. And it was in Jordan that the cry of "witch hunt" was heard—not for the first time, but in a manner that commanded national attention.

And so the media had discovered the backlash. Articles appeared on other cases that had fallen apart, but more important, there were articles suggesting how easily *anyone* could be accused of sexually abusing a child, and how difficult and expensive it was to defend oneself. The old cautionary statement, first declaimed in seventeenth century England by Lord Chief Justice Matthew Hale and until recently read to many juries before they began deliberating rape charges, was repeated: "Rape is an accusation easily to be made and hard to be proved, and harder to be defended by the party accused, though never so innocent." Such a backlash had been avoided by adult rape victims largely because there was frequently medical evidence to corroborate their accounts and juries found them credible witnesses. But medical evidence is rare in child sexual abuse cases and often children make poor witnesses—when they are even deemed competent to testify.

There were stories about the incompetence and arrogance of child protective workers—sarcastically referred to as "child savers." Horror stories about adults who said they were falsely accused began appearing almost as often, it seemed, as those about sexual abuse victims. VOCAL was mentioned in many of the articles. The organization sprouted chapters in more than thirty states, and began lobbying for changes in state laws, seeking among other measures to make it more difficult to remove children from the homes of allegedly abusive parents, and to make prosecutors and investigators accountable for accusations that prove unfounded. Some of their efforts have succeeded.

Most recently, VOCAL has contended that a great many child sexual abuse allegations arise out of divorce and custody proceedings where one parent falsely and maliciously accuses the other to gain an advantage in court. The accuser then "brainwashes" the child to testify accordingly. In other cases, VOCAL asserts, investigators are so sure the crime has occurred that they browbeat children until the abuse is "admitted." In the end the children *are* abused—but by the investigators, not the accused, says VOCAL. Articles have appeared in professional journals (written for the most part by psychiatrists) arguing this position and outlining what the writers suggest is the proper way to determine whether a child has been sexually abused.

Whither the Pendulum?

Has the pendulum swung all the way back, then? And *is* there a witch hunt? We will return to the second question in chapter 6, where the backlash will be examined more thoroughly. As for the first, the answer is an unequivocal no.

Despite the controversy—and in part because of it—child sexual abuse is part of the national consciousness. It has always been a volatile subject; that much remains true. And it is a subject most people prefer to avoid. That too has not changed. But in the late 1980s, fewer and fewer people found themselves able to avoid thinking and talking about it, however much they would have preferred to. It seems safe to assume that articles will continue to be written, studies will continue to be conducted, and debates will continue to rage in the decades to come. The past ten years have brought an increased public awareness that is not likely to disappear, although it will undoubtedly blow hot and cold with the political weather.

As the subject has attracted wider interest, the diversity of the professionals involved has expanded, and it has grown increasingly difficult to divide combatants into camps. This is most apparent at national conferences on child sexual abuse and related topics. Joining the fray at the larger ones are judges, social workers, prosecutors, defense lawyers, psychiatrists, police officers, researchers, pastors, parents of victims, professors, FBI agents, politicians, doctors, journalists, therapists, and teachers, among others.

Given this variety, conflict is not surprising; what is, perhaps, is the quiet evolution over the past few years of some important general agreement in a field with many more questions than answers. Although not everyone will agree with any list of statements on this subject, the majority of "child advocates" as well as members of VOCAL would probably agree with the following (as did several leaders interviewed from each group):

1. Child sexual abuse exists and has always existed.
2. It is more common than once believed.
3. A child is not capable of "consenting" to sex with an adult.
4. Many children who have been sexually abused do not disclose the abuse.
5. Under pressure, children who have been sexually abused sometimes falsely recant.
6. Adults sometimes make false accusations of sexual abuse and children are sometimes prompted to repeat them.
7. The criminal justice system sometimes convicts individuals who are innocent, and sometimes acquits those who are guilty.
8. Children may be badly damaged by sexual abuse. The criminal justice system may add to a child's trauma, sometimes causing more harm than the sexual abuse did in the first place.
9. Child abusers rarely stop abusing children voluntarily and without external pressure.
10. Child abusers should undergo therapeutic treatment, or should be punished, or both.
11. The field of child sexual abuse is in its infancy. A great deal more research and training is required to improve investigation, prosecution, treatment, and prevention.

The Rest of the Iceberg

But such agreement, as far as it exists, is only the tip of the iceberg (to borrow a tired metaphor from the profession). The rest of the iceberg, ever ready to rise above the surface, is conflict and bitter disagreement.

VOCAL believes the problem is not as extensive as the "child savers" would have us believe. In this climate of "hysteria," social workers and police investigators are only too ready to believe in the guilt of anyone accused, regardless of the facts. For this reason, VOCAL leaders say, it is impossible to get a fair investigation, much less a fair trial. And this presumption of guilt means that a child can be removed from the home and a family can be torn apart while the state "investigates" for months or even years. They are also unconvinced that the majority of children who are abused are seriously damaged as a result. They acknowledge that some may be but add that treatment by therapists may prolong rather than ameliorate the condition. "Wouldn't it be better just to let them forget?" they ask.

To child advocates, this sounds familiar. It is a lot like the way it was before anyone started talking about pendulums. It is not déjà vu, they say, only because there has never been a time when denial and minimization did *not* exist. They do not have to look to VOCAL to see the phenomenon. The importance of child sexual abuse is often minimized even by forces within the system that is supposed to be handling the cases. To cite but a few examples:

—A Philadelphia criminal court judge was the subject of a federal investigation. Court administrators thought he should be removed from hearing criminal cases, so what did they do? They transferred him to family court, where "all" he would be responsible for was cases of child abuse and neglect.[1] "I think the public sees this as comparable to a policeman being assigned to a desk job," commented a local child abuse expert.[2]

—The status of professionals in this field is often apparent in the facilities they are provided. One Sacramento county counsel has been working for years out of a temporary trailer, waiting for the permanent office he has been promised. Down the driveway is a large green sign that he says is symbolic of the state's priorities. In large white letters it reads: REFUSE COLLECTION. And just below: YOUTH SERVICES CENTER.

—A policeman in Westchester County, New York, spent more than a year investigating and gathering evidence for a major day care trial.

Social workers who worked closely with him said that although he had little background in this area, he was extremely dedicated and spent long hours educating himself. Back at the station house, however, he was stigmatized by fellow officers, who viewed him as a "prima donna."

—A Wisconsin judge, in sentencing a 24-year-old man to 3 years' probation on a first-degree sexual assault conviction, said of the 5-year-old victim: "I am satisfied that we have an unusual sexually promiscuous young lady and that this man just did not know enough to knock off her advances."[3]

And the Home of the Brave

In some ways denial and minimization are eminently understandable, given certain traditional American values. Our society has always been more willing to pay lip service to its responsibility to protect those who cannot protect themselves than to pay cash. And children are the least powerful constituency, unable to organize, speak out, or vote. Our national optimism and naiveté make it difficult for us to suspect that people who look "normal" may be child molesters. And even when our suspicions are aroused, as a rule we do not believe in turning in our neighbors—even when "turning in" means only that our suspicions will be investigated. But even that rubs against the grain, because our criminal justice system is built on the precept that an individual is innocent until proven guilty. We also believe that a man's home is his castle and what he does within its confines, his own business.

All of this is not to say that Americans support child molesters. When we read about one in the newspaper, we are enraged. We are especially angry if he is some skid row psychotic who never should have been released from the mental institution where he was confined. Somewhere on the other side of the country.

But the battle for acceptance is not only waged *there*, on the other side of the country. It is waged *here*. And that is when it truly hits home.

2

It Can't Happen Here

THEY were employed by the same bank in San Francisco and happened to meet in the train after work. He was getting off first—in a bad neighborhood. She asked where he lived, and he told her he lived in the suburbs but parked his car near the station. Wasn't he nervous about that? she asked. Hadn't he heard that a fellow bank employee had been beaten recently in that neighborhood and was now in a coma? He'd heard, he said, but his car was close and he rarely returned past dusk. The next morning the bank was buzzing with the news. Mr. Itcanthappentome had been jumped on the way to his car and was in the hospital with three cracked ribs and a broken nose.

The story is true but not unique. We never have trouble believing such stories until we are forced to play the lead role. Perhaps we prefer to believe we lead charmed lives. More likely we need to believe that, despite evidence to the contrary, justice will prevail—and when it does we will not merit broken ribs.

Then again, when most of us think of evil, we think of something or someone distant, cold, and powerful—Machiavellian. Evil is not something we encounter during the short, familiar walk to the car. And its face is not that of our neighbor in the big house on the hill—the one who throws extravagant Christmas parties every year. Until we discover that this neighbor has pleaded guilty to sexually assaulting his own granddaughters, ages 5 and 7. But even that does not mean we have to believe it.

The man who lived in the big house (and whose case is examined in the next chapter) eventually went to jail, but not many of his neighbors knew that. It was not reported in the press. When several neighbors were informed during interviews, they refused to believe that he had committed the crimes to which he confessed. They did not wish to see documentation, either; they *preferred* not to believe.

The phenomenon is not rare; there are countless examples. During an interview, a physician told of an allegation that a counselor had sexually abused a camper at a summer camp owned and operated by a well-known national charity.[1] The physician, who cofounded a hospital-based program to identify and treat abused children, sits on the charity's advisory board. Following the allegation, the board met and asked the doctor for advice. What they wanted to know, however, was not how they could protect children from abuse, but how they could protect counselors from what they assumed to be false allegations.

Even more troubling was a 1984 PBS broadcast on child sexual abuse that included the story of a pediatrician in a Midwestern city who had molested a number of his young male patients.[2] The doctor left the area after he was convicted but retained remarkable support within the community. Several parents interviewed on camera said they firmly believed in the man's innocence and would send their children to him again if he returned.

A minister who was convicted of sexually abusing five children at a Bronx, New York, day care center run by his church also maintained a remarkable following. Fellow clergymen raised more than $70,000 in defense funds and proclaimed their support even after he began serving a 15- to 45-year prison sentence. One clergyman was quoted in the press as calling the accusations "the worst travesty of justice in the history of the United States," and he used his church's newsletter to solicit defense contributions.[3]

"It Was Almost Like I'd Heard It for the First Time"

Denial is not limited to outside observers, however. Parents of victims and even victims themselves may deny the reality of sexual abuse. Ed Clark, for instance, couldn't believe his daughter had been abused at a day care center owned and operated by Jeanette Martin, who led the church choir in which he once sang.[4] The night his wife met with a group of parents whose children had also been abused at the Martin Day Care Center in Mount Vernon, New York (not to be confused with the McMartin Preschool in California), Clark, a police officer, was sitting in Mrs. Martin's living room, talking about the "crazy charges" and assuring her that he knew she wasn't involved. (She was eventually convicted of child endangerment, while her employee, James Watt, was convicted of seventeen counts of felony rape.) When Clark returned home, he told his wife: "You know, you're going to burn in hell for what you're doing because it ain't right. That woman ain't got nothing to do with this mess."

It was months before he changed his mind and even longer before he recognized the true impact of the abuse. The night he finally understood, he was home alone with his 5-year-old daughter, who was sitting on her bed, clutching a Cabbage Patch doll. There was a blank look on her face and he asked if she was all right. "Uh huh," she said. But when he returned to check on her five minutes later, she hadn't moved. Only now there were tears in her eyes.

"Something hit me wrong," Clark continued. "I said, 'Come here, baby.' I picked her up and when I did, her bottom was wet. I looked at the bed, and the bed was soaking wet. She'd urinated on herself. Just sitting there. And she wouldn't let go of her doll. And this is a kid who used to be able to sit by herself and play. I said, 'Baby, what's wrong?' And all she said to me was, 'Jimmy hurt me, Daddy. Jimmy hurt me.'

"Up until that moment, I never realized how badly it affected the children. It was almost like I'd heard it for the first time. I just felt numb."[5]

Other parents whose children were abused at the Martin Center refused to cooperate with the investigation, continuing to suppress what they could not accept.[6] The same phenomenon was noted by Jan Hollingsworth in her book on a Florida day care case:

> The core group of parents who had bonded on that first horrifying night . . . became and remained cautiously committed to following the path that led to a courtroom.
>
> Their numbers were few compared to the ones who closed their doors to [the police investigator] in the beginning and now only cracked them occasionally in order to shoo off any additional inquiries from the law. Most didn't want to get "involved."
>
> Some continued to deny, even to themselves, that they were.

A few announced intent to help "clear the Fusters' [the per-petrators who were ultimately convicted] name," a resolution that began to fade as their children's "peculiarities" became too pro-nounced to ignore in this new and revealing context. Nightmares. Masks. Monsters. Excessive masturbation. French kissing. Insert-ing toys into rectums. Irrational fear of the bathroom. Unusual toilet and bathing habits. Regression. It was the mosaic blueprint of a Fuster victim.

Yet still some parents denied. Even those who knew without question what had happened to some of the children—would not accept that it had happened to their own.[7]

A parent whose daughter was abused in another case made a dual discovery when she learned of the abuse. It was only then, the woman said in an interview, that she recalled her own childhood abuse. Previously, she had utterly repressed her father's repeated sexual assaults.[8]

Therapists say that repression by adults of childhood trauma is not uncommon. There have been many accounts written by sexual abuse "survivors" attesting to the fact. One of the most powerful begins:

> I didn't have any memory of being sexually assaulted. The first time I had sex I was surprised that it didn't hurt, and I thought that his penis looked small. When I was pregnant, I had a lot of strange feelings. I always thought it was the pregnancy. Then when I was in labor, they strapped me down. I felt like I was being ripped apart. Suddenly I was three years old. I was crying, saying, "I'll tell my mommy. You can't do this." And then I was screaming, "Please don't kill me, I'll be good." I remembered everything.[9]

Denial of this sort is a subconscious coping mechanism that allows a victim to survive, to carry on with her life. In the most extreme instances of denial, in response to the most extreme forms of abuse, victims may develop multiple personalities. Virtually all individuals with documented cases of this disorder have a history of severe and protracted childhood abuse, often involving physical and sexual torture. The "personalities" are the individual's desperate ef-fort to seal off the pain resulting from overwhelming trauma.

More often when victims deny, they do so consciously. In his widely cited article "The Child Sexual Abuse Accommodation Syndrome," Dr. Roland Summit explains that children are often manipulated or forced by their abusers into denying the abuse.[10] Writing specifically about the typical (female) incest victim, Summit says: "Most ongoing sexual abuse is *never* disclosed, at least not outside the immediate family. Treated, reported or investigated cases are the exception, not the norm."[11] (Emphasis in original.) When there *is* disclosure, frequently it occurs long after the abuse is initiated and is met with the perpetrator's denial and society's disbelief.

"Unless specifically trained and sensitized," Summit contends, "average adults, including mothers, relatives, teachers, counselors, doctors, psychotherapists,[12] investigators, prosecutors, defense attorneys, judges and jurors, cannot believe that a normal, truthful child would tolerate incest without immediately reporting or that an apparently normal father could be capable of repeated unchallenged sexual molestation of his own daughter. The child of any age faces an unbelieving audience when she complains of ongoing sexual abuse."[13]

As a result, Summit says, children are under overwhelming pressure to retract the allegation—and often do.

> In the chaotic aftermath of disclosure, the child discovers that the bedrock fears and threats underlying the secrecy are true. Her father abandons her and calls her a liar. Her mother does not believe her or decompensates into hysteria and rage . . . . The girl is blamed for causing the whole mess, and everyone seems to treat her like a freak. . . . *Unless there is special support for the child and immediate intervention to force responsibility on the father, the girl will follow the "normal" course and retract her complaint.* . . . The children learn not to complain. The adults learn not to listen.[14] (Emphasis in original.)

Even parents who want to be supportive may send subtle (and not so subtle) cues to children, encouraging denial. It is common for children, if they do disclose, to tell their stories a little at a time. One of the reasons is that they read the reactions they get when they tell—or try to tell. Patricia Doe, whose daughter's story is the subject of the next chapter, said in an interview long after her daughter had first told her about the abuse, "I'm sure there are things she's still holding in. She watches my reaction, and I can hardly keep myself together." One time, she recalled, her daughter started telling her about sexual devices the abuser used—devices Patricia knew nothing about. The child looked at her mother and quickly dropped the subject.

What Patricia now realizes she was saying to her daughter was, "Don't tell me this, I can't handle it." Patricia, who has not seen a therapist but says "it's something I have to do," was attempting to deny the reality of what she knew would cause her pain and guilt. One hears that guilt when parents ask themselves: "Why didn't I see what was going on? Why didn't my daughter tell me? What could I have done to prevent it?" These are questions parents may compulsively ask not just for days or weeks following disclosure, but sometimes for years. Patricia asks them still.

But Patricia did not know then what she knows now. She has learned about herself. And through reading and conversations, she has learned a great deal about child sexual abuse, including the pattern in her daughter's behavior that she feels should have made her suspicious. That reasoning, though—and it is shared by many in her situation—is based wholly on hindsight.

What Mandate?

For parents or children to deny the horror of their experience is one thing. But denial by professionals who have a special responsibility for children is another. Some of them, like teachers, school administrators, and physicians, are so-called mandated reporters, required by law in all fifty states to report any suspicion of child abuse because they are in a special position to detect it. Theoretically, at least, they can even be prosecuted for failure to do so, although such laws have rarely been enforced. There are other professionals, like religious leaders, who in some states have a legal obligation to report but, one would presume, would everywhere have an ethical responsibility to protect child victims. How have these professionals responded to this difficult and uncomfortable issue? All too often they too have denied.

Many examples could be cited from each profession. Certainly Roman Catholics, for example, have no monopoly on sexual abuse cases; no religious group is immune. But a number of cases involving Catholic priests have come to light in recent years and were examined in depth in an investigation by the *National Catholic Reporter*.[15] The stories, which focused on both the abuse and the church's response, revealed that priests have been convicted of multiple sexual assaults of children in Louisiana, California, Oregon, and Idaho, and charges have been filed in five other states (two of them involving two priests each). Even more troubling was the reaction of the church leadership in case after case. As the paper editorialized:

> These are serious and damaging matters that have victimized the young and innocent and fuel old suspicions against the Catholic church and a celibate clergy. But a related and broader scandal seemingly rests with local bishops and a national episcopal leadership that has, as yet, no set policy on how to respond to these cases. As the articles in this issue show:
> —All too often, complaints against the priest involved are disregarded by the bishops, or the priest is given the benefit of the doubt.
> —Frequently, local bishops exhibit little concern for the traumatic effects these molestations have on the boys and their families—even though mental disturbances and, in one recent case, suicide, have followed these molestations.
> —Only legal threats and lawsuits seem capable of provoking some local bishops into taking firm actions against the priests. In some cases reported here, the priests, once identified for their offenses, have been moved to other parishes and again placed in positions of responsibility.

The callousness of the church's response to many of the initial complaints was cited as the reason for several of the civil lawsuits. One lawyer was quoted as saying, "I hate to sound harsh about it, but had they (the church authorities) shown a caring attitude, the parents would never have been interested in filing a lawsuit." A parent who filed another suit told the paper: "I feel the Catholic church is one of the great forces for good in the world. But it is a huge organization that sometimes views the members of the laity as unimportant. My feeling is that the suit was the only language they could understand."[16]

A parallel can be drawn to the school environment. There have been many cases of teachers' sexually abusing students, but few administrators informed of allegations ever report them, even though by law they must do so. Noteworthy because it is an exception, a

high-ranking Los Angeles school district administrator was convicted
of failing to report suspected child molestation, a misdemeanor, in
July 1986. It was the first successful prosecution in the area, according to a news account.

The administrator first learned of the complaints in 1982, when
the teacher was transferred to his school following similar allegations
at his previous school. Yet it was not until late 1984 that action was
taken, despite numerous complaints in the interim that the teacher
was molesting girls in his third grade class.

The administrator's attorney was quoted as saying, "It's a shame
they set up this one guy," and indeed one of the jurors called him
a "guilty scapegoat," adding, "We think they were all guilty as hell.
We wish we had the whole LAUSD (Los Angeles Unified School
District) up here." The story continues: "The case sent shock waves
through the district, which was the target of a district attorney's
investigation into a possible coverup, and faces a multimillion-dollar
lawsuit filed on behalf of the victims."[17]

What makes this kind of denial, whether by church or school
officials, so reprehensible is that it endangers countless children to
whom the perpetrators have daily access. It should be noted that the
law does not require "mandated reporters" to investigate; they are
only obliged to report their suspicions. They may do so anonymously
and may not be held civilly liable for the consequences of their
reports. In general, investigations are supposed to be conducted by
social workers (if the alleged abuser is the child's parent or caretaker),
or by police (if he is not).

"The problem . . . is that organizations, rather than reporting
suspected abuse to the agencies responsible for investigating (as required by law and regulation), conduct their own investigations and
decide themselves whether there's anything to the charges," said Dr.
E. Peter Wilson, a physician who heads a child abuse program at
the Children's Hospital of Philadelphia.[18] "That happens all too often
in a variety of settings including schools, where it is common, if a
teacher is implicated, for a report to be made to the principal and
then for that principal to conduct an investigation and reach his own
conclusion." The way it is justified, Wilson added, is that the principal will claim he did not have "reason to suspect" until he
investigated.

Why do professionals fail to report? There are no hard answers, just as there are no hard statistics kept of how many educators and clergymen do and do not report allegations passed along to them. It seems likely, however, that their failure is due to a willingness to believe and support their colleagues (and to discount the word of children), and to a desire to protect their reputations as well as those of the institutions they represent. And it may also be attributable to their desire to believe it never happened.

Is There a Doctor in the House?

Of all mandated reporters, physicians may be the most important. According to one commentator, "The medical profession was the first, and remains the foremost, target of these mandatory reporting statutes. Doctors are considered the professionals most likely to see injured children and are presumed most qualified to diagnose the symptoms of abuse and neglect."[19]

But frequently doctors fail to make the diagnosis or fail to report it. Nor is this failure an isolated phenomenon. A parallel can be drawn to the frequent failure of doctors to report sexually transmitted diseases in adults, which they are also required by law to do. So common is it for doctors to treat symptoms of gonorrhea without reporting or without running the lab tests to confirm the diagnosis (and thus technically circumventing the reporting law), that the Federal Centers for Disease Control estimates the actual number of gonorrhea cases in 1985 to be double the nine-hundred-thousand cases reported, according to a spokesman there.

Doctors have rarely been charged with failing to report child sexual abuse, however, although there have been cases. One of particular note was a 1984 New Hampshire case that may have been the first time a doctor was charged under the state's misdemeanor reporting law. Ironically, the doctor had previously helped establish a local child protective team and lectured church and community groups on child abuse.

According to news accounts, a mother brought her daughters, ages 3 and 4, for an examination after learning that they had been abused by their 15-year-old baby-sitter. The pediatrician decided that the children had not been physically or emotionally damaged and advised the mother how to avoid future abuse. He then suggested the baby-sitter seek counseling and dropped the matter.

But the mother later learned that her children had been abused over an extended period, that more than one perpetrator was involved, and that her son had also been abused. She felt that her children would have received the counseling they ultimately required much sooner had a thorough investigation been conducted. And the reason there was no investigation was that the doctor never reported the abuse; that was why she wanted the doctor charged, she said.

In the end, however, the charges against the doctor were dropped despite the mother's protest. The prosecutor was quoted as saying, "I don't say he's getting off. I see punishment. I see him donating or giving up significant amounts of his time and energy. This has been a tremendous hassle, burden, or whatever you want to call it, to him." But less than three months earlier, when the charges were first brought, the same prosecutor had said, "It's very unusual for anyone to be charged with failure to report. I find it a very difficult charge to bring, since it deals with a professional. But the incidents in this case are such that it just had to be done."[20]

What made this case unique, however, was not the dropped charges. It was the charges, period. And the reason doctors are rarely charged is not because failure to report is a rare occurrence. Although here, too, no hard statistics are kept, ample evidence exists. At least one study was done several years ago by a team at the University of Washington School of Medicine that mailed three hundred questionnaires to a randomly selected sample of local pediatricians and general practitioners. The team's findings appeared in the *Journal of the American Medical Association:*

> Even though the trauma of the victimized child tended to be serious, only 32% of the physicians indicated that they urged the family to report the incident. Of all the [96] physicians responding, 42% indicated that they would report any child abuse case involving sexual activity. This pattern of limited reporting is supported by the Child Protective Service statistics. Since the Child Protective Service receives only 11% of their reports from physicians, physicians are not considered an important source of cases. Reasons provided by the physicians for not reporting sexual abuse cases to the proper authorities were in two categories. Two thirds of the physicians believed either that reporting would be harmful to the

family or that the problem could be handled more easily privately. The other third was dissatisfied with the manner in which state social service agencies handled such cases.

The findings of this investigation support the hypothesis that physicians are not reporting cases of child sexual abuse to the state as directed by law. These results tend to support the view that the actual frequency of child sexual abuse far exceeds reported cases.[21]

Other studies that have examined physicians' reporting of all child maltreatment (not limited to sexual abuse) have yielded similar results.[22] (And because physical evidence of sexual abuse is relatively rare, it is likely that underreporting of sexual abuse exceeds that of physical abuse.) One study found that the majority of 120 physicians surveyed said their medical training in this area was "minimal" or "inadequate." The study went on to say:

> Two doctors had no intention of ever reporting and 11 would report only if there were "a definite proof" of abuse or gross neglect. Many respondents claimed their strongest reason for not reporting suspected cases was lack of information about reporting requirements and procedures. Further analysis indicated, in fact, that about 35 percent of the physicians were not fully aware of legal mandates and sanctions. Several complained about lack of procedural information, inefficiency of child protective services workers and time-consuming court procedures.[23]

The studies only repeat what has been said for some time. More than a decade ago Dr. Ray Helfer, a pioneer in the field and a colleague of Henry Kempe's, wrote a ground-breaking article entitled "Why Most Physicians Don't Get Involved in Child Abuse Cases and What to Do About It." In listing eight reasons why physicians do not get involved, Helfer, a physician himself, placed at the top: "Medical school training was insufficient." Further, he says, doctors are not adequately compensated for their time in such cases, and it is often difficult for them to cancel all office activity in order to testify in court. Nor does any of their training prepare them emotionally or legally for the court process.

> We have fears about going to Probate or Juvenile Court too because we do not understand the workings of these courts and are not

prepared to wrestle with the questions of an astute attorney who may "wish to rake us over the coals." I believe requesting such testifying is analogous to asking a physician to do his own cardiac catheterization without ever training him in this skill.

For example, a lawyer once asked me, "Did you examine the child completely?" Now think for a moment about that question. A "yes" answer would set me up for a barrage of picayune questions, one of which would surely be deadly. On the other hand, an answer of "no" would make me appear rather ridiculous. If one has experience in testifying in court, the stance that must be taken is to pause, look nervous, act flustered and then with great confidence say, "My examination was sufficiently complete to permit me to make my decision." Then the lawyer will pause, look nervous and act flustered.[24]

The solution, Helfer argued more than a decade ago, is general training in medical schools and in residency programs. But interviews with a number of doctors from around the country suggest that medical school training still is virtually nonexistent—often limited to one optional lecture on physical abuse. Training of residents in pediatrics, at least, seems to have improved somewhat, but it remains deficient in most programs.

"We have not begun at all to train medical students in terms of child maltreatment," said Gloria Powell, a child psychiatrist who, as a faculty member at U.C.L.A. since 1974, has been active both in training child psychiatrists and treating sexually abused children.[25] "We have failed to provide adequate training to postgraduate students in general—particularly in the area of child sexual abuse," said Powell, adding, "I would dare say that 95 percent of pediatricians coming out of their training have not dealt with child sexual abuse at all, and I would say that 99 percent of child psychiatrists coming out of their training do not know anything at all about child sexual abuse and child maltreatment."

Asked how she knows, she said that as one of the first child psychiatrists to become involved in this area, she has attended numerous conferences and has conducted many seminars around the country. In addition, she said she is often telephoned by doctors who have no training in sexual abuse and are desperate for advice. Even at U.C.L.A., which trains about twenty child psychiatrists a year in one of the largest such programs in the country, the twenty are the only trainees at the school who receive specific instruction in sexual abuse and "not to the extent that we would like," Powell said.

What it all boils down to is, in the often repeated words of another pioneer in the field, Dr. Suzanne Sgroi, *"Recognition of sexual moles-tation of a child is entirely dependent on the individual's inherent willingness to entertain the possibility that the condition may exist."*[26] (Emphasis in original.) If the diagnosis does not occur to a doctor, it will not be made.

How important is this? Dr. Jeffrey Gilbert says it is crucial. Gilbert is an internist who heads the child sexual abuse unit at the New York City Health Department's Bureau of Sexually Trans-mitted Diseases. Prior to 1980, he had had no contact with child abuse, he said, but then he attended a seminar by Sgroi, who is also an internist with a background in working with sexually transmitted diseases. During the six-hour presentation, Gilbert grew impatient. He simply did not believe that child abuse was as common or serious as this woman was saying it was.

"What are you talking about?" he said to himself.[27] "I know kids. I know adults. This doesn't happen. I don't see it. Where is it?" Upon further reflection, he realized that children were brought to his clinic but were referred by the clerks to the pediatrics department. He obtained permission to see them and quickly found himself talk-ing to children with gonorrhea and herpes "who were telling me these horrible stories of their family members doing sexual acts on them.

"I really started seeing kids to prove to myself that [Sgroi] was wrong," Gilbert said. "And what I came out with was the realization that not only was she not wrong, and not only was she right, but it was even worse than what she told me."

Since then Gilbert has repeatedly seen doctors miss diagnoses and fail to report suspected abuse. For example, he diagnosed several of the children who were abused in the Mount Vernon day care case as having sexually transmitted diseases. Previously, several who ex-hibited symptoms that might have tipped off a physician trained in this area were examined by pediatricians who simply never thought to run lab tests.

A "60 Minutes" broadcast on the McMartin case raised this very question, although in a manner that undoubtedly misled many viewers.[28] Mike Wallace asked the chief prosecutor in the case, Lael Rubin, why, if so many children had been abused at the center over such a long period, none had been diagnosed by a pediatrician.

> RUBIN. Do you really think that there were doctors out there who two, three, five years ago, pediatricians who were really trained to examine young children in their genital areas? Many of the doctors suggested either alternatives or other reasons for pain, discomfort, urinary infections, vaginitis, all sorts of other problems.
>
> WALLACE. Is it possible, Miss Rubin, that they are better trained to understand than are you?
>
> RUBIN. Well, they're medical doctors and I'm not, but what I'm saying is that not only they but parents and a lot of other people in this case were not willing to believe and accept that, in fact, children were being molested.

What happened at the McMartin Preschool will be debated for a long time. Few aspects of the case are clear, but it requires no strain of credulity to believe that children could have been abused at the facility without being diagnosed by a pediatrician. The Mount Vernon case seems a clear enough example that it can and does happen. When asked for his comment on the above exchange, Gilbert said he agreed with Rubin's statements.

In support, he cited case after case. In New York City, every time a lab test on a child under the age of 11 comes back positive for a sexually transmitted disease, Gilbert and his colleagues investigate to learn the background. Time and again they find it was not reported. There must be some mistake, doctors say. A doctor in Chinatown says that such things do not occur in a "nice Chinese family." "In Russian families this doesn't happen," they are told by a doctor in another part of the city. And time and again they hear the same excuses: they thought it was from the bedsheets, or the bathwater.

There is another important reason that may explain why doctors frequently fail to report. It is the status of the clients. Children simply do not have the knowledge or resources to demand competent service. Moreover, children are only nominally a pediatrician's clients. The real clients, of course, are the parents who pay the bills. If a pediatrician reports a child as having been sexually abused, an investigation may well begin by scrutinizing the child's parents, which is not likely to inspire loyalty and affection in the hearts of these tax-paying citizens or the friends in whom they confide. And the kind of publicity that could be generated by media coverage is not most physicians' idea of a public relations coup. (Similarly, when a doctor reports a sexually transmitted disease in an adult and the patient's sex partners are contacted, a great deal of ill will may be generated, especially if the patient is married.)

Getting down to Business

Put most cynically or crudely or practically (depending on one's perspective), reporting child sexual abuse is rarely good for business. That is one reason doctors in private practice report sexual abuse less often than do doctors in public clinics or hospital emergency rooms.[29] Few people relish the thought of having their names linked to a child abuse case, no matter what the link. Many doctors may fear guilt by association, in the most general sense. The public, as we know, sometimes forgets the details.

In that sense, perhaps the last type of business that would wish such a connection is a private charity that depends on the public's good will—and children—for its existence. A charity like the Fresh Air Fund. And that may help explain why this charity that undeniably is well-intentioned and provides an important service to needy children could find itself denying and attacking and covering up to avoid association with child sexual abuse—as we shall see in the next chapter.

3

Case Study: The Fresh Air Fund

T HIS *was* a story about an organization that, when confronted with evidence of abuse in its program, denied it had a problem. It was an all too familiar story. But something remarkable happened literally after the ending was written. This organization that for years had tried to ignore reality and shield itself from scrutiny, granted an interview and admitted it had been naive.[1] The interview also revealed for the first time that this charity, which had been locked in an adversarial relationship with lawyers litigating a third successive child abuse lawsuit against it, joined with those same lawyers in forcing the criminal indictment of the alleged abuser in the most recent suit—four years after he had made a deal to avoid prosecution. And then it invited the lawyers, whom it credited with "raising its consciousness," to participate in the interview and comment on the victory—and the troubles that preceded it.

And so this "familiar" story had been transformed into a two-part account that may be unprecedented. It is a story of ignorance exacerbated by denial but finally faced and defeated by the courage it takes to say, "We were wrong."

1. Denial

Sexual abuse of children on Fresh Air Fund vacations? It sounded impossible. It was like saying the Red Cross promotes malaria or CARE causes malnutrition. Yet there was growing evidence, buttressed by several lawsuits, that children left in the care of this venerable charity were in danger of sexual assault.

The Fresh Air Fund provides free summer vacations for New York City children who could not otherwise afford them. Each summer it sends about 9,000 underprivileged children to stay with host families in so-called Friendly Towns scattered in more than a dozen states and Canada. Another 2,500 stay at four camps in upstate New York.

Private and not-for-profit, the Fund is one of New York's oldest and most revered charities. Its directors represent a Who's Who of New York society, and it has the backing of some of city's—indeed, the country's—most powerful and prestigious companies and individuals, including Con Edison, David Rockefeller, and The New York Times Company (which contributes more than $75,000 a year). All told, donors contribute about $3 million annually, and the charity's net worth is more than $25 million, according to its 1986 tax forms.

But the Fund's most valuable supporter is undoubtedly *The New York Times* itself. *Times* publisher Arthur Ochs Sulzberger is chairman of the Fund's board of directors, and every year from May through August the newspaper runs laudatory articles and editorials and free full-page ads exhorting readers to contribute to the Fresh Air Fund. Given this kind of support, the charity's reputation has been nearly sacrosanct.

But the patina had faded—and had begun to look suspiciously like tarnish. Critics said that the Fund's program was in dire need of revision. It was a system, they said, that relied totally on volunteers and the "goodwill" of its participants. And although the system may have worked beautifully in 1877, when a Pennsylvania clergyman brought nine children from New York City's slums back with him to the "fresh air" of his congregation's farms, critics questioned whether the same system could work in today's world.

The focus of the criticism was three civil lawsuits filed between 1981 and 1984 charging that the Fund's negligence in its screening and supervision caused children to be abused. All three children named in the suits were black (over 80 percent of the children the Fund serves are black and Hispanic), and two cases involved white host families.

The latest was a $70 million suit, filed in State Supreme Court in Manhattan, alleging that a 10-year-old child was sexually abused and photographed in "kiddie porn" poses by her host during two consecutive Fresh Air Fund "vacations" in New Hampshire.

Criminal charges were not filed until December 1986 because the New Hampshire prosecutor who handled the investigation agreed not to charge the man in return for his guilty plea in the sexual assault of his own granddaughters, who were 5 and 7 years old at the time he attacked them. For those offenses the man served 8 months of a 12-month jail sentence (the remaining time was suspended). There is evidence that the molester, who is now believed to be living in Arizona, has attacked other children as well.

Lawyers for both sides said during the interview that the $70 million lawsuit will be settled as soon as the Fund resolves technical problems involving insurance (its carrier from the time of the abuse has filed for bankruptcy). The other suits have already been settled. In 1985, the Fund paid an undisclosed amount to settle a suit charging that a 10-year-old Brooklyn boy was sexually assaulted by his counselor at a Fresh Air camp four years earlier. The terms could not be learned, and the settlement has not previously been reported in the media because the court file was sealed at the Fund's request.

The other suit was settled in 1983, when the Fund paid $125,000 to an East Harlem girl who three years earlier, when she was five, was beaten and tormented during her four-week stay with a Vermont couple. The couple ultimately pleaded guilty to criminal charges in connection with the beatings.

Critics have called the Fund a natural target for pedophiles—adults whose sexual orientation is focused exclusively on children—and predicted that further abuse was inevitable until the charity made substantive changes in its program. Their charges seemed to be supported by interviews with convicted pedophiles.

One man now in prison for the felonious sexual assault of a 13-year-old boy was asked during an interview in a prison visiting room if he knew what the Fresh Air Fund was. He nodded. "They're the group that sends kids from New York away for the summer." Would he be surprised to learn that a pedophile had obtained children from the Fresh Air Fund? "I'm not naive," he answered in a memorable understatement. "It must happen in all the groups—scouting, camping, Big Brothers."[2]

The prisoner was undoubtedly right. All those groups are vulnerable. The scandals that have swept the country in recent years have made it clear that child abuse can and does occur in virtually

all institutions. The Fund's dependence upon volunteers and its iso-
lation of children from their parents seemed to make it particularly
vulnerable to penetration by pedophiles. But what was most troubling was the charity's initial response to the problem.

Many child-care agencies similarly struck were shut down—at
least temporarily. But the Fresh Air Fund did not even slow down,
much less shut down. And it was not inclined to discuss the matter
with critics or the press. Ultimately, it managed to shield itself from
inquiry.

The charity backed by *The New York Times*, whose landmark
victory in the Supreme Court *(Times* v. *Sullivan)* made it the First
Amendment's greatest champion, obtained a gag order prohibiting
the lawyers litigating the third lawsuit from speaking to the press.
The gag order, it should be noted, was aimed at the adverse publicity,
in no way stemming the flow of praise in *The New York Times*.[3]

Following an appeal, the gag order was affirmed in 1985 by New
York County's appellate court. Although the court issued no opinion
explaining its decision, to heap irony upon irony, the presiding justice
of the court had argued with passion and eloquence precisely the
opposing position seven months earlier. In a speech at a child sexual
abuse conference at Fordham Law School, a transcript of which
appeared in the *New York Law Journal*, Justice Francis T. Murphy
said, "Children have neither power nor property. Voices other than
their own must speak for them. If those voices are silent, then children who have been abused may lean their heads against window
panes and taste the bitter emptiness of violated childhoods."

He concluded with this exhortation: "Badger every legislator
from every county in this state, let no editor or reporter sleep, until
the remedy you want is granted. For you are the only voice of the
violated child. If you do not speak, there is silence."[4]

"Kiddie Porn" in a "Friendly Town"

In an effort to break that silence, an investigation was undertaken
with the most recent lawsuit viewed as a case study. Fund executives
at the time repeatedly refused requests for interviews and instructed
Fund volunteers in New Hampshire and elsewhere not to talk to the
author. Some of the details, therefore, remain sketchy. But the following account emerged from dozens of interviews, including many

with Fund volunteers who, although still strong supporters of the charity, were sufficiently concerned about the child abuse cases to grant interviews despite the Fund's admonition.

"Patricia Doe" sent her daughter "Jane" on Fresh Air Fund trips in 1981 and 1982.[5] Jane had just turned 10 and was away from home for the first time when she arrived in the "Friendly Town" of Pittsfield, New Hampshire, to spend two weeks in the home of Don and LaDonna ("Johnni") Tynan, who were 49 and 46 years old respectively that first summer. Also placed with the Tynans was a young boy named Pedro.

If the other Fresh Air Fund children had seen the Tynans' house, they might well have been envious. Don Tynan was a commercial airline pilot who made about $80,000 a year,[6] and he and his wife lived in one of the area's largest and most luxurious houses. Built in 1773, the eleven-room, seven-fireplace ranch house offers a panoramic view from a mountain overlooking Pittsfield. And among the Tynans' extensive additions to the property were a stone wall, intercoms, and a master bedroom suite complete with a spiral staircase and a Jacuzzi. Postcards featuring a color photograph of the house are still sold in a downtown drugstore.

But the other children's envy would have been short-lived. According to Jane's therapist and her mother, the child is still suffering the effects of what happened to her in that beautiful house, although she has made considerable progress in therapy.

As the child's mother and therapist tell it, the abuse started with baths in the Jacuzzi. Tynan would bathe the girl and then play games like "hide-and-seek." Later Tynan began exposing himself and eventually got into the Jacuzzi with her. Tynan's former daughter-in-law, the mother of the grandchildren he sexually abused, said in an interview that sexual contact with her daughters was also begun in the Jacuzzi. (Her name and those of her children have not been published in order to protect their privacy.) Such use of play and games is a common way pedophiles initiate sexual contact, according to Flora Colao, Jane's therapist and a specialist in treating children who are assault victims.

Jane told Colao that after one week Tynan's wife discovered what was going on and, following a loud argument, insisted her husband leave home and not return until Jane was gone. The former Mrs. Tynan, now remarried, admitted she asked her husband to leave the house. She denied, however, that it had anything to do with sexual abuse. (She also denied that her ex-husband ever abused their granddaughters, despite his guilty plea.)

Interviewed in her Ohio home in May 1985, Johnni Tynan Bates said she asked her husband to leave because they were having "problems" that predated Jane's visit. When asked what those problems were, she said, "That's personal."

Asked whether her husband ever photographed naked children, she said she herself had photographed him with children in the Jacuzzi. "Don had a swimsuit on. And most kids take baths naked," she said as she scanned a bookshelf for a photo album—one of forty she has from those days, she said—and, finding it, flipped through about twenty pages of Polaroid photographs. In some photographs children—including Jane—were in the Jacuzzi alone. In others Tynan was with them, arms around the children and smiling broadly. It was impossible to tell whether Tynan was wearing a bathing suit; the children wore bathing suits in some pictures, but in most they were naked. Several photographs showed Tynan with the granddaughters he sexually abused. There were no pictures of Pedro among those shown, and it is not known whether he was involved in any abuse.

During the second week of her stay, Jane had no direct contact with Tynan, although he called to apologize, according to therapist Colao. The apology, Colao said, was one of the reasons the child returned the next summer. Jane believed Tynan was sorry for what he had done, and she was reassured by cards and letters he sent her during the year. And she believed she could count on Mrs. Tynan to intervene if there were trouble again. But the most important reason Jane returned, Colao believes, is that she was emotionally incapable of disclosing the abuse. And because she could give no reason not to return, she felt she had to go.

But it was a different household to which Jane returned July 22, 1982. There was no Mrs. Tynan to protect her. Johnni said she left her husband for good in May—more than two months before Jane's arrival—returning to the house one last time on July 2 to pick up her car and clothes before driving to Ohio.

Tynan was coping that summer not only with a recent separation but also with severe financial difficulties that led to the foreclosure on his house a year later. Yet Jane was left alone in his care (Pedro

He had agreed, he said, not to prosecute Tynan again unless he was shown evidence that there had been a "greater degree of penetration" in Jane's case than in the cases involving Tynan's granddaughters, adding that he would not reopen the case until he was presented with that evidence. In a separate interview later that month, New Hampshire's attorney general questioned the propriety of Johnson's decision.[8]

As for the $70 million lawsuit, Patricia did not realize at first that she could sue the Fresh Air Fund. When she first called the Fund's Manhattan office in November 1983 to inform them of the abuse, she said she spoke with Associate Executive Director Tom Karger (then assistant director of camping), who was eager to meet with her. When they met, Karger told her he had never heard of abuse on a Fresh Air Fund trip and that the Fund would be happy to help in any way it could, Patricia said. She never heard from him again.

Patricia was bitter at the way she and Jane were treated by the New Hampshire authorities and, particularly, by the Fresh Air Fund. Of the Fund, she said, "They lied. They just don't care. If [Karger] knew that they had cases in the past, I think he could have at least called and said, "How's things going with your daughter?" If they care about children, they should help you after something goes wrong."

(In a recent interview, Karger explained that he had been chosen to meet with Patricia because he had a Master's degree in social work and was viewed as best able to handle the situation. He said his intention was to learn the name of the alleged abuser [so that the Fund could avoid sending him another child] to find out whether the proper authorities had been contacted, and to offer assistance to the family. When Patricia said she had been in touch with the New York police and had been told to contact the police in New Hampshire, which she intended to do, it sounded to Karger as if the necessary steps were being taken. As for his remark about child abuse, Karger remembers saying that he had never heard of a case like it in the Fresh Air Fund, referring to sexual abuse in a Friendly Town—of which there had been no reported cases.

Of Patricia's question why no one called to find out how Jane was doing, Karger said, "It's a good question." Since then the Fund has changed the way it responds to cases of abuse, he said, and a

Fund lawyer who was present during the interview added that the decision not to contact the family again was made not by Karger but by a group of Fund officials.)[9]

Although the Fund refused to comment on Patricia's criticism at the time she made her comments, citing the pending lawsuit before the gag order was in place, it had not always been so reticent. In response to the first lawsuit, Fund spokespersons said initially that the child might have been abused but that her own mother was the perpetrator. The Fund, they added, was merely a travel agent and was not responsible for the children it transported.[10]

Finally, after the abusers pleaded guilty to criminal charges and the Fund paid to settle the lawsuit, the charity issued a brief public statement: "The Fresh Air Fund deeply regrets this incident. It would be a pity if this isolated incident were to be taken out of perspective, potentially limiting the success of our drive and therefore the number of children we can help this summer."

Despite the reference to an "isolated incident," there are indications that the Fund began to recognize systemic problems as early as 1985. A *Times* article said: "Committee members interview prospective hosts *at their homes* and ask whether the family has pets, where the child will sleep and how the families discipline their own children *(the fund does not permit corporal punishment)*. Those families who wish to continue participating in the program are *reinterviewed every three years.*"[11] (Emphasis added.)

These policies were different from those stated in the 1982 "Friendly Town Chairman's Manual"—obtained from a source— which is the primary body of information available to Fund volunteers. Although on the surface the policies suggested increased vigilance, critics said that they did not go nearly far enough. Moreover, they said, the Fund had no way of knowing whether they were even implemented. No system is perfect, they said, but the Fund's placed children at risk unnecessarily with the distinct possibility, if not likelihood, that in the majority of cases the Fund would never even learn of the damage that was done.

The System

Patricia registered Jane at one of the forty community centers and agencies around New York City that process applications for the

Fresh Air Fund. The Fund made no attempt to screen the children; it merely required an application and a doctor's examination before busing them, in shifts, to and from the 320 Friendly Towns. The shuttles began in July and continued through August.

On the other end, volunteer committees—usually composed of longtime Friendly Town hosts—were responsible for recruiting and screening host families. Committees were usually small, and often the chairperson did the vast majority of the work, which theoretically included advertising in newspapers and on the radio, processing hosts' applications, checking references, and interviewing new hosts. Neither committee members nor hosts were compensated for work or reimbursed for expenses, and many held additional full-time jobs.

According to several former chairpersons, the only training provided for the position was the "Chairman's Manual" and an optional one-day workshop (offered in at least some locations) given by a local representative and an executive from the Manhattan office. As far as could be learned, none of the volunteers or those who instructed them had professional training in child placement or protection.

Although the Fresh Air Fund said that interviews and home visits were required prior to placement, critics have asserted that the Fund had no way of knowing whether this "policy" was followed. No interview forms were sent to the central office, for example. Volunteers were required only to send in forms listing the names and addresses of hosts, their hobbies, and the age, sex, and number of children requested.

There is evidence, moreover, that hosts have received children without having been interviewed at all. The court record of an unsuccessful 1978 lawsuit charging that the Fund was responsible for a child's illness contained the plaintiff's account of how the child was placed: "No one came to her [the host's] house. No one investigated anything. One phone call. . . . No interview. No application. . . . You want to take two children from New York City? Yes. All right, and that is about it."

Nor did the Fund's attorney dispute this account: "There was a telephone conversation with . . . the chairlady from that particular area who spoke with [the host] on the telephone and arranged with her and found out where she lived and found out who she was and how many people in her family. Basically told her right there on the telephone to be a host you have to treat the kids from New York like your own and she as a chairlady was convinced that [the woman] was the kind of host that she would recommend to the Fresh Air Fund and she did."[12]

When a personal interview *was* conducted, there was no uniform procedure that all volunteers followed in making an assessment. Most often they spoke of a "gut feeling" they got from a visit. (In this respect, as in most others, the program in New Hampshire seemed quite similar to programs described by volunteers in Vermont, New York, and Massachusetts.) Roger Stone, whose wife, Teresa, was chairperson of the Concord (New Hampshire) committee for eight years, explained, "We turned a number of people down, and we just went by gut instinct. We're not trained psychologists. We're volunteers—like in the Boy Scouts and Girl Scouts."[13]

Similarly, Audrey Ordway, who also worked on the Concord committee, recalled turning down a widower who wanted a 12-year-old boy. "He wanted to know exactly what he was getting," she said. "It didn't hit me right. Sometimes you just have the intuition."

But representatives did not always agree on what was permitted and what was not. Asked how marital status would affect her placement of a child, Ordway said, "I wouldn't place a little girl with a widower, but someone else might. But a divorced man with children of his own? I wouldn't hesitate." As for spanking, Ordway said she told hosts to "do what you do to your own."

Teresa Stone, however, had a different view. "Usually there's no problem getting the same kid back," she said. But "if [the hosts] have gotten divorced or something, that's a whole different story." Of spanking, she said, "I would tell people, 'You can't hit these kids.' To some a spanking is a slap on the leg; to others it's hitting hard."

On two policies, however, there seemed to be unanimity. First, volunteers felt that in order to turn down a host, they had to have good reason. Said Stone of one placement: "We gave him a child. We didn't have any reason to turn him down." Ordway echoed, "We can't refuse anybody that's on the up and up." Second, hosts did not have to be reinterviewed if they reinvited a child. As Susan Picard, former chairperson of the Rochester (New Hampshire) committee, said, "[Hosts] don't have to do another thing except say they want [the children] back."

Beyond such screening—when it was done—there was no supervision during a child's visit or a follow-up after a child left. Often a child's only contact with Fund volunteers was on the day of arrival and the day of departure. The reason they did not visit to see how the children were doing was that "you'd never have enough time to visit all the homes," said Stone. And there were no interviews with the children or the hosts after the children left to determine how the program worked.

What the Pros Say

The professionals in child placement and protection interviewed for this chapter were sharply critical of the Fresh Air Fund's methods.

"I don't think you can any longer just have neighbors looking at neighbors saying, 'They seem nice enough and they want to take a kid,' " said Susan Sabor, director for professional issues at the New York State Council of Voluntary Family and Child-Care Agencies, which she said was responsible for placing 90 percent of New York's children currently in child care. "That may have worked a number of years ago," she continued. "Empirically, it doesn't seem to be working now.

"I think we have to take a new look at our social services systems, includng places like the Fresh Air Fund, given a whole new set of social variables," she added.

Bennington Police Chief David Mancini said he thought the Fund's view of New Hampshire was naive. "We raise cows, go fishing, and watch the sun set—I think people in urban areas think that's the way it is out here in the woods," he said. "It isn't that way at all.

"If you could work it out on paper, you'd probably find that sexual abuse occurs as frequently here as it does in the city. The only difference is that there are smaller communities where it's all kept quiet."[14]

Ignorance of such matters endangers children, said Don Rabun, the New Hampshire social worker who first investigated the reports of abuse lodged against Tynan. "A pedophile is going to seek out children as a means of sexual gratification. It's only logical that they're going to go to the sources of children." Those, he said, are jobs at day care centers, YMCAs, summer camps, and similar organizations.

But such jobs increasingly require a thorough background check, Rabun said. To obtain a child from the Fresh Air Fund, however, is far easier, and there is presumably less risk of being caught than there is when the pedophile and his victim live in the same community. To minimize the danger to children, Rabun suggested that host families be treated as foster homes. "Instead of looking at them as host homes, [the Fresh Air Fund] should look at them as short-term foster homes and have them licensed and go through the process. It's more expensive, it's more of a nuisance, but the probability of children getting hurt is lessened—probably considerably."[15]

All of those interviewed spoke of the difficulty of child placement, the impossibility of ever being absolutely certain a child is safe, and the need for professional training to mimimize the inherent dangers. Marie Miccio, executive director of Big Brothers/Big Sisters of Greater Manchester (New Hampshire), said professional training was "essential" in child placement and that an organization that did not provide adequate training would be "negligent."[16] The director of New Hampshire's Division of Children and Youth Services, David Bundy, called such training "crucial—necessary at a minimum."[17]

There was general agreement that at a minimum the Fresh Air Fund should hire professionals in each geographic region to train the volunteers and supervise their work.

"You have to have the background to investigate," Chief Mancini said. "The perfect background would be an investigator trained in youth services or someone experienced in child abuse cases." Someone like Don Rabun, he added, would be ideal. If the Fund hired one such investigator/supervisor for each state, that person could train the volunteers and critique them, Mancini said. The volunteers should also be given forms to fill out in assessing applicants and these, he said, should be reviewed by the supervisors.

Hiring professionals would also provide an accountability that could help enforce performance standards. "If you get someone who is hired and trained and his job is at stake," said Mancini, "he's going to do a hell of a lot better than an untrained volunteer." Miccio added, "If I make a lot of bad decisions, I don't have a job anymore, where with a volunteer, that wouldn't be the case."

Along with criticism of the training—or lack of training—of those doing the placing, there was also criticism of the Fund's placement methods. All spoke of the need for thorough screening, supervision, and follow-up and suggested procedures by which they could be accomplished.

"If you want to absolutely guarantee as best as you can the children are going to be safe," said Bundy, "you should have up-front interviews [with hosts], police checks, record checks, reference checks, do unannounced visits while the kids are there and exit visits [with them] after the children leave, and periodic updates and interviews with the [hosts]."

Said Mancini: "I don't think it would be that complicated to investigate, once you set the criteria." He suggested the best method for doing so would be to hire professional consultants. "It would take several trained investigators a couple of weeks to set it up," he said, "but then you'd have some pretty good criteria."

In addition to case-by-case review, regular evaluation of the entire program was also suggested. Sabor suggested assessments to identify and remedy problems in specific regions, as well as general reviews of the program. A general evaluation would consider such questions as: Would the program be better if fewer children were involved? Are the families generally adequate? Where could improvements be made?

These and other questions ought to be raised regularly, Sabor said, and are particularly important when an organization learns of abuse within its program. "I would like to see [the Fresh Air Fund] socially responsible," she said. "I would like to see them available to the [abused] kid and the family.

"I think [the Fresh Air Fund] should at least be willing to look at the case honestly and say, 'Was there something we could have done to prevent this?' "

What It Could Have Known and When It Could Have Known It

It is impossible to say what the Fund actually knew about the Tynans. It is not even certain who was responsible for screening them, but it seems likely it was Jeannie Walton.[18]

Patricia said she was told by a secretary at the Fund's Manhattan office that her daughter was assigned to the Northwood committee, which was closest to the Tynans' home in Pittsfield. The committee chair in 1981 and 1982 was Walton, according to Susan Picard, who chaired the nearby Rochester committee those years and who worked closely with her.

Walton declined to be interviewed. Speaking through the screen door of her residence in East Rochester, she said, "I've been told not to talk to you." She would not say who gave her those instructions. Asked if she had placed children in Pittsfield, as Picard said, she replied, "No comment."

When Johnni Tynan Bates was asked who, if anyone, interviewed her in 1981, she said she could not remember the woman's name, only that someone from the Fund had come to her house. Unless the case comes to trial, which seems unlikely given the assertion by lawyers for both sides that it will be settled, the full story may never be known. But there was a wealth of information the Fund could have learned about the Tynans.

The most obvious and important was that Tynan's wife had left him before Jane arrived in 1982. Should the Fund have known this in a town of about three thousand? Mancini said it should. He knew Johnni had left, he said. Referring to whoever allowed Jane to return after Johnni was gone, Mancini said, "Someone should have that person by the short hairs."

Aside from the possible instability of a man whose wife has just left him and the questionable advisability of placing a girl with a single man, there was another factor to consider. Tynan's job as an airline pilot frequently took him out of town. During Jane's visit, he was gone for several days, according to his former daughter-in-law. She remembers, she said, because Tynan left Jane with her—in violation of Fund rules.

The information available in 1981 was less unusual and more difficult to obtain. But there was a good deal a trained investigator— or someone consulting with one—could have learned.

"The local police are always a good reference," said social worker Rabun, who suggested that the police be required as one of the three references hosts are asked to supply. The police are a particularly valuable source in rural areas, where they are likely to know everyone personally, Rabun added. That would seem to apply to virtually all Friendly Towns.

Mancini said he would have been happy to discuss the Tynans and other prospective hosts from Pittsfield with Fund representatives. What could he have told them? That the Tynans were having financial problems, that Mrs. Tynan had written bad checks, and that at least one of their own six children had been in trouble.

"Anybody who knew them would be expected to know they were having money problems," Mancini said. In fact, the Tynans were heavily in debt—so heavily that in September 1981 they filed a Chapter 7 petition with the U.S. Bankrupty Court in Manchester, and two years later their house was foreclosed on. According to a claim filed with the court, they even owed $3,107 in child support payments to their own daughter, who stayed in California when the family moved east.

The youngest of the five Tynan boys was in trouble with the law, Mancini said, for persistently driving without a license and registration—until he was finally jailed. "He just wouldn't quit," said Mancini, who called the boy "flaky." Mancini described another son as "screwed up."

Given this information, even a highly trained investigator probably could not have predicted what Tynan would do to Jane. But a prediction is not required in placing a child. Writing bad checks and raising children who get into trouble indicate an attitude, according to Mancini. "That's basically what you're working on—is an attitude," he said. "That's all you're going to get.

"In this case, you don't have to prove anything," he said. "You can just pass on a host family." In theory that is true. The Fresh Air Fund is not required to explain a rejection, as a social agency turning down a foster home must do under New York law, for example. But Fund volunteers said they felt obliged to place a child in a home unless there was a good reason not to.

Was there a good reason not to place Fresh Air Fund children with the Tynans? A Fund representative apparently decided not. But had that representative asked Mancini the same question in 1981 or 1982, he said he would have answered yes.

20/20 Hindsight, Foresight

There are those who will say that Mancini spoke with 20/20 hindsight. What is the use, they will ask, of dredging up the past?

But for Jane, the past is not over. According to her therapist, while her peers are talking about dating, Jane is terrified of having a relationship with a male. She still has occasional nightmares, and until quite recently she had trouble concentrating on school work. She was irritable and often picked fights with her siblings. And she asked questions her mother could not answer—questions like, Why hasn't Don Tynan been punished? Since the indictment, the question that has most troubled her is, Why did God let this happen to me?

Jane has been receiving therapy, thanks to the efforts of her mother and lawyers.[19] Most experts agree that early intervention and treatment offer abuse victims the best chance of recovery. Big Brothers/Big Sisters of Greater Manchester refers children for professional counseling, if needed, even when a relationship is severed amicably, according to Miccio. If a case of child abuse occurred, Miccio said, the child would be referred for counseling, and the agency would report the incident to the local Social Services Department and would aid them in any way possible. The Fresh Air Fund, by comparison, had not shown a willingness to provide children with therapy or to report the abuse in the first two cases (although it said it would have in the third, had Patricia not already done so).

There were those who said that a strong dose of hindsight was precisely what the Fund needed. If the Fund did not take a hard look at its past, further cases of abuse were inevitable, they said. And even some supporters saw a need for improvement.

"This program is a good program," said former chairperson Susan Picard. "All those kids wouldn't have any way of getting out of the city and seeing how other people live and what their options are, nor would our people here have an option of finding out that these kids that they almost think of as ghetto kids or zombie kids are kids that they can love.

"But I can definitely see restrictions need to be tightened up," she said. Of the Fund's screening methods, she added, "It's a loose arrangement—no two ways about that.

"I think that now you're running into the problem of a lot of women working, which ten years ago they didn't do so much," Picard said. "And so you're having people doing this on a part-time basis because they're trying to be real nice and they believe in the program. But let's face it, if you're already working forty to fifty hours a week, and if you have any size to your program—we put through ninety kids—that would be tough part-time."

Picard agrees with suggestions that the program could be improved if the police and Social Services provided information for background checks and training for volunteers. "You need some kind of training," she said, "and you certainly need some kind of review system.

"I can't be sure that one of our children that came through wasn't abused," she continued. "And we were a good committee. I'm sure other committees weren't as on top of things."

Along with the other professionals interviewed, Chief Mancini foresaw difficult but necessary decisions in the Fund's future. Speaking from behind his desk at the Bennington police station, located in a cramped basement beneath City Hall, he said, "People don't like getting investigated. They get belligerent. You're going to lose a lot of volunteers and hosts if you go to that method. But you've got to do something. The problem is not going to go away.

"Doing nothing," he added, "is like saying you don't need a juvenile officer because sooner or later the juveniles are going to be adults."

2. Redemption

The change began during the settlement of the second lawsuit, according to C. Stephen Heard, Jr., a lawyer and an officer on the Fund's board of directors. During a three-and-a-half hour interview in Heard's Manhattan office, he and Fund counsel Robert Gaynor spoke for the charity, while Vachss and Borowka provided their own perspectives. What Heard and Gaynor discovered during that settlement was that the opposing lawyers were neither lunatics nor mercenaries—two possibilities that had occurred to them before they met face to face.

That first meeting was in July 1985. The Fund lawyers were surprised to find that it was not money that seemed to drive Vachss and Borowka. Nor did what they say seem unreasonable. Heard recalled a question Vachss posed as a kind of turning point: " 'How would you view it if it happened to one of your children?' I didn't have to think very long," Heard remembered. " 'I'd kill the son of a bitch,' " he said.

It is crucial to an abused child's recovery that she be told what happened was neither her fault nor a figment of her imagination, Vachss explained to them. The clearest and strongest way the message can be communicated, he said, is by telling her that society has punished the person responsible—when it has. "If you're prepared to change your position and see this for what it is, let's work together to see that [Tynan] is indicted," Vachss challenged.

The Fund's attitude had already begun to change by this time, according to Gaynor, who pointed to the difference between the charity's response to the first suit and the third. In the first case, remember, the Fund denied any responsibility and even accused the mother of having abused the child. Heard said that the disaster of the first case led to a change in lawyers that brought in Gaynor. In the Doe case, there was immediate acceptance of the situation as Patricia related it and an expressed willingness to help. The charity had come a long way, Gaynor said. But it was not there yet, and they knew it. That was why they decided to accept Vachss's challenge.

It was extraordinary for a number of reasons. It is rare that adversaries unite, especially in the middle of an emotionally charged lawsuit. They united in order to do what all agreed was truly in the "best interests of the child" (although the New Hampshire prosecutor has strongly questioned those motives). It was also in what they agreed was the best interests of the Fund and the literally millions of children it would serve in the future. Prosecution would send a message not only to Jane, but to the Tynans out there who contemplated molesting or otherwise maltreating Fresh Air Fund children.

The message he wants them to hear, Heard said, is this: "People who abuse in any way children of the Fresh Air Fund are going to be pursued by the Fund and its board and its lawyers to the full extent of the law. And if there's any misconception in anyone's mind that we're going to look the other way because it's easier or more convenient, they should look at the history of Mr. Tynan in New Hampshire. They're going to be very sadly mistaken."

The final pages of that history have not yet been written, but it has been a remarkable story so far. It has also stirred strong and bitter feelings in at least one New Hampshire resident.

Back to New Hampshire

"Michael Johnson was a brick wall," Gaynor said during the interview. But the New Hampshire prosecutor did not appear to be a wall at first—or at least not an insurmountable one, Gaynor added.

Vachss had already asked Johnson to indict Tynan on criminal charges. He was convinced Johnson never would and was ready to implement another strategy, but the Fund lawyers thought they might persuade him if they took the lead. In August 1985, Gaynor and Heard flew to Concord and met with Johnson to "insist" he reopen the case. "Johnson's response was, 'Don't call us, we'll call you,' " Gaynor said. But Gaynor *did* call—repeatedly.

Johnson was no longer talking about a "greater degree of penetration"; he said there had to be a "greater degree of culpability." There was talk of his sending an investigator down to New York to interview the child and her therapist. It did not happen. Finally, a videotaped interview of the child was suggested. Gaynor said he was led to believe that if he just had a videotape that met Johnson's evidentiary requirements, an indictment would be obtained.

Vachss arranged for the interview to be conducted by an assistant district attorney from a suburb of New York City who had experience interviewing children in sexual abuse cases. The prosecutor had never met Jane, and the entire session was supervised by FBI agents, at their headquarters, to ensure there was no coaching or other contamination of the evidence, Vachss said. Gaynor flew back to New Hampshire to hand-deliver the tape.

When Johnson viewed it, he professed he found it credible, Gaynor said. He just wanted to talk to the assistant district attorney who had conducted the interview. It was part of a pattern, according to Gaynor: "He was always raising the hurdle on us." After Johnson talked to the A.D.A., he wanted a sworn statement from Patricia expressing her wish to see Tynan prosecuted along with an opinion from Jane's therapist that prosecution would not harm the child. They were delivered—both stated that the child needed and wanted Tynan to be punished—but still no indictment. In their last phone conversation, Johnson told Gaynor: "I'm not going to tell you what the status [of the case] is and don't call me anymore." Gaynor described the entire effort as "a year and a half of frustration."

Vachss was more scathing in his criticism: "To me, the real horror is this: Michael Johnson knew that our child was molested, knew that other children had been molested, knew our child was a Fresh Air child, and never notified the Fresh Air Fund that a person to whom they were entrusting children had been convicted of sexual crimes against other children."[20]

When the criticism was relayed to him during an interview, Johnson said he would not comment on the merits of the pending case, but he did respond to the accusations.[21] He did not take issue with the basic facts Gaynor described, but he objected to the way his behavior was characterized. He began by explaining his view of prosecutorial discretion.

"Fortunately for our liberties," he said, "the criminal justice system and the civil justice system are separate and distinct in regard to determining who gets charged, prosecuted, and punished for crimes. And that is fortunate, I say, because we are a free society. Prosecution, in this country, takes that freedom away. And that should not be in any way commingled with financial interests, regardless of how sincere those interests might be. Now I tried to impress that to the Fresh Air Fund."

Explaining those interests, he continued: "Seventy million dollars at interest, when there is a question as to whether or not Mr. Tynan would be responsible for the financial liability as opposed to the Fresh Air Fund, in my opinion discounts the kind of input one might get from all of the civil litigants, and that's why the civil process is not part of the criminal process." While Tynan has not been sued in connection with the alleged abuse, Johnson was apparently referring to the possibility that he will be, and to the presumed effect a criminal conviction would have on such a case as well as on the lawsuit against the Fresh Air Fund.

As to the evidence he deemed necessary to proceed, Johnson responded: "The distinction between the offenses in New Hampshire under our criminal code is the question of penetration. So I indicated to you that if this accusation was of a greater criminal culpability, i.e., a more egregious offense because of the nature of the penetration—which is the distinction between a misdemeanor, Class A, and Class B felonies—then I would consider going forward with it, because that was the understanding left with Mr. Tynan's initial attorney," he said, referring to the agreement made during the case involving Tynan's granddaughters.

"Mr. Gaynor was never led to believe that the state's prosecution would or would not occur," he continued. "It's apparent that Mr. Gaynor . . . sees the criminal justice process as sort of like a Monopoly game. If you get from square one to square ten, you get an indictment. That obviously is not the system in this country—thank

God . . . In terms of the hurdles that Mr. Gaynor addresses, they are not hurdles. They are responses to Mr. Gaynor's insistence that we indict. The indictment is not the goal; justice is. It's the criminal justice system, not the criminal indictment system."

Responding to the charge that Tynan could have obtained another Fresh Air Fund child, Johnson said that the man had been in jail, followed by carefully supervised probation. After his conviction, he had a record that could be checked by any organization considering placing a child with him. "There's no way that this individual could be properly considered for any type of child supervision, period," he said.

Finally, Johnson questioned the motivation—particularly Andrew Vachss's—that prompted the effort to seek prosecution. "Ask Mr. Vachss what his percentage of the $70 million will be when and if a judgment is rendered," he challenged.

"In my opinion," he continued, "Mr. Gaynor and Mr. Vachss were using the child and her trauma to attempt to convince this office to prosecute, therefore . . . their continuing efforts to make input on the process were discounted because of what obviously was in the best interests of the child at the time. The comment from them was that the child needed closure, the child needed to know that the defendant had been punished for what the child went through. It was clearly explained to them that the man had been punished and the child could be informed of that to provide the closure that they wished. However, they didn't wish closure under those circumstances . . . It certainly was not, in my interpretation, the kind of support that would be normally offered to the child victim in this jurisdiction. Keeping a case alive for three or four years is not the kind of thing that assists the child in getting over the trauma and providing the child with a closure."

Vachss responded, "If Michael Johnson is saying my motivation arose from the lawsuit, his problem is that the prosecutorial duty arose way before there was any concept of a lawsuit . . . way before this ever came to my attention." Patricia contacted the New Hampshire police in November 1983, Tynan pleaded guilty to sexual assault the following month, and the lawsuit was filed ten months later, he observed. "For Michael Johnson to say, 'Well, the child should have contented herself with the fact that Tynan had been prosecuted' seems ridiculous to me when the only way the child found out about the prosecution was due to our investigation." Vachss added that Johnson never contacted the family and never disclosed to them or to him the agreement he made with Tynan's attorney.

"For him to talk about what's in the best interests of the child," Vachss continued, "when he has exactly contrary information from the child, the child's family, and the child's therapist is to me indefensible. As far as what percentage we get of any recovery, the percentage is fixed by the court. We're limited to a third of the recovery, but that's an outside limitation. A lesser amount can be fixed by the court in an infant's compromise order."[22]

Vachss had encountered a similar situation before. In the case that led to the first lawsuit against the Fresh Air Fund, as a matter of fact, the prosecutor never brought criminal charges. He said he needed more evidence. Vachss went public, the press reported their heated exchanges (not dissimilar to those above), and ultimately Vachss turned to the Vermont attorney general, who took over the case and successfully prosecuted. Vachss believed it was a legitimate and effective way to force prosecution in a case where there was sufficient evidence to proceed and where a prosecutor refused to do so without presenting legitimate reasons.

Rather than turn to the press, the Fund officials (no doubt seeking to avoid unwanted publicity) preferred to take the case to the New Hampshire attorney general themselves.[23] By the time they approached the attorney general, they had the videotape and a stack of evidence. An assistant attorney general was quickly assigned to the case, and within a few months Tynan was indicted on three counts of aggravated felonious sexual assault.

How does Jane feel about that? She said she was "happy" and "satisfied" during an interview in the presence of her therapist, Flora Colao.[24] Colao said that Jane's therapy improved dramatically after the videotaped interview (Colao said she told Johnson as much in her letter) and that Jane improved even more after she learned of the arrest. Making the videotape was not easy, Jane said. "At first I thought it was embarrassing, but then I said, 'It's life, you know? It happened. I have to get through it. I have to face it. It happened.' So it wasn't so hard to do after a while."

Jane, now 15, said she never doubted Tynan would eventually be arrested. She feels she has helped others by her action. "If I would have never told, like, many kids would have still been going to Tynan and the same thing probably would have happened to them. I'm glad I stopped it." She also understands that her experience helped bring about changes of attitudes and policies at the Fresh Air Fund. "I feel good that I'm helping the kids," she said.

A New Awareness

Heard and Gaynor described those changes during the interview. "We have to be vigilant," Heard said. "We can't pretend it doesn't exist because we were wrong in Myrick [the first lawsuit]. Forget the fact that we had to settle the case. The child was hurt. We didn't believe it could be so . . . We were too trusting."

The changes have included computerizing records,[25] hiring more full-time professionals, training regional representatives more thoroughly, and insisting that chairpersons carefully screen host families. The new attitude has met some resistance, as Chief Mancini predicted it would. "We lost some very good people out in the field because they just weren't going to do it the new way," Heard said. There are no illusions that such measures will eliminate all abuse, however.

Said Heard: "You can't handle many kids in thirteen states and a large camping area and not have incidents [of abuse]. It's going to happen. But we think we've now got a response mechanism and we think we've begun to learn something about the people who are . . . expert in this area.

"We think we're operating today in a much more aware environment, a more responsive, reactive environment, rather than just saying, 'No, no, it couldn't be us, no one would do that to our kids,' which, as you know, basically was the response we had seven years ago . . . We're not all the way there yet, but we're making an effort."

The Fund is determined that cases of abuse be handled immediately and professionally, Heard said. The New York office is now available around the clock for emergencies, and Heard and Gaynor said they are personally notified. When circumstances have dictated, Fund officials have traveled to a site to ensure a child is safe and that proper authorities are notified. But its involvement does not end there. The New Hampshire experience has taught the Fund that it must be proactive, not reactive, Gaynor said. The Fund now follows up with therapy for a child and family members, when necessary. It no longer assumes that simply notifying the authorities is sufficient.

As "a fringe benefit of doing the right thing," the Fund is much less likely to be sued when it follows such a course of conduct, Gaynor said. Vachss and Borowka agreed, since the victim and family are likely to see the Fund as a covictim. Furthermore, they said, an agency can only be successfully sued if it is liable. So long as the Fund is acting to the best of its ability to prevent abuse, and to help victims in response to it, a suit is unlikely to succeed.

The new approach has already proved effective in handling a half-dozen emergencies, including sexual abuse, in the past couple of years, Heard said. He openly and warmly credited Vachss and Borowka who, he acknowledged, "sometimes beat us over the head with a stick" before they struck a responsive chord.

Asked near the end of the interview why institutions commonly deny abuse, Heard said people have an aversion to the subject and find it easier to say 'Well, that was *their* charity, that was *New Hampshire*, that was *that* lawsuit. Here . . . we're all friends and neighbors, good Christian people.'

"By God," he warned with the conviction of one who has learned his lesson well, "if you don't see that seamy underbelly, there'll be more Tynan cases before there are less."

4

The Courts

Passions run high when the subject turns to prosecution. Even those who are ambivalent seem passionately so; their feelings may be mixed, but the feelings themselves are strong. And this is understandable. Lives are often in the balance.

To some, the prospect of a child's testifying in court and not being believed is so painful to contemplate that they question whether it is even worth the risk. Others believe not *having* a day in court—not even having a case investigated, as we saw in Jane Doe's case in the last chapter—is much worse. It is the cases that fall between the cracks (or are pushed into the abyss) that they rail against.

Still others believe the system is so stacked against the defendant that if a child is halfway presentable in court, the jury's sympathy is all but guaranteed.

Some of these assessments are predictable. Defense attorneys typically decry what one of them calls "the presumption of guilt" in child sexual abuse cases. Prosecutors talk about the difficulty of prosecuting these cases, often calling them the hardest of all in which to get a conviction. And therapists worry about the damage the criminal justice system does to already damaged children.

Members of VOCAL (Victims of Child Abuse Laws) who have been accused themselves often talk about their own cases, which they typically describe as marked by gross abuses of power, revealing how easily and arbitrarily innocent adults can be victimized by incompetent investigations. They and other critics of the system also talk about child protective workers' breaking up families. When they do, however, they generally are referring to an entirely separate process that occurs in a different court.

Child Protective Investigations

Basically, there are four arenas in which a child sexual abuse case can be heard. There is the criminal court, where a perpetrator is charged with a crime for which, if convicted, he can be penalized. And there are three kinds of civil proceedings. These cannot result in criminal penalties for any party, but a judge or jury may be called upon to determine whether a child has been abused and to take appropriate action.

First, there are civil lawsuits. A parent or guardian, acting on a child's behalf, may sue an alleged perpetrator for damages the child has suffered (as in the case study in chapter 11). Or, a negligence suit may be brought against a third party that had a duty to protect the child (such as the Fresh Air Fund, in the last chapter). Second, allegations of sexual abuse may arise during a divorce proceeding (or may be incorporated into one, as we will see later in two case studies). In order to determine who should have custody of the child, and with what visitation agreement, the court often must decide whether the allegation is true.

Finally, there are proceedings specifically for hearing allegations of abuse and neglect of children by parents or guardians and taking whatever action the court deems "in the best interests of the child." The court's options in such cases are myriad. If there is a finding of abuse, a child may be removed from a home and the parent's custody may be temporarily or permanently terminated. Or the court may, for example, insist that an abusive parent attend counseling and have contact with the child limited to supervised visits until there are signs that the counseling has proved effective.

Cases of this type are held in courts that are known by different names in different jurisdictions, most often juvenile court and family court. (For convenience, we will use the second to refer to all such courts.) When VOCAL talks about social workers' "destroying families," it is generally referring to proceedings in these courts, where social workers are often the key witnesses.

The following general description of how a case is investigated and litigated in family court will not apply to every jurisdiction, but interviews conducted around the country suggest there are many more similarities than differences. When a report is made to a state's central registry that a parent, guardian, or caretaker (such as a day care worker) is suspected of having sexually abused a child, the local Social Services Department[1] must investigate within a prescribed time (usually twenty-four hours, if the alleged abuser still has access to the child). Most of the larger localities, at least, have a special unit called child protective services that does initial investigations.

Three experienced child protective services workers in Westchester County, New York, discussed how they investigate a report.[2] Their methods, described during a lengthy interview, were similar to those outlined by social workers in other states. First, they contact the individual who made the report—usually by telephone. They try to learn how the allegation came to light, what the current situation is, and who the child is with. Next, they seek to interview the child in a neutral setting, when possible, to minimize factors that may inhibit a child from speaking openly. One of the caseworkers said she usually picks up the child and drives back to the Social Services office for the interview. Another said he usually interviews children in their homes, preferably in their rooms, away from parents who could influence what the child says. In other states (Iowa, for instance), a common site is the child's school. Some states have laws requiring school officials to cooperate with social workers' investigations, but New York is not among them. The New York caseworkers said that they rarely interview children in schools because sometimes the principals insist on attending, often inviting a teacher, a guidance counselor, and the school nurse, almost guaranteeing that the child will be intimidated. Other times principals have refused access to the child until they obtained parental permission. Then they called the parent, who sometimes was also the alleged perpetrator, tipping that person off to the fact that there was an investigation.

If the social worker decides from preliminary interviews that the child is in "imminent danger" of further abuse or neglect, in most states the child may be removed from the home immediately, so long as a court order authorizing the emergency removal is obtained within a prescribed period (usually seventy-two hours). In some states (Iowa, for example), a court order must be obtained before the child is removed. Who actually removes the child varies from state to state. In California a police officer must do it; in Iowa it is a juvenile intake officer; in New York and in many other states, it is the social worker.

Whether or not the child is removed, the caseworker then completes the investigation, and if he or she finds "any credible evidence" that the child has been abused, the case is designated "founded" or "indicated." Theoretically, in order to make such a determination, the worker tries to interview all parties who may have information. The Westchester workers said that after interviewing the child, they would next try to interview siblings (again, in a neutral setting), followed by the parent who is not accused, the accused parent, and any other children named by those already interviewed as having been abused. Others who might be interviewed include relatives, teachers, pediatricians, and neighbors. But a variety of factors sometimes prevent a worker from investigating thoroughly. Social workers frequently carry overwhelming caseloads with mandates requiring that other emergency reports be investigated promptly. They may fear the prospect of interviewing potentially hostile parents, who sometimes react violently or hysterically (especially if one has been accused of the abuse). Or a caseworker may be an incompetent or biased investigator and may thus overlook sources who could prove valuable.

All or most of the interviews in a priority case should be conducted in the first two days, the Westchester caseworkers said. If there are indications the child was abused recently, then a medical examination should be scheduled the first day; if not, then the second day. Following the investigation, the worker decides whether the case is "indicated." What happens next is entirely discretionary. The worker may negotiate an arrangement with the family to provide services designed to alleviate the problem, may ignore the matter, or may file an abuse or neglect petition with the family court, which would then schedule a trial.

That is the investigator side of the social worker. But in the sometimes strange world of social work, in some cases the same worker may provide services to the families he or she investigates on an incest report. This is good cop, bad cop all over, but in one "cop." And in a sense, such "schizophrenia" is written into most states' regulations, which require social workers—and family courts—to "reunite" and "rehabilitate" families whenever possible, and, simultaneously, to protect "the best interests of the child." What the laws do not say is what social workers are supposed to do if these ends prove mutually exclusive.[3]

One of the Westchester workers put it this way: "The whole set-up—your frame of reference—is to reunite the family. And to think the unthinkable, that you're going to separate this mother and child— I mean I've been thinking about it in terms of this little girl who was really screwed up. I don't think that mother should ever have that kid back. She let her oldest daughter be abused twice and now she let the younger one get abused, and I don't think she should ever have the right to have that kid and expose her to that again, which inevitably is going to happen. But to think that goes totally against my brain because I'm thinking in terms of: this is a family, what right do I have to make that judgment?"

His co-worker, on the other hand, while acknowledging the potential conflict, saw no easy solution. Assigning separate workers to handle child protection and family rehabilitation, she said, would likely create more conflict and delay, and more mandates and tasks for an already overburdened system.

To avoid this very conflict, however, the *Federal Standards for Child Abuse and Neglect Prevention and Treatment Programs and Projects* suggests that Social Services Departments "assign specific staff for the purpose of *intake* (receipt and evaluation of child abuse and neglect reports) when the Local Unit has two or more child protective service workers" and "assign specific staff for the purpose of *treatment* (provision and/or obtainment of services and resources to meet the needs of the child, individual members and the family as a unit)."[4] (Emphasis in original.) And there does seem to be a trend around the country toward establishing specialized child protective units that are trained to investigate.

Family Courts

But investigating, filing a petition, and providing services do not end a social worker's involvement in a child sexual abuse case. The worker will likely be called to testify if and when an indicated case comes to family court and, depending on the result there, may well be called on to monitor the home after the case is resolved. Although the social worker's testimony may be key to the case, workers are rarely trained in courtroom demeanor (any more than doctors are). Most often they learn under fire. In that respect, they are not alone.

The assistant county attorneys (or, in some places, assistant attorneys general) who represent the Department of Social Services in family court are typically a year or two or three out of law school. The high turnover of social workers makes it likely a beginner will be testifying, and the judges who sit in family court are often beginners themselves. In New York, children in abuse proceedings are represented by lawyers formally known as law guardians. Their poor quality was amply documented by a study that found 45 percent of the representation "seriously inadequate or marginally adequate" and just 4 percent "effective."[5] Similar complaints have been made of law guardians elsewhere.[6] Consequently, these cases are often investigated by beginners, litigated by beginners, and heard before beginners.

For these reasons, one of the Westchester social workers called family court "a joke." "It's not taken seriously," he said, "and the court cases are looked at differently. . . . Even when cases are not appropriate for a criminal court, what happens in family court is not appropriate. Nobody takes it seriously. The attorneys look at it as training grounds for criminal court. The judges in the family court are looking to get out and move up to supreme court [New York's superior trial court]. The level of argument in the courts is ridiculous. If I was a defense attorney on some of my cases, I could have ripped my case apart—with a little bit of effort. But they don't even make an effort, half the time."

Certainly the quality of family court proceedings varies in New York, and that state's court system does not necessarily reflect the quality of such courts nationwide. But neither are the above remarks isolated. Disparaging comments about family courts are common in many states. The transfer of a judge who was the target of a federal investigation from criminal to family court in Philadelphia (chapter 1) conveys nothing if not an attitude.

At the same time, real power is vested in these courts. Although they cannot send anyone to jail (except for violating a court order, such as an order of protection), they can see that a parent's rights are permanently terminated, in the most extreme instances. They can see that a child is protected and gets the counseling and support that he or she needs, which is more than criminal courts can do.

They are much more likely than criminal courts to validate a child's experience by finding that abuse has occurred. And they are in a better position to protect vulnerable children from further abuse.

There are several reasons why this is so. First, the standard of proof in family court is much lower than in criminal court, requiring only that a case be proved by a "preponderance of the evidence" in many states, or "clear and convincing evidence" in others, whereas criminal courts require "beyond a reasonable doubt."

Second, hearsay testimony as to the out-of-court statements of a child victim is allowed into evidence routinely in many family courts (although usually it must be corroborated by other evidence). Hearsay is an out-of-court statement that is not made under oath, is not subject to cross-examination, and is offered for its truth. According to child advocates, the importance of hearsay in a child sexual abuse case is that if a parent, teacher, therapist, or doctor is permitted to repeat what a child said concerning an allegation, then the child may be spared the trauma of having to repeat the story in a courtroom full of strangers. Children rarely have to testify in family court, and when they do, since cases are almost always tried by a judge rather than a jury, the judge (in at least some states) may question the child alone in chambers, rather than in the more intimidating courtroom setting.

Third, family courts can issue orders of protection, barring a father accused of abuse from seeing a child at all or without proper supervision. Or, if a child has already been found to have been abused, the court can prescribe conditions that the abuser must follow in visiting the child and that the nonabusing spouse must follow to maintain custody. If both parents are found to be unsuitable custodians, the court may declare the child a ward of the court and place the child with a relative, in a foster home, or in some other environment it deems appropriate.

The importance of lawyers appointed by family courts to represent children in these proceedings should not be overlooked. Not all states appoint law guardians, and when they exist they are not always used, nor are all lawyers who are appointed qualified, as we have seen. There is not even uniformity in what they are called.[7] Yet these lawyers are the only litigators whose sole function is to represent the best interests of the child. At their best, law guardians fulfill that function by conducting their own investigations. They make sure that undermanned Social Services staffs monitor the child during and after the trial to ensure that all court orders, including those barring the abuser from the home, are enforced. They must also act to ensure that the state does not lightly sever a child's tie to her family, but does so only to protect the child.

What makes their tasks doubly challenging is that law guardians must determine not simply what the child *says* she wants, but what is *best* for the child, which may be very different. As law guardian Andrew Vachss pointed out, bonding between a parent and child may be negative as well as positive.

"If you take the Stockholm syndrome principle," Vachss said, referring to the name given to the bonding that sometimes occurs between a terrorist and his hostage, "and you accelerate it to the one hundredth power," he continued, "you've got incest. No crime bonds the victim and the perpetrator closer." If an incest victim says she wants to return to the home in which she was abused, even though nothing has changed there, does that mean her law guardian should adopt that position? Not at all, said Vachss. But what gives the law guardian the right to oppose the child's wishes? The court does, Vachss replied.

The role of the law guardian is to present to the court a professional assessment of what is best for the child. That opinion does not necessarily have to coincide with the child's wishes, Vachss said. His job is to *protect* the child, not serve as the child's mouthpiece. Although he always consults with the child, he said, not every child is capable of contributing a competent, informed opinion as to her best interests—any more than the child was capable of informed consent to sex. However, Vachss added, if a child is older (say, in her teens) and, in his judgment, competent to determine her own best interests, then he will present her wishes to the court so long as he agrees they represent at least a minimum level of safety. If he believes they do not, he will explain why and allow his client to choose between modifying her position or finding a new lawyer, which he will help her do.[8]

Critics have suggested that the courts have no business assigning children lawyers and effectively splitting up families. They object as well to the liberalized rules of evidence that permit hearsay. The balance has been tipped, they say, in favor of those making the accusations (and often, they believe, the child has been put up to it).

Others have argued that no such imbalance exists. And still others claim an imbalance is proper in these cases. One judge, for example, said she viewed the court's primary obligation as protecting the child. The risk to the respondent (the accused), she said, is that there will be an unjust finding of sexual abuse causing "embarrassment, discomfort and maybe even a temporary loss of the child." But dismissing a case when a child has actually been abused, she continued, risks the far more serious possibility of returning the child to an environment where the abuse will continue and "the child may be destroyed."[9]

Arguments such as this spur VOCAL and its proponents to demand that defendants' rights be protected. But the real target of their fury is the emergency removal of children from the home. Such actions, they insist, are tantamount to a presumption of guilt. Their complaints have clearly struck a chord. Articles with headlines such as "False Accusation of Child Abuse: Could It Happen to You?" are attention grabbers,[10] without a doubt, but beyond the sensationalism, they raise serious concerns. The questions that seem to draw readers to these articles are, Why should anyone be allowed to take away a parent's kids? and, Even if it is proper at times, why should it happen before there is proof of wrongdoing? The it-could-happen-to-you approach is extremely effective in this kind of story. For example:

> The police often strike at night. Your children are seized and taken to a secret location. They are placed in the hands of state doctors who strip them down and give them thorough examinations, focusing attention on their genitalia. Meanwhile, you are hauled into court to face an inquisitorial hearing into your character. Your accusers enjoy complete anonymity and full legal protection. Your guilt is essentially assumed. Many standard rules of evidence are tossed out, including the hearsay prohibition. Also unavailable to you are ancient privileges such as husband-wife and patient-doctor confidentialities. Even among those who, against all odds, manage to prove their innocence and recover their children, many escape only by agreeing to state-directed psychological counseling, where therapists work to restructure one's mind and values.[11]

Despite the hyperbole, there are substantive issues at the heart of the controversy. We will return to them when we examine the entire backlash movement in depth in chapter 6. But let us turn now to the issues and controversies in the criminal courts.

Criminal Courts

One of the most obvious differences between family court and the criminal courts is that we have heard a lot more about the latter. And it is not just because no television shows are set in family court, or that violent crimes do not wind up there. Violent crimes are described daily in family courts around the country. In fact, some cases tried in family court then move to criminal court and can end with a civil lawsuit. There is nothing in most states to prevent the same set of facts from being litigated in all three forums with the object of achieving three different results. For example, if a father sexually abuses his daughter, the case may go to family court first, where (let us say) a finding of abuse occurs and the daughter is removed from the home and placed with a relative. Then, in a separate trial, the father is convicted of criminal charges and placed on probation (a not uncommon result). Finally, his daughter files a civil lawsuit for damages resulting from the abuse. The purpose of the first case is to protect the child from further damage; the second, to punish the offender; the third, to compensate the victim. This scenario corresponds precisely to the facts in the Angela Doe case—the case study in chapter 11. (There are also many cases in which the results are not consistent, such as a finding of abuse in family court and an acquittal in criminal court.)

Why then do we hear so much more talk about criminal court cases? The reason, which will sound at first like a tautology, is that they are reported more often in the media. Family court cases, on the other hand, are rarely reported. The ostensible reason is that family court cases involve children whose identities the courts are obliged to protect. But as more and more criminal cases—especially high-profile day care scandals—appear in the media, it is clear journalists are willing and able to report stories without revealing the names of child victims. And in fact reporters have not only written about family court cases, but have attended family court as well. In many states the judge has the authority to grant access to the media, but also may establish ground rules concerning use of names and identifying information. Or the judge may deny access to the courtroom but divulge pertinent information in response to media inquiries.

We can only speculate why the media have not been more vigilant in reporting on this area. One possibility is that such reporting requires more work and greater enterprise. Initial inquiries for information may meet resistance, convincing a reporter that further effort will be fruitless. Editors may perceive the cases to be lacking in drama and significance since there are no criminal penalties, the names of litigators must be withheld, and children are the central figures. A certain amount of denial may enter into the editorial process as well. Editors, like their readers, sometimes do not wish to believe that sexual abuse is widespread, or they believe it but do not want to trouble their readers with daily reminders (just as editors know that murders occur regularly in certain neighborhoods of large urban centers but do not deem murder newsworthy until prominent people from very different neighborhoods are killed).

Whatever the reasons, it is clear that the media attention to the one arena and not the other affects each profoundly. The lack of media attention to family court means that much of what goes on there is unknown to the public. The claim that cases must always be kept confidential may be used by Social Services Departments, prosecutors, defense lawyers, law guardians, judges, and even perpetrators to shield themselves from accountability and unwanted publicity. Mistakes and abuses within the system often continue uncorrected, and perpetrators may have continued access to children because their neighbors lack critical information about them. VOCAL's insistence that the process by which cases are investigated and litigated in family court be opened for public scrutiny may well prove persuasive and, if their efforts succeed, salubrious.

But that is not to say that media attention is an unmitigated palliative. Parents of victims are sometimes told by prosecutors that they should not discuss their cases with anyone or they may well find their names—and those of their children—splashed across the morning papers. Such comments are sometimes well-meaning advice. But other times they are threats that can convince parents to remain silent in compliance with those who may not wish to prosecute a case for reasons of their own, which may have little to do with their professional responsibilities.[12]

The authors of *The Politics of Child Abuse*, one of the most biased (and superficial) books on this or any subject, argue that prosecutors of child sexual abuse cases have most often been motivated by politics and the desire for "job security."[13] It is undoubtedly true that prosecutors in all states are sometimes motivated to prosecute cases, child sexual abuse among them, for political reasons. This, of course, says nothing about the merits of those cases. But the authors either failed to understand or found it inconvenient to acknowledge that it is equally clear prosecutors sometimes choose *not* to prosecute cases for political reasons.

Prosecuting a mass molestation case can make a name for an entire office. It can keep a district attorney and several assistants in the news for months. Winning the case can lead to reelection, prestige, lucrative jobs in private practice. But losing the case can do untold damage to those same careers. And there are very few "sure things" in prosecuting child sexual abuse cases. They are almost always heavily dependent on the testimony of child witnesses who at their best will remain question marks until they take the stand. Medical evidence is usually absent or equivocal. Other corroborating evidence is often circumstantial and sketchy. So there are often motives for not prosecuting a sex abuse case. A prosecutor who is overly concerned with a conviction record can find many cases far more appetizing.

There are prosecutors with reputations for avoiding these cases, although their reputations are often known only to those in the field, since the public almost never hears of cases never filed, and the victims can rarely publicize their plights. A Westchester County, New York, prosecutor[14] who has said she has a perfect conviction record (50–0),[15] has been criticized by social workers who say that she seldom makes a good faith effort to prosecute even the strongest cases they investigate. One child protective worker who has personally investigated more than fifty cases over five years says not one has been criminally prosecuted.

"When you go through it a couple of times," he says, "and you bring the witnesses up there and they interview them at length and nothing ever happens, after a while you get the message. Nothing is ever going to happen."[16] The caseworker's two colleagues agreed with this assessment, as did two former child protective supervisors.[17]

The prosecutor replied that she had established an award-winning, innovative unit with a statewide reputation, and she was defended by colleagues she brought with her to an interview. "It's a shame that if a person does well, that that's somehow interpreted to work against them," she said.

But a number of prosecutors experienced in child sexual abuse cases said that losses are inevitable. "If you're not losing some cases, you're not taking tough cases to trial," said Jan Hansen, a prosecutor in Sacramento, California. Asked what she would think of a prosecutor with a perfect record, she responded, "Something's wrong."[18] Nan Horvat, a prosecutor from Iowa, agreed. Her office is not concerned with its conviction rate, she said. Perhaps that was in part because her boss, the county attorney, was running unopposed in the primary and general election.

"We try lots of cases that we lose," Horvat said. "We try them for the sheer inconvenience of the defendant." When asked if that was fair to the defendant and the taxpayers paying for the trial, she replied, "We believe our witnesses are testifying to the best of their ability and truthfully, and we believe that we can get past a directed verdict and submit the case to the jury, but we also anticipate what the defense arguments are and sometimes we know that we don't have a very good case. But it puts the defendant through a trial."

"I've never tried anybody that I didn't think did it," Horvat added. "There's always a question in marginal cases about whether you'll get a conviction. And if I lose, well, I lose."[19]

There are many reasons why a prosecutor may lose, even if the abuse occurred. Successful prosecution is dependent on a chain of people. If any link on the chain is weak, the case may be jeopardized. This is not to say that mistakes cannot be overcome, or that extraordinary performances by key players cannot compensate for the deficiencies of the supporting cast, but a case can easily be hampered, sometimes fatally.

The first link, and in many ways the most fragile and the most important, is always an amateur: the child. Child victims are often pressured by perpetrators to remain silent, and there are sometimes threats of harm to the child or the child's parents. The child is almost always inhibited from reporting the abuse initially and often has difficulty repeating what happened over and over through the investigation, preparation for prosecution, preliminary hearings (if there are any), and the trial. If pressure is applied by family members and others who may sympathize with the abuser, the child may well recant. Even if the child is supported, there are likely to be some inconsistencies if the child is required to repeat a story that may have its beginnings several years earlier. The limitations of children's verbal skills may jeopardize their credibility as witnesses, as may their difficulties recalling elements relating to time. Children can rarely remember in what month an event occurred and often have difficulty recounting how long an event lasted.

Social workers involved in investigations are often inexperienced, overworked, and undertrained. The police may be trained investigators, but they often have little knowledge of the special problems presented by a child abuse case and may have no experience interviewing young children. If a policeman conducts an interview with a young child in the same way he interviews adult victims, he is unlikely to elicit useful information. As one social worker put it, "They [the police] need to learn social work skills probably as badly as we need to learn police skills."[20]

But the reality is that police and social workers rarely work well together. That much is widely acknowledged by professionals in both fields. It is not difficult to understand why, either. Their general orientations are almost polar opposites. Although a quick description of the professions will necessarily be oversimplified, in general social workers strive to help people who voluntarily seek assistance. Their method is cooperation. The police strive to enforce standards on people who seek to elude them. Their method is confrontation.

Yet in many jurisdictions, social workers and police officers conduct joint investigations in sexual abuse cases. In fact, that is considered by many to be the ideal way to investigate. And it does seem to work well in some places. The advantage, when it works, is that social workers can use their skills interviewing children and police officers can use their investigative skills in building a case. Also, the child may be spared at least one interview, since parallel investigations often require each agency to interview the child. The situation can be even more difficult in large cities, where the police and Social Services may each investigate, as may the prosecutor's office. The skill and experience of the investigators may vary widely, and the ultimate result of multiple investigations and interviews may be contradictory information and a badly traumatized child.

The trend in many places has been to establish specialized teams of social workers and police officers to investigate sexual abuse cases and to have regular formal meetings at which all involved agencies are represented and encouraged to discuss problems. King County,

Washington, and Polk County, Iowa, both have such arrangements, although they are quite different. The Iowa program deals primarily with incest cases that do not go to trial. (Most are processed through a so-called pretrial diversion program in which offenders plead guilty with the understanding that they will not be incarcerated if they enter treatment. There are many such programs around the country, as we will see in chapter 10.) In Polk County, child protective investigators and special police officers often investigate jointly, if initial reports suggest the case may be suitable for prosecution—although sometimes schedule conflicts make such cooperation impossible. Weekly meetings are attended by social work supervisors, police officers, prosecutors, victim and offender therapists, and a group coordinator, among others. Because the community is so small, the group can literally discuss every case.[21]

Such is not possible in King County. Meetings there are monthly and, given the number of cases it handles, the group has time to discuss only general issues. During one meeting, for example, the topics included problems the police were having telephoning child protective workers; unrelated changes child protective services was planning; the pros and cons of prosecuting people who failed to report child abuse; and the failure of hospital personnel to report cases to the police as well as to Social Services. This was followed by a discussion of proposed changes in state sex crimes laws.[22]

Like Polk County, King County conducts joint investigations, but the composition of its team may be unique. A preliminary investigation is usually done by social workers. Then, if the case looks sufficiently strong for prosecution, an assistant district attorney, a police officer, and sometimes the child protective investigator as well, conduct a joint interview with the child. The prosecutor asks the questions, and the police officer generally takes notes. This is to minimize the use of leading questions and to ensure that, if there are any, the individual responsible risks suffering the consequences in court.

But even a thorough and professional investigation is no guar- antee of a conviction. If the prosecutor is inexperienced and unsure of the subject or cannot establish a rapport with the child, then a case may quickly fall apart. And assistant district attorneys are fre- quently inexperienced. In addition to learning how to interview chil- dren for information, prepare them for trial, and question them on the stand, a prosecutor must have knowledge of medical evidence, behaviorial indicators of abuse, and psychological tests and evaluations that may be performed on adults as well as children. The prosecutor must be ready to argue the admissibility of certain hearsay evidence and for the competence of the child to testify, and he or she must be prepared to call experts—if only to rebut a defense attorney's expert. And all may be for naught if a child refuses to talk on the stand, as may happen at any time.

Mass molestation cases may be daunting even to prosecutors experienced in trying sexual abuse cases. Barbara Egenhauser successfully prosecuted the Martin day care case in Mount Vernon, New York. She had previously tried a half-dozen sexual abuse cases and many more cases of adult rape. "I thought that I knew a lot about it," she said in an interview a couple of months after the conclusion of the eleven-month trial, "but I was to learn that I was really just sort of scratching the surface."[23]

"Nothing can prepare you for a mass abuse case," she said, adding that it was "the hardest thing I've ever done in my life by far." Preparing child witnessess is much more difficult and time consuming than working with adults, she explained. And every contact with the child is scrutinized by the defense and becomes part of the court record.

"I'm used to criticism," Egenhauser said. "That comes with the territory. However, the type of criticism that's leveled at you in a child sexual abuse case is of a different degree and of a different nature . . . Every single thing you do in conjunction with the child is criticized, no matter what methodology you employ. I should have foreseen it. I did not foresee it to the degree it was true."

The defense in these cases is typically designed to convince a jury that the abuse did not happen, Egenhauser said, and in attempting to explain the allegations, defense lawyers argue that the parents, or prosecutors, social workers, police, therapists, or a combination of the above suggested the charges until the children repeated them. "I can't imagine any case going to trial today, in 1987, where that is not part of the defense," she said.

What makes the prosecutor's job particularly challenging, she added, is that the cases that go to trial are typically not the strongest. "Where you have a very strong case, where you have adult witnesses, a confession, corroborating evidence, the case does not go to trial.

Invariably defendants at that point will plead guilty as charged and take their chances on sentencing. The cases that go to trial are the cases where you're lacking in one of those three areas, which should be recognized and understood."

Defendants' Rights

But many defense attorneys say the system places a heavy burden on defendants to prove they are innocent. "I think for this particular crime, unique to our general concept in criminal law—in California, at least, and I presume the rest of the United States—it's hard for a sizable segment of our society to say they truly believe in the presumption of innocence," said Michael Sands, a Sacramento defense attorney who estimates he has handled at least fifty sexual molestation cases over the past twenty-one years. "The burden, really, as a practical matter, shifts to the defendant," Sands continued. "[The jury is] coming in there with a basic feeling that if this kid says so, it's probably right. What's the man got to say about it?"[24]

Sands and others have criticized child sexual abuse investigators as being at worst, biased and at best, gullible. "The fact of the matter," said Sands, "is that we have documented that the so-called experts—and this includes cops, and the psychologists, and the sex molest support teams—do not do an objective job of questioning the kid. They slant these kids, some of them. I'm not saying everyone." Michael Frost, a Seattle defense lawyer who has also been active in this area, agreed: "There is a certain kind of social worker mentality that comes into play in these cases and that mentality is a gullible one. They have a tendency to believe the accusations without a critical view of the motives. . . . The first place where you have a genuinely critical review of the accusations is when you get to the courthouse."[25]

This investigative bias, they said, necessitates close cross-examination of the child. "I think that it is necessary," Sands said. "There's nothing improper about subjecting the child to careful scrutiny on their statements, on whether they say the same things and if they change, what do they change and why do they change it. And there's no harm in pushing them and if the police officers won't, and the therapists won't, and the support people won't challenge this, and their policy is not to challenge—you do not challenge the

child, you support the child—somebody has got to raise this challenge. If the child says, 'He did this to me' on one occasion and on
another occasion he says, 'He didn't do it to me,' somebody's got to
find out why." On the other hand, said Frost, "no defense lawyer
worth their salt would go into a courtroom with a confrontational
attitude toward a child." It backfires, he said. Juries are much more
likely to convict than acquit in response to such a strategy.

The Bottom Line

There are many more arguments and issues to which we will return
in chapter 6, but proponents and critics of the criminal justice system
each have one basic complaint. For child advocates it is that the
process can be as traumatic or more traumatic than the original
abuse—even if it results in a conviction. And an acquittal, some say,
is society's ultimate denial of the child's reality. For their part, defense attorneys and critics of the system say that, in a sense, defendants cannot win a sexual abuse case. Even when acquitted, they
are often left bankrupt and stigmatized for life.

It is certainly true that innocent people are sometimes convicted
of child sexual abuse. It is inevitable, as it is with all crimes. That
in no way mimimizes the horror for those to whom it happens. In
the articles and book previously cited, there are certainly examples
of victims of the system. It is important for those responsible for the
implementation of that system to be aware of such mistakes. But
examples of injustice do not necessarily mean that the laws themselves are unjust. When an innocent man who has served ten years
in prison for murder is exonerated by new evidence, ordinarily we
acknowledge the mistake, try to compensate him with money, knowing it is small compensation indeed for his suffering, but we do not
change the laws against homicide. If mistakes can be shown to be
systemic, on the other hand, that is another matter.

It is also true that child victims are not always believed, nor
should they be. They are not always worthy of belief. Sometimes
a jury tends to believe that the child is telling the truth and may
believe that the child has almost certainly been abused, but may not
think there is sufficient evidence beyond a reasonable doubt to convict the defendant. Prosecutors like Nan Horvat understand that.
They understand that some cases are weak, even though they may

believe the child is telling the truth and the defendant is guilty. Horvat also believes prosecution is most often therapeutic for child victims.

Egenhauser agreed. "Testifying in court can be positive for a child," she said. "I've seen kids come out of it stronger, better than they were before. I've seen almost a cathartic effect—an alleviation of some of the behavioral indicators. . . . I almost see it as a form of fighting back, of empowerment for the child. . . . And I see the start of the healing process. . . . I had eighteen child witnesses [in the Mount Vernon case] and I saw it in almost all of the children."

What about when the child is not believed? "What I always tell the kid," replied Horvat, "is, 'It's not that they didn't believe you. It's that the state didn't prove their case beyond a reasonable doubt.' You tell the kids, 'Testify to the best of your ability and if we can't prove it, it's not your fault.' " The child benefits, Horvat added, by seeing that the prosecutors, investigators, and parents believe her and take her seriously. That in itself is important validation of the child's experience by the adult community regardless of the result, Horvat said.

Is it enough? Only the child can say, and responses undoubtedly vary dramatically and change over the years. Sometimes even successful prosecution is not enough. Eileen Wolfe (see appendix), an incest survivor, obtained a transcript of her father's sentencing years after the abuse ended and was amazed to find not one reference to the nature of the crime. Her father was given probation, returned to the home, and the abuse continued. The lesson she learned from this "successful" prosecution, she said, was that nobody cared what her father did to her.[26]

When we talk about these cases, it is important to remember that relatively few ever come to any court. A conservative estimate, based on virtually every recent study on the subject, is that at least as many cases are never disclosed as those that are; and only a fraction of those disclosures ever come to court. There are no statistics— nationwide or otherwise—on how many cases that are disclosed appear in courts. But there are some statistics that suggest an answer.

Becky Roe heads the Special Assault Unit in the King County Prosecuting Attorney's Office and has a national (and local) reputation as an aggressive prosecutor—especially in the area of child sexual abuse. Her office maintains detailed statistics (see table 4–1),

Table 4–1

SEXUAL ASSAULT UNIT: 1985 STATISTICS, OFFICE OF THE PROSECUTING ATTORNEY, KING COUNTY, WASHINGTON

	Sexual Assault of Children (Less than 18 years of age)					
	Exploit. Minors	In-Family	Live-in Nonfamily	Acquaintance	Stranger	Total
Total Filings	27	147	36	142	17	369
Declines	8	256	49	233	11	557
Pleas						
Felony, as charged	8	88	11	70	4	181
Felony, D/W deleted[a]	0	0	0	0	0	0
Felony, reduced	2	10	3	14	1	30
Misdemeanor, as charged	0	0	0	2	1	3
Misdemeanor, reduced	3	11	2	9	4	29
Insanity acquittal	0	0	0	0	0	0
Total Pleas	13	109	16	95	10	243
Trials						
Found guilty, felony	2	17	2	12	2	35
Found guilty, misdemeanor	0	0	1	0	1	2
Found not guilty	0	6	1	11	1	19
Hung jury (not retried)	1	7	2	2	2	14
Total Trials	6	30	6	25	6	70
Dismissals	3	24	6	12	5	50
Dispositions						
Jail only	7	8	2	13	5	35
Treatment, specialized	0	17	1	11	1	30
Jail and treatment	1	50	6	32	1	90
Jail and in-patient treatment	0	6	3	4	2	15
In-patient treatment only	0	0	0	2	0	2
Prison	3	18	2	21	2	46
Probation only	0	2	1	2	0	5
Total Sentencing	11	101	15	85	11	223

[a]Deadly weapon allegation.

	Sexual Assault of Adults			Physical Assault of Children		Domestic Violence	Total
Sig. Other	Acq.	Stranger	Total	In-Family	Other		
17	63	44	124	17	6	109	625
13	141	12	166	58	12	126	919
0	22	24	46	11		38	276
0	0	0	0	0		1	1
1	9	2	12	5		20	67
0	0	0	0	1		3	7
1	7	2	10	3		21	63
0	0	0	0	2		0	2
2	38	28	68	22		83	416
3	11	13	27	2		22	86
0	2	0	2	1		0	5
1	5	3	9	0		6	34
1	2	1	4	0		0	18
5	20	17	42	3		28	143
3	13	5	21	1		12	84
1	16	8	25	5		44	109
0	3	0	3	3		12	48
1	3	1	5	4		13	112
0	1	4	5	1		0	21
0	0	0	0	0		0	2
2	16	18	36	3		17	102
0	4	0	4	0		9	18
4	43	31	78	16		95	412

including the total filings on all sexual assault charges and the total declines, that is, the cases declined for prosecution. The statistics are broken down by children (under 18) and adults. In 1985, the most recent year for which statistics were available, there were 369 filings and 557 declines in cases of child sexual assault. According to Roe, the reason there were so many declines is that reporting was improved. Cases her office would not have heard about in the past were showing up. But in at least half the cases, prosecutors could not get the child in for an interview. The reasons varied, she said. Some parents did not wish to prosecute because the offender was a friend or relative. The statute of limitations had expired in some, and in others the family had left the jurisdiction. In still others the child was named as a victim by another child, but no follow-up was possible. These statistics prove nothing. Some may well be false allegations. But they seem to support the suggestion that even when there is disclosure, there are many reasons why a case may "fall between the cracks"—even when a system with a reputation for aggressiveness and efficiency is in place.

The next chapter will look at two cases where there was no such system. One case seemed too large to fall between the cracks. But it did. The other seemed small enough to slip quietly through. But it did not.

5

Two Case Studies: West Point and Judy Coletti

1. West Point

WALTER and Mary Gray are angry.[1] But their anger is not as acute as it once was. It has become part of their lives, just as child sexual abuse has. It was a subject they knew little about in August 1984, when their daughter, Donna, first told them she had been molested at the West Point Child Development Center.

No court has ever validated the abuse. The Grays do not need convincing, but the failure of the authorities to obtain indictments has made them angry. Donna has been clear about what happened, they said, but it has been suggested that she was questioned in a leading manner by a therapist in a videotaped interview. And at the time of the alleged abuse, she was only 2½ years old.

But the Grays' daughter was not the only child allegedly abused. Although there are many ways a single case can founder, it seemed inconceivable that a case in which as many as 50 children may have been abused—and there was even medical evidence in one case—could simply die. But it did. Although it got off to a shaky start, before the investigation was completed 17 FBI agents worked on the case full-time and 950 potential witnesses were interviewed, including 50 children (aged 2 to 8). But no one was ever indicted. The reasons, say the Grays, are many. Ignorance and incompetence undermined the investigation early on, they say, but denial was perhaps the most devastating response of all. It was what they viewed as denial that made them most angry and it was denial that led Capt. Walter Gray to decline a promotion and resign from the Army.

Col. John Yeagley, a spokesman for West Point, responded, "There were allegations of child abuse. As far as I know, there never was any child abuse that occurred at West Point." The FBI investigation, he said, "was never able to substantiate the parents' allegations."[2]

Rudolph Giuliani, the U.S. attorney for the Southern District of New York, whose office presented the case to a grand jury, wrote in a letter to West Point made public at the conclusion of the grand jury hearing: "We concluded that although there were indications that children may have been abused at the Center, there was insufficient substantive evidence to prosecute anyone as the perpetrator of that abuse. Thus, the grand jury has concluded its hearings without indicting anyone in connection with this investigation." To a reporter's suggestion that "it seems that abuse occurred in that center," Giuliani responded, "There isn't much question about that."[3]

The Grays, who say they spent thousands of dollars of their own money to see that the allegations were thoroughly investigated, were deeply disappointed that no indictments were forthcoming. But they were incredulous at the reaction of West Point.

"I fully expected that West Point was going to make an announcement asking that anybody who suspected anything to bring their kids in," said Walter Gray.[4] "That never happened." Instead, Gray said, West Point "covered it up." There were rumors that the whole thing was a misunderstanding over a diaper rash. Officials seemed bent on waiting for the "problem" to blow over, he said.

"The way West Point dealt with things was just to cover the things up, or transfer people, or kick them out of the Army," Gray said.[5] "Maybe I'm a naive, idealistic person, but I just couldn't believe that's the way they did things up there. But that's the way the whole thing transpired." Of the community at large, Gray added, "Our next door neighbors, when we walked out of the house, would run inside. I mean, people that I had taken care of in the hospital would walk up to me and walk away, and give me the silent treatment like they gave cadets that were, I don't know, honor violations.

"The worst thing, I think, about child abuse is for the kid to feel that they're abandoned, and that their parents are unsupportive.

Just like we feel abandoned by authority. I think this is the hell we go through."

Yeagley said that charges of a cover-up were "absolute nonsense. There was no cover-up. There was no reason to cover anything up." Gen. Willard Scott, West Point's superintendent at the time, talked about the investigation in his annual address about three weeks after the first allegation surfaced, Yeagley pointed out. The announcement itself, he said, was evidence that the Army was not trying to cover up. Yeagley acknowledged that Scott said at the time that there was no reason to believe children at the center were unsafe. That statement has never been contradicted by the evidence, he added.

A memorandum to parents who used the center telling them whom to contact with questions or information about alleged abuse was issued a month after Scott's speech. By the end of September, two months after the first allegation, two of the day care teachers who were suspects had been reassigned to administrative duties. Beyond cooperating fully with the FBI and, eventually, the U.S. Attorney's Office, Yeagley said West Point instituted more stringent screening procedures in the hiring of day care workers, along with a new rule requiring the presence of two adults with any child or children at the center, although he could not say when these were initiated.

Walter Gray, 35 years old, is a large, stocky man who can quickly become emotional—especially when discussing West Point. Gray, who describes himself as "a good amateur wrestler," joined the Army on a scholarship program and chose West Point because he wanted to help out on the wrestling team. Mary, also 35, is tall and, like her husband, strong-willed. Walt makes a point of saying that she is "more intuitively smart" than he. Both are deeply religious and say that their faith has helped them through this difficult time.

It began Friday, July 27, 1984. That night a 3½-year-old came home from the child care center with a bloody vagina. She told her alarmed parents that a teacher at the center had jabbed her repeatedly with a pen. The parents took the child to the emergency room of the base hospital where she was examined and her injuries were confirmed: vaginal lacerations. Her father reported the abuse immediately to West Point's Criminal Investigation Division as well as to the local and state Social Services Departments. West Point decided that since the teachers at the center were civil servants, not military personnel, the Federal Bureau of Investigation should take over, which it did. The only problem was that the child care center was still open for business.

"I'm Afraid Our Daughter Might Be Involved"

The Grays' case illustrates how parents can come to be convinced their child has been abused despite the fact that there was no criminal conviction, that no charges were even filed. And parents can be just as sure even when there is an acquittal in a case. That is partly because the evidence sufficient for a parent's personal conviction may have little to do with that required for a legal one.

In the Grays' case, suspicion was by no means immediate, however. They returned from vacation on August 12 and, of course, had heard nothing of the assault two weeks earlier (since the first official word was Scott's speech, five days later). But Mary soon heard neighborhood rumors and asked Walt if he had heard anything at Keller Army Community Hospital, where he worked and where the child with the injured vagina had been treated. He had not.

"I asked a few people at the hospital," Walt remembered, "and they didn't know anything about it, which struck me as strange because I would think that people at the hospital would at least have been told to have a high index of suspicion for potential other cases— just to be on the lookout. So I talked to my boss. He knew nothing about it, and he's the head of internal medicine. I went and talked to the guy who's in charge of the emergency room. He knew nothing about it. So I'm saying, 'Gee whiz, maybe this didn't even happen, maybe it's just gossip . . .' I asked my secretary, and she said, 'Oh yes, Dr. Gray, that happened,' and she brought me somebody that was there in the emergency room that night."

At home, Walt and Mary discussed it. "I'm afraid our daughter might be involved," said Mary. Walt was not sure. Donna only went to the facility Sunday mornings, while the Grays were in church. (Their son, who was almost 5 at the time, attended Sunday school instead.) West Point had encouraged them to use the center rather than take her to church with them, but the Grays had stopped doing so in late March or early April, when Donna had had, as Walt put it, a "hysterical reaction going down there one day and said she didn't want to go there anymore, and we honored her wishes." They had not given the center much thought since, but now it struck them that the abuse had occurred on a Friday night, when the weekend shift was on duty. They decided to talk to the child.

"Has anybody touched your 'heinie'?" Mary asked Donna. The child nodded. Who? Her parents had, her grandmother, others who had bathed her. Anyone down at the child care center? Yes, the child answered. Arlene[6] had. Arlene was her 20-year-old teacher.

Walt and Mary were upset, but they tried not to show it. They were not quite sure what to think, but to Mary it rang true. She remembered Donna's behavior around that time, and she remembered her reaction the last time Donna was to stay at the center. Unsure what to do next, Walt went to work that night. He was with a patient when Mary called. Donna had come to her unsolicited and said, "You know what? Arlene made me touch her 'heinie,' too."

Walt had heard enough. "I mean, that was it for me. At that point I was convinced. I hadn't been, but I was convinced." He immediately got in touch with the hospital's chief of staff, who said he knew nothing about the July 27 episode. Walt called the chief of pediatrics, who at first said he knew nothing. "You're the chief of pediatrics!" Walt said. "Wait a minute," the doctor said. "I do remember a 3½-year-old with vaginal lacerations, but I had no idea it had anything to do with the child care center." At that point Walt was "damned suspicious."

The chief of pediatrics suggested Walt bring Donna in and he would examine her himself. There was no physical evidence of abuse (not surprisingly). No cultures were taken, Walt said, but a history was, and the doctor indicated on the chart a history of abuse. He suggested the Grays consider suing the child care center. But Walt had more important concerns, like: Were the same teachers still there? And who was investigating?

He called the West Point Criminal Investigation Division and was told the FBI was in charge. He called the FBI and finally got through only to learn that the agent assigned to the case was on vacation. "Fine," said Gray, "let me talk to the other agent working on it." There *was* no other agent working on it. Wait a minute, he told them, do you know that the teacher my daughter identified is not the same teacher the other child identified? He knew this because just that morning he had called the other girl's mother and asked her to give him the initials of the teacher who abused her child. He was eager to inform the agent because he was convinced they had the wrong teacher, but the person on the phone told him Arlene had already been questioned and released. The FBI had given her a polygraph, she had passed, and she was back at work.

Since there was no one to talk to at the FBI, Gray called the Orange County Department of Social Services. He got a child protective worker and told her the whole story. "Dr. Gray," she said when he was through, "I don't see what you're so amazed about." He was amazed, he said, that the hospital officials claimed ignorance, the FBI agent released the teacher and went on vacation, and the center was still open when it should have been closed down immediately, or else infiltrated. "Well," the social worker responded, "how do you expect an organization like West Point to deal with it honestly when they let a murderer go?" "What?" said Gray. "A child was murdered at West Point," she said, "and they covered that all up, so how do you expect them to deal with a little child abuse?"

Gray was stunned. He called some friends to check the story out and was amazed to learn it was true. It had even been reported in the local paper.[7] An Army staff sergeant killed a 22-month-old infant his wife was baby-sitting by punching her in the stomach. He was given a military trial and sentenced to 18 months' hard labor. And if that was not shocking enough, Gray learned that the man never even completed the sentence. He was simply given a dishonorable discharge and released.[8] (Colonel Yeagley said the Army accepted a plea bargain because it was the opinion of the staff judge advocate that the evidence in the case was weak. However, the man was reported to have confessed to state police officers who initially investigated that he had punched the girl the night before she died.)[9]

Now Gray decided to call back the FBI. He was told again that the agent was on vacation and was given the number of his superior. He called the superior, repeated the story, and was told that the agent would be back on Monday and he was welcome to call back then. Gray told the man that the woman his daughter had named was still at the center, that she worked on weekends, "and you're telling me to hold on to it for another weekend! I don't think I can do that," he said. "I'm not in the FBI, so I don't know how the investigation should be run." "Well, listen," the man told him, "I can't do anything more than you can do. I'm just going to give him the information when he comes in on Monday." "Are you familiar with the Sergeant Poole case?" Gray asked. "No, what's that?" "That was about the 22-month-old that was murdered last year up at Stuart Army Subpost. "Oh," said the agent, "I heard that that child died of natural causes." That was when Gray began thinking, "This really smells to high heaven."

There was only one other avenue to try. Mary told the whole story to the assistant chaplain. At last she had found someone who believed her! He said he would see what he could do and get back to her the next day. When she did not hear back, she approached the man again. "Well?" she asked. The assistant chaplain was reluctant to make eye contact. He had spoken to his immediate superior and then to the head of all chaplains, who also happened to be the head of all child care centers. The FBI had already investigated, he was told, and had found that no one at the child care center was involved. The assistant chaplain shrugged. "What could I do," he said, "call my boss a liar?"

Later, when Walt was leaving church, the assistant chaplain said the same thing to Walt. "I believe you," he said, "but I would have had to call my boss a liar." "Well," Walt responded, "if your boss is a liar, call him a liar." "I couldn't do that," he said. "No," said Walt, "but you can let kids get abused, is that what you're telling me?"

The assistant chaplain is currently stationed in Germany and could not be reached for comment. The head chaplain declined to respond, citing pending civil litigation and the advice of Army counsel.

Enter the FBI

When the Grays finally made contact with the FBI agent, they were less than impressed. "This FBI guy," said Walt, "basing the thing on the polygraph test—when he started telling me that, I just was not impressed with the guy. . . . I said, 'Well listen, I'm a physician, I know what a polygraph test is. And he said, 'Well, we believe in them,' and stuff like that. I said, 'Well, listen, it measures the pulse, a piloerector response, and a blood pressure response, and they're not reliable and that's why they're not admissible in courts. of law. This is preposterous!"

After the conversation with Walt, the agent said he wanted to talk to Mary. According to her account, the agent asked Mary a number of questions, and then, in the middle of the conversation without introducing himself or preparing the child or even stooping down to her level, he turned and said, "Well, did someone hurt you at the child care center? Who was that?" Donna was intimidated, Mary said. She started walking away and said "Arlene" in a small voice. "I can't hear her very well," the agent said. But his real concern, he said, was that he had never heard of a 2½-year-old who distinguished between her genitals and her anus. "None of *my* kids did," he said. "My husband is a physician," Mary told him, "and that's just the way we've always done that." "Well," the agent told her, "when you come up with something concrete, you get in touch with me," and left.

When the Grays' account was repeated to him, the agent said he would check with his superiors to find out if he could respond. He never called back with his response, however, and he did not return subsequent phone calls.

While they were getting nowhere with the authorities, the Grays were learning a great deal from their daughter. The same day the FBI agent conducted his interview with Donna, Mary saw her daughter playing with her doll. She had heard something about using dolls to help young children explain what happened to them, so she said, "Show me what Arlene did to you on the doll." Donna said, "I'll be Arlene." She took the doll and said, "Arlene did this and this and this." Up until then, the Grays did not know how bad it was. They were beginning to find out.

Over the ensuing months Donna slowly began to tell them. And, sometimes more slowly still, they began to understand. Some of the disclosures were obvious. Donna had a male and a female doll that she played with. When the Grays found the dolls coupled in a sex act, they knew Donna had not learned that from them or from television, since they closely monitored her viewing. Other revelations were retrospective. One day Walt called up Mary, excited. "Do you remember the Fourth of July?" he asked. "Yes," she said, "you mean when Donna saw Arlene at the parade?" The Grays had been enjoying the parade when a woman walked up to them and said, "Hi, Donna! You look so sweet!" And Walt said, "Say hello to Arlene, Donna." But the child refused. Instead, she ran behind her father's back. They could not understand. "Why is Donna acting so rude?" Walt asked Mary. "Walter," said Mary, "she's 2½ years old!

How can she be rude?" He realized she was right, but he was puzzled by the child's behavior. She had not even seen Arlene for over three months.

Evidence of this sort is probably the most powerful of all for parents. It was an event that they knew was utterly genuine, that they both observed, and it was inexplicable until the missing knowledge was supplied. It is doubtful that anything a juror or a district attorney or a judge could say would change the mind of a parent who has had such an experience. It is no longer simply a matter of supporting their child or believing her, but believing what logic and their own observations dictate as well. In fact, courts even have a hearsay exception that applies to similar circumstances. It is called the "excited utterance" exception. It says that when a person is in a particularly excited state and blurts something out, he or she is more likely to speak the truth than under normal circumstances. Donna's excited utterance was nonverbal, but its message was as loud and clear to her parents as the most piercing scream.

As the Grays understood more and more—or believed they did—their frustration at the failure of others even to begin to fathom grew unbearable. Walt's medical training had taught him to begin a diagnosis by ruling out the most dangerous possibilities; West Point, he said, seemed to be operating under the theory that if there was no diagnosis, there could be no disease. The Grays finally decided to contact a lawyer.

"We went with him," Walt explained, "only after nobody would close down the child care center, nobody would listen to us, and it got passed around that our daughter's problem was a diaper-changing incident," a rumor they heard from a number of sources. Lawyer William Crain, whose practice is limited to civil litigation, was recommended. Although technically they retained him to initiate a lawsuit, the Grays later pulled out of the suit (which by then other parents had joined) and maintain that their primary goal all along was to see that a proper investigation was conducted that would result, they hoped, in the conviction of the perpetrators.

Crain arranged for a child psychologist reputed to be an expert in the field to interview Donna. The therapist, Anne Bush Meltzer, was recommended to him by the Bronx District Attorney's Office (which had handled a highly publicized day care case of its own).[10] Meltzer conducted videotaped interviews with Donna, with the first child who disclosed abuse, and with several others. The Grays believed these interviews validated the abuse, but there were suggestions behind the scenes that the interview techniques were leading and suggestive, and could be impeached in court. With the permission of the parents and in Crain's presence, the author was permitted to view Donna's interview and part of the first child's.[11]

The children were both interviewed on September 11, 1984, in what appeared to be a living room. Crain had hired a private production company and had bought a two-way mirror behind which the video camera was concealed. The interview with the first child started as soon as the child and therapist entered the room. Meltzer asked the child what happened at the center that made her have to go to the doctor. The youngster readily spoke about how her "toochie" was hurt and, asked how that happened, said her teacher had hurt her. Her answers were clear and her attention never wandered. She appeared comfortable with Meltzer. Within the first minute, Meltzer picked up a doll and began asking the child to demonstrate what had happened.

"Did your teacher pull up your dress?" she asked. Meltzer pulled up the doll's dress and pulled down its panties. The child chose a crayon she was holding and demonstrated what she said happened. Meltzer turned the doll over. "What do you call this, your butt?" she asked. "Did she do it on your butt too?" The child said she had and demonstrated. Some of the other questions were: "Did she have her clothes on or were her clothes off?" "Did she touch you just with the pen or did she use her hands also?" "This is the [Carol][12] that's your teacher?" "Did she tell you not to tell your mommy?" "How did it feel when she did that?" "Did it hurt?" After about ten minutes, Crain stopped the tape. During the remaining minutes (less than five, he said), the child named other children who she said had also been molested, Crain explained.

Donna's interview lasted about fifteen minutes. Again, questions began immediately. Donna's attention seemed to waver slightly at times. After a few minutes she appeared uncomfortable talking about the abuse and abruptly walked around the room, but she soon resumed her seat and continued to answer the questions until shortly before the session was concluded. At the outset, it was impossible to hear Donna's response to the question of what happened. Meltzer said, "Oh, she touched your private parts," presumably repeating

Donna's inaudible words. Again, Meltzer introduced the doll almost immediately. Some of the questions she asked were: "Let's pretend this is [Arlene]." "Can you show me how she touched your private parts?" "She did it with her fingers?" "Show me with your finger what she did." "She moved it around like that?" "She put it inside?" "And did she do something on this private part too?" "Did you ever see [Arlene's] private parts?" "What did you do to hers?" "Did she touch your private parts with something else besides her hand?" "What else?" "Did it hurt?" "How did it feel when she did that?" "Did you cry when she did that?" In this interview too Meltzer lifted the doll's dress and asked Donna to demonstrate, which she did.

Meltzer said in an interview with the author that she had spoken with the parents for about an hour prior to the videotaped sessions to obtain information about them and their children.[13] She asked the names the children used for anatomy. She said she had discussed the abuse with the parents, but in speaking with the author, two and a half years after the events, she said she could not recall whether it had been before or after the sessions with the children. She met with the first child for a brief time before the interview and met with Donna, along with her family, for about an hour earlier that day, she added.

Asked if she had heard comments that her techniques were leading and suggestive, she said she had heard through Crain that either Giuliani or someone else in the U.S. Attorney's Office had made such comments.[14] Crain declined to discuss the matter.

"It's best to avoid leading questions as much as possible," Meltzer said, "but with very young children . . . you have to come closer to crossing that boundary than you would have to with an older child—if at first you don't succeed with a more general question, and you often don't with young children." She said it was difficult to remember the videotapes, since she had not seen them recently,[15] but added, "I don't remember at that time thinking that they were leading questions in such a way that the children could have been fabricating it, that the children were incredible. I was very much struck by actually how articulate the young children were, how open they were without my having to ask concrete questions like that."

She said that she had not been informed of the abusive acts that were alleged, and so did not have the information required to lead the children. (At this point, she said she recalled that in these two cases she had not discussed the abuse with the parents prior to the interviews.) When it was suggested that some of the questions appeared to lead the children toward certain answers, Meltzer said, "But you see, if you just ask a child, 'Well, what happened?' or 'How did something feel?' you often get, 'I don't know" or 'It's okay.' " But there were few open-ended questions that were not immediately followed by more concrete ones. And the children were almost always responsive to the questions—when they were given time to answer before another was asked. Meltzer said it was her practice to use dolls with young children even when they were not having difficulty talking. Young children find it easier to demonstrate acts that they sometimes do not have words to describe, she explained.

Finally, asked for her response to criticism of her techniques, she said even if questions were sometimes leading, that did not discredit the children's accounts. "I think it's an unfortunate distraction from the real issue as to what's going on, and of course at that time we knew a lot less than we know now about interviewing children. It was at the time when it was just starting to gain more widespread attention, and people in the mental health profession have since paid a lot more attention to it in attempting to standardize interviews."

It is impossible to assess what effect, if any, Meltzer's interviews had on the case. Grand jury proceedings are secret, and the assistant U.S. attorney who handled the case said for that reason he would not comment on any of the evidence.[16] But the tapes probably helped Crain push the investigation along. The Grays made the tape of Donna available to a newscaster they trusted. After steps were taken to conceal the child's identity, a short portion was broadcast. Crain and a number of the parents also appeared on television and were quoted in the print media. The publicity was aimed at focusing attention on the investigation's perceived inadequacies, and it apparently did. Giuliani's office entered the case, and the FBI called in its pedophile unit to join the investigation. And when that happened, the Grays thought they had succeeded at last. Important people were taking the charges seriously. Something was happening.

The Investigation Expands

But it was not what they had hoped. First, the assistant U.S. attorney assigned to the case, although well-intentioned, had virtually no experience handling a child abuse case, the Grays said (and he confirmed). They believed that he never did fully grasp the nature of the abuse.

The FBI hired Flora Colao (Jane's therapist in chapter 3), who had experience interviewing children for court proceedings. But even Colao has acknowledged that the arrangement was difficult. The first day was reportedly the worst. There were a number of FBI agents present, along with parents and a video camera, all in the large room in which Colao was trying to interview small children. The FBI agents wanted her to get certain information in a certain way, Colao explained.[17] The forty-five children she interviewed (for a total of 110 interviews), however, were chosen partly because all had exhibited strong emotional reactions to the center. Many had become hysterical, for example, when asked about their experiences there. But all were young; they ranged in age from 2 to 8, Colao said, and most were under 5. As a therapist (although not *their* therapist), Colao felt it was important not to push the children for information they were not ready to divulge. But the FBI needed evidence. It was a problem that took some time to work out. Only two children were interviewed the first day, Colao said, and it was somewhat chaotic. One parent came to the Grays afterward in a highly agitated state, complaining about the session, they said.

But the arrangement improved after a time, according to Colao. The FBI learned to trust her when she felt a child could not be pushed further. And she adjusted to the way they wanted the children questioned. The number of people in the room was reduced, and the video camera was well concealed. Even so, several children grew extremely upset when they caught a glimpse of the camera, leading investigators to speculate that a sidelight at the center might have been videotaped "kiddie porn."

The results, however, were extremely frustrating. "We knew something happened," Colao said, "but we couldn't be sure what." The children talked about certain games, but investigators could not determine precisely what they were. Sex play was described, but it was unclear what it was and who was involved. Some children named older children as their abusers, but used only first names that were shared by several children.[18] Further complicating the situation was the fact that the center was open long hours, seven days a week, was attended by a great many children, some on regular schedules, some not, and there were lots of teachers. It was not uncommon for children (and their parents) to be unsure of or to confuse the teachers' names.

Colao, who treats child victims, parents, and adult survivors of abuse in her private practice, also spoke more generally about the problems families have dealing with the trauma of sexual abuse.[19] It is most important, she said, for parents to maintain the equilibrium and stability of the home environment in the face of such a crisis. The child has almost always been involved in the situation for some time prior to the disclosure. If the parents react radically, Colao said, the child will perceive it as a reaction to the disclosure, not to the abuse. In the wake of an experience that may shake a child's sense of reality to the core, it is especially important for the child to feel that the world at home is intact. Parents should not change their rules, should not indulge their children because they have been abused, should not treat them like "damaged goods." Children need to feel that there are controls and that their parents are in charge.

And yet, Colao continued, parents are also victimized; they are the secondary victims of child abuse. They too suffer grief, a sense of loss, and guilt that they did not perceive what in many cases not even the professionals who were supposed to be experts were able to perceive. It is a grief that is particularly acute because it cannot be expressed in front of their children, for whom they must be strong, and it is not easily shared with friends or even family.

"Any other kind of grief, in this society, you can openly share," Colao said. "This you can't. And it is very important to demystify the grief around a child who's been sexually assaulted so that the kid can go on. But how many parents can openly talk about this? If a kid's in a car accident and is not killed, you can talk about it at dinner, at a PTA meeting. But not this. You think: 'What will they think of me as a parent? What will they think of my children? Will they let their kids play with mine?' "

At the Grays' house, the subject of the abuse "got so it became dinner conversation," Mary said. They would sit around the dinner table and talk about what happened. "One time," Mary said, "I remember I took a pillow and I said, 'I could just kill [Arlene],' so I started beating on the pillow in front of [Donna], and she said, 'Can I do it, too?' And I said, 'Sure.' " Together they proceeded to beat the pillow to a pulp.

Some of Colao's insights the Grays knew intuitively; some they learned by reading and attending conferences, and, to a lesser extent, by talking to other West Point parents. It was only in a support group that Mary organized for West Point parents who believed their children had been abused that they realized the number of alleged victims far exceeded anything they had previously imagined.

Over time the Grays came to believe that there were only two or three women involved who worked at the center, but that there were also men involved who did not work there. They also believed there were ritualistic elements to the abuse. At one point Donna kept talking about the firemen, but what she meant were men who burned people with fire, Mary decided after listening closely.[20] And Donna was talking about being photographed. In fact, one time soon after they stopped taking her to the center, the Grays were going to have Donna's photograph taken by a professional, but she became "hysterical" and they decided not to. This had been another of those small mysteries—she had previously had her photograph taken many times without objection. After she had disclosed the abuse, Donna was able to show her parents the sexually suggestive poses she was taught.

Burning? Photographs? Mary kept wondering how this could have happened at the child care center. Finally she asked. "Oh, I wasn't there," Donna replied, just as naturally as could be. "I was somewhere else." "Show me where you were," Mary demanded, and they got in the car and Donna directed her straight to the local high school. Mary believes that the children were regularly transported to the school, which was near the center and on top of a hill, commanding an excellent view of the area. There would not have been much traffic on a Sunday, and even if they had been noticed, the Grays figured there would have been nothing suspicious looking about a group of children being transported to or from the school. There was even a preschool located in the high school.

Donna was afraid when they arrived, but her mother assured her she was safe. The child then led her mother to a part of the school Mary had never seen, so she was sure they had never been there together. Donna pointed to a room. Painted on one of the walls was a mural of a fire truck and a fire dog. The room next door was painted completely black—a photography darkroom.

"That's where they took off my clothes and took my picture," the child said. Then she led her mother to the back of the school. "That's where they killed the dog and that's where they buried it. That's where they fired people," Donna said, only now Mary under-

stood the child meant "burned." She said they fired Arlene (the first
time Donna had said this, Mary had assumed the child meant that
Arlene had been removed from the child care center and placed in
another job, as her parents had told her). Where did they fire her?
Mary inquired. On the bottom of her feet. Of course, Mary thought.
The easiest place to conceal any kind of mark. Donna showed her
mother where they were made to change clothes and where the
marriage rituals were held. It was Mary's impression that an adult
couple was paired with two children, and somehow the little bride
represented the big bride. Some sort of ceremony was involved, and
there was fire and burning, Mary said.

The Grays believed they were finally beginning to put some of
the pieces together, and they dutifully reported everything they
learned to the FBI. Their phone bills from this period, they said,
were astronomical. But they never got the impression that either the
FBI or the U.S. Attorney's Office fully understood what they were
up against—at least not as the Grays understood it.

Some of what they had uncovered seemed to be corroborated
when they read in the paper that the chief of military intelligence
at West Point was arrested in nearby Highland Falls in September
1984 for asking a 10-year-old boy and 14-year-old girl if he could
take nude pictures of them.[21] According to a 1986 investigation conducted by the Army's inspector general, in response to a letter Gray
wrote accusing the Army of covering up child abuse, "the incident
was alcohol related," and following the officer's successful completion of an alcohol rehabilitation program, all charges were dismissed.
Furthermore, the report said, the FBI investigated his possible involvement with the child abuse case, but "no connection was ever
established, and the officer was never determined to be a 'prime
suspect.' "[22]

What particularly interested the Grays at the time, though, was
a rumor that the man frequented the same bars as the day care
teachers the children had named.

Walt decided to contact the man directly. It was a gambit inspired
by frustration and should not be seen as a model for others in his
situation. At best it was potentially dangerous to himself and the
investigation. He called the man, told him that he believed children
had been photographed naked by child care workers, and said that
he wanted to talk to him. The Grays had come to believe that the
only way the case would ever be broken was if someone confessed.

The man agreed, and they met in a restaurant. Donna and Mary were watching from a distance. If the man did not confess, the Grays were hoping that at least Donna would recognize him. That part worked, the Grays said. "He's not hurting Daddy! He's not hurting Daddy!" Mary said her daughter exclaimed. "He said he'd hurt Daddy!" It was a turning point in the child's recovery, her parents said. It was clear to them now that she had been threatened, and she could see for herself that they were all safe.

While the Grays' efforts apparently proved therapeutic for their daughter, it should be emphasized that such actions might have different results for others. Despite their intelligence, their knowledge, and their good intentions, the Grays were amateurs. Another child could have become hysterical. Another man confronted as this one was could have reacted with violence. The perceived inadequacies of the professionals with whom they dealt did not make the Grays any more professional. And had their case been prosecuted, their questioning of Donna (with or without the doll), not to mention their freelance investigation, might have destroyed a potentially strong case.

Herein lies a conflict that troubles many in the field (and one to which we will return in chapter 8). Prosecutors in cases like the Grays' often advise parents not to press their children for information, but to take note of what they say and to respond with questions like, "And then what happened?" so as to avoid suggestions that the children have been prompted. But parents and therapists are not trained in the law and often are much more concerned with the health of the child than the strength of the case. They believe it is important for children to be encouraged to express their feelings and their fears, and to be rewarded for doing so, while prosecutors feel such encouragement and reward are vulnerable to attacks by defense attorneys.

The Lawsuit

The Grays' personal investigation was the result of their frustration not only with the government's investigation, but with their lawyer as well. They believed Crain was not fully cooperating with the government because he had been retained by eight families, on behalf of eleven children, to sue West Point and the individuals believed to be involved for $110 million. (Crain freely acknowledged that his interests in representing his clients were not identical to the interests of those conducting the criminal investigation.) The Grays' own goal in hiring Crain had been to see that a thorough investigation was performed, and although they still had misgivings about its competence, it was certainly full scale.

The Grays briefly considered staying in the suit if they could donate the proceeds—and they believed they would be substantial—to an organization that combats child abuse, they said. Crain told them that the money would have to be placed in a trust fund for Donna, though. The Grays talked about it, agonized over it, and decided to pull out. Said Mary: "Walt and I didn't want her impression of why we were pursuing this to ever be tainted—that the money was an issue. We didn't even want it to be considered. And the biggest thing was we didn't want to worry about it for the next sixteen years [until their daughter reached majority] . . . The money . . . wouldn't take care of anything . . . I grew up in a town where a lot of my acquaintances and friends came into nice fat trust funds at age 21, and not one of them has made much of their lives, and I have to believe my daughter doesn't—neither of my children need that."

In addition, the Grays said Crain sometimes advised his clients to work through him and not to speak directly to the criminal investigators or the press. The Grays, however, thought that it was important to speak out.[23] And they came to resent the fact that only they paid for Crain's initial investigation (whereas the others will be charged a percentage of whatever money is obtained from the lawsuit, as is customary in such cases). Some of the money the Grays paid was required for such expenses as the videotaped interviews. The rest they were charged only when they pulled out of the suit, Crain said. The final total was in the neighborhood of $5,000, all agreed.[24] Crain said it was far below what his normal fee would have been.

A Parting of the Ways

And so there had been a parting of company even before the Grays' physical departure. The parents' support group that they initiated met only twice before the Grays moved to Fort Dix, New Jersey, in April 1985. (Had they had their way, the Grays would have left much sooner. In November 1984 Walt tried to resign, but as a former scholarship student, he still owed time to the Army. His request for an early discharge was approved by the ascending chain of command, but not by the top. Instead, he was allowed to transfer to Fort Dix, where they remained until his discharge in June 1986.)

In October 1985, the U.S. Attorney's Office announced there would be no indictments. What most angered the Grays was the wording of Giuliani's statement that "children *may* have been abused at the Center" (emphasis added). As far as they were concerned, there could be no doubt that children were abused.

But Walter and Mary Gray are not just angry at the U.S. Attorney's Office. They are angry at the FBI, particularly at the first agent assigned to the case. They are angry that he resorted to polygraph tests and assumed the children were mistaken, or worse. They are angry that he went on vacation while children were at risk. Most of all, they are angry that he entered the case knowing little or nothing about child abuse and did not accept responsibility for that.

"I'm an internist, okay?" said Walt. "I know nothing about brain surgery, okay? Now when there's a tumor in the brain, and somebody has got to cut it out, if all the other doctors in the world died, then I become the most capable. But this agent had a moral responsibility to bring in the FBI pedophile team, and say, 'Hey, Jack, I need help on this one.' "

The Grays' harshest criticism, however, is reserved for West Point. A year before his discharge, Capt. Walter Gray was offered a promotion to major. In a public gesture that was widely publicized, Gray declined the promotion, a decision of which he and Mary are proud. In a prepared statement, he said: "I cannot accept promotion in a system that at first refused to acknowledge and now refuses to deal with the victims of extensive child abuse that occurred at the West Point Child Development Center.

"The irony is not the refusal of a promotion. The irony is that the U.S. Army designated 1984 its 'Year of the Child' and has declared 1985 'The Year of the Family,' and there are presently numerous families at West Point and scattered around the world who have not received the proper counselling and support that they need."

2. Judy Coletti

In most respects Judy Coletti's case bears little resemblance to the Grays'.[25] There were no allegations of mass molestation. The only victim was Judy's daughter, Lisa (if you do not count Judy herself, and her friends and relatives, who were also affected), and the perpetrator was her ex-husband. The case was never prosecuted criminally, but it was successfully litigated in civil courts and had a conclusion that was rare in its finality: Judy's ex-husband's parental rights were terminated. If that makes it sound simple and relatively "clean," it was neither.

From beginning to end, the case was heard in various courts in two states for nearly five years. Judy estimated there were at least fifty hearings at which she was represented by a succession of eight lawyers. At one hearing a judge actually ordered her to move back to Illinois from Minnesota, where she had moved (or, more accurately, fled) following the breakup of her marriage. At a later hearing the same judge said she could stay in Minnesota, provided she regularly transport her daughter (at her own expense) back to Illinois for weekend and vacation visits with her ex-husband. Accordingly, for more than a year she and Lisa regularly flew to Chicago and drove to the house of her ex-husband's parents, where he had supervised visits; then she picked up her daughter and flew back to Minneapolis that night.

Lest one conclude that this was simply a divorce proceeding in which the wife charges the husband with sexual abuse in order to gain an advantage in a custody battle (as many have suggested is becoming more and more common), it was not. First, the allegation of abuse was not made until several months after the divorce was final. Second, at the time the allegation was first made there was no custody battle. Judy was granted custody from the outset. Her husband, Tom, was trying to gain more frequent and longer visits, but it was not until relatively late in the day that he first requested custody. And third, the abuse was substantiated by separate investigations by the Illinois Department of Child and Family Services and the Minneapolis Police Department, which contributed to a finding of abuse by the Hennepin County (Minnesota) Juvenile Court.[26]

And yet this was a case that might easily have died, gone the way of West Point. A woman without Judy's emotional, intellectual, and financial resources might have given up during the many times the case seemed destined to disappear between the cracks—either those in Lake County, Illinois, or the larger ones that gaped like a geological fault between Illinois and Minnesota. The case is particularly instructive in that it illustrates some of the problems courts frequently have in determining the truth of these allegations, especially under circumstances obfuscated by divorce proceedings and the involvement of courts in two or more states.[27]

"Pillar of the Community"?

Even without these complicating factors, the difficulty for courts in these cases is often twofold. Men who sexually abuse children may be successful "pillars of the community," who appear not only normal in other areas of their lives but outstanding. And the crime itself is difficult to prove because there is rarely any corroborating evidence in addition to the testimony of the child victim. When the child is very young—Lisa was not yet 3 at the time she was first abused—she may have difficulty giving coherent and reliable information, and she may be unable or unwilling to tell what her father had done (as children much older may be). Thus, the court must judge whether a man who appears beyond reproach has violated a child who not only is reluctant to tell but may also be literally at a loss for words.

Although Tom Coletti was a lawyer, educated (as was Judy) at the University of Chicago and employed for a number of years at the Illinois State Attorney General's Office, he was not a "pillar of society." He was a man who not only sexually abused his infant daughter, but who also had a history of mental problems, had serious problems with drugs and alcohol, was fired from a succession of jobs, was by his own admission obsessed with pornography—including child pornography—and who beat and threatened to kill his wife and infant daughter on more than one occasion. Among the Minnesota court's "Findings of Fact" were:

Prior to the marriage of [Lisa's] parents and specifically during periods prior to the birth of [Lisa], the Respondent Father, [Tom Coletti], had undergone psychiatric and psychological evaluation and treatment by a number of persons. During that period of time, the use and abuse of alcohol and drugs was a contributing factor to many of his psychological problems.

Following [Lisa's] birth, [Tom Coletti] began to drink heavily and was frequently intoxicated, engaged at various times in the use of drugs, and evidenced interest in pornography, including child pornography. This interest in pornography became one of the major aspects of his personality.

[Tom Coletti] began to exhibit abnormal sexual interest in [Lisa] and this, along with his dreams about killing [Lisa], his physical abuse of the infant, and the mother's fears for both her safety and that of the child, contributed to the mother's decision to leave the Respondent Father and move from Illinois to Minnesota with the child.[28]

According to Judy, Tom abused her physically and emotionally during the last eighteen months of their nearly twelve-year marriage. The Illinois court that heard their divorce found that there was "sufficient evidence to establish the grounds of extreme and repeated mental cruelty without cause or provocation by the petitioner."[29] The court believed "that [Mrs. Coletti] did not leave the State of Illinois with the intent in mind to deprive her husband of his ability to see his child; rather, I feel that her concern or her feelings at the time she left Illinois were genuine, in that she felt herself to be in danger and, possibly, even her child to be in danger, and I am convinced that she honestly went to the State of Minnesota with the expectation that in so moving away from her husband she would avoid any physical abuse to herself and, possibly, even to her child."[30]

Yet the same court later refused to believe that Lisa was at risk with this man. Why? There are many possible explanations, but two important factors were probably that the court did not see the man described above when Tom Coletti appeared before it; and that the man that it did see, an intelligent and well-educated lawyer (no less) who had worked for many years in the Attorney General's Office, also happened to be the child's father. The combination of lawyer and family man undoubtedly weighed in Tom's favor.

Judy herself did not see the man described above when she married Tom Coletti in 1969. They had met in college and were married when he was 21 and she was 20. Over the course of the marriage Judy recognized that her husband had problems, but she believed he would get better and that it was her responsibility to support him, she said in an interview.[31] "I thought he was sick and that one of the jobs of being a wife is that you stand by somebody when they're sick," she explained. In the end, however, she realized he was destroying himself and would destroy her and Lisa as well if she stayed.

Tom has claimed that Judy's several failed attempts to have children during the course of their relationship caused him great trauma.[32] Prior to their marriage, she had aborted their child against his wishes, he said. During a decade of marriage before Lisa was born, Judy had two miscarriages and then gave birth to a fourth child who died hours later. These contributed greatly to his anxiety and depression, Tom maintained.

But ironically, Lisa's birth was the most traumatic experience of all for her husband, according to Judy. From the day she came home from the hospital in February 1979, Tom began drinking heavily every weekend. By the following November, she said, he was drinking every day and spent much of his free time in bars. He often expressed jealousy of his daughter, and when she was 18 months old, he insisted that she was sexually attracted to him. He was frequently verbally abusive of Judy, telling her she was crazy and accusing her of not loving him. Beginning in late 1979, he grew increasingly threatening and violent toward both his wife and daughter. In the summer of 1980, Tom punched Judy twice, threatened to kill her if she ever left him, and then, on August 11, he told her he had purchased a gun. In a court deposition, Tom denied ever owning a gun but admitted he had threatened to kill Judy with one.[33] Two days after he made the threat, she left.

Before she fled to Minnesota, where she had a brother who offered her shelter, Judy filed for divorce. That was a mistake, she said. If she had it to do again, she would wait the six months it takes to become a legal resident and file in Minnesota. She certainly could not have predicted, however, that the Illinois judge would take it upon itself "to decide whether she stays [in Minnesota] or whether or not she comes back to the State of Illinois. In so doing," the judge expounded, "I pull out my own chemistry table with a tray on each side and put the pros and cons of the issue on different trays and see which side is ultimately heavier."[34] The cons won, and he ordered Judy to move back to the "Land of Lincoln," although at a later hearing the judge was convinced that his chemistry table did not wield the power he had imagined.

The issue that was not so easily resolved was visitation. An Illinois judge insisted that Judy make Lisa available to her father in Illinois, no matter where she chose to live.[35] And so for a year, beginning in September 1980, Tom had twenty-nine visits with Lisa, most of them requiring Judy to transport her daughter to Illinois. But because Judy had fears and suspicions concerning Tom's potential for abusive behavior, she convinced the judge to make them supervised visits to occur only during the day and in the presence of at least one of Tom's parents. Following more hearings, however, a judge ruled that Tom had the right to spend weekends with the child. A schedule was established, but only three of the visits actually took place. The first was an unsupervised weekend in Minneapolis, the second a week of supposedly supervised daytime visits in Illinois, and the last a weekend of daytime visits, again in Illinois. As it turned out, one was too many.

A Weekend "Visit"

Lisa was just 2½ during the first visit. According to the Minnesota court, this is what happened:

> During the period of visitation, Respondent and the child stayed at the University Inn, a "Best Western" motel, in Minneapolis, Minnesota. When Respondent returned [Lisa] from the visit, [Lisa's] hair was wet and matted, she appeared dazed and stared vacantly, and would not respond to her mother's questions. Shortly thereafter the child informed her mother that the father had hurt her vagina while she was "crouching" in the motel bathtub, and that he had been wearing a necklace and shirt, but no pants.
>
> On September 8, 1981, [Lisa] was brought to the office of a pediatrician where, as a result of examination, his records reflect a complaint by the child that "Daddy hurt my vagina." An examination by a gynecologist revealed that the hymen was intact at that time.

Following the visit in September, 1981, the child began to have substantial regression in her behavior, including night fears, bed-wetting, lack of toilet control, and crawling rather than walking. While on a trip to the North Shore of Lake Superior in late September, 1981, [Lisa] became hysterical when taken to a "Best Western" motel with a "Crown" logo in front. She stated it was "daddy's motel" and asked if he was going to come and hurt her.

As a result of continued regression and traumatized behavior following that visit with the father, the child was taken by the mother to see Dr. Stanley W. Shapiro, a child psychiatrist, for medical attention. At Dr. Shapiro's initial interview with [Lisa] on November 6, 1981, she described being frightened during the visitation with the father in the motel by an object that looked like a caterpillar and indicated that her father had a "purple stick," that she had seen his penis, and that her father rubbed his penis.

During a second interview with Dr. Shapiro on November 12, 1981, the child told him that her vagina had been hurt in the bathtub. She picked up a doll and a purple crayon and tried to put it into the doll's mouth, stating that the purple stick had rinsed her tongue and that it had scared her. She also stated that the father had hurt her vagina with a stick. Based on his interviews with [Lisa] and his observations of her, Dr. Shapiro testified that he believed that the minor child had been sexually molested by the father during the September, 1981 visitation.

Between September 4 and September 7, 1981, during the course of his visitation with [Lisa Coletti], Respondent [Tom Coletti] sexually abused said child by inappropriate touching of her genital area and by touching his penis to her mouth.[36]

The pediatrician never reported the abuse, Judy said. But Shapiro did. The social workers she dealt with were concerned and helpful, she added, but there was no investigation to determine whether abuse occurred—probably because the perpetrator was neither a resident in nor a visitor to the state at the time. Nevertheless, Judy sought protection from the Hennepin County (Minnesota) Family Court. And thus began the "battle of the family courts."[37]

The Battle of the Courts

Illinois claimed jurisdiction because the divorce was filed there and it was the first court to hear the matter that eventually led to allegations of abuse. But Judy claimed she and Lisa were residents of Minnesota and entitled to the protection of its courts. All of a sudden there were motions being filed by lawyers in two states. And there were contradictory court orders. And much confusion.

Illinois prevailed. The court had threatened Judy with an order of contempt, warning that she could be fined and jailed if she refused to cooperate. Her own lawyers there ultimately convinced her that she would be jeopardizing her case if she refused to appear for hearings. So in April 1982, she acceded to the pressure and appeared for a hearing. When the court asked if she had brought Lisa, she told the truth, and the court immediately demanded she produce the child in order to grant Tom another of his long-awaited visits. She felt she had no choice, so she did.

The court granted Tom one week of daily visits, again in the presence of at least one of his parents. Judy could not remain that long, but her mother agreed to shelter the child. Although afterward Judy was fearful of what might have happened, Lisa offered no overt complaint, and her mother and her grandmother avoided asking the questions they were afraid to hear answered. To this day Judy is not sure what, if anything, happened that week.

The next visit—which was also the last—occurred under similar circumstances. A hearing was scheduled, and Judy brought Lisa with her. She was convinced by the court to allow Tom another weekend visit prior to the hearing, again during the daytime only. On the first two days, when Lisa returned to Judy's parents' home (where they were staying), she said she was fine. But when she returned on the third day, the child again appeared dazed and did not respond to questions. According to the Minnesota court:

> She then began again to react abnormally by running around the room, striking out at those present, banging her head on the furniture and threatening to cut her mother into pieces. Later that evening, while assisting [Lisa] go to the toilet, the maternal grandmother . . . noticed that [Lisa's] genital area was red. [Lisa] prevented her grandmother from "wiping" her, saying that the father had hurt her vagina. The child then asked if her father would go to jail if she told what he had done to her.
>
> On the same evening after returning from visitation, the child told her mother that the father had inserted his finger into her rectum, put his penis into her mouth, had put her head into his

lap while he was not wearing pants, and rubbed her vagina and told her that this would make her feel "hot and good."[38]

Judy debated taking Lisa to an emergency room that night, but decided that it was already late, that they might have to spend hours waiting, and that Lisa was too agitated and needed to rest before the hearing that was scheduled for the next morning (!). She did take her to a pediatrician in Minneapolis the day after they returned. The doctor concluded that it was "very questionable" that Lisa's hymen was intact. In addition, Lisa saw Dr. Shapiro again and told him the same things she had told her mother, adding that her father's "purple stick" was his penis.[39]

At the Illinois hearing, Judy told the court as much as she had learned of the previous day's "visit." The judge, however, was skeptical. Why would a man risk such behavior, knowing that he would be appearing in court the very next day? And how could he perpetrate such acts in the home of his parents, who were present the entire time?

These were logical questions. And that was the problem. They were rational questions asked about irrational behavior—compulsively irrational. Time and again in these cases questions such as these are raised. Time and again courts seem to be searching for a rational motive for an irrational crime. Perhaps that is why the notion that child abusers are merely reenacting behavior that was inflicted on them as children seems comforting, in a way. At least it provides an explanation. But it does not apply to all offenders and it does not answer the question, Why would an intelligent man who knew he was going to appear in court the next morning commit the very act that was least likely to get him what he wanted? Speculation would suggest two answers: he had no choice, or what he really wanted was just what he did. It is also possible, of course, that he counted on no one's believing he would do it—including his parents.

The judge was also in possession of psychological tests that he believed supported his view that the abuse had not occurred. Several months earlier, he had ordered psychological evaluations of Judy, Tom, and Lisa and had appointed Francis Petrauskas, a marriage and family counselor, to perform them. Which Petrauskas had done— with one small omission. He had not evaluated Lisa. He "chose not to see the child because the child is too young," he explained. He added, "It is very difficult to differentiate fact and fantasy when you are working with such a young child." Asked if he felt that was proper, since the court order included the child, Petrauskas replied, "Well, I wasn't specifically aware of the order to evaluate the child."[40]

He administered a Szondi test to each of the parents and interviewed them. When asked under cross-examination why he did not choose a Rorschach test[41] instead, he said, "Well, first of all, it is very time consuming." "Are you aware of any literature that has thoroughly discredited the Szondi Test?" Judy's lawyer asked. "Yes," said Petrauskas. "I can't refer to any specific literature, but there is a lot of literature that discredits it. There is a lot of literature that supports it, and this applies to the Rorschach Test, also."[42] When asked how the test led him to his conclusion that Tom was not sexually deviant in his behavior with Lisa, Petrauskas explained:

"Well, maybe I should explain a little bit about the test. There is one factor there which involves a homosexual picture and indicates the—It is a reflection of the intensity of need for love and affection, and that factor was not elevated . . . [T]here were only three selections of the pictures. There are six generally that can be chosen; and if it goes to four, five, or six, then that is an indication that there is something seriously wrong in that area."[43] Under further questioning, he was asked what makes a picture a homosexual picture. "They were diagnosed as homosexuals," he responded. "There is extensive history on each photograph. It is a clear cut diagnosis."

And a little later he explained, "This test is genetically based. The assumption is that we all as human beings possess the characteristics in varying intensities that these diagnostic pictures represent. . . . You have to understand what homosexuality in this case means. It represents a need for affection."[44] And then the following exchange occurred:

Q. Well, how would you determine that he was not a sexual deviate, Mr. [Coletti] I mean, because he didn't choose the picture of that sexual deviate?

A. Because at this particular time the intensity wasn't there.

Q. Now, the intensity meaning that he didn't choose the picture of that sexual deviate?

A. That's right, yes.[45]

Of Judy, Petrauskas concluded: "Well, it worked out that she is under a considerable amount of pressure, and she is highly threatened, and there is a potential for panic." Judy's lawyer: "In other words, she is a normal human being?" Petrauskas: "That's right."[46]

Termination

While the circuit court, along with Petrauskas, remained unconvinced that Tom's behavior had been deviate, the Illinois Department of Child and Family Services determined there was credible evidence that he had sexually abused Lisa. But that finding was not what foiled the efforts of the Illinois court to enforce visitation.[47] A legal tactic in Minnesota did.

While the matter was in the Minnesota Family Court, the Illinois court had a legitimate claim to jurisdiction. However, a new action was brought in Minnesota that was independent of the previous litigation and took precedence over it. A law guardian was appointed to represent Lisa in a dependency and neglect action brought in juvenile court.[48] The previous actions in both Illinois and Minnesota all had emanated from the Colettis' divorce. This was entirely separate. It was an action brought on Lisa's behalf to determine whether she had been abused and required the state's protection.

The key to the strategy was that Minnesota courts would not be bound by Illinois court rulings, since Lisa was not represented by counsel in the later Illinois hearings (Judy's specific request that a law guardian be appointed was denied), and thus Lisa was not a party to the decisions. Also, actions in Minnesota's juvenile court are "superior" to those in family court; that is, if there is a conflict between the two, it is resolved in favor of the juvenile court ruling. This applied to a conflict between juvenile court and family court in Minnesota or circuit court in Illinois. The reasoning behind the protocol is that the resolution of matters before family court does not necessarily affect the state—as, for example, the division of property in a divorce. However, the welfare of its residents is in the direct interest of the state, and in Minnesota such matters are heard in juvenile court. Thus, In Re the Marriage of [Judy Coletti and Tom Coletti] was superseded by In the Matter of the Welfare of [Lisa Coletti].

In December 1982 Lisa was adjudicated a dependent of the Hennepin County Juvenile Court, and her father was restrained from all contact with the child until "he can show competent psychiatric testimony that he is amenable to visitation."[49] All prior orders were vacated.

Tom, meanwhile, continued his unsuccessful effort to gain visitation through the Illinois court and also filed a counterpetition in Minnesota alleging that his daughter was indeed a dependent and neglected child, but that the cause was her mother's psychiatric illness, which led her to inculcate in the child the belief that she had been abused. The matter came to trial in February 1984. Following seven days of testimony, the judge rejected Tom's allegations and continued the protective order barring him from all contact with his daughter.[50]

In a hearing the following July, the court ordered both parents to submit to case plans. Judy was required to provide Lisa with psychological counseling, and to seek counseling herself, if it was deemed appropriate. (It was not.) Tom was to submit to psychological evaluation by a professional approved by either the court or Lisa's Minnesota law guardian. He was required to follow all recommendations resulting from the evaluation including therapy, if indicated, and to submit to regular reevaluation. He was also ordered to undergo tests for chemical dependency and treatment, if required, as well as neurological tests and treatment.

There is no evidence he did any of it, nor did he pay any child support, and in 1985 Judy moved to terminate his parental rights. Tom failed to appear at the first hearing, and at a second hearing, on February 21, 1986, his parental rights were terminated.[51] Two months later, Lisa was legally adopted by Judy's new husband (whom she had married two and a half years earlier).

Lisa was in therapy once a week for about ten months. Her mother said she improved dramatically during that time. Shortly after she turned 8, she at last stopped wetting her bed. In early 1987, her therapist said Lisa was no longer in need of treatment, adding that the child will probably require further counseling later, possibly when she reaches puberty.

The stories of the Grays and Judy Coletti end on positive notes. Their children were injured and are injured still, but they have been supported by their parents and have received help. In that respect they are lucky—or rather, fortunate (the efforts of those who helped them cannot be ascribed to luck). It was the children's ill fortune to have been abused, but many who share that experience do not have the good fortune to be believed. The Grays believed their daughter in the face of general denial. But for them, that was not enough. They became convinced that there was a need for people who have had their experience, and who have taken it upon themselves to learn from it, to educate those who have not. Acting upon these convictions has not always made them popular, but popularity was not what they sought; justice was.

Judy Coletti was also deeply changed by her experience. Following her protracted legal battles, she went to law school. At this writing, she has taken her bar examination and plans to join a firm in the fall of 1987. "The reason I wanted to be a lawyer," she said, "is to help other women who don't have families that are supportive like mine was, because I felt there were a lot of women out there who this is happening to and who just give up. It's so hard to keep fighting it." She has been working part-time at a legal clinic associated with her law school. What she tries to give the women who seek her assistance, she said, is what she herself did not get from the system: "That person who believes in them. I didn't really get that from the system—I got it from family and friends.

"Even when the judge signed the termination order, he took me aside and he said, 'I know what you said up on the stand, but tell me, how is Lisa really doing?' And I thought, 'Here, even this person doesn't quite believe me.' Here's this person who sat through all this testimony and everything. And I said, 'Well, she's really having a bad time now,' and he looked startled."

She had warm feelings for the judge, she added, and she recalled the incident with an ironic smile. But she did not smile when she remembered the rage and frustration that preceded it. "It's the most frustrating thing to realize you can't protect your child," she said. The next most frustrating experience has been trying to convince people that the problem exists. "There's so much more education to be done," she said.

The Grays would understand.

II
The Backlash

6

The Backlash

Jordan

A TELEVISION script could hardly have been more dramatic. In the lead role you had R. Kathleen Morris, a prosecutor who had established a reputation by aggressively pursuing sexual abuse cases and who had publicly stated that children almost never lie about sexual abuse. It was a battle cry that many took up, only without qualification, asserting that children never lie about sexual abuse, or simply: children never lie. The setting was Jordan, a small town of about three thousand, thirty-five miles out of Minneapolis. And those cast as the villains seemed from a distance to be practically the whole community. Actually, about sixty adults were questioned during the investigation, and twenty-four adults and one juvenile were ultimately charged, but among them were average, church-going, respectable citizens—even a police officer and a deputy sheriff. These were people who were supposed to be home watching Johnny Carson, not out molesting children and producing "kiddie porn."

Add to this scenario a dramatic trial during which the 6-year-old son of defendants Robert and Lois Bentz testified from the stand that his parents sexually abused him. When asked by a defense attorney if he feared his father would sodomize him, the child turned to his father and said, "You won't do that no more, right?"[1] But another witness, an 11-year-old, contradicted himself several times on cross examination, admitting that he had lied during his testimony. And in what was perhaps the biggest blow to the prosecution, James Rud, a convicted child molester who had confessed to molesting more than a dozen Jordan children and had agreed to testify for the state, could not identify Robert Bentz in court. All of his testimony was eventually stricken from the record. Amid tears and television cameras, the Bentzes were acquitted of sexually abusing their son and four other neighborhood children.

But the drama hardly seemed over. After all, this was scheduled to be at least a miniseries. There were twenty-one other defendants waiting to go to trial. But less than a month later, on the eve of the second installment, the series was abruptly canceled. Scott County Attorney Kathleen Morris dropped all charges against the remaining defendants. Only this was not television. These were real people whose lives were indelibly altered. And no matter what you believe happened in Jordan, innocent people were damaged by the system.

Rarely has the turning of a tide had such a clear demarcation. The child sexual abuse backlash began on September 19, 1984, the night the Bentzes were acquitted. Twenty-five defendants had been accused of participating in two sex rings that abused dozens of neighborhood children. In the end only James Rud, who had twice been convicted of sexually abusing children elsewhere, was convicted. In exchange for a reduction of the charges against him, Rud had pleaded guilty and agreed to testify against the other defendants. Ultimately, however, he recanted his 113-page sworn statement detailing sex parties involving children and adults, including his own parents. He never denied his own abuse of children, though, and is now serving a 40-year prison sentence.

The acquittal and dropped charges by no means answered all questions. They were the beginning, in fact, of two official inquiries, and the case will doubtless be the subject of intense investigation and speculation for years to come. We will not attempt either here. But a review of what is actually known and what Jordan has come to represent are crucial to an understanding of the backlash.

Unfortunately, Kathleen Morris did not respond to repeated messages left for her requesting an interview, so her reactions to the inquiries and her current perspectives on the case could not be reported.

Mistakes and Malfeasance

Shortly after Morris dropped the charges, the FBI and the Minnesota Bureau of Criminal Apprehension began investigating alleged homicide, child pornography, and sexual abuse in Jordan. Morris then formally requested that the state Attorney General's Office assume responsibility for all pending family court cases (twenty-six children had been removed from their homes) and for any criminal charges uncovered by the federal and state investigations. Four months later, Attorney General Hubert H. Humphrey III issued his report. Basically, it concluded that: (1) There was no credible evidence that any murders had occurred in Jordan; none of the children who told of murders was credible, and all eventually recanted. (2) There was insufficient evidence to bring new sexual abuse charges against any defendants. (3) The many mistakes made by the police and the county attorney had destroyed the opportunity to prosecute successfully those who may have victimized children and had caused the suffering of those who may have been falsely accused.

The report enumerated some of those mistakes. Among the most egregious were the questioning of children who had been removed from their homes dozens of times by many investigators, the failure of investigators to file written reports following many of these interviews, and the "cross-germination" of child witnesses.[2] "Cross-germination" in this context meant that children were sometimes informed of other children's statements, two children were sometimes interviewed together, and often children were permitted to discuss the case privately—all tending to reduce the witnesses' credibility.

A further criticism was that the investigators failed to gather evidence corroborating the children's statements. This was largely attributed to the filing of criminal charges before the cases were thoroughly investigated. Background checks were rarely performed, and neighbors, friends, spouses, and, indeed, suspects themselves were rarely interviewed prior to arrests. Although there were allegations of victims' having been photographed in "kiddie porn" poses by their abusers, no search warrant was obtained at the time any suspect was arrested. Nine days after Rud was arrested, a Jordan police investigator observed a stack of videotapes and a large box of what he believed to be pornography in Rud's trailer. The investigator was ordered to leave by Rud's parents, however, and when he returned the next morning, all of it was gone.[3]

The attorney general's report took pains to emphasize that children had definitely been abused. The issue was addressed near the beginning of the document:

> It should be emphasized that some children in Scott County were sexually abused. One individual has already been convicted as a result of a guilty plea. Other offenders received immunity and are undergoing treatment. In one instance the abuse occurred outside the period of the statute of limitations. In another instance a woman admitted sexually abusing her son, but the Scott County Attorney decided not to file charges. In that case there were no indications of any connection with a sex ring or other adults. With respect to all other allegations of abuse, however, it is impossible to determine whether such abuse actually occurred, and if it did, who may have done these acts.

The issue was reemphasized near the end of the report, which then added, "The tragedy of Scott County goes beyond the inability to successfully prosecute individuals who may have committed child sexual abuse. Equally tragic is the possibility that some were unjustly accused and forced to endure long separations from their families."[4]

A month after the report was released, Gov. Rudy Perpich appointed a special commission to investigate charges that Morris's conduct during the investigation and prosecution constituted malfeasance.[5] The commission began with a list of charges compiled by a woman who had been scheduled to be tried just before Morris dismissed all the cases, and who presented the allegations in the form of a petition requesting that the governor remove Morris from office. The commission completed its report seven months later, in October 1985.

It found that Morris had committed two acts of malfeasance, which it defined thus: "When an official consciously does an *illegal* act *or* a *wrongful* act which infringes upon the rights of another to his/her damage, and the act is outside the scope of the officials' authority."[6] (Emphasis in original.) According to the commission, Morris kept from the Bentz defense team potentially exculpatory evidence—specifically, children's stories of murder and mutilation that might have raised questions about their credibility. And during the trial, she violated the court order to sequester witnesses by housing children in a single hotel and allowing them to discuss their testimony. Both of these, while not illegal, were deemed "wrongful acts."

In addition, the commission found that five other charges had been proved by clear and convincing evidence, although these did not constitute malfeasance. Morris dismissed complaints against twenty-one defendants despite her belief that the cases had been properly investigated and that they could be successfully prosecuted, the commission said. She lied when she told the media that children had not been subjected to dozens of interviews, and lied when she told the Bentz trial judge that the defense had never asked for notes that she had previously told them did not exist. She failed to inform the judge that child witnesses were housed together. And she physically and verbally abused employees.

The commission did not recommend that Morris be removed from office, though. It decided that so drastic a measure was not warranted by the damage done—noting that the Bentzes had been acquitted. (The governor said at the time that the people would decide whether Morris should be removed in the next election; a year later Morris was defeated by a political novice who, after practicing law for only a year, won 64 percent of the vote.)[7]

More troubling than the malfeasance, the commission wrote, was the decision to dismiss charges against the twenty-one defendants:

> [T]he Commission found that it would be reasonable to conclude that some of the cases could have been successfully prosecuted. Once all of these cases were dismissed by Kathleen Morris, however, the prospect of recharging by herself or by the Attorney General represented a difficult task at best. . . .
>
> In many ways the dismissal allegations were the most troublesome of all for the Commission. Those defendants who were guilty went free, and those who were innocent were left without the opportunity to clear their names. Those children who were victims became victims once again. The Commission has concluded that the wholesale dismissal of the twenty-one cases was not justified.[8]

However, the commission added, "despite the fact that the Commission has concluded that the dismissals by Kathleen Morris were unjustified it cannot find this action to constitute malfeasance. Under our system of justice the County Attorney has such broad prosecutorial discretion that the power to dismiss cases without regard to whether or not a conviction could be secured is practically absolute."[9] In conclusion, the commission said, "Kathleen Morris did not respect the rights of the accused" and "did not see that the guilty were prosecuted."[10]

What Happened, What Did Not, and What Is Remembered

The backlash was born in Jordan for a variety of reasons, including what happened there, what did not, and what the public was left believing. Most people who remember Jordan probably think of it as that small Midwestern town where a "witch hunt" occurred. Even some people who followed the case closely for professional as well as personal reasons—like Leslie Wimberly and Lee Coleman, both of whom have ties to VOCAL—even they said they did not remember that the attorney general's report stated that children were molested by people other than Rud.

Although they may not remember all that happened, most people who remember Jordan at all almost certainly remember the allegations of murder. Children told stories of stabbings and shootings of adults, other children, and infants. There were tales of decapitations, of ritualistic torture and mutilation, of bodies being dumped in the Minnesota River. No bodies were ever found, and many of the children who described them later recanted. One child reportedly told state investigators that the reason he lied was to avoid having to go home. Another reportedly told them he lied because he wanted to please the investigators.[11]

Since Jordan, other children who were allegedly abused have told stories of murder and mutilation—many of them remarkably similar.[12] And there have been ritualistic elements in many children's stories that do not include murder (as we saw in the last chapter). Could these children—even very young ones—somehow have picked this up from the media? Were they coached by investigators?[13] By parents? By abusers who knew they would not be believed?[14] Or did they actually see something (or think they did)?[15] The stories are puzzling and disturbing, and suggest at least that the full explanation of what occurred in Jordan (and in many other places since) may not yet be available. But at the time, nothing like these stories had been heard before, and Jordan had the nation's ear. The public probably concluded that the children were telling some pretty big whoppers.

And that may well have been so. But as we have seen, that was by no means the whole story. Most people who even remember Jordan probably have a mental snapshot. Snapshots in an area as complex and confusing as child sexual abuse can be worse than no picture at all—much worse. There are lots of things that should be remembered from Jordan. It should be remembered that the original investigators were inexperienced. According to a lengthy investigation conducted by the *Minneapolis Star and Tribune*, "Morris has said the officers assigned to her had 'never gotten any experience in investigating any of this stuff.' One had just become an investigator in August [the investigation began in September]. Another had been a road deputy. Two assistant county attorneys working closely with Morris also were relative novices."[16]

Jordan is rightly remembered for the poor investigation that was conducted. The fault was not that there *was* an investigation, but in how it was done. It should be remembered that children who had been removed from their homes and who grew increasingly dependent on the investigators for support and affection were questioned by them repeatedly over many months. It should be remembered that these inexperienced investigators apparently had no standard protocol for interviewing children and documenting evidence.

But two things Morris did following the Bentz acquittal were devastating and probably more responsible than anything else for the way Jordan is remembered. First, she announced to the world right after the trial: "This means we live in a society that does not believe children."[17] This remark hardly seemed calculated to reassure the children. Compare the approach of Nan Horvat (chapter 4), who said that when she loses a case she reassures the child by telling her that the acquittal was not attributable to the jury's failure to believe the child, but rather to the state's failure to prove its case beyond a reasonable doubt.

Looking at the broader ramifications, Morris's statement was poor strategy. What she was saying, in effect, was that if you did not believe that the Bentzes were guilty—or, more precisely, that Morris had proved their guilt beyond a reasonable doubt—then you did not believe that children are ever sexually abused. Such a statement could help Morris, but it could not help the cause she professed to support; in fact, it did a great deal of harm. As Morris had undoubtedly learned from painful firsthand experience, many people do not wish to believe that sexual abuse exists. This has always been true and always will be. To say that an acquittal in one case means that society does not believe children is to make believing all children at all times an article of faith. With that philosophy, there would be no need for investigations, no need for courts. You simply interview the children and believe. That is not a position most Americans are willing to buy.

Then Morris compounded the error by the explanation she gave for dropping the charges against the twenty-one remaining defendants. She said she did so to protect "an active criminal investigation of great magnitude" and to avoid putting children through additional trauma and stress. The governor's commission analyzed in great detail the many problems Morris had during the Bentz trial and those her office would likely have faced in the second trial.[18] The *Star and Tribune* article also makes clear that the murder allegations, when they surfaced, were not taken very seriously by investigators and that it was questionable whether there really was "an active criminal investigation" of any magnitude when Morris made her announcement.[19]

But the ultimate damage was that Morris's actions and statements almost guaranteed that whatever came out of the murder investigation was what Jordan would be remembered for. And it is. Jordan is remembered for the Big Lie.

VOCAL

On October 19, 1984 [precisely one month after the Bentz acquittal] a group of people in Minnesota who had been falsely accused of abusing children joined together and formed a non-profit group, V.O.C.A.L., Victims of Child Abuse Laws, to represent their concerns and experiences.

After becoming VOCAL, we soon found that many others across the country were also being caught up in the witch hunt for child abusers. The cries for help began pouring in. We not only sent out information on what we were doing, but also encouraged people to contact others in their own state who had contacted us.

Those who had been feeling the frustration and despair of going through this alone found strength in each other, and began to work together. Many were motivated to form chapters of VOCAL in

their own states. Presently, there are 62 chapters formed or forming. Not every state has a chapter of VOCAL, while others have
several. (Calif. has 8 chapters!)

Thus began the first VOCAL National Newsletter, dated May–
June 1985. The organization's first board of directors included Robert and Lois Bentz as well as one other former Jordan defendant.
Although there have been some changes in the organization's leadership of late, there are now more than one hundred chapters in
more than forty states, and Lois Bentz is still a director. The newsletters are still bimonthly and, although more professional looking
now, contain substantially the same material. Virtually everything
in them focuses on child sexual abuse (as opposed to other forms of
maltreatment). Typically, there are articles about cases from around
the country, with attorneys' names and addresses and case citations
for further information. Recent books and newspaper articles are
cited and briefly reviewed. VOCAL members sometimes report on
conferences they attended. Letters, poems, and drawings are printed
from people accused and/or convicted of child abuse—occasionally
written from jail. Lawyers, doctors, psychologists, and others who
say they have had contact with cases (without having been accused)
write letters of sympathy and encouragement. There is usually a
bulletin board where meetings and events are advertised and new
VOCAL chapters announced.

As the organization's name implies, VOCAL has always taken
an interest in state child abuse laws, and many chapters make a
concerted effort to see that they are represented at pertinent legislative hearings. Some state chapters publish their own newsletters
with detailed reports of legislative efforts. California does so, and
recently the northern California chapter, based in Sacramento (the
state capital), has acquired the assistance of a lobbyist, who, according to the newsletter, has had some success.

But the organization's chief complaint is not so much about the
laws as about their implementation. As a position paper published
by the national headquarters states, "The intent behind the child
abuse laws is basically good. However we believe that a blatant
disregard of the laws is largely to blame for many of our situations."[20]
Although some of the arguments supporting their positions can be

complex, the basic positions themselves can be stated quite simply. The most important points, drawn from newsletters, the position paper, and interviews with VOCAL members, are these:

1. Justice is not being done. The system that is supposed to handle cases of child sexual abuse too often allows molesters to go free, while jailing the innocent.

2. The presumption that an individual is innocent until proven guilty has been thrown out the window in these cases. The accused are not always given an opportunity to respond to allegations, and in some instances are not even informed of their existence.

3. No one takes the side of the accused parent(s). Although there are often "child advocates" appointed to represent the best interests of the child, there are no "parent advocates" who help the accused adult or adults through the system and advocate on their behalf. There should be.

4. Children are frequently removed from their homes on the basis of mere suspicion, indelibly stigmatizing an individual or family even if the accusation proves groundless. With increasing frequency, such allegations arise from divorce proceedings during which a parent tries to use the charge to gain an advantage in a custody dispute.

5. Investigators—whether social workers, police officers, or prosecutors—begin by assuming abuse has occurred. Then they look for evidence that proves what they have already decided, insuring that the investigation will be biased. The result is often inappropriate prosecution.

6. Investigators often encourage and sometimes teach (or "coach") children to disclose abuse—whether the abuse occurred or not. They do so by asking leading questions, by using highly suggestive "anatomically correct dolls," and by rewarding children for certain answers under the guise of "victim support."

7. All interviews with children should be taped—preferably videotaped—so that the investigative techniques are documented and can be used at trial. In cases where rehearsing or coaching of children by prosecutors or investigators is exposed, all charges should be dropped.

8. There is a whole network of mental health professionals who make their livings "finding" and "treating" child sexual abuse. This "child abuse industry" has created the present atmosphere of hysteria and has a financial interest in maintaining it.

9. Courts charged with determining whether a child has been sexually abused are all too eager to defer to these same mental health professionals and allow them to decide. When they do so, however, they are shirking their own responsibilities.

10. The so-called experts who interview and/or evaluate children for the courts have no way to know for sure whether a child has been abused. In many cases their own biases make it less likely they will arrive at the truth than would an honest, reasonable layperson.

A number of these issues will be examined in detail in the next two chapters. But let us focus on the issue that is at the heart of VOCAL and the backlash: investigations. VOCAL says it supports thorough and unbiased investigations, and more and better training of investigators, particularly of social workers. Although some of VOCAL's critics have come out punching—one, commenting on the charge that Jordan was "another Salem witch hunt," responded, "The only thing wrong with Salem is there were no witches!"[21]— other critics have been more circumspect. Prosecutors, police officers, and social workers who were interviewed did not argue with at least some of VOCAL's positions and admitted—grudgingly in some cases—that the organization may ultimately help improve the system. It has already made professionals approach allegations arising from custody disputes with greater caution, some said.

But there has also been sharp criticism of other positions the group has taken and the information—some would call it "disinformation"—it has disseminated. For example, Sacramento prosecutor Jan Hansen and California VOCAL coordinator Leslie Wimberly had some polite, if not overly flattering, words to say about each other during separate interviews. But when Wimberly wrote an article in the paper published by the law school from which Hansen graduated, Hansen wrote a response. Wimberly's article begins with a personal account of her husband's battle for custody of his daughter by a previous marriage, during the course of which he was accused of sexual abuse. She goes on to describe her founding of the VOCAL chapter and the many abuses she has discovered in the system.[22] Hansen privately said she does not doubt that Wimberly's husband was the victim of a false accusation and believes Wimberly means well. But the most positive statement she makes about Wimberly's article in her own response is, "It is unfortunate that V.O.C.A.L. provides this obviously distorted information to the public and makes their bias so apparent—because they have some valid points to make and they express some legitimate concerns that we all share."[23]

In an effort to focus the debate, Lieut. Michael Hash, commander of the Sexual Assault Bureau of the Sacramento Sheriff's Department, was asked in an interview to comment on the following paragraph from Wimberly's article, chosen because it contains a number of specific complaints about law enforcement:

> The situation gets worse after a report is filed. Arrests can take place without warrants under the Welfare and Institution Code of California, at the request of Child Protection Agencies within the jurisdiction of suspected abuse. At any time day or night, law enforcement can come into your home, threaten you, belittle you, take you into custody without informing you of your rights or of the crime you have alleged to have committed, book you and in many of our cases not allow you a phone call or notification of your family for as long as four days. The jailers offer no caution as to allowing other prisoners the knowledge of the crime of which you are accused and often the accused is physically abused while in custody. There is an immediate assumption of guilt before you are tried in these cases. You are considered a "baby-raper" immediately upon the report of "suspicioned [*sic*] abuse."[24]

To take the complaints sequentially, Hash said the report referred to would be a child protective report filed by social workers, who might initiate proceedings to place the child in protective custody under the welfare and institution code.[25] An arrest, however, would have to be made under the penal code, and the officer must have probable cause to believe the suspect has committed a crime. The arresting officer must tell the individual what he is being arrested for but need not advise him of his rights (with a *Miranda* warning) unless he wishes to question him. After the suspect is charged, he has to be allowed a phone call within three hours. What if he isn't allowed a call for four days? "Then bye-bye case," said Hash. As to the assumption of guilt, Hash said, "By whom?"

When Wimberly was presented with this information, specifically Hash's response to the failure to permit a phone call, she acknowledged that the charges against the woman in the (single) case she was referring to had been dismissed.

During a wide-ranging interview Wimberly, who has appeared on radio and television, is often quoted in newspapers, and has given many speeches on the subject, discussed VOCAL's image and philosophy.[26] Asked why, if VOCAL is as concerned about the guilty going free as about the innocent accused (as she maintains), the newsletters contain articles only about the latter, Wimberly said she was unaware that the group was known only as supporting the falsely accused. "This is an interesting thing to know," she said, "because VOCAL is always contending . . . that people who abuse children should be punished to the fullest extent of the law." She cited the example of a protest she organized in a northern California town where a man prostituted his 13-year-old daughter. Wimberly said first that three men who admitted having sex with the child were granted immunity from prosecution in exchange for their testimony; later she said they pleaded guilty to a bargained charge.

"It was an outrage," she said. "You know, I could understand even one witness getting some kind of immunity to that degree, but three—that just blew me away. If what they're really after is trying to convict child molesters, then why did they imprison one of them and let three go? That doesn't make sense to me." She was also angered by the press coverage of her protest. "Two of the newspapers . . . took our pickets to solely and completely defend the defendant instead of taking up our issues that we were outraged over the three that pled guilty and got a plea bargain." Asked if, in fact, she had supported the defendant, she said, "Well, the defendant, in that particular case, had come to VOCAL and asked for some investigation into his background, and we steered him to an attorney and a private investigator. And the private investigation report that came out of that case showed us a lot of information and evidence that seemed to point to the father's innocence in that case."

A frequent criticism of VOCAL is that they defend the guilty,[27] that they have no way of even knowing which of their members were falsely accused and which were not. "I believe that some of the people in there are legitimate victims of the system," said Sandi Baker, executive director of the Sacramento Child Sexual Abuse Treatment Program, which treats both victims and offenders. But others, Baker said, are child molesters. "Some of the ones that I know of that have joined, we work with their victims. They're just using that group to reinforce their pathology. That is not what I think of Leslie [Wimberly], however, and some of the other ones who I do believe—I mean there's a place for Victims of Child Abuse Laws. There is enough wrong with this field for that to be a legitimate concern. But to have it run by people naive enough to believe that anyone that says they're not guilty is not guilty is setting up a 'Rationalizations United' group," she said, playing on the name of Parents United, the popular self-help organization for incestuous families.[28]

Wimberly acknowledged that there have been members who were convicted child molesters, asserting, though, that they were "people who we have supported through trial, people who were accused who we felt were falsely accused, prior to conviction." She claimed that her chapter has expelled three members who had prior records on similar charges and whom she came to distrust. But to the charge that she has heard often—"You really have no way of knowing how many of your members are guilty"—she retorted, "Neither does Boy Scouts, or church groups, or the general public. I mean you could be a child molester for all I know, right? See? I mean that's a silly question, isn't it?"

Asked if the situation were not different, since VOCAL aids and abets its members' defense (as opposed to the groups she mentioned), she answered with an analogy. "Look," she said, "say we are a support group for people falsely accused of burglary. . . . The first thing that VOCAL wants to do in its job is to make certain that all investigations into burglary are done thoroughly. We want finger-prints, we want photographs, we want crime scene investigation, we want times and places, we want stolen goods, we want witnesses, we want more thorough investigation. Now you tell me how many self-respecting burglars are going to want to join an organization that pushes for thorough investigation. . . . So when they tell me, 'You've got child molesters in your group,' well, if we do, they won't stay around very long."

But one convicted child molester stayed around long enough to become the VOCAL coordinator of Washington State (although he has apparently since left). Gerald Maloney was convicted in 1984 of statutory rape. He was sentenced to 3 months in the county jail, and was required to have outpatient counseling and to pay for his victim's therapy. In a telephone interview, Maloney said he had been VOCAL coordinator since March 1986 and had been involved with the organization for about eighteen months prior.[29]

He said (and investigation confirmed) that he had been in a Texas penitentiary for burglary, had been arrested once for shooting some-one (although charges were later dropped), and that he had also been involved in drug trafficking. "But I'm not a child molester!" he declared. "My side of the story is that I have an action against the state," he said, explaining that he is suing for a "massive violation" of his civil rights. "I pled guilty because I was immediately released from jail [having already served the time] and they did not attempt to arrest my wife for aiding and abetting—a felony."

Maloney added that "the vast majority of all child abuse is com-mitted by the agencies designed to stop child abuse." He speaks often on the subject, he said, for which he receives no compensation. Asked how he makes his living, he said, "I'll have to take the Fifth Amendment on that."

VOCAL is not the only organization that defends the falsely accused in Seattle. The Coalition of Concerned Citizens, founded in February 1984, was around before the Bentzes were acquitted. As its founder and director, Marilyn Gunther has had occasion to work with Gerald Maloney and knew that he was sometimes a dif-ficult personality to get along with. She knew too that he had been convicted of statutory rape of a 15-year-old who was baby-sitting in his home, but she did not know about the alcohol with which she had been plied or about the nude photographs he had taken of her. His story, she said, was that he had not realized she was under the age of consent.[30] Technically she was a child, but physically she was not, Gunther said. Gunther knew nothing about Maloney's prior run-ins with the law and was troubled by them, she added.

Of the people she helps, Gunther said, "The primary function we perform is not to determine whether these people are guilty or not guilty, but whether or not these people have received due process in their case." After a moment, she added, "Of course we like to know whether they are telling the truth because that will affect how we go on the case. But most people will tell us the truth." Asked how many people she thought had lied to her of the eight hundred cases she estimated she had reviewed for people from around the state, she said none, so far as she knew, but acknowledged that it may have happened.

Of molesters, Gunther said, "Sometimes they make excellent parents. There are a lot of people who sexually offend their own children who are excellent parents, despite that one little hangup. It's not as if they abuse them all the time. It may be two or three times a week over a prolonged period." She said the children were not necessarily damaged by the experience. "Usually all they require is to be told, 'Hey, it wasn't your fault, and we're going to see that it doesn't happen again. Forget about it.'

"People think the worst thing that can happen to you is sexual abuse, but it's not. It's being removed from your parents," she said. Asked how the abuse can be stopped if neither child nor parent is removed from the home, she said, "That is the $64,000 question."

Although Gunther's attitude may be extreme by VOCAL standards, it does not seem to be isolated. There is no way of knowing how many VOCAL members agree with her opinions, and she herself is not a member of the group, but there are professionals in the field with whom VOCAL has ties who express similar sentiments.

LeRoy Schultz, for example, was a featured speaker at VOCAL's first two national conferences[31] (and circulated a questionnaire at the first that we will discuss in the next chapter). A professor at West Virginia University's School of Social Work, Schultz had for several years been writing articles that foreshadowed the backlash. Gunther might well agree with them. Many VOCAL members talk about the vague definitions of child abuse, but few seem to have problems defining *sexual* abuse. Schultz does. Most VOCAL supporters at least implicitly acknowledge, as the law makes explicit, that children do not have the ability to consent in sexual relations with adults. Schultz does not:

> Including sexual abuse or misuse within the definition of physical child abuse may prove to be an unfortunate historical alliance. It wrongly conveys a victim-offender dichotomy that does not always

hold in sexual interactions, it wrongly conveys physical damage which is true in only 5%–10% of child sex-abuse, it does not deal with voluntary consenting reciprocal sexual activities that may be non-damaging, it does not acknowledge that children and adolescents are sexual beings and that sexual expression is a minor's right if it does not risk pregnancy. . . . The very labelling and intervention in child/adolescent/adult sexual interaction may themselves be victimogenic or traumatogenic. . . . Early learning that occurs in sexual interaction, unless repeated over time, is no more than a link in the child's developmental chain. . . . It is no longer defensible to apply diagnostic and intervention models, appropriate to those victims who are truly victimized, to the large majority who apparently are not.[32] (References deleted.)

Later in the same article, Schultz suggests that an important area for future study is "boy-man sexual activities that may be either constructive, nurturing or neutral, or adult-child incest activity that may be non-damaging."[33] These are not ideas one finds in VOCAL's newsletters, although they are staples in the newsletters published by NAMBLA (the North American Man/Boy Love Association). One of Schultz's statements probably would not even be defended by NAMBLA: "All children are sexual beings from birth, and all children will mature to view sexual activities as normal, healthy, and worth striving for in themselves and others."[34] It is difficult to see how *anyone* could defend a statement that *all* children will grow up to have a positive view of sex.

And yet both Schultz and VOCAL have thus far avoided being dismissed as fringe elements. Schultz was a member of the editorial board of the publication in which the article quoted above appeared, and if some of his ideas roiled the waters, he swam in the mainstream. So did Douglas Besharov, the keynote speaker at VOCAL's first conference. Besharov was the first director of the National Center on Child Abuse and Neglect and most recently has been director of the Social Invention Project at the American Enterprise Institute for Public Policy Research, a conservative Washington think tank. He has conferred upon VOCAL a certain air of respectability, especially in the media's eyes, it seems. His writing, which has attempted to expose the excesses of the system, particularly in the area of inappropriate investigations and removal of children from homes, has been widely cited by VOCAL and its proponents.

We will return to Besharov's work in the next chapter, but before we do, let us focus on examples from the center of the storm. Following are brief descriptions of two investigations that were inappropriate for opposite reasons. Most people would probably agree that both cases warranted some level of investigation—and that neither received the degree it deserved.

Those who assert that there is a witch hunt point to a case that vaulted from the pages of VOCAL's newsletter to *Woman's Day*.[35] According to the magazine, it is the story of how a 5-year-old California child was removed from her home for two weeks and was subjected, along with her family, to a six-month investigation, although ultimately the court determined that she had not been abused by her father (as alleged by social workers) or anyone else.

It started when her mother took her to the pediatrician to check a vaginal discharge that turned out to be Gardnerella vaginalis. The child was examined by a local physician, reputed to be an expert, who found she had a "dilated hymenal ring," a finding unsupported by other physicians who subsequently examined the child. The case was further complicated by a second lab test on the child's discharge which indicated that it was a common bacteria not transmitted sexually. Evidence presented in court revealed that Gardnerella vaginalis is also commonly transmitted nonsexually. But the case dragged on, forcing the child to undergo two psychological evaluations and numerous physical exams, before the court ruled that she had not been abused. There have certainly been many more cases like this one; three examples were cited in the article.

On the other side, perhaps the best example is an "investigation" that was done by a Florida caseworker sent out on a report that children were being sexually abused at the notorious Country Walk Baby-sitting Service. (The couple who ran the service were ultimately convicted of heinous crimes against numerous children.) According to a book on the case, the "investigator" was a seven-year veteran who was investigating her first "sexual harassment" complaint. Under questioning by the defense, she explained that she dropped in at the center unannounced and asked the woman answering the door whether she had been "sexually harassing" any children. "As the young woman said no, and the house was 'immaculate,' and there didn't appear to be any 'sexual harassing' going on, she believed the complaint to be 'unfounded.' " Under questioning by the prosecution, the woman revealed the extent of her inquiry:

> Did she speak to any of the children?
> "No."
> Did she speak to any parents?
> "No."
> Did she get any *names* of any children or parents?
> "No."
> Did she try to track down the source of the complaint?
> "No."
> Did she do anything other than ask the woman who answered the door whether she was "sexually harassing" children?
> "No."[36]

Clearly there are investigations that are overly aggressive and those that cannot even be called investigations. Children may be injured by either. Jordan was undoubtedly an example of a very bad investigation. There are many more that we never hear about. They come in different sizes and shapes. We never would have heard about the Country Walk "investigation" if children had not been badly damaged there and if the parents and children had not insisted on prosecution. But lack of publicity would not have made the social worker's efforts any better. VOCAL has helped expose some of the incompetence. Its attitudes and motives have been questioned and criticized, and it has questioned and criticized its critics. At first glance, there does not seem to be a great deal of common ground. But there is this small swatch: incompetence. When you think about it, it is not small. Incompetent investigations make it less likely the innocent will go free and the guilty will be punished.

And that is, after all, what all responsible parties say they want.

7

A Morass of Statistics

Founded, Foundering, Unfounded

M ANY stories on child sexual abuse, excluding breaking news
of an arrest or trial, follow a general pattern. They open with
a dramatically described horror story. It may involve a false accusation or an actual crime, but its power is in the raw human emotions
it describes. Then the reporter pulls back and attempts to place the
story in a context. The paragraph (or two or three) in which this is
done usually begins with a sentence like, "Unfortunately, this is not
an isolated instance." It is followed by statistics of some sort, demonstrating that the problem is widespread. (For a modified version
of this formula, see chapter 11).

It is not easy to use statistics in a fair and responsible way. It is
easier just to use them. And using statistics concerning child sexual
abuse is particularly difficult because it requires qualifying what we
say, which takes some of the bite out of a story. We journalists
should say that statistics in this field are suspect, that they may be
inaccurate for a variety of reasons, that there is much that is simply
not known. We probably do not say so often enough. Nor do others.

Much of the battle and the backlash, as it has appeared in the
media at least, has been fought with statistics. And these are not
statistics that the reader is likely to snooze through—not when someone says that 500,000 families in this country are inappropriately
investigated for child abuse each year, or when a San Francisco study
finds that 54 percent of a randomly selected group of women said
they had been sexually abused.[1] These statistics are grabbers, all
right, but can you believe them? A lot of things are said and written

in the heat of battle; it is all too rare to see them examined in the aftermath.

One of the largest issues that merits scrutiny is the controversy involving so-called unfounded cases of child sexual abuse. The problem has been attacked most forcefully by Douglas Besharov, who, as noted in the last chapter, was the first director of the National Center on Child Abuse and Neglect and was the keynote speaker at VOCAL's first conference.

In a lengthy 1985 article entitled " 'Doing Something' About Child Abuse: The Need to Narrow the Grounds for State Intervention," and in several shorter versions of it, Besharov argues that over the past twenty years the creation of mandatory reporting laws, accompanied by massive publicity, has drastically increased the number of child abuse reports.[2] Ironically, however, the success of child advocates in convincing the public that the problem really exists and that something has to be done about it—namely, that it has to be reported—has left children even more vulnerable than they were before. Along with the increased reporting has come a proportionately even greater increase in the number of "unfounded" cases— that is, cases that are investigated by social workers and are not substantiated. The unfounded rate is up to "more than 65 percent," Besharov says,[3] which means that the system can no longer respond expeditiously to cases in which children are in serious danger. As Besharov put it in his speech at the VOCAL conference, "The system now is like a 911 emergency phone call system that cannot distinguish between a murder in progress and littering."[4]

The dual result, Besharov says, is that children who are not in danger are needlessly removed from their homes—sometimes for months or even years—and, at the same time, "[e]ach year, over 500,000 families are put through investigations of unfounded reports. This amounts to a massive and unjustified violation of parental rights. As more people realize that hundreds of thousands of innocent people are having their reputations tarnished and their privacy invaded while tens of thousands of endangered children are going unprotected, a backlash is sure to develop that will erode continued support for child protective efforts at federal and state levels.

"Already, a national group of parents and professionals has been formed to represent those falsely accused of abusing their children," he continues, describing the genesis of VOCAL (see chapter 6).[5] It should be noted that Besharov is writing about all forms of child maltreatment, not just child sexual abuse. Although that means the numbers are much larger than those he would have cited for the more limited category,[6] we will examine his arguments as they relate to sexual abuse alone, as VOCAL has done.

The first problem with Besharov's thesis is his contention that "the determination that a report is 'unfounded' can only be made after an unavoidably traumatic investigation."[7] We saw at the end of the last chapter just how painless an "investigation" can be. The social worker who "investigated" the Country Walk Baby-sitting Service asked a few questions and bingo, "unfounded." Was it typical? One would hope not. It makes clear, however, that not all investigations are traumatic.

Then, before we even get to the numbers, there is disagreement over the meaning of "unfounded." In the popular media, Besharov has loosely referred to unfounded reports as "inappropriately made."[8] And he has been quoted as saying of the unfounded rate, "That means the system makes 700,000 inappropriate investigations each year."[9] Others have gone further, interchanging the terms "unfounded" and "totally false."[10] But as Besharov himself has acknowledged in his articles, at least, every report that is labeled unfounded is not false and is certainly not inappropriately made.

In his articles, Besharov is careful to say that some overreporting is necessary since the law requires the reporting of "suspected" cases.[11] He admits that sometimes "child protective workers wrongly determine that a report is unfounded, and that sometimes they declare a report unfounded as a means of caseload control."[12] Nor does he contradict the assertion that "if child protective agencies had more investigative staff, they would find that more reports now labeled unfounded are, in fact, valid."[13] But, he argues, "unfounded rates of the current magnitude go beyond anything reasonably needed."[14]

Others have argued that "unfounded" statistics include cases in which abuse may very well have occurred. In a footnote to a 1986 report, the Child Welfare League of America explained:

> Substantiation means that the investigating caseworker assessed the report as "founded" or "indicated." It should be noted, however, that "unsubstantiated" does not always mean a report was proven false. Approximately 11% of unsubstantiated cases are categorized

as "unable to investigate," for such reasons as the family has moved to another location. . . . Moreover, recent evidence concerning extremely high caseloads of investigation workers in state agencies indicates that many cases go unsubstantiated simply because the worker cannot get to them.[15]

Further complicating matters, the term does not mean the same thing in all states. And there is often plenty of room for discretion within a state's definition. For example, in California "an incident can be unfounded only if it is proven to be a false report, inherently improbable, an accidental injury, or not within the definition of child abuse."[16] This clearly allows a great deal of latitude. And a child protective administrator added that if an alleged child victim could not or would not talk to an investigator, the case would be unfounded, even though the child may have been abused.[17]

In New York City, cases are sometimes labeled unfounded even when there is medical evidence of abuse. This is because the reporting system in some instances requires that the alleged perpetrator be named in order to indicate a case. Thus, if a child has a venereal disease but is not verbal, the case may be called unfounded.[18] In Iowa, a case is labeled unfounded if the child names as the perpetrator someone who is not a caretaker.[19]

The safest thing we can say about the term is that it is in need of clarification. As one commentator has written, "It would be useful to evaluate the nature of the unsubstantiated reports. Are they at risk? Are these inappropriate reports? Does the public have adequate knowledge to make informed reports? Is this relationship changing over time?"[20] Much of the confusion might be eliminated if there were standardized terms used by Social Services Departments in all states. There also seems to be a need for expanded terminology to distinguish reports that are false (and malicious) from those that are baseless or unfounded (with no evidence of malice), those that could not be investigated, those that appear indicated although no perpetrator was named, and so forth.

Aside from the disagreement over definitions, Besharov's figures have been challenged. The introduction to the Child Welfare League of America survey cited above says, "CWLA reviewed its survey findings in light of recent reports, most notably those of Besharov, Gelles and Straus, that have led the public to believe that child abuse is leveling off or that, as reports increase, the level of substantiation decreases. CWLA's results indicating a substantial increase in reports and stable substantiation rates challenge the interpretations resulting from these studies." The results? "As the number of reports has increased, the substantiation rates have remained relatively constant. CWLA's survey found a substantiation rate of 47% for 1983 and 45% for 1984 for all forms of abuse and neglect. The substantiation rate for sexual abuse reports was 55% for both 1983 and 1984, based on data provided by seven states."[21] (In other words, in 1984 the unfounded rates were 55 percent overall and 45 percent for sexual abuse.)

The end of the last sentence quoted raises another problem with statistics in this field. Frequently we are dealing with smaller samples than we would like. And the seven states do not even include the country's most populous.

But even if Besharov's figures are too high, what he says is still disquieting. A substantial number of investigations may involve innocent people. Would it be less troubling, however, if the unfounded rate were, say, 2 percent? Critics would be absolutely furious. Investigations, they would say, are merely rubber stamps. And they would probably be right. So it is possible to look on this same 65 percent unfounded rate (if that is what it is) as indicative of thorough and professional investigation.

In all probability, that is not the case. All too often investigators are neither professional nor thorough. When social workers and their supervisors were asked during interviews around the country how long it takes to become a minimally competent child protective worker, the answers ranged from one to three years. The estimates on the low end came from supervisors, who were probably mindful of their own inexperienced staffs; the higher estimates were from the social workers themselves.[22] Although supervisors try to help inexperienced workers and it is common for beginners to be paired with veterans, it is still clear that a lot of caseworkers are learning on the job. And what makes this problem even larger is yet another statistic: the high job turnover that plagues so many child protective agencies. It is not unusual to hear of a 50 percent turnover in a year or two. That means that there are a lot of beginners and not many veterans to send them out with. Mix in the huge caseloads that Besharov mentioned and you have a recipe for incompetent investigations.

But Besharov does not talk about social workers' investigations. He talks about removal of children from homes. What does this have to do with the unfounded rate? As more and more reports come in, he says, social workers are swamped and because they have to investigate them all, they are throwing out a lot of cases that may be abuse, while removing children from homes where little or no abuse has occurred. It is the worst of both worlds.

And then he gives us a very big statistic, one that has been quoted in a number of articles. He says of the children social workers have been removing from their homes: "[A]ccording to data collected for the Federal Government, it appears that up to half of these children were in no immediate danger at home and could have been safely left there."[23] That is a major league statistic. It is at least the springboard that leads him to the conclusion that the laws that are supposed to guide social workers in these vital decisions are too broad. In the absence of such guidance, he argues, it is apparent that social workers and judges who must approve emergency removals simply are not equipped to make sound judgments.

So what is the crucial "data collected for the Federal Government" upon which these arguments are based? The footnote tells us this 50 percent figure is: "Author's estimate, based on: US National Center on Child Abuse and Neglect, National Analysis of Child Neglect and Abuse Reporting: 1979 47, Table 17." In other words, it is based on Besharov's estimate of a table in an analysis of reporting in the year 1979. Given the unreliability that we already know about reporting (see chapter 2), this seems a shaky foundation on which to build such an important argument, but let us look at table 17 (see table 7–1).

Katie Bond is an information specialist at the American Humane Association, which issued the report. Even before she was asked about Besharov's interpretations, she said, "You are not likely to get hard answers from our statistics. We will be the first to tell you that they are not what we would like them to be." The reason, she explained, is that the number of cases the table was based on was only a small percentage of the total reports, and the information the states report does not necessarily correspond precisely, since they have different systems and their definitions sometimes differ. The association does the best it can to put the information together, Bond

Table 7–1

DISTRIBUTION OF SERVICE INDICATIONS ACROSS TYPE OF MALTREATMENT[a]

(N = 55, 339)

Type of Maltreatment	Investigation Only (%)[c]	Casework Counseling (%)[d]	Court Action (%)[e]	Crisis Services (%)[f]	Long-Term Services (%)[g]	Other Services (%)	Percent of All Maltreatment
Major Physical Injury[b]	4.05	4.83	4.91	3.23	5.00	10.00	5.02
Minor Physical Injury	21.51	16.23	15.58	17.41	12.63	3.68	14.71
Physical Injury—Unspecified	0.82	0.32	0.13	0.34	0.25	0.26	0.29
Sexual Maltreatment	5.62	6.26	12.93	7.90	6.80	3.21	7.00
Deprivation of Necessities	42.73	33.60	17.74	25.56	29.70	39.33	30.96
Emotional Maltreatment	5.25	6.76	4.08	8.37	7.36	7.40	6.74
Other Maltreatment	1.87	3.91	5.57	7.13	5.30	9.11	4.81
Multiple Maltreatment	18.14	28.09	39.06	30.06	32.97	27.02	30.47
Total Services	100.00	100.00	100.00	100.00	100.00	100.00	100.00

[a] Note that the data reflect indications or frequencies rather than reports; thus one family could have received more than one service.

[b] Includes minor physical injury when it was indicated in conjunction with major physical injury.

[c] It is important to point out that "investigation only" refers to those cases that remained open after the investigation, and services are planned or expected but have not yet been provided. It is included in the services category in order to account for more of those families that remain involved with protective services.

[d] "Casework counseling" represents those cases with which the child protective services worker remained involved, as opposed to referring the family to another type of treatment provider. It is significant that casework counseling was provided to 87.3 percent of involved families who received services. This reflects a continuing increase in the proportion of families reported to be receiving casework counseling over the past few years.

[e] "Court action" refers to any activity whereby the authority of the judicial system is invoked, and it represents the range of uses of this authority from temporary placement of the child to termination of parental rights. Criminal prosecution of the perpetrator is also included. Court action was indicated for 16.0 percent of involved families.

[f] "Crisis services" refers to short-term emergency medical or shelter care, and it was indicated for 9.5 percent of involved families.

[g] "Long-term services" refers to long-term, support services, such as foster care or homemaker services. It was indicated for 67.1 percent of involved families. Approximately 8 percent of the reports indicated services that could not be described accurately by other service categories.

Note: When the distributions are compared, some interesting differences are revealed. When minor physical injury was present, investigation only (services planned or expected) was indicated more frequently than the other service categories. In sexual maltreatment, court action was the dominant service category. The opposite was true for deprivation of necessities, for which court action occurred less frequently. Surprisingly, while not significantly higher, crisis services was the dominant service category for emotional maltreatment. Court action was also the dominant service category for multiple maltreatment.

said, but "if you're trying to prove something by these statistics, you're going to find it very difficult," she cautioned.

Asked if it was possible to estimate from the table the number of children who were removed from their homes but could have been safely left there, she said it was not. "The information is not there," she said. When she was read Besharov's statement, she added, "I've known Doug for a long time, and I'm not saying that he is not valid in a lot of things that he is saying, but what I am saying is that he has used our statistics in this case to prove a point when they simply can't logically do it."[24]

When Bond's remarks were conveyed to Besharov, he declined to comment, saying that he stood behind his analysis.[25]

Hard Talk, Soft Data

It should be apparent by now that statistics can be a quagmire. While such a statement is hardly original or limited to child sexual abuse, it is particularly relevant because this is a new field and our ignorance is vast. And that very ignorance makes statistics especially dangerous. They can be molded into foundations on which knowledge is built; but they can also be fashioned into facades that project the illusion of knowledge.

Statistics are commonly used not so much to support beliefs as to prop them up. For example, very little research has been done on false accusations of child sexual abuse. It is a very hard subject to study. First, it is hard to know whether an accusation is false or not. How do you define "false"? Does an acquittal in a criminal trial mean an allegation is false? It may and it may not. Sometimes there is an acquittal in criminal court and a finding of abuse in family court. There have also been successful lawsuits for damages resulting from incest even when there had been acquittals in criminal court. And a child recanting an accusation is all too common in these cases (see chapter 2). So the truth of the matter may be difficult to arrive at, and that is undoubtedly one of the reasons why so little research has been done and why virtually all that has been done is based on extremely small samples.

But this has not prevented people from making lots of claims about false accusations and supporting them with far from reliable studies.[26] Those claiming there is an increasing number of false allegations have supported that position by citing a study by Elissa Benedek and Diane Schetky of eighteen allegations that arose during custody disputes.[27] The authors decided that ten of the eighteen cases they evaluated were false allegations, although they do not explain how they made the determinations. There are a number of problems with the study,[28] but even if there were not, it is necessary to approach with extreme caution any study with so small a sample. No caveats are issued by the authors, however. And there were none—not even mention of the sample size—in an article by a law professor who wrote, "In fifty-five percent of the cases studied, the psychiatrists concluded that the allegations of sexual abuse brought by one parent against the other were false."[29] A journalist went completely overboard, reporting that the study indicated that as many as 55 percent "of reported sexual molestation cases might be the result of a false allegation."[30] The study did not purport to say anything of *all custody* cases, much less of *all reported sexual molestation* cases.

The other side has been guilty as well. In a speech at a conference, Lois Haight Herrington, then an assistant attorney general in the U.S. Department of Justice with a reputation as a strong and effective child advocate, said, "An American Bar Association study . . . will soon publish some shocking findings. . . . In its comparative look at the sentences given to adults versus those given to children, the study found that 68 percent of convicted child molesters are given probation. *Moreover, if* they were incarcerated, they generally served one year or less."[31] (Emphasis added.) While technically true, the statistic was at least partly misleading. The implication (at least through the grammatical construction in italics) is that 68 percent of the convicted molesters got *only* probation. But a close look at the study reveals that only 6 percent received probation alone; 64 percent received some jail time. And although it is an interesting study, these numbers are based on just ninety-three cases, and the entire study looked at only three counties.[32]

A study by David Jones entitled "Reliable and Fictitious Accounts of Sexual Abuse in Children" was widely circulated and quoted with few caveats when still in preliminary form and incomplete, despite specific warnings to that effect and the absence of a description of methodology. It is interesting that in the final version, Jones and his colleague include an even stronger warning than that in the earlier one:

We suggest caution with the interpretation and use of these results, as the DSS survey was a pilot and the clinical survey was uncontrolled. The definition of *fictitious* used in this study was that professionals did not consider that abuse had occurred. This is subject to error. . . . We therefore suggest that the results be used as a base for further study and not as a definitive basis for proving that a case is or is not "true." (We are aware that our study has already been misused in court for this latter purpose.)[33]

David Finkelhor, a sociologist who has done a great deal of research and writing on child sexual abuse, said in an interview that false allegations are hard to study and that the preliminary Jones effort (the full version was not yet available) and one other he was aware of were not very good or complete. "I'm sure there are false allegations," he added, "and I'm sure when people are caught up in false allegations that it's terrible. . . . In all areas of social control, and particularly in criminal areas, there's always the possibility of false allegations, and I don't think they're more severe in the area of child abuse than they are in, say—I want to say something innocuous—people making false allegations about having had money stolen from them, or false allegations about embezzlement."[34]

But in truth, we do not know how many false allegations there are in this area. In the absence of hard data, generalizations are easily made and not easily contradicted, and speculation can sound like fact. For example, this pronouncement in an article on sexual abuse written by a psychiatrist who has published widely on the subject may sound plausible: "Placing a child in foster care is not treatment. This, however, is the most common outcome when a father is accused. He is usually jailed."[35]

Whether one accepts the unfounded rate argued by Besharov or that of the Child Welfare League, a fair proportion of these accusations will prove unfounded. If even a small percentage of the founded cases do not involve foster placement of the child (as in cases where the father no longer lives at home or when he voluntarily leaves), then it is clear foster care is hardly "the most common outcome." As for jail, the statement is preposterous.

Given the unfounded rate, it is likely that those who are accused will never even be charged, much less convicted. Look at Becky Roe's statistics (see table 4–1, pp. 74–75). Even an aggressive prosecutor may decline to prosecute many more cases than she files. And those are only the cases brought to her office. Many cases that do make it to court are heard in family court, where an individual can be jailed only for contempt of court. Many cases never make it to either arena. Clearly, accused fathers are not "usually jailed."

Perhaps the most remarkable of all articles on false accusations is an unpublished paper by LeRoy Schultz who, as noted in the last chapter, circulated a questionnaire at VOCAL's First National Conference. The paper, "Fifty Cases of Wrongfully Charged Child Sexual Abuse: A Survey and Recommendations," is based on fifty responses completed by conference attendees who claimed to be innocent and said they had been found not guilty of the criminal charge of child sexual abuse. Although Schultz adds the caveat "No pretense is made for the 'scientific' nature of this survey,"[36] he apparently was willing to call the cases "wrongfully charged" based solely on the word of the respondents and without even asking them if there had been findings of abuse in family court, for example.

Of the scant research, none has been done—reliably or otherwise—in the area that is allegedly rife with false charges. There are no statistics on sexual abuse allegations coming out of divorce and custody disputes, although there have been suggestions that *most* allegations now come out of such situations. Benedek and Schetky seem to say as much in their article. "In our experience," they write, "allegations of sexual abuse have been most common in child custody disputes that arise after a divorce has been granted and center around issues of visitation."[37] A study was conducted by the American Bar Association, in cooperation with the Association of Family and Conciliation Courts, to determine, among other things, the frequency of allegations during custody disputes. The results, made available to the author in draft form, unfortunately contain no hard data. The anecdotal information, however, based on interviews with court personnel and observers in five cities, several nationwide surveys, and informal questioning at conferences and the like, revealed that there was "a small but growing number" of false allegations arising under such circumstances. "The perception of these cases as far more common may reflect the fact that such cases are particularly vexing cases for court professionals and their impact is disproportionate to their occurrence," the authors wrote.[38] They are currently tracking these cases in eleven courts and will eventually have six months' statistics from each court.[39]

That Slippery, Suspect Recidivism Rate

False accusations and the unfounded rate are the high-profile debates, but they are not alone in the statistical trenches. An impassioned debate (which has not received adequate coverage in the popular media) has emerged in response to the questions, Can child molesters be cured, and How effective is therapy as a treatment? The resolution of these questions will undoubtedly have a profound effect on the sentences offenders receive in courts.

Interviews with a half-dozen directors of the country's leading treatment programs for sexual abuse offenders and a review of the literature shed light on the subject and also raised a number of questions about how statistics are used and what they mean.

First, there seems to be general agreement among professionals who treat offenders on the subject of a cure. "Don't use that word," said William Prendergast, who has been treating sex offenders for a quarter of a century—the past eleven years as director of the Adult Diagnostic and Treatment Center at Avenal, New Jersey. "There *is* no cure. We don't believe sex offenders are ever cured. They go into a remission state, but they can very easily recommit."[40] But Prendergast and the others interviewed believe that with proper treatment, the likelihood that offenders will recidivate—that is, will recommit—can be greatly reduced.

Sociologist Finkelhor, in his most recent book, reviewed the research in the entire field. In his review of the research on offender treatment, he prefaced his remarks with the observation: "This research is so flawed with conceptual and methodological problems that there is good reason to question virtually everything this accumulated work reveals."[41] Of the recidivism rates in particular, he wrote:

> Another serious shortcoming in the sex-offender literature is the scant attention given to the study of sex-offender recidivism. The most important public policy question for judges, prosecutors, defense attorneys, and therapists who work with sexual abuse cases is how likely child molesters are to reoffend after they have been caught and punished. One point of view within the criminal justice community tends to see child molesters as incorrigible; long prison sentences for offenders, then, are the only way to protect the com-

munity. Others, however, take a more optimistic view. They hold that being caught deters many offenders from risking the crime again and that, especially when treated, these offenders have a fairly high probability of long-term reform. Unfortunately, there is painfully little evidence to resolve this debate fully. Only a few efforts have been made to follow up identified child molesters over a period of time to find out whether or not and under what conditions they do continue to offend. Those few attempts are badly flawed and, probably for that reason, not well known.[42]

Perhaps the most salient flaw, Finkelhor points out, is that recidivism rates are routinely based on the number of reoffenses that were reported to the authorities—and sometimes just those that resulted in a conviction. "We know from many other sources of evidence," he writes, "that the vast majority of sexual offenses never are reported, never come to the attention of the authorities, and, even when they do, the probability of conviction is still low. So it is virtually certain that some and perhaps many of the offenders committed subsequent offenses that were not detected and not counted in the studies."[43]

One of the recidivism studies Finkelhor cites was conducted by Northwest Treatment Associates in Seattle, which found a reoffense rate of 3 percent for a group of 126 child molesters treated as outpatients and followed up for an average of two years. The men were tracked not by a check of official records but by self-reports or reports from family members or police, which, Finkelhor speculated, "may partly explain the low rate."[44] Tim Smith, who coauthored the study and is a cofounder of Northwest (where he works as a therapist), spoke during an interview of recidivism statistics in general.

"The statistics in this field are terrible and are real suspect," Smith said.[45] "I'm suspicious of follow-up statistics I see because I know how difficult it is following offenders. . . . When I see follow-up research, I'm skeptical that only people doing well will cooperate with the research."

Smith explained the importance of accurate statistics to his program and others like it: "What we're dealing with in this field is we're not getting any feedback. We're applying treatments that make sense to us, but then we're not able to get the last part of the circle—the feedback to see how that treatment has worked ten years down the road. . . . The problem with this kind of a disorder is it's not something we can say, 'There, we fixed it.' It's not like a broken leg where you can take off the cast and see it's fixed."

He agreed with Finkelhor's suggestion that long-term follow-up is essential and that self-reports are a dangerous source of information. People molest children when they are in their sixties, seventies, and eighties, according to Smith. "We see them in our program," he said. As to self-reports, he added, "Every day we have clients lie to us—that's the nature of the disorder. As a treatment center, we're at a disadvantage because we have no way of knowing when people are lying to us." The other offender therapists who were interviewed agreed it was dangerous to rely on self-reports.

One problem Finkelhor did not mention is that the statistics of most programs are further skewed by dropouts. Many programs screen offenders before accepting them. Northwest, for example, accepts only 40–50 percent of those who apply. In many programs, if offenders fail to complete the treatment—either because they drop out or are ejected—they are not counted. (And one cannot help wondering what most programs do with offenders who recommit during treatment.) Thus, the statistics are automatically cast in a better light than they might be.

But an even larger problem that Finkelhor omitted is the temptation for programs to tout figures they know are (at best) unreliable in order to promote their programs and raise funds. Perhaps the greatest danger in this indulgence is that it calls into question all figures in a field composed largely of, in Tim Smith's words, statistics that are "suspect." The potential damage may be compared to the loss of credibility suffered by organizations that publicized missing children statistics that have been shown to be at best inflated and at worst false and misleading.[46]

Sandi Baker, executive director and founder of the Sacramento Child Sexual Abuse Treatment Program, which treats victims and offenders, said that her program's recidivism rate was less than 5 percent, but then quickly added that the number was for reoffenses and that she did no follow-up whatsoever (due to lack of funds). When questioned further on the matter, she added that about 10 percent of her clients are expelled from the program because they are deemed too high a risk for treatment and that an accurate assessment of recidivism would probably reveal a rate of between 10 and 20 percent. Even a 20 percent recidivism rate would be excellent, she said: "When you're talking about 80 percent of it being successful in something like this, that's phenomenal."[47]

All of those interviewed agreed that a 20 percent recidivism rate was excellent. And all of them agreed too that programs claiming unrealistic rates hurt them all. The clearest example is the well-known Child Sexual Abuse Treatment Program of Santa Clara County, California, funded by the state as a model program and widely imitated around the country. The program was developed by Henry Giarretto, a pioneer in the field who founded Parents United, a self-help group for victims and offenders that is an essential component of Giarretto's treatment approach and now has dozens of chapters nationwide.

Giarretto has for years maintained that his program has a recidivism rate of less than 1 percent (0.6 percent, to be precise). It is a figure that has been dutifully quoted in many newspaper and magazine articles and that was allegedly confirmed by an evaluation of the program commissioned by the state and later published as a book by Jerome Kroth.[48] But it is a statistic that nobody who treats child molesters believes—including Giarretto's staunchest supporters. One of those supporters is Bob Carroll, who worked for Giarretto for nine years and who maintains close ties in his current position as coordinator of child abuse services for Santa Clara County, Carroll said in an interview that he has long tried to talk Giarretto into dropping the number.

"I get very angry at that statistic because it is not accurate," Carroll said. "It may have been accurate at one time, but it's far from accurate now. A recidivism rate of 25 percent may be a good program now. If we can turn around 75 percent of the cases, we're doing a great job."[49]

Giarretto himself backed off from the number during an interview. Early in the conversation he was asked what percentage of offenders he deemed treatable. His answer was 90 percent—emphasizing that he was speaking only of incest offenders, who many believe can be more successfully treated than other offenders. Asked why his estimate was so high compared with others, he said, "Nobody has been able to show me that the less than 1 percent recidivism rate is a wrong figure."[50] Pressed on the matter, he acknowledged that his statistics were based solely on police reports of reoffenses and that he would not know of cases in which the client moved to another state or even another county. Told of the opinion of the statistic held by the others interviewed, he said, "I know, and I hate even to say—what I'm saying is the only figure I've got. I can speculate too and say 5, 10, 15, 20 percent, and that's pretty good too, you know. All I'm saying is that the reported recidivism rate is a hard number." He mentioned the Kroth evaluation, but when it was pointed out that Kroth simply embraced Giarretto's numbers without question and endorsed a review of unnamed "European studies" that found an expected recidivism of 2 percent to be normal,[51] he acknowledged, "Kroth's stuff is not necessarily convincing to me because I know the statistics."

It is clear that reliable statistics are needed. As Finkelhor wrote, "The study of child molesters is not an easy task. Such individuals do not make enthusiastic or cooperative subjects, and the matters of most interest to the researcher are often the exact ones the subjects are least interested in divulging. Yet there is perhaps no more important need in the field of sexual abuse."[52] The information is essential both in assessing the efficacy of treatment and in enhancing the quality of programs.

Baker said she believes research would prove the effectiveness of her program, "but if it proves something different, then we need to know that for the field also and change and modify what we're doing to be more effective." Ideally, she said, researchers should be independent but not adversarial. She would like to see her program evaluated by such researchers but does not know where the money would come from. "I would welcome it," she said. "I would love to see it happen. And I wouldn't want it to come out of my treatment budget. I would want it to be independently funded. I have five families waiting to get in here right now; I don't want to turn down five families to do research projects. I want that to be funded separately and let us do what we're good at doing."

Without independent research independently funded and conducted by disinterested experts, statistics in this area will remain suspect. And to be sure of unbiased results, it is important that researchers approach the work without even the assumption that treatment is more effective than no treatment.

The Big Picture

Although offender treatment is one of the most problematic areas, as we have seen there is uncertainty concerning virtually all statistics in the field. We know more about victims than we do offenders, but we do not have anything resembling an accurate picture of how widespread sexual abuse is in this country, or what its effects are. "The situation is confusing," writes Finkelhor. "The reality is that there is not yet any consensus among social scientists about the national scope of sexual abuse. No statistics yet exist that fully satisfy the request that journalists and others so frequently make for an accurate national estimate."[53]

The quality and quantity of the research is not alone to blame. The criminal justice system must also accept responsibility. As Lois Haight Herrington said in a speech a few months before she resigned (in September 1986) as the assistant attorney general who headed the Justice Department's Office of Justice Programs:

> The Justice Department has not done a very good job of keeping statistics on these issues. The FBI's Uniform Crime Report measures reported crime nationally, but has no information on child sex abuse and very little on family violence. The only crime for which it records the relationship of victim to offender is murder. . . . For crimes less than murder and for those against children, there are no reliable statistics from the justice system. The other national measure of crime, the National Crime Survey of the Bureau of Justice Statistics, is a well-respected source, but has inherent problems. It doesn't ask questions of subjects under 12. Interviews are often conducted in the presence of the entire family. What child would report being abused or molested under these circumstances?[54]

Herrington added that efforts have been initiated to rectify these deficiencies, but how soon better statistics are available and how much they tell us remain to be seen.

While the country awaits better federal statistics, there is no reason why prosecutors' offices cannot track at least their own cases, as Roe has done in Seattle. One of the reasons why the big picture in this field is so fuzzy is that it is composed of thousands of small snapshots that are themselves out of focus. The debate will not end when the images are clearer; there will always be differences of opinion on how to interpret what they mean. And there will always be those who choose to manipulate and distort data to suit their own purposes. But in this young field there seems to be a growing recognition, at least among those who are truly committed to its maturation, that an acknowledgment of ignorance is a prerequisite to knowledge.

This chapter has examined for the most part what we do not know. The next chapter will look at what we *do*—or, more precisely, at what those who claim to know claim they know.

8

The Experts

Who and What

WHO are the experts in this field and what is their expertise? These sound like simple enough questions, but they are at the center of some of the most intense debates.

There are so many disciplines involved in handling child sexual abuse cases that a list of the professions, each of which has specialists who may be experts in their own right, is daunting:

1. Police officers
2. Social workers
3. Therapists who treat victims
4. Therapists who treat offenders
5. Prosecutors
6. Defense lawyers
7. Law guardians
8. Doctors
9. Nurses
10. Researchers
11. Educators
12. Program administrators
13. Writers and theoreticians

To these we can add judges and legislators, who may be extremely knowledgeable but do not exactly specialize in sexual abuse. There are also child molesters themselves and their victims, who in some instances are the most expert of all. And finally, there are advocacy groups and what we will call, for lack of a better name, the ombudsmen. There are a variety of child advocacy groups, and the North American Man/Boy Love Association (NAMBLA) could be described as an advocate for the other side. VOCAL too is basically an advocacy group—for defendants. The ombudsmen are those who oversee the field and try to hold it accountable. People like Douglas Besharov fall into this category (although Besharov could also be placed in category 13).

It is safe to say that the attitudes and skills among these groups vary. Some groups violently disagree with attitudes commonly found among others. For example, many police officers who specialize in sexual abuse question whether offenders can or should be treated, preferring to see them incarcerated. Some would question whether offender therapists are experts at all, and they would find support in other disciplines. This kind of infighting is not uncommon in the professional world, but there are few fields in which so many disciplines that are so disparate are also interdependent.

And yet the biggest disputes have not been internecine. The pitched battles have been between VOCAL and its supporters on the one side and the social workers and therapists on the other. Members of other groups have taken sides and joined the fray, but the focus is still on the original combatants. Why? It comes down to power and vulnerability. Social workers are the frontline investigators who decide whether a case is founded or not, and the results of their investigations often determine whether a case goes to family court and what happens when it does. Therapists may also have a lot to say about the outcome of a family court case and sometimes are the key witnesses in criminal court as well. That makes these groups undeniably powerful.

As to vulnerability, social workers are often inexperienced and overworked, and the combination often leads to marginally competent work, as noted in the last chapter. But that is only a small part of it. Lawyer Andrew Vachss points out that VOCAL and others of their persuasion rarely raise issues related to physical abuse. There is a reason, says Vachss:

> [W]e should note that backlash advocates largely confine their focus
> to cases of child *sexual* abuse. The reason for this is simple: the
> techniques by which child sexual abuse is proven differ widely

from those used in cases of physical abuse. While the "battered child syndrome" is now an accepted part of medical terminology, the process by which a diagnosis of "child sexual abuse syndrome" is made is still thought of as a "soft" science. And while rhetoric which raises the spectre of a child "fantasizing" sexual abuse comes easily to those accused, no such comfort is available to a perpetrator confronted with an X-ray of his child's broken bones.[1]

Two points seem clear. Backlash proponents *have* focused almost exclusively on sexual abuse. And since there is rarely medical evidence in these cases, there is more lattitude for dispute. The process by which a diagnosis of "child sexual abuse syndrome" is made is indeed a soft science. In fact, it is more of an art than a science. There are even some respected therapists specializing in this area who do not believe there is such a thing as child sexual abuse syndrome, although they do believe a child can be diagnosed as having been sexually abused. There is plenty of room for disagreement even among specialists who often agree.

This is not to denigrate the skill required to make the diagnosis. Quite the contrary. But because there is nothing as definitive as an X-ray, the conclusions of a therapist are subject to dispute. Just as a social worker's investigation is subject to dispute. And they *are* disputed—regularly. There is nothing in the least bit surprising about that. After all, there are other professionals whose job is to find flaws in the work of social workers and therapists: defense attorneys. Their job may also involve finding experts who will testify that the system is flawed.

The experts who routinely testify for the defense are a controversial group. Some would insist on placing quotation marks around the word *expert* when it is applied to them. Their testimony, among other factors, has made some of the therapists and social workers whom they have opposed controversial as well. And as the controversy has heated up, so has the language. The defense experts are usually called "hired guns" by the opposition. The therapists and social workers have been derisively called "child savers"; their techniques have been characterized as everything from manipulation to out-and-out child abuse.

The public criticism and controversy have been engineered largely by VOCAL, which has assiduously cultivated media contacts. The emergence of the defense experts has underscored VOCAL's importance as the only network linking them with defendants and defense lawyers. The VOCAL newsletters have been the medium through which they have exchanged business cards. Those newsletters, which have provided and still provide psychologists and psychiatrists with what is tantamount to free advertising, have now begun to accept paid advertisements as well. An announcement of the availability of advertising space (with the caveat "only ads of interest to the special character of our readers will be accepted")[2] has yielded results. An organization that calls itself Men International placed the following ad:

> There are over 700,000 false reports of child abuse in America each year.*
>
> Growing numbers of people and professionals have come to appreciate the hysteria about child abuse that is gripping our nation. Only twice in America's history have there been issues so volatile that due process rights of defendants have been so abused. The first was the Salem Witch Trials and the second was the Communist scare of the McCarthy era.
>
> The current trend is extremely dangerous. Innocent people are being sent to prison.
>
> False abuse allegations have become, arguably, the most popular tactic in divorce cases today. False abuse allegations in child custody disputes have become institutionalized. Child care professionals have become targets as well. This can strike anyone.
>
> *There is a great deal of deceit in the child abuse evaluation process.* Most people, confronted with allegations against them, make the mistake of not taking the allegations seriously enough.
>
> Perhaps the most serious problem an accused faces is the unpreparedness of local defense counsel. The problem of false abuse allegations developed so fast, like wild-fire, that the Defense Bar was caught off-guard.
>
> But there is a new hope. We have developed a specialized team, capable of assisting on cases anywhere in the nation. The team is made up of the best experts available in the United States. We call it the "Annihilation Team" because our aim is to destroy false

---

*SOURCE: Dr. Douglas Besharov, former director, National Center for [*sic*] Child Abuse and Neglect.[3] (Emphasis added.)

allegations. You can call it the "A-Team" for short. We mean business. We can help if you'll take the time to call, or have your attorney call to find out how we can help you.

The focus, as is clear from the advertisement, is the "deceit" in the evaluation process. Who are the evaluators? Most often they are social workers and therapists. Some of the complaints about the process are that evaluators do not always talk to the accused or to collateral witnesses who may have information about the case. But primarily the controversy has centered around the interviewing of alleged child victims.

It is a controversy that achieved national prominence in Jordan, as we saw, and is likely to persist for some time. It is multifaceted, and a number of the issues have divided therapists who normally see eye to eye. Some of the basic questions that frame the argument are: Who should interview child victims? What should an interviewer know about the case before the interview? When is it proper to use leading questions and to what extent? Are drawings and anatomically correct dolls legitimate tools to use when interviewing young children? To what extent should evaluators encourage children to "tell the secret," when there may be no secret to tell, and how does such encouragement affect the results of the interview?

The arenas in which the battles have been waged are the courts and the media, although not always in that order. The weapons have been words and lawsuits. Perhaps the most discussed case, after Jordan, is the McMartin Preschool case in Manhattan Beach, California. At this writing the trial has not been completed, but it has received a great deal of attention both in the field and out. Although charges were dropped against five of the original seven defendants in the case, it is interesting to note that a defense lawyer representing one of the two remaining defendants told a reporter: "I believe there were some children who were molested," then added that his client was not responsible.[4]

Much more will be written about the McMartin case when it is concluded, but it is of particular interest here because of the charges and countercharges concerning the investigation. McMartin and Jordan are often cited by both sides as examples of investigations gone wrong. Without examining the McMartin case in depth, certain parallels can be drawn between at least the preliminary investigation there and the Jordan investigation. In both instances there were allegations of mass molestation that were unprecedented and for which—perhaps of necessity—the investigators seemed ill equipped. In the McMartin case, as in Jordan, the alleged perpetrators learned of the investigation (in this case, through a letter sent by the police to parents whose children had attended or were attending the school) before search warrants were obtained, even though there were allegations that children had been photographed in sex acts. And charges were filed before a thorough investigation had been completed.

Investigator or Therapist?

The thrust of the defense in Jordan was that children had been unduly influenced, even "brainwashed," by the interviews investigators conducted. The same defense is likely in the McMartin case, as is clear from a conversation with Walter Urban (see appendix), a lawyer who represented one of the defendants against whom charges were dropped. Ironically, the interviews were conducted by therapists the Dictrict Attorney's Office hired specifically because they were considered to be experts in interviewing young sexually abused children. Many were conducted by Kee MacFarlane, who has worked in the field since 1970 and is considered by most of her colleagues to be a pioneer and a true expert. MacFarlane and her co-workers at Children's Institute International undertook the monumental task of interviewing about 400 children over a period of ten months. The interviews were videotaped and, following a court battle during which the therapists tried to prevent the release of the tapes, fearing they might be used by the press (leaving the confidentiality of the children unprotected), 220 tapes were turned over to the prosecutors. They were then made available to the defense, under the rules of criminal discovery.

The defense lawyers' comments on these interviews, and the comments they solicited from others they asked to review the tapes in preparing their cases, have formed the basis of the criticism. The criticisms of the techniques are similar to those that have been made in many other cases, including the interviews of children at West Point conducted by Anne Bush Meltzer (see chapter 5). The general thrust is that the techniques used by interviewers are intrusive and suggestive, tainting the interview and rendering the information produced unreliable. The techniques most frequently criticized include the interviewers' use of dolls, toys, and drawings—which, it is pointed out, children commonly use to create fantasies—for the purpose of eliciting truthful accounts of reality. The use of leading questions to focus attention on sexual abuse, especially following a child's repeated denials, has been sharply criticized. And critics have attacked interviewers' asking children if they have been threatened, reassuring them that they are safe and that it is "okay to tell," and then praising them if they disclose any abuse. According to this theory, the interviewers who use these techniques may be well-intentioned and the children may have no intention of lying, but the effect is that children are taught what to say. In the end, they do not lie but rather grow so confused that they can no longer distinguish between what they have been taught to believe and what actually occurred.

The criticism does not end there. Therapists' involvement in the legal end of these cases is not always—or usually—as investigators. They may be asked to testify in court, sometimes as expert witnesses. When qualified as experts, their function is to educate the trier of fact (either the jury or the judge, if a nonjury trial) in matters that are not common knowledge and that a layperson could not be expected to know. The special knowledge an expert possesses may be of a particular child the therapist has treated or general knowledge of the field. Such testimony is not uncommon in criminal courts.

In family courts, on the other hand, psychiatrists, psychologists, and social workers are sometimes asked to evaluate children to determine whether abuse has occured. Their testimony often includes a catalogue of behavioral symptoms children have exhibited, and some jurisdictions have accepted the diagnosis of "child sexual abuse syndrome," although many courts have refused to do so on the grounds that a scientific foundation for the diagnosis has not been adequately demonstrated. Whatever the diagnosis, evaluators' opinions may weigh heavily on courts' decisions.

A number of critics have argued that therapists have no business either investigating cases for law enforcement agencies or testifying in court. The critic who has made this case most consistently, and cogently, is Lee Coleman, a California psychiatrist who was the keynote speaker at VOCAL's Second National Conference and who was hired by defense lawyer Urban to review a number of the McMartin tapes before charges against his client were dropped. He has testified for the defense by critiquing videotaped interviews in a number of high-profile cases, including the Country Walk case in Florida. During a lengthy interview, Coleman described how he first became involved in these cases:

> I have for fifteen years been a student and a critic of the role of psychiatry in our legal system. I have written a book about that.[5] So it was with that background . . . that I first had this problem brought to my attention. . . . I was not working specifically in the area of child sexual abuse . . . Somebody who was an accused person called me up and said, "I heard about what you think about psychiatric methods in the courtroom, and based on that maybe you'd be interested in what's happening to us." I said, "Sure, if you want to hire me to review your case, I can do that." So I did and I was immediately appalled by what I saw going on because you don't have to be—you don't have to have been interviewing children who have been alleged to be abused or any of those things to see certain things that are very, very wrong with what is happening.[6]

Coleman's position is that mental health professionals have no way to tell whether a child has been sexually abused and no reliable information to convey to a judge or jury to help them decide. Furthermore, he argues, so many of the therapists and others who interview children begin with the belief that the child has been abused that they do a worse job eliciting reliable information than a reasonably intelligent layperson would. "The conclusion that I formed," Coleman testified in the Country Walk case, "is that in none of the cases where the courts ask psychiatrists and psychologists to give expert opinions do we actually have the methods that the courts think we have. . . . In fact, I would go even further. My conclusion is that we are actually worse than ordinary lay people because of some of the biases which are built into our training."[7]

Are there *ever* times when Coleman believes it is proper for such professionals to testify in court? "There are a few such situations," he said in the interview, "but not in this area, no." When? "Malpractice cases, because there you're talking about the standards in your field. There may be certain cases where medical issues come up that are overlapping psychiatry, such as brain injury, things like that." Why, then, does Colemen testify frequently in court? "But I don't testify about what we're talking about," Coleman countered,

explaining that he has never and will never examine a child to determine whether the child has been sexually abused. "In other words,"
he continued, "I only testify because they testify, and I'm trying to
give my opinion on the methods that they're using to give some
perspective on that."

Although at first he agreed that he would not testify if psychiatrists did not testify for the other side, he quickly added, "Now
you have a special thing going on in this child sexual abuse area.
Psychiatry's theories and methods from this child sexual abuse arena
are influencing the way their investigations are being done, even
though psychiatrists may not testify. So, therefore, it is important
for a court to hear a different—you know, if there are other opinions
about these theories and these methods, because if a social worker
or a police officer goes in and interviews a child and has been influenced by the training that they've gotten from the people in mental
health, then you might say that psychiatry is in the case, and it is
in all these cases because there's an amazing uniformity of belief and
practice in these cases across the country."

One of his primary targets is Roland Summit and his child sexual
abuse accommodation syndrome (see chapter 2). Coleman has written, "In cases which fit this description"—that is, when the model
is applied to incest allegations in intact families—"Summit has made
a real contribution by vigorously pointing out how a victim may be
invalidated and thereby further victimized, and why professionals
should support the child."[8] But the syndrome does not adequately
describe allegations that arise when the parents are already divorced,
Coleman says. "Nasty divorces, followed by angry custody disputes,
do not find one parent rushing to the other's aid, as is described in
the accommodation syndrome. Far from defending the accused person (usually the father), the other parent (usually the mother) is
typically the chief accuser."[9] The model is also inappropriate when
applied to extrafamilial cases and day care cases like McMartin,
Coleman adds.

There is no question that Summit's paper has been influential
in the field. According to Coleman, its influence has been positive
when applied to cases where the facts match the model and pernicious
when misapplied. (In an interview, however, Summit took issue with
Coleman, asserting that although his paper did not say so, the syndrome can be applied to cases other than incest.)[10] Coleman has

focused on two distinct ways in which the accommodation syndrome has invaded the courtroom and, in his view, has done untold damage to defendants. The first is directly, through expert testimony; the second indirectly, through tainted investigations conducted by those who subscribe to its biases.

Experts in Court

To take the first way, Summit and others who have been influenced by him have been qualified as experts and have testified in court as to why a child may delay for days, weeks, or even years before disclosing abuse, and why she may retract under pressure even when the disclosure is truthful. Such testimony has generally been admitted into evidence only when the credibility of the child's allegation has been attacked by the defense. Under such circumstances, the prosecution is sometimes permitted to call an expert to rebut such an attack by explaining that many sexual abuse victims blame themselves and disclose abuse slowly, piecemeal, and often retract—information that may not be familiar to the judge or jury. Coleman's objection to such testimony is not only that it is sometimes applied to cases where incest is not alleged—Summit himself has testified in such cases—but that the purpose of such testimony is not so much education of the jury in a matter that Coleman says mental health professionals have no special information to offer, as it is advocacy on behalf of the child. In fact, as Coleman points out, Summit's paper specifically calls for clinicians to engage in legal advocacy for child victims. The use of experts bent not on informing but persuading the jury that children do not lie about sexual abuse is improper, Coleman argues.

But the broader issue is the training of police, social workers, prosecutors, and therapists who investigate these cases. Coleman sees Summit's influence in workshops in which the techniques he criticizes are allegedly taught:

> In hundreds of workshops for police, protective service workers and prosecutors, the leading lights from psychiatry, psychology and social work are training investigators to believe that when it comes to alleged sexual abuse, the child's statements are unimpeachable.

Ignored at such workshops is the fact that the experts developed their ideas by studying incest in intact families, while the major arena of false allegations is divorce/custody battles. In the former the child may be pressured to drop a true accusation, but in the latter the pressure may go the other way—to "remember" something that never happened. The young child may easily be led to the point of sincerely believing in things that did not take place.[11]

In addition to Summit, Coleman has frequently and sharply attacked Kee MacFarlane, who conducted many of the McMartin interviews. In response to questions about how experts should be used in court, MacFarlane said during an interview,

> I don't think that so-called experts should be used to go into court and say, "I think it happened and I think he did it." Even though I'm on the expert panel in L.A. and play that role, because of everything I do, it makes me most uncomfortable if I ever have to do it—it makes me feel like playing God.
>
> I think the role of experts in this field should be to come into court and educate judges and jurors about the nature of this problem, because they don't know about it, they shouldn't be expected to know about it. And those people would assume, for example, that if you or I got our house burglarized and the police come in and we told them all about it, and two weeks later we took it back, and said, "No, I didn't really get my house burglarized, I was just fooling," they would then have serious reason to question all our credibility. The instructions to juries are—in California anyway, there's an instruction that says if the witness contradicts themself, either in court or in the statement, that should have a major effect on the jury's judgment of their credibility. Not so. This is a major exception to that, because it's so frequent. That's the kind of thing I think experts report.[12]

Further qualifications of the proper role of expert testimony were offered by Lucy Berliner, a social worker at a hospital-based sexual assault center in Seattle who has written and lectured widely on the subject over the past fifteen years. Berliner is one of those who does not believe there is a child sexual abuse syndrome. During an interview, she explained why:

> There is not any characteristic way that all abused children behave. Roland Summit is describing a clinical phenomenon that is seen

in some kinds of situations of abuse. It's an eloquent, beautiful description of a psychological process and he says it as well as anyone can, and all of us have seen some of that. It doesn't appear in even the majority of cases of abuse. It's an exception. Now I think it's fine to go in and say, "Here's why a child might behave in this way, here's an explanation for it." But to say, "It means the child's molested," I don't think you can do it.

You really don't scientifically have the basis for it, and I think lawyers are looking for ways to improve their cases, which is exactly their job to do. I think the unfortunate problem is that we experts take ourselves too seriously and go beyond what we—we don't really understand always the legal system, and what they're doing and how they're doing it. So we, because we feel strongly and we really believe that this really happened, we cannot resist the temptation to spout off in court about that and to give it something more—greater meaning than it should have. Roland Summit knows perfectly well that that's the case. I think he probably testifies just that way. It's the lawyers who try to say that because you see this pattern of behavior, these behavioral indicators, that means it happened. No expert should say that, because it's not true. It doesn't mean it happened.[13]

The courts themselves have had something to say about the proper testimony of experts. In criminal court cases, a series of appellate decisions around the country have sent a generally consistent message that there are two kinds of testimony experts cannot properly present. They cannot pass judgment on the credibility of a witness—the child who was allegedly abused, for instance—and they cannot testify as to the guilt or innocence of the defendant. Both are improper in that they call for a witness to "invade the province of the trier of fact." In other words, it is up to the jury, not an expert, to judge the credibility of each witness and to decide whether the defendant is guilty beyond a reasonable doubt.

The Iowa Supreme Court reviewed the matter in a decision reversing the conviction of a man charged with having indecent contact with an 8-year-old child. The defense objected to expert testimony from the principal of the girl's elementary school, who testified, "Children do not lie about this type of matter," and from the child protective investigator, who stated, "It is my opinion that it is very rare for a child to lie about this subject."[14] The court noted that a number of jurisdictions deemed inadmissible testimony con-

cerning trauma suffered by rape victims because its scientific reliability had not been established or because it implied a judgment on
the alleged victim's credibility. One court, while holding that testimony about rape trauma syndrome could not be used to prove that
a child had been raped, held that expert testimony on the emotional
and psychological trauma a rape victim suffers may be admissible.[15]

"In summary," the Iowa court wrote,

> it seems that experts will be allowed to express opinions on matters
> that explain relevant mental and psychological symptoms present
> in sexually abused children. Unlike the holding in *Kim* [*State* v.
> *Kim*, 645 p.2d 130 (Hawaii 1982)], though, most courts reject expert
> testimony that either directly or indirectly renders an opinion on
> the credibility or truthfulness of a witness.
>
> Expert opinion testimony is admissible pursuant to Iowa Rule
> of Evidence 702 if it "will assist the trier of fact to understand the
> evidence or to determine a fact in issue." The ultimate determi-
> nation of the credibility or truthfulness of a witness is not "a fact
> in issue," but a matter to be generally determined solely by the
> jury . . .
>
> A witness is not permitted to express an opinion as to the
> ultimate fact of the accused's guilt or innocence. *Oppedal*, 232 N.W.
> 2d at 524. In this case the trial court admitted expert testimony
> relating to the truthfulness of the complaining witness. We believe
> the effect of the opinion was to improperly suggest the complainant
> was telling the truth and, consequently, the defendant was guilty.
> We conclude the opinion crossed the "fine but essential" line be-
> tween an "opinion which would be truly helpful to the jury and
> that which merely conveys a conclusion concerning defendant's
> legal guilt." *Horton*, 231 N.W. 2d at 38.[16]

Although there have been criminal court cases in which both
Summit and Coleman have appeared for the opposing sides, and
such "battles of the experts" are likely to occur with greater frequency
now that Men International has joined the fray, the use of experts
in family court is likely to receive more and more attention. This is
because custody cases have been touted by the backlash as the area
of the most false allegations and because family court is the arena in
which experts often have the most influence and may be most vulnerable. On the other hand, it is also the arena in which incest cases

involving intact families are most likely to appear—the cases for which even Coleman agrees the accommodation theory makes sense.

The "Validation Interview"

Child protective investigators are sometimes qualified as experts in court (as we just saw in the Iowa case), but in family court as well as criminal court most often the experts are therapists. It is in family courts that mental health professionals are most often asked to testify as to whether a child was sexually abused. Although she says she has mixed feelings about such testimony, Lucy Berliner has testified in these courts "where they, in effect, to a great extent, leave the decision making to mental health professionals, and they base their legal decisions on mental health opinions.

"I have very mixed feelings about that," Berliner continued. "There are no standards among mental health professionals, so there are many, many risks when a judge is looking at a whole series of evaluations and then saying, 'I think this one is better than that one.' " One of her qualms, Berliner said, is about therapists' claiming special insight. "Any individual mental health professional has to be darn careful about setting themselves up to say, 'I have some special ability and insight into the truth that no one else has.' I mean all you are doing is forming an opinion that will be a piece of the mosaic." The ultimate decision rests with the judge, who must put the mosaic together, she said.

But according to many in the field, the construction of the mosaic damages children when it involves multiple interviews. In some jurisdictions, a child is routinely required to repeat her story as many as half a dozen times or more to social workers, physicians, prosecutors, therapists, and others. Although many jurisdictions have reduced the number by conducting joint interviews and by using audio– and videotape, they are working at cross-purposes when a court requires two, three, or more expert evaluations (see the next chapter).

Coleman notwithstanding, courts are not only permitting mental health professionals to evaluate children but are requesting them to do so. Once a court makes such a request, however, can it then limit the number of evaluations, or must it permit each side to hire its own expert (or experts)? And what if the accused, for example, is not satisfied with the results of an evaluation? Can he order another?

In a memorandum of law submitted to a family court in New York, law guardian Andrew Vachss argued against a respondent's motion for a second "validation interview" of his daughter, whom he was alleged to have sexually abused. (The term *validation interview* is taken by Vachss from Suzanne Sgroi's *Handbook of Clinical Intervention in Child Sexual Abuse*.[17] The term seems to have fallen out of favor—more often *evaluation* is used today—but the concept is still very much alive.) Therapists like Berliner, MacFarlane, and others are asked by family courts to interview children and to testify as to their findings. Why should the respondent not have a right to have his own expert as well?

It was to that basic question that Vachss's memorandum responded. The facts presented in the memorandum (and in the court's decision in the case)[18] are these: Tara H., age 5, was diagnosed as having infectious gonorrhea. When interviewed by social workers, the child described taking baths with her father and of playing "games" with him. Vachss sought the validation "because 1) corroboration of the child's statement to caseworkers would be required in the event she could not testify at trial; 2) an expert opinion from an objective source could illuminate the issues for the Court; 3) such an interview would also indicate the child's need, if any, for immediate initiation of therapeutic treatment."[19] At the time, the respondent offered no objection to the validation or the expert chosen, but after the results indicated that the child's symptoms were consistent with "intra-family child sexual abuse syndrome" and after the child stated that she had been threatened by the respondent, he demanded a second validation, claiming that unless he was permitted to duplicate the test and obtain a "second opinion," his due process rights would be violated.

Vachss argued (successfully) that validation is not a scientific test that can be duplicated, as fingerprinting or ballistics tests can, but is "a complex event, depending for its integrity and accuracy more on the experience of the interviewer than any other component."[20] He added, "Perhaps the most significant concern in validation is objectivity as to result, coupled with concern for the child."[21] In this case, Vachss contended, the validator must be considered objective and nonpartisan since she was chosen by the law guardian, who represented neither the state nor the respondent. The law guardian was appointed by the court to act as independent counsel for the child. As such, wrote Vachss, "the Court must assume, absent specific evidence presented, that said independence remains intact."[22] And "when a Validator . . . is selected by a competent Law Guardian, acting upon competent information and or advice, the Court should deem said Validator to be cloaked with the same mantle of objectivity as the Law Guardian himself."[23]

The "second opinion" sought was not to further the best interests of the child, as the respondent claimed, but was actually an attempt to conduct an "examination before trial" in order to gather information the respondent hoped would bolster his defense, Vachss said. But far from being in the child's best interests, a second validation would be needlessly traumatic. Even one such interview may be traumatic, since "validation requires that, to some extent, the victim re-experiences the original trauma, yet absent such validation, properly targeted therapy cannot go forward."[24] (Similar arguments were used to bar a second validation of Lisa Coletti [chapter 5].)

The memorandum offered a proposed reform to obviate the need for the court to relitigate this issue every time a second validation was demanded. The court would designate a panel of expert validators, all of whom possess the "training, background, education, and expertise sufficient to qualify as expert witnesses before the Court."[25] They could be private practitioners or publicly employed, and when the need arose they would be chosen by the court on a rotating basis, to prevent either side from bargaining for its own experts. The court could also insist that the panel be subjected to ongoing "peer review," to assure quality and expertise.

Coleman must have nightmares about such proposals. To him they must seem an attempt to institutionalize mental health professionals in the courts. It makes others uncomfortable as well. Berliner viewed such a system as unnecessary: "I think you have to justify to me why there is more reason to believe that a child who says that they were molested by their parents has to have an independent validation as opposed to using the ordinary procedures of investigation."

MacFarlane was also skeptical. The expert panel (for family court) that she is on in Los Angeles has "big problems," she said. The experts on it all have impressive credentials, but they do not have a background in child sexual abuse, and the pay is so low that "I haven't done one that I haven't lost hundreds of dollars in my time," she said. But the Los Angeles system does not prevent a child from being interviewed by several experts both before and during the proceeding; it only provides the court with a panel from which to choose when it orders an evaluation.

Flora Colao is an author and therapist who has been qualified as an expert in both family and criminal courts in New York. (She was also Jane's therapist in chapter 3 and interviewed children for the FBI in chapter 5.) Colao has fashioned her own solution to the problem of second validations. She will conduct a validation for a court only if both sides and the court agree in advance that hers will be the only validation in the case, she said. Experts who do validations for courts should not only have the requisite training and experience, but should also have a track record demonstrating that they do not find that every child they examine has been sexually abused, according to Colao. At least some of their evaluations should prove inconclusive or should indicate that a child has not been abused, she said. Colao estimated that about 20 percent of the evaluations she does result in a finding of no abuse or are inconclusive, and, she added, she sees a select population. The children she evaluates often exhibit many of the behavioral symptoms consistent with sexual abuse, she said, so her percentage should be higher than that of someone evaluating a different population.

Colao described her validation method during an interview.[26] She talks to the child "cold," she said, with little or no information about the case so as to avoid unconscious bias. After her evaluation, she said she reviews any other information available, including police reports and court files, and she may interview the parents. She tries to avoid leading questions, instead asking general questions and following up on information provided by the child. If she does not obtain information about abuse, she sees the child again or she decides the result is inconclusive. Children can be coached, they can have symptoms that appear to be indicators of abuse but are not, and they can tell stories that are false, but a trained "true expert" can see through them, Colao said. Always? No, she acknowledged. But she believes it is more likely that she would reach an inconclusive result incorrectly than an incorrect validation. It is possible, she said, to decide that a child has been sexually abused when it was a previous instance, not the one ostensibly being investigated. Her evaluation is not designed to determine who the perpetrator was, she said— only whether abuse occurred. The rest is up to the court.

Colao recalled a false allegation she evaluated involving a 4-year-old. "I'm supposed to tell you that Grandpa touched me on my tootie," the child said. (Colao later learned the child was supposed to accuse her father, but she could not bring herself to do so.) "Did that happen?" Colao asked. "She paused for a long time," Colao remembered, "and she wouldn't make eye contact and she said, 'Yes.' 'What did it feel like?' And then she said the fateful words: 'I don't know the right answer.' And I said, 'Who knows the right answer?' And she wouldn't answer me and then she asked if she could go out and see her mommy." The child had a number of symptoms— nightmares, nausea, and others—"her symptoms, however, were around the fact that she was either going to be accusing Daddy, which she didn't want to do, or she was going to be disappointing Mommy, which she didn't want to do," Colao said.

The allegation arose at the end of a custody dispute, Colao later learned. The reason why she believes she is not fooled by coaching is that children who have not been abused cannot fully describe the experience. They can be taught to say they were hurt, but they cannot describe the pain. She asks children about the progression of sexual activity that one almost always finds in these cases and will ask the child what else was going on the day an incident allegedly occurred. She will ask for peripheral details: What were people wearing, where did the attack occur? Children are rarely coached in such matters, she said. And she will observe the child's nonverbal cues, such as pauses, shaking, and tears, all of which she will describe in her court testimony.

The problem Berliner and others have with this approach is not specifically with Colao, but it is contained in one of Colao's comments. A big problem, according to Colao, is that experts should be objective, but all too often they are not. This makes it hard for courts to find experts and to know whether those they do are presenting reliable information. And biases, it should be added, can lead to mistakes both in finding abuse and in not finding abuse. In their study on "fictitious" reports (discussed in the last chapter), Jones and McGraw noted, "All too frequently, we saw cases where it appeared that the professional mind had been made up well before sufficient information had been obtained." Playing off of Suzanne Sgroi's well-known remark that the diagnosis of sexual abuse can only be made if the professional entertains the possibility that it exists, they added, "Fictitious cases can be diagnosed only if the evaluator entertains the possibility that such a situation is feasible."[27]

Berliner, for one, would rather see efforts devoted to seeing that the "normal" investigative system works than to establishing a special method of investigating incest allegations. But one of the reasons, of course, why special methods have been devised is that the "normal" methods have not always worked. MacFarlane, for example, did not submit an application requesting permission to interview four hundred children who had attended the McMartin Preschool. She was called in because it was felt she had special expertise. And although that case was clearly extraordinary, many people consider all child sexual abuse cases extraordinary and difficult enough to warrant special measures. Even among those who believe this, however, the question of what those measures should be is likely to be debated for many years.

Who Should Investigate and How?

Coleman approaches child sexual abuse investigations the way some people approach art. "I don't know what it is," they say, "but I know what I like—and what I don't." Coleman, like most critics, has been a lot more successful articulating what it should not be than what it should.

He has testified as to who does not have special expertise in this area and what methods are not reliable. The prosecutor in the Country Walk trial asked him, "In fact every case you consulted with you've never seen a good interview or interview you feel was well done?" Coleman: "That's true. I have not seen any videotaped interviews that did not show essentially the same kind of manipulative, leading, bias[ed] techniques that I've seen in this case."[28]

Many of Coleman's criticisms are of investigative techniques. His justification for commenting on these is that the mental health professionals are investigating or they have trained those who are. The second premise is questionable at best. Social Services agencies and police departments have been talking for years about giving investigators special training of the type, perhaps, Coleman alludes to. But interviews with workers and supervisors out in the field—and those who work with them—indicate that there has been a lot more planning than implementing and that turnover, burnout, and *lack* of training are constant complaints.

But the real question is, How should an investigation be conducted? When Coleman and others who criticize current practices are asked the question, their answers are generally that the interviewer should be unbiased, should not know a great deal about the case, should ask open-ended questions, and should neither hammer away with repeated questions nor reassure the child that he is now "safe."

But Coleman is not an expert in criminal investigation. Surprisingly, however, he now claims to be—at least in the area of child sexual abuse investigations. "Why would I be willing to claim I'm an expert on investigation when I'm not a police officer or trained like that?" he asked rhetorically during an interview.[29] "The crucial thing you have to realize is they're not going out and using their traditional investigative techniques. They're going out and using investigative techniques that they've learned from us—meaning mental health."

It is notable, however, that in response to questions demanding how he would conduct an interview (something he clearly states he has not done and would not do), Coleman's answers are vague. Nor has he attempted to identify an interview he finds satisfactory, which he might be more likely to find among unfounded cases, as opposed to the select group of criminal cases he is asked to review. Although he objects to children's being reassured that they are safe, on the grounds that the defendant's guilt is implied, it is difficult to understand why it is acceptable for a witness in a Mafia trial to be given a new identity, a new job, a new home, and round-the-clock protection but wrong for a child to be informed that the man who allegedly abused him is in jail.[30] After all, if the child were old enough to read the newspapers, he would not have to be told.

Alan Nudelman agrees with some of Coleman's ideas about the role of mental health professionals in the courtroom but disagrees with some of what Coleman says about investigations. Nudelman is the supervising deputy district attorney for special operations in the Santa Clara (California) District Attorney's Office, where the primary units he supervises are homicide and sexual assault. He has worked on sexual assault cases for twelve of his fourteen years in the office, he said, and has handled literally thousands of felony cases, from which he estimated he could pick out about three hundred that were badly investigated. There is nothing extraordinary about investigating child abuse cases, he added.

"I have seen bad techniques utilized from time to time in any number of different types of cases," Nudelman said.[31] "But do I think that there's anything systemic? I think that's patent nonsense." Furthermore, he asked, "why should an investigator be neutral? When a police officer comes to my house after it's been burgled, I hope he has an open mind with respect to the options—who did it, what happened—but I don't want him to be neutral." He would like an officer who is bright, perceptive, and can assess the child's veracity, he said, but "there's no such thing as listening neutrally. You listen sympathetically." A good interview, he continued, is one in which the officer does a lot more listening than talking. Asking many questions—leading or otherwise—is a bad technique for eliciting information. And that, he added, is the purpose of the interview. "Essentially, you want the truth regardless of whether it supports a position or doesn't support a position."

Of leading questions in particular, he said, "Very often when you're dealing with very, very young children, leading questions are necessary. The problem is to the degree that they are informationally leading, they undermine the strength of the statement. . . . A leading question is not an evil in and of itself. If it's used to focus attention, it's fine. If it's used to elicit certain information, it's not fine."

Pat Alvarez estimated it took her a year and a half on the Sexual Assault Unit of the San Jose Police Department before she had "a grip on the situation." And then, after another year and a half, she was rotated out of the unit, as required by department policy. But she has returned for a second tour and teaches seminars on sexual assault investigation at the Criminal Justice Training Center (a police academy mainly for Santa Clara County). For many officers the most difficult aspect of interviewing young children is feeling comfortable doing it, according to Alvarez. "You have to be comfortable with it. If you're not, the kid will clam right up," she said.[32] Many officers are afraid to talk about sexual abuse. Their discomfort makes them more likely to ask leading questions, she said, just to get the interview over with.

One recurrent problem Alvarez identified was with social workers who were "doing investigations" although "they're not calling them investigations and they aren't trained to do proper investigations." Typically, no reports are written, and the police officer must try to find out what the child has been asked (and what may have been suggested to her) prior to the officer's first interview. This lack of coordination, Alvarez said, can be detrimental to the child and to the case.

Despite the difficulties, Alvarez and Nudelman both said it was easier to teach a police officer (trained as an investigator) to interview children, than to teach a therapist (trained to interview children) to be an investigator.

Asked about that, MacFarlane said she was experiencing "sort of a raging ambivalence on this subject because I've really been in the middle of it. I think at this point in time, the best answer to that is probably: the jury is out. . . . What we've got for the most part is clinicians who have never had any training in investigations doing their best and messing up the cases legally. As I have done. Inadvertently learned the hard way on cases. And we have a bunch of investigators who know zip about children, child development, child abuse, you name it. They took these two-hour courses, if that, and therefore, neither side—to say therapists are lousy investigators is, you know, no more valid than to say investigators can't be sensitive to children."

Later in the interview, after further reflection, MacFarlane resolved some of her ambivalence: "My bias is the opposite of what you were just telling me. It's a hell of a lot easier to teach people how to investigate a case than to teach them how to be comfortable with 4-year-olds. . . . And the contrasting damage between having a clinician mess up a legal case that may get dumped versus somebody who messes up a child who may either end up back in an abusive situation, or may end up with doubt over the investigative process, is not comparable to me at this point."

MacFarlane's struggle with these issues is apparent not only from the interview but from several articles she wrote that were published in the 1986 book *Sexual Abuse of Young Children*.[33] Passages in the chapter "Interviewing and Evidence Gathering," coauthored by Sandy Krebs, seem to be direct responses to the criticism of her handling of the McMartin interviews and to the more general criticism Coleman has leveled in articles and court testimony. To cite a few:

> [A]long with being sensitive and skilled with children, interviewers must educate themselves to the many aspects of the legal system that take on significance following a child's disclosure of abuse. These often go far beyond the mandated reporting of sexual abuse, and interviewers can no longer afford to be naive to the process . . . [T]hose who take on the task of evaluating alleged child victims must also be prepared to become the objects of attack when cases enter the legal system and their conclusions and techniques are challenged . . . (p. 99).

> [T]he interviewer's role is different from that of a trial attorney. An interviewer should not be trying to "prove" that a child was or was not molested; a diagnostic interviewer gathers data in order to try to determine whether or not sexual abuse occurred (pp. 93–94).

> It is time to recognize that child sexual abuse is not comparable to other types of adult crimes, and should not be investigated as though it were. . . . In the best of all possible worlds, it would be advisable not to ask children leading questions, in order to avoid the concern that children are responding to suggestions that certain things occurred or that they are being compliant and acquiescent to an adult authority figure. But, in the best of all possible worlds, children are not sexually assaulted in secrecy, and then bribed, threatened, or intimidated not to talk about it. In the real world, where such things do happen, leading questions may sometimes be necessary in order to enable frightened young children to respond to and talk about particular subjects. Although they may present legal problems later on, leading questions, on the other hand, should not be viewed as some form of illegal activity on the part of an interviewer (p. 87).

> Although there has been some criticism about the use of puppets and dolls, which centers around the concern that they encourage fantasy in children, even young children know that hand puppets are not real and that they cannot talk unless someone talks for

them. . . . Establishing that the puppet's job is always to tell the truth about what happened to the child, and not to make anything up, can be a non-threatening way of getting a child to open up initially and talk about what he or she is really feeling (p. 77).

Have MacFarlane's perceptions been skewed by her traumatic experience? How could they not? Do her comments say more about one case and one jurisdiction than about the rest of the country? Probably not. While her experience cannot be considered representative, the entire field has struggled, as she has, to learn from it, just as the field continues to struggle with Jordan. Although the advice she offers, and the Coleman criticisms to which she seems to be responding, may well be salutary for the profession to consider, not everyone feels the need for a dramatic reassessment of the therapist's role in the legal system. Berliner, again, draws a very different lesson from the McMartin case.

"We learned some things," she said of the case, "some important things, which are: you don't get mental health professionals to do the legal system's job, and it really is very consistent with the philosophy of this program [in King County, Washington], which is, you separate. Investigative interviewing is quite different from therapeutic interviewing." On the question of who is best qualified to interview children, Berliner added, "That's assuming that it's a big, complicated, terrible thing. It's not that big of a deal in most cases. Our prosecutors do it to the tune of one thousand interviews a year. And it's not that hard. When you're talking about 3- and 4-year-olds, it's a little bit more complex, and then in that situation you might want to have someone the child knows, who's worked with the child, in there in the interview. . . . I don't want to go back to an old era when we just spent ten years convincing people not to be so worried that when a 9-year-old says something, they should wonder about it."

Up Close and Personal

It is impossible to move on without at least taking note of the personal attacks that have accompanied the "battle of the experts." Coleman has been routinely labeled a "hired gun," who is "getting rich off the backs of children." His supporters have criticized professionals they claim rubber-stamp as abused every child they examine for child protective services and make a fortune in the process. Cries of "mercenary" are inevitable—and in some cases they are proper. For example, Ken Pangborn, president of Men International, said in an interview: "Believe me, I've had a number of professionals that if— there's this one guy in Chicago that, for a price, and there's another guy in New Jersey by the way, too—I'm just thinking of the two of them that have made it quite clear. We slip some money under the table to him, *x* number of bucks, he'll go in and swear to God that you couldn't possibly be guilty of sexual abuse of a child. Those are not the people we're dealing with," he added, declining to name them.[34] "We deal with people with some integrity," he said, citing William McIver, Daniel Schuman, and Diane Schetky, among others.

The genuine corruption Pangborn revealed about the unnamed "experts" may help put the sniping in proper perspective. And the venality is likely to expand as the system is flooded by an exponentially increasing number of cases. These new clients bring to the system more money and an increasing demand for the services of experts—and "experts." Whether Vachss's proposal for a rotating panel is a cure will undoubtedly be debated, as will other suggestions involving the regulation and certification of professionals in this field (see chapter 12). The issue of second validations seems certain to be widely litigated. If evidence of the need to do so is required, the following worst-case scenario should prove more than convincing.

If ever a case demonstrated that more is not necessarily better, it is the case study in the next chapter—a quintessential "battle of the experts" in which everybody lost.

9

Case Study: The Battle of the Experts

Dramatis Personae

Treated and/or evaluated children

Gisela Dengel	pediatrician
Ann Webb	psychologist
Anne Carter	psychologist
Cora Lynn Goldsborough	psychologist
R.W. Lutz	pediatrician
Gwen Steeley	gynecologist
Mark Davis	physician

Treated and/or evaluated parents

Meredith Green	psychologist
A.C. Kiczales	psychiatrist
William Zuckerman	psychologist

Evaluated children and parents

Gregory Lehne	psychologist
Ruthellen Josselson	psychologist
Eileen Higham	psychologist

Investigated case

Phillip Pate	social worker
Suzanne Rossiter	social worker
Richard Keyville	state police trooper

Evaluated evaluation
   Sheila Deitz   psychologist

Tried case
   Douglas Napier   lawyer for Social Services
   Thomas Schultz   lawyer for father
   John Fekety   lawyer for mother
   William Sharp   lawyer for children
   Henry Whiting   judge, circuit court

T HIS is the story of a divorce and custody case in which the mother charged that the father had sexually abused their two young children. The list above is by no means exhaustive of everyone involved in the case. It does not even include all of the doctors consulted during the year from the time the allegations surfaced to the court's final decision. The twists and turns the case took during that time are boggling.

If there is such a thing as a "standard" case in which a mother falsely charges her husband with abuse in order to gain an advantage in a custody battle, this is not it. The allegation preceded the divorce—in fact, it was not the wife but the husband who filed for divorce. The wife claimed she still loved him and wanted him to "get help" in order to preserve their marriage. When he denied the abuse, she filed for custody.

During the year that followed, two separate child protective investigations were conducted; both determined that the charges were unfounded. A parade of physicians and mental health professionals treated and evaluated the parents and the children. Some were hired directly by the parents, one was chosen by the court, and a team of three was chosen by the Social Services Department. A police investigation was begun, then closed at the request of the mother's lawyer. That investigation uncovered no evidence of abuse, according to the police.

At the end of the year, following five hearings at which more than forty witnesses testified and an additional twelve depositions were entered into evidence, the judge granted the divorce and awarded custody to the father, allowing the mother limited supervised visitation. According to the judge's ruling,[1] the mother had "intentionally, or unintentionally due to a mental or emotional condition, falsely accused the father of sexual abuse of their children." Although he said the mother had "orchestrated the charges," the judge added, "I do not find the mother acted in a spirit of malice but only in an effort to obtain custody of these children."[2] How it is possible to orchestrate such charges without malice is but one of many questions the case raises.

For this is the story of a case gone amuck. It is much easier to pick the losers than the winners. The biggest losers were undoubtedly the children, who were guaranteed to be losers long before the final outcome and no matter who had won. There is blame enough to go around and how it is assigned will probably depend largely on one's attitudes. But on this much the various camps should agree: there can be no justice when the system itself causes this much suffering.

The story has been reconstructed entirely from the reams of court documents.[3] The names of the parents and children—but no others—have been changed to protect their identities.[4] There has been no effort to pass judgment on the guilt or innocence of the father but rather on the process by which a determination was reached.

"Daddy Gets Me"

Sarah Fahrnhorst had just bathed Tammy, her 2-year-old, and was putting on a diaper. "I had turned around to get a diaper," she later told a social worker in a tape-recorded interview, "and when I turned around she said, 'Daddy gets me' and I thought it was a game they played 'cuz they played a game, Daddy gets Me, and he chased her around and I thought, 'I'll play with her,' and I said, 'Well, how does Daddy get you?' And she pointed down to her genitals, and I said—I just turned away from her and I said to myself, 'Well this isn't right,' so I turned back around and I said, 'How did Daddy get you?' And she inserted her finger into her vagina."[5]

That was in October 1984. Sarah and Gerald Fahrnhorst, then 40 and 36 years old respectively, lived in a town of about ten thousand in northern Virginia. They had been married five years and had a 4-year-old boy, Billy, in addition to Tammy. Although the marriage was not perfect, each had been married previously—he once and she three times—and they were content with what they had (as they later told a social worker in separate interviews). In recent months, however, the relationship had been somewhat strained. Gerald had been working long hours with increased responsibility at the automobile supply store, where he had been made manager. He was making more money, but they had extended themselves with several recent purchases. Sarah had begun taking night classes in accounting and often studied in the evenings. Her husband was sometimes resentful and, with increasing frequency, there was an atmosphere of tension. There were more arguments and there was less intimacy.

And then came the allegations. They were not the first time sexual abuse had been mentioned in the Fahrnhorst home. Several years earlier, Sarah's daughter by a previous marriage (who by 1984 was grown and living in another town) had been fondled once by a friend's father. Sarah confronted the man and he agreed to leave town, she said. And in 1982 Sarah came to believe that Billy had been molested by Gerald's brother.

She had suspected something was wrong when the child started wetting his bed—something he had not done for a long time. Sarah began checking on him during the night, and one night she found him masturbating on his pillow. She was even more disturbed another night when he crawled on top of her as she was watching television. "And then," she recalled, ". . . [he] put his hands like here [indicated around shoulder area] [and] started rocking back and forth. And he got that strange look on his face. And I thought, 'What are you doing?' And I took him off. I said, '[Billy], where'd you learn that at?' . . . He made no comment. Of course he was not vocal. . . . And I said, 'Don't do that, don't do that.' I was, I mean [the] look on his face and the way he was rocking, I just—I couldn't believe—I just went into shock."[6]

She was concerned, she said, but did not know what to attribute the behavior to. The incidents occurred after the Fahrnhorsts had spent weekends in the brother's company, and she suspected a connection, but she was not even sure that the behavior was abnormal. When she went for her regular appointment with Dr. Gisela Dengel (she was pregnant with Tammy at the time), she asked. No, the doctor said, it was not normal. Dengel suggested Sarah return with Gerald to discuss the situation. When she did, the doctor recommended that they confront the brother jointly. Gerald, who was quite angry, readily agreed. The uncle denied he had abused the child (although he admitted it was possible that Billy had seen him masturbate). Dengel suggested the uncle stay away from Billy for several months, until everything "cooled down."

And that was the way it was resolved, only when the rest of the family heard, it created a lasting schism between Sarah and the Fahrnhorst family. (Later, when Sarah believed Gerald was molesting Billy, she thought she might have blamed the wrong brother—a point that Gerald's lawyer emphasized in attacking Sarah's credibility.) As for Billy, by the time of the new allegations, he had stopped wetting his bed and had not repeated his behavior with Sarah, although he had one lingering problem. "He's putting his finger up his anus," Sarah told the social worker. "And it's a continuous thing. He does not want to do it."[7]

The Professionals' Response

After the diaper-changing incident, Tammy began saying "Daddy gets me" or "Daddy gets my bottom"—the child's word for her genitals—frequently, Sarah said. And she began wetting her bed and having nightmares. The child grew more and more frightened, and Sarah became convinced that something was terribly wrong. She brought it up at Tammy's next appointment with Dr. Dengel. The pediatrician examined the child and noted "some irritation of the vaginal area."[8] Later, when asked in court by Gerald's lawyer whether she had an opinion of the cause, she testified, "I had to find out if there was any type of infection involved."[9] When the lawyer asked if the redness was of the kind caused by diaper irritation, she replied, "Yes, sir."[10] She did a vaginal culture that was negative and testified that she was unable to obtain a urine specimen for a urinalysis.

At that point, she referred Sarah and Tammy to Meredith Green, a local psychologist, and scheduled another appointment for "follow-up." Sarah met with Green, explained the situation, and planned to meet with her husband in Dengel's office several days later. On the day she did, Tammy had an appointment with Dengel in the morning, during which Sarah asked her to show the doctor what her father did to her, but the child did nothing. In the afternoon, Sarah confronted Gerald, with Dengel's help. But Sarah was deeply ambivalent, as she later explained to the social worker: "Dr. Dengel sent me to Dr. Green . . . [who] said it can either go through court or it can go through therapy, it's a treatable thing. That's what happened there. I love my husband very much. I love my home. I like going to school. I like the yard. I just like the whole thing, you know? And the two kids. And if it were treatable, I wanted to go that way. And see Dr. Green was gonna—I think go out of town or something and so that she didn't feel she could confront him or I didn't feel I could get him over there without some suspicion. So we decided to let Dr. Dengel confront him . . . He denied it, of course—well I say of course—he denied it. He was embarrassed, appalled, upset. When Dr. Dengel wasn't in the room he was furious. And when she came back in he was upset."[11]

What is glaring here—and this separates the Fahrnhorst case from most of the cases it superficially resembles—is not only that the allegations preceded the custody dispute (and, in fact, caused it), but also that nobody has taken issue with Sarah's claim that she loved her husband and wanted to save her marriage. Nobody has claimed that the accusation was an underhanded way of seeking retribution for real or imagined injuries, or a way to break up the marriage. In fact, nobody identified any motive at all to explain why Sarah would falsely accuse her husband, if that is what she did. And although her lawyer never raised the issue, Sarah had strong motives not to accuse her husband of anything, since her uncontradicted statements were that she still loved him and wished to preserve the marriage.

In the beginning, when she first began talking about the abuse, Sarah was neither believed nor disbelieved. While Dengel did help Sarah confront Gerald, and neither Green nor Dengel simply dropped the matter, neither reported suspected abuse to Social Services, either. Why not? Dengel was asked that question under cross-examination by Sarah's lawyer:

> Q. Did you at any time report this allegation of sexual abuse to Social Services?
> A. No, sir, I did not report the case.
> Q. Why didn't you report the case?
> A. From my standpoint there was no reason to report the case to Social Services because there was no physical evidence of any sexual abuse, nor did the child show any unusual behavior during the examination . . .
> Q. Are you aware that the Code requires the reporting of a suspicion of sexual abuse or physical abuse?
> A. Yes, sir.

Q. And you still did not report it despite Mrs. [Fahrnhorst's] concern of sexual abuse.

A. No, sir. I immediately referred the mother and the child for professional services of the psychologist.[12]

Green's response was similar. Asked under cross-examination whether she too would have to be sure before reporting, Green said, "I think if I suspect that abuse is taking place I would do so. I think . . . there was a feeling about this that just, I wasn't convinced that we weren't going to do something like blow this marriage apart. I had not seen the husband, Dr. Dengel knew this couple, she had seen them and had not made a referral to Social Services, had sent them to me.

"I felt, again, that we better get somebody else in, someone that could listen to this, again and see whether they should immediately refer them to Social Services, or whether they should try to get the couple into therapy, or what should be done."[13]

And so Green also passed the case along. She sent the couple to A.C. Kiczales, a psychiatrist who saw the couple twice and saw Gerald, who was the designated patient at all sessions, twice more alone. He too failed to report the case, but no one bothered to ask him why.[14] Although Kiczales said he had treated parents who sexually abused their children, Dengel and Green were quick to admit they had little or no experience working with sexually abused children. Green said flat out, "I have not worked with a child who has been abused."[15] Dengel estimated she had treated between five and ten children, adding that all had suffered physical trauma—a "deep redness, real bruises, bluish in color"—in the genital area. Asked if she believed such trauma is usually present in sexual abuse cases, she answered, "Most of the time."[16] But later, Sarah's lawyer asked:

Q. Dr. Dengel, would it come as a surprise to you that people, experts in the field of child sexual abuse, say that in the majority of cases there is not trauma when a child has been sexually abused?

A. Could you please repeat the question again, or the statement?

Q. Would it come as a surprise to you that people who are considered expert in the field of child sexual abuse say that in the majority of cases there is not trauma when a child has been sexually abused?

A. Do you mean physical or mental trauma?

Q. Physical.
A. That could well be.[17]

But before the couple even went to see Kiczales, several crucial
events occurred that had a lasting effect on the case. The same day
Sarah confronted Gerald in Dengel's office, she took the children
and drove to Massachusetts without telling him. During the month
she remained, she refused to tell him where she was, although she
called him nine times. She left, she said, "when my husband ex-
ploded in the night. Because he was really mad and I realized he
wouldn't confess. And I knew for [Tammy's] sake that I would have
to get some kind of proof."[18]

During the time she was gone she stayed with her sister and
brother-in-law and looked for a mental health professional to evaluate
her children in a manner she felt they had not been in Virginia. She
found that person in psychologist Ann Webb. Webb saw Tammy
for three hourly sessions and saw Billy once. She was able to elicit
little from Billy, but of Tammy, Webb wrote in a two-and-a-half-
page report:

> After three evaluation sessions I have very little doubt that this
> child has been sexually abused by her father. Specifically, she
> recalls being manipulated in the genital area by her father. [Tammy]
> remembers this as a negative experience. It is highly unlikely that
> she would fantasize this experience at her stage of develop-
> ment. . . . The client's mother has responded quite appropriately
> to her child's crisis. She has removed the child from the dangerous
> situation and has sought professional help. She continues to reas-
> sure [Tammy] that she is not responsible for her father's inappro-
> priate actions and that she is not a "bad girl."

The report also included the following exchange from Tammy's
first session:

> DR. WEBB. "Does he get mad?"
>   [TAMMY]. "Um hum (positive)."
>   DR. WEBB. "Does he spank the little girl?"
>   TAMMY. "Um hum (positive)."
>   DR. WEBB. "What else does he do?"
>   TAMMY. "He touches her."

DR. WEBB. "Where?"

Tammy points to the doll's genital area, and continues to stare at the dolls in position of father leaning over daughter on changing table.

DR. WEBB. "What does it feel like?"

TAMMY. "Um (noncommittal)."

DR. WEBB. "Does she like it?"

TAMMY. "No (emphatic)."

DR. WEBB. "Does your daddy ever touch you?"

TAMMY. "Um hum (positive)."

DR. WEBB. "Where?" No answer. Question repeated.

TAMMY. Points to doll's genitals.

DR. WEBB. "Does the daddy ever kiss her?"

TAMMY. "Um hum (positive)."

DR. WEBB. "Where?"

TAMMY. Points to mouth.

DR. WEBB. "Where else?"

TAMMY. Points to knees. Changes subject.[19]

Following the second or third session (she was not sure), Webb reported suspected child abuse to the Massachusetts Social Services Department and an investigation was initiated.

In some respects Sarah had gotten what she wanted—she was safe, and she had found an evaluator who was able to elicit information from Tammy that seemed to validate the abuse. In retrospect, however, the trip to Massachusetts probably did more damage to Sarah's position than good. The evaluation itself—at least according to the skeletal account found in the report—was hardly definitive. The defense argument that Sarah influenced the child to say and do the things described was by no means laid to rest by this report. Nor was the predictable issue of leading questions. And it later emerged that Webb had never previously testified as to whether a child had been sexually abused and had never even examined a child in order to make such a determination.[20]

But more important, Sarah had raised a number of questions about her own personality that would ultimately—rightly or wrongly—prove devastating. As she was later portrayed by Gerald's lawyer, Sarah was a woman who was capable of taking her children and fleeing when she was not assured of having her way. And she was willing to shop around until she found an "expert" she could hire to adopt her position. Her credibility was questioned, and it was a question the judge found persuasive. As he wrote in his decision,

> I don't believe [Mrs. Fahrnhorst] left because she was afraid of [Mr. Fahrnhorst]. She had been quite successful in her management of him up to that time, and while he admits he was angry at what he said was a false and unjustified accusation, he told her he agreed to see Dr. Kiczales, as requested by [Mrs. Fahrnhorst], and she never denied it. I find that she left because she suspected that neither Dr. Green nor Dr. Dengel would be willing to accept her accusations at face value and wanted more information before taking drastic steps and she wanted to find some expert who would immediately support her position.[21] (References omitted.)

Sarah and the children returned to Virginia in early December and moved in with Sarah's other sister, who lived near where the Fahrnhorsts had resided. Within several days Sarah had delivered a copy of the Webb report to Green's office, hired a lawyer, and filed for custody. Gerald began visiting, but he was not always permitted to see the children. And finally, child protective services opened an investigation of Gerald's alleged abuse of Tammy.

Enter CPS

A caseworker with nine years' experience investigated for about a month before determining that the case was unfounded. He met with Tammy and Billy several times and with both parents. His primary focus was Tammy, and he described his evaluation of her in his court testimony: "[I]n the initial sessions with the child, I generally try to stay unstructured to see what the child will produce without my having influenced it in some way. In the later structures, then, I try to push more specifically for what it is I want to know. When I talked to [Tammy] about how the dolls play with each other or what do they do, again it was generally unremarkable. I didn't see a whole lot of anything that stood out as being particularly significant.

"The other thing I wanted to find out," he continued, "was how [Tammy] responded in the presence of her father in an unexpected situation."[22] With the cooperation of the parents, he arranged to have Gerald enter unexpectedly at the end of a session. "Her first reaction," the social worker recalled, "was one of just basically a blank reaction, as if she didn't at that moment see who it was; that was maybe a second. Then she had a look of very pleasant surprise; she smiled, her eyes grew big. She didn't say anything; she gave a little kid squeal of delight. Mr. [Fahrnhorst] came into the room and began to play with [Tammy]. She asked to climb on his back and they did some playing around the room, and that was my final session with [Tammy].[23]

He also testified that the child had said she hated her father, but that on another occasion she said the same thing about her mother. Under cross-examination he acknowledged that he had advised Sarah not to seek custody of the children, suggesting that she wait until his investigation was complete (she did not take his advice). He was never asked during the February or September hearings what specific questions he asked Tammy, and his case notes were never entered into evidence, although the notes of the caseworker who investigated subsequent allegations were.

But while the caseworker was conducting his investigation, and after he had finished, there were a number of other evaluations in progress. Gerald was seeing Kiczales, and Sarah joined them for two sessions. Gerald also saw Green and took a polygraph test, which he passed. The children had been referred by Green to psychologist Anne Carter for therapy, and Tammy was examined by a gynecologist.[24] In the midst of all this, there was a second trip to Massachusetts in mid-January, shortly after Gerald filed for divorce. And, if possible, the second trip had a worse effect on Sarah's position than the first.

Sarah has said she returned on the advice of a California attorney she telephoned who told her to get a "trauma team" to examine the children. She had them examined, she said, in the emergency room of Boston Children's Hospital, but the results of the examination have never been entered into evidence.[25] During the week they were there, Sarah brought Billy back to see Webb, in the vain hope (as it turned out) that he would disclose abuse. She also went to court to obtain a restraining order barring her husband from entering her sister's property, taking the children, or harming Sarah during her stay in the state at any time (effective for one year). The judge specifically told her that the custody matter would have to be resolved in Virginia, where she was a legal resident, and that she could not take up the matter in Massachusetts unless and until she met the one year residency requirement. Sarah has acknowledged that she obtained the restraining order by filing an affidavit containing information she knew to be false.[26] She has blamed this admitted blunder on the bad advice of the California attorney.[27]

When she returned, in short order Sarah dismissed her first lawyer, hired a second, and made appointments for the children with yet another psychologist, Cora Lynn Goldsborough, canceling two others previously scheduled with Carter. On the advice of her new lawyer, she arranged to be evaluated herself by psychologist William Zuckerman.

In mid-February, the first court hearing was held to consider Sarah's motions for temporary custody and support for herself and the children; they were granted. However, the court did not find that the sexual abuse allegation had been established; nor did it label the allegation false. It simply granted Gerald supervised visitation (meaning that another adult, which could include friends and relatives, had to be present), and deferred resolution of the matter. After the hearing, Judge Henry Whiting (who has since been appointed to the Virginia Supreme Court) said he appointed a law guardian to represent the best interests of the children,[28] although none made an appearance until three months later. He also appointed Anne Carter to act as an independent evaluator (or, in her words, "impartial expert")[29] charged with interviewing the children and parents and reporting back to the court.

Four days later Sarah was back in court to explain why she had refused Gerald visitation. Judge Whiting told her she would lose temporary custody if she continued to violate his order. The same day, a second child protective investigation was opened, based on a new report submitted by Cora Lynn Goldsborough, who had seen the children four times by then.

March was hectic, to say the least. The children were seeing both Goldsborough (for therapy) and Carter (for evaluation), and Tammy was examined by another pediatrician who became convinced that she had been sexually abused.[30] Social worker Suzanne Rossiter was interviewing Sarah and Gerald for the child protective investigation, William Zuckerman was preparing an evaluation of Sarah, and Sarah complained that her children were returning from overnight visits with their father in a highly agitated state. Psychologist Carter requested that the judge terminate overnight visits, and he did. Although Gerald had only daytime visits and they were supervised by his mother or family friends, Sarah reported that the children were still being molested when chaperones left Gerald alone. Meanwhile, Gerald passed another polygraph, and, on the advice of her lawyer, Sarah refused Social Services' request that she take one.

Just when it seemed as if no more professionals could possibly become involved in one case, two more did. Billy had been returning from visits with anal irritation, according to Sarah, and at the end of March he returned with more redness than usual. She asked him if "Daddy put peepee in bottom."[31] He answered affirmatively, she said, and she took him to a hospital emergency room on the advice of Goldsborough. Sarah requested that the doctor examine Billy with a proctoscope, but he refused, saying an external examination had made it clear that the child had not been penetrated with a penis and that the examination itself would be both painful and traumatic. The redness, he suggested, could have resulted from poor hygiene. A state trooper was called, and he interviewed the child. Billy did not appear traumatized, and the trooper found no evidence of abuse. He closed his investigation several days later, at the request of Sarah's lawyer.

The allegations continued to escalate in April. Both children reported oral sex with their father, their mother said. Sarah took the children on one more week-long trip to Massachusetts, which was the subject of some dispute. And then the Department of Social Services took action that proved decisive.

The Last Expert

They decided to make the expert game "sudden death overtime." Just a month earlier Anne Carter, the "impartial expert," had sent the court her report recommending that full custody be granted to Sarah, with limited supervised visitation to Gerald. Yet despite that fact—or, as there is reason to believe, because of it—the department chose one more evaluation team. The final evaluators were a three-person crew associated with Johns Hopkins University, who the department said (and both Carter and Goldsborough agreed) were "national experts" on sexual abuse. In April 1985 Gregory Lehne, Ruthellen Josselson, and Eileen Higham evaluated the entire Fahrnhorst family, interviewing each parent, observing the parents with the children in the waiting room, and then interviewing the children. Individual follow-up evaluations were done with the parents three weeks later.

Social worker Rossiter consulted with the Lehne team twice in May and, based on their findings, decided emergency removal of the children was required. As she explained in a letter to the judge: "[Tammy] and [Billy Fahrnhorst] were in imminent and extreme danger of substantial psychological damage due to their incorporation into Mrs. [Fahrnhorst's] delusional system." And "[t]here was an imminent and substantial danger that Mrs. [Fahrnhorst] would flee with the children."[32] On that basis, on May 18 the department declared all allegations against Gerald unfounded, lodged an allegation that Sarah had emotionally abused her children, and founded that allegation. The children were placed in foster care and then, following a hearing four days later, were placed with Gerald's mother.

The Lehne report was not finished until August. When it was, all that was left was the final parade of experts and the judge's decision. It was a marathon. The September 14 testimony ran from early morning to past midnight. And a number of additional witnesses testified earlier by deposition, including four key witnesses whom one would have thought the judge would have wished to hear in person: the Lehne team and Anne Carter.

Although Sarah's lawyer hired one more expert—this one to testify on the Lehne team's expert testimony—all the issues before the court came down to one question: Did Gerald sexually abuse the children? Lehne (who did the evaluation with his colleagues, but wrote his report alone) said no, and based his diagnosis of Sarah and his subsequent recommendations to the court on that belief. As he wrote in his report, "This diagnosis presupposes my belief that the allegations of sexual abuse are not founded in fact."[33] In his deposition, under cross-examination by the children's law guardian, Lehne was asked:

Q. Let's assume here, just for the sake of this question, that it could be conclusively proven that Mr. [Fahrnhorst] had abused the children sexually.
A. Yes.

Q. Would that, in any way, that fact alone, would that affect your evaluation of Mrs. [Fahrnhorst]?

A. Okay. If that was the case I think that it would affect my evaluation of her, because while she may have been what we consider paranoid, or excessively involved in the issue of abuse, outside observers, such as myself, would say that although her concern might have been excessive that it was appropriate in terms of her need to protect the children from further abuse, and so on.

Q. And, hence, would not pose a threat to the interests of the children, or the welfare of the children?

A. Correct.[34]

What did Lehne base this belief on (and it was, remember, a belief that Social Services used in unfounding its case)? He seemed to suggest at first, under questioning by the law guardian, that the psychological tests were a key element in his diagnosis. "Was the paranoia indicated in the testing alone?" the law guardian asked. "Yes," Lehne replied. "From the testing alone and the interviews, the evidence was that she suffered from a paranoid disorder and that she was both anxious and depressed at various times as a result of the experiences that she had been through in pursuing her belief that the children had been sexually abused."[35] But a moment later he said, "The M.M.P.I. test results for both [Fahrnhorsts] were basically unremarkable."[36] But the more important question his first answer raised was whether he was measuring the personality of a woman who, based on the reality of her situation, had every reason to be disturbed or no reason at all.

As for the evaluation of Gerald, Josselson, Lehne's colleague, was asked in her deposition, "And, are you familiar with the personality structure of an incest offender?" to which she responded: "[T]he state of our knowledge is such now that we really are not. It is not only I who am not, but it is the whole field who is not. This is a new field. We really do not have very much data on it. Just beginning to elicit that. To my knowledge there is no information that there is a general profile of an incest offender if there is anything such as that which does exist."[37] There are few responsible professionals in the field who would disagree with her position. Perhaps this was why so much of the testimony centered around Sarah, not Gerald.

The children were seen by Higham, Lehne's other colleague, together in one session (and a brief individual session with Billy). Higham testified that the children had said "Daddy is going to get me" in her office, but added, "They could not elaborate on it. They could not tell me more about what it meant for the most part, except these kind of stereotyped, what appeared to me well-rehearsed statements about what that meant. And they were very minimal statements, I assure you." She did not address, nor was she asked to, the possibility that the statements sounded well-rehearsed because the children had repeated them so many times to so many "experts." She continued: "However, this is a game that they play. I heard the father and the children playing 'Daddy is going to get you.' Running after them with a plastic mouse, or something. Perfectly normal, healthy father-child play. The kind of thing that every father says to his kid, probably."[38] Indeed, it was that very game to which Sarah thought Tammy was referring six months earlier, when she first heard her daughter say those words while she put on her diaper.

Higham was then asked by Sarah's lawyer, "Did the children make the statement that 'Daddy is going to get my bottom'?" When Higham said yes, he asked, "Do you know what [Tammy] calls her vaginal area?"

> HIGHAM. [Tammy] was not able to express that to me in clear and equivocal *[sic]* terms. She doesn't even know what a vaginal area is. This is a very young child, hardly verbal.
>
> LAWYER. You don't think that she can differentiate between her buttocks area and her genital area?
>
> HIGHAM. Certainly. But, not if you use those terms. They didn't use those terms. They just talked about "my bottom." That is the only word that they were able to use.
>
> LAWYER. And, then, you had no feeling from [Tammy] as to whether she was referring to her vaginal area when she was saying bottom?
>
> HIGHAM. No. There is no evidence of one or the other. They did not differentiate between. They didn't even know the word that I was using. I have worked with children for thirty years. I know how to phrase things at a developmental level of any child. And, so it *[sic]* is a lot of doubt in my mind of what she could and couldn't have meant.[39]

Strangely, Sarah's lawyer did not think to ask why Billy, who was 5, was no more able to differentiate than 3-year-old Tammy. His next question was, "To confirm a case of molestation [in a child] this young, what evidence do you think is required?"

"Well," said Higham, "I think you have to, you know, consciously use the law. Can't use a shotgun. You have to find evidence of sperm. You have to find evidence of a sexually transmitted disease. You have to find evidence of real conclusions. That has never been verified for these children. They have been repeatedly examined. Nobody has ever found those things. Now, there are instances where children do actually—where they find sperm. Now, that is pretty clear evidence, isn't it?"[40]

Higham's own belief, as one might guess, was that the children had been coached. Asked by the lawyer what her opinion was based on, she said, "Well, my opinion on that is that it is entirely possible for children to be influenced by the adult upon whom they are dependent and upon whom they identify, and are affectionately related. The children are young and impressionable, totally dependent upon the adult world for any ideas that they have whatsoever. And, therefore, it is very easy for them to be influenced, swayed, given the impression that does not necessarily have the consensus of opinion among adults."[41] Given these incredible circumstances, the unintentional irony of the last statement is striking: if anything was lacking in this case, it was a consensus of opinion among adults.

Lehne's report as a whole was criticized by William Zuckerman, hired by Sarah but praised by the judge for his genuine attempt to be objective. Lehne spoke of Sarah's paranoia and elements of depression (as quoted above). But according to Zuckerman, "the one thing you have to rule out in paranoid disorder is depression. And one of the criteria for paranoid disorder is to say that there's no depression, the reason being that in depression very often there are paranoid delusions."[42] Zuckerman's evaluation identified depression as the primary diagnosis, and he testified, "I could find nothing that led me to believe that sex would be an important issue around which she would build a delusional system. I found delusional paranoid things, but it didn't seem to me to be in that area.[43]

"[W]hen you're talking about delusions," he continued a little later, "it's a very touchy subject. How do you know they're delusions or they're not? . . . At this point, if she comes in and says, 'My children have been abused,' there's reason for it—and there's three people and there's a bunch of psychologists who support that allegation, and there's a pediatrician who supports it, and the children are supporting it, that seems to me to be indications from three different directions. I'm not sure that counts as delusional. I wouldn't rule it out, but I'm not sure that that counts as delusional. And I'd feel funny about saying that—I wouldn't want to start with the premise that that was delusion."[44]

Which, of course, was precisely what Lehne did. Summing up his thoughts on the Lehne team, Zuckerman added, "I thought Dr. Josselson's report was a pretty good report, actually. I thought Dr. Lehne, to me reading it, looked as though he made up his mind and then set the facts to fit what he thought."[45]

Some of the problems Zuckerman had with the Lehne report can be found in Josselson's testimony as well. "You see," she told Sarah's lawyer, "the important thing here is that paranoids do not act terribly differently from normal people, except that what they believe doesn't happen to be real." To which he responded, "Who determines whether it is real or not?"

"Well," Josselson continued, "these are very complicated metaphysical questions and I—When Joe McCarthy was saying that there were Communists under every porch, for a long time the country believed him. And indeed, did accuse all manner of people of being Communist until this society caught up with it and decided that, indeed, Joe McCarthy was a paranoid rather than that all of these people are Communists. Who was to say what was real there? These are metaphysical, philosophical problems that can't be determined in a simplistic way, because I think if you really get into it it is the kind of thing, well, what is reality? Reality is what other people say reality is."[46]

But a trial is not a metaphysical discussion; it is an adversarial proceeding that must yield a result. The two most important issues the court had to consider in weighing the conflicting testimony of the experts was their knowledge and objectivity. Neither was easy.

Several of the doctors acknowledged their inexperience in dealing with sexual abuse cases, and both Dengel and Green had an interest in denying the abuse, since neither had reported it. Kiczales clearly sided with Gerald, who was his patient. Zuckerman seemed genuinely interested in doing an objective evaluation, and his report seemed quite balanced, but he was hired by Sarah, as was Webb, who was the first psychologist to interview the children and who had never before evaluated children for this purpose. Goldsborough was also hired by Sarah, and the judge discounted her opinion because of her contact with Webb (a telephone call), her "credulity" in accepting some of Sarah's and the children's statements that the judge found hard to swallow, and her having asked Tammy a leading question (while the child was playing with an anatomically correct doll): "I pointed to the penis and said, 'Has your daddy ever asked you to put that in your mouth?' or something like that, just pointing to the area, and she said yes."[47]

The "Disinterested Third Party"

That left Carter and Lehne, basically. But it is probable that the person most responsible for the ultimate decision, after the judge, was no expert at all. It was Suzanne Rossiter, the social worker who began the case with just four months' experience on the job. There are two myths about child protective workers. One is that they are always biased against the alleged abuser, which is basically VO-CAL's position. And the second is that they are impartial, which is not even what they are supposed to be (they should be advocates for the best interests of the child),[48] but is often the way they portray themselves and are portrayed by attorneys who agree with them (as Thomas Schultz portrayed the whole Social Services Department in his summation).[49] Suzanne Rossiter was neither biased against the accused nor impartial. As the law guardian wrote in his report to the court:

> I have not placed any significant amount of weight, in my review of this case, to any of the conclusions the Department of Social Services reached with regard to the allegations against [Gerald Fahrnhorst]. Frequently, in a case involving a custody dispute between the parents, the Department of Social Services is called upon to make a report to the court as a disinterested third party. Under those circumstances, I find such reports to be useful and valuable in examining the circumstances of the case. . . . Unfortunately, the Department's advocacy before the Court of Mr. [Fahrnhorst's] position, or, perhaps more clearly stated, the De-

partment's defense before the Court of its conclusions, has colored the weight I have given to those conclusions. It appears to me that the Department's position is not unlike permitting Dr. Carter or Dr. Lehne, or any of the other professionals involved in this case, to appear before the Court by Counsel, and to present witnesses, defending their reports against the attacks made against them by the interested parties in this case.[50]

There are many examples of Rossiter's clear advocacy in the case, but perhaps the most flagrant and far-reaching is found in her March 22 interview with Gerald, during which they discussed the Carter report that was highly unfavorable to him.[51] Early during the conversation, they discussed Rossiter's prior suggestion (it is unclear when it originated) that Gerald make an individual appointment with Dr. Lehne—the same Lehne who did the final evaluation. This discussion, however, took place twelve days before Rossiter first contacted Lehne to set up the evaluation of the whole family (according to her own written chronology), and it was apparent that that idea had not yet occurred to her. Gerald seems to have been unenthusiastic about seeing Lehne. Now she told him "there is no choice." Why? Referring to the Carter report she has described as "devastating" to him, she said, "My reasoning is—this cannot be unanswered."[52] Gerald: "So you feel very strongly that I should see this Dr. Lehne . . ." Rossiter: "Yeah." Gerald: "That's good enough for me."[53] Later in the interview on several occasions she slips into the first person when discussing strategy, as if they were in this together. If Gerald can get a better result on a retest of the M.M.P.I., "then *we've* got something," she said.[54] (Emphasis added.)

But by far the most important moment of the interview was when Gerald revealed he had already contacted Lehne. He had called and left a message on Lehne's answering machine, and Lehne had called back. According to Gerald, they had had a ten- or fifteen-minute conversation:

> I told him I had been accused of sexually abusing my 2-year-old daughter [and] that through Social Services had been asked to contact him and possibly set up an appointment. . . . I tried very quickly—I mean you can't hardly do it very quickly—to explain some of the things that happened. . . .

And he said, "Well, let me just say one or two things." He said, "Number one, in most cases, people are sent to me once they have admitted that they are guilty. And it is my job or whatever, to help people, you know the—that have a problem." He said, "Now whether you have a problem or not I can't say." He says, "If you've taken a polygraph and so forth and so on, I'm not saying you have lied or are lying now, but if you did lie, and lied on the polygraph, then you can come down here to me and I'm not going to be able to tell the difference." He said, "What I'm telling you is that, if you are coming to me for an answer of yes, he did sexually abuse his daughter, or no he did not sexually abuse his daughter," he said, "I will not be able to give you that answer. A cut and dried answer." He said, "What I can do is do a—an evaluation on you and determine such factors as whether you would have any tendencies towards—sexual tendencies towards children." And I told him, I said, "Well—let me talk to the people at Social Services and let me consult with my attorney"—and he said he did know Taz [Thomas] Schultz—"and see what they think."[55]

But somehow Lehne did manage to give Gerald and the court "a cut and dried answer," and at the same time he managed to forget this entire conversation. In his deposition, he testified that he had never spoken to Gerald before April 20, a month after Gerald described their conversation. When pressed by Sarah's lawyer, Lehne said he had no record of such a conversation, although "usually I do keep notes of telephone calls from people with their names, if they give them, but some of those—a number of situations people are not always willing to leave their names. So it is possible. But, you know, I do not have any memory."[56] What makes this particularly strange is that Gerald had absolutely no reason to lie, and he specifically remembered that Lehne called *him* after he left a message on Lehne's answering machine.

Furthermore, Gerald probably did not know that Lehne was acquainted with his lawyer—an association one would think would have helped Lehne remember the conversation. Gerald probably did not know, either, that Schultz had hired Lehne one year earlier to evaluate another man charged with sexual abuse whom Schultz was defending. Or that Lehne testified on behalf of Dr. Byron Timberlake on June 5, 1984, before the same judge. Or that Judge Whiting had thrown out the psychologist's entire testimony on the grounds that Lehne did not qualify as an expert witness because his field was not "sufficiently advanced."[57] Or that Lehne testified in that case that he had examined Dr. Timberlake and concluded he was not a pedophile,[58] testified further that if he were a pedophile, it would have been in his best interest to admit it to Lehne,[59] and that "pedophiles have typically been, you know, gotten in trouble, been convicted of these types of problems"[60] (while, of course, Timberlake had not).

Lehne had concluded his testimony in the Timberlake trial by offering no fewer than three answers to what was undoubtedly the most important question he was asked (and if it did not invade the province of the jury, it came close). Asked if it would be impossible for a person who was not a pedophile, or was not addicted to drugs or alcohol, to engage in sexual activities with young boys, he first answered yes.[61] Then he amended his answer, stating that a normal male would not be capable of engaging in such activities.[62] His final answer was that it is impossible for a person who is not a pedophile or intoxicated or on drugs to engage in a sexually motivated act with a child.[63] Gerald probably did not know all that. But the local paper covered the trial closely. It was in the headlines at the same time Suzanne Rossiter became a child protective worker for Warren County.

It is only possible to speculate on Rossiter's motivation in becoming Gerald's advocate. First, her agency had already investigated the case once and had deemed it unfounded. To reverse itself would have been tantamount to admitting it had bungled the first investigation. Second, Gerald was a cooperative "client" who acted innocent (and again, we do not presume to judge whether it was an "act" or the truth), took polygraph tests when asked, and apparently got along well with the department. It seems likely Rossiter became convinced of his innocence, grew personally involved with the case (as can easily happen with a novice), and was genuinely alarmed that an innocent man might lose his children.

Sarah, on the other hand, was not cooperative. She had no confidence in Rossiter and made that clear in their very first appointment. Her trips to Massachusetts undoubtedly alienated not only Social Services but the judge as well. And her sisters wrote letters to a variety of public officials up to and including the White House, complaining about the handling of the case. In return, they received sympathetic letters from afar and hostility closer to home. One of Sarah's sisters also suggested to a local newspaper reporter that she write about the case. The reporter declined, informed Social Services, and testified to the fact in court, completing what amounted to a public relations disaster.

The Envelope, Please

But what of Anne Carter, the only "impartial expert" appointed by the court? Why was her opinion ignored? Again, we can only speculate. First, there were suggestions that she was not impartial after all. She had treated the children as a therapist before she agreed to the evaluation and, the judge noted, "it is unfortunate that she had received opinions from professionals on both sides of the issue before drawing her own conclusions. . . . I believe it preferable that such an expert form her opinion without knowing what the other opinions have been."[64] (And, although the judge did not mention it, under cross-examination by Schultz, Carter could not state with certainty that she had not expressed concern for the children's safety prior to her evaluation.)[65]

But Lehne had had much more contact with the experts than Carter ever did. There were the prior contacts with Gerald and Schultz, which raised serious questions about his objectivity. He was essentially hired by Rossiter, as opposed to Carter, who was hired by the court. And Lehne received all of Rossiter's notes, her disputed chronology (without Sarah's corrections), and he met with Rossiter twice, whereas when Carter specifically requested a meeting of the experts to discuss their differences, she received a letter from the Social Services' lawyer denying the request "so that no question of [the Department's] impartiality can be raised."[66] Finally, Lehne had evaluations or letters to the court or depositions from Carter, Goldsborough, Lutz, Green, Kiczales, Dengel, Zuckerman, Webb, and Sarah.[67]

Judge Whiting's decision probably came down to four factors. First, and probably least, Carter herself had warmly endorsed Lehne, as had Goldsborough—two of Sarah's strongest witnesses. Second, Gerald had taken the stand and Sarah had not. The judge already had doubts about her credibility (as he expressed in his opinion), and in a civil action it is not improper to draw a negative inference when a party does not take the stand to rebut damaging testimony. Third, the court had expended considerable time and expense on the Lehne team. To have done so and then thrown out its report and gone with Carter's would have been an admission that it was all a waste. All the momentum—and a case this long and complex has nothing if not momentum—was moving in Gerald's favor. And then the law guardian boarded the bandwagon.

The law guardian was singled out for commendation by the judge in his decision. His opinion seemed to carry weight with the judge, and he and Zuckerman were the only participants the judge seemed to think were objective. And what was the law guardian's final determination concerning the abuse? He could not say whether it happened or not.

And yet a decision had to be made. "Harm is also done to the children by not making a final resolution of this situation," he wrote, "especially considering that it appears that all reasonable avenues of investigation have been exhausted. Under these circumstances, I believe that it is in the best interest of the children to make a determination regarding custody at this time, even though all suggestions of abuse cannot be absolutely refuted or proven. Further, I am sufficiently unconvinced by the evidence of sexual abuse to believe that that should not be a consideration in determining the custody of these children."[68]

And so, at least in part because Sarah's lawyer never addressed the issue of custody independent of the abuse allegation, the law guardian threw his cards in with Gerald. And so did the judge. No one tried to weigh the comparative risks if they were wrong. The law guardian came closest when he wrote, "To remove these children from the custody of either of their parents will cause some harm to the children. The question the Court must resolve is whether or not the risk to the children in not removing them is greater."[69] But he missed the point. Clearly the children were going to be removed from one or the other. But the question of risk, *if* the possibility of abuse had *not* been resolved, was, What is the risk if the children are placed with the mother and the abuse did not occur, versus the risk if the children are placed with the father and it did? But then, despite some lingering doubts, the key players decided it probably did not.

In a case with so many questions, it seems only fitting to close with one more. Who won the "battle of the experts"?

III

Conclusions, Solutions, and Future Directions

10

Legal Reforms and Trends

The Tribulations of Trial

IMMENSE progress has been made over the past decade in this field. Yet the mass media never seem to focus on potential solutions—or on those already in place. A commonly voiced complaint is that too often we journalists are, in the immortal words of Spiro Agnew, "nattering nabobs of negativism." Most stories about sexual abuse have focused on the negative. Some have also exposed the need for change (as the last chapter was intended to do). Ironically, however, when the publicity does bring change, the improvements receive a fraction of the coverage the horror stories did—when they are covered at all.

But there is no dearth of progress to report. As noted in chapter 1, there is a consensus even among bitter antagonists on issues that were controversial as recently as five years ago. And what may be most amazing is that the legal system, steeped in precedent and tradition, has changed with remarkable alacrity in adopting measures aimed at minimizing children's trauma while maximizing their opportunities for protection and redress. In some cases, change has resulted from legislation. In others, judges have learned and adapted, or have been persuaded by increasingly knowledgeable lawyers to accept arguments that were not raised a few years ago.

To be sure, there are still daily horror stories. Children are still traumatized by courts, and innocent adults are sometimes prosecuted and become victims of the system as well. Time and again one hears people who have had contact with the system complain that it was not what they thought it would be. Parents of victims say they expected understanding and support from the police and prosecutors to whom they turned, only to find insensitivity and arrogance instead. They speak of the vagaries of a system in which prosecutors decide what cases to file and victims have to live with their decisions. Those who claim they were falsely accused say they thought the "misunderstanding" would be cleared up in short order. They complain about huge legal fees and the arrogance of investigators who had made up their minds before they asked the first question. These complaints are not unique to child sexual abuse.[1] People charged with crimes they did not commit are, at a minimum, unfairly stigmatized and may be unfairly impoverished and convicted. Victims whose cases are not prosecuted may be victimized again by the system. And the stakes are very high indeed. This is not petty theft. The stigma and injury resulting from a false accusation can be devastating, as can the damage of victimization. Our criminal justice system will never be infallible, but when it fails in one of these cases, the cost may be incalculable.

For years the talk in the profession was of the difficulty—which sometimes sounded like impossibility—of taking these cases to trial. Now one hears more about custody cases and less of the tribulations of trial, even though there have been more than a few high-profile losses. One begins to hear prosecutors—aggressive prosecutors—say for the first time that further reform is not necessary. Not all of them would agree, and when pressed most can think of some additional legislation they would like to see, but one does not hear the laments about the system being stacked against the victim that were common a few years ago. Sexual abuse cases are difficult to win, most say, but that will not necessarily be changed by more legal innovations.

Sacramento is a jurisdiction that has been looked to as a model by some in and outside of California. It has a specialized unit and vertical prosecution of sexual abuse cases—that is, the same prosecutor handles a case from beginning to end. "We've had some big cases that have turned out less than desirably," acknowledged Jan Hansen, the deputy district attorney who supervises the Sexual Assault and Child Abuse Unit, "but overall we're generally considered a model type of program . . . We're growing all the time, we're getting better all the time. I've done conferences, and we get people from other counties and even some people from out of state that will call with questions about how we do this or that, so to that extent, I think that we're pretty successful, but we have a long way to go. It's an area that's always changing, and we're always refining our approach.

"Everyone always wanted to be innovative before," Hansen added. "I think we've got plenty of legislation to be innovative, but we need to kind of work with and develop within the parameters that we have right now."[2]

The Technological Revolution

Some of the innovations that seemed important to many prosecutors a few years ago seem less so now. Laws have been passed in a number of states permitting children to testify in criminal cases via closed circuit television from a location outside the courtroom. The purpose was to minimize the child's trauma by allowing testimony outside of the intimidating presence of a roomful of strangers and, more important, the alleged abuser. To warrant this special measure, the child must be deemed by the judge to be psychologically fragile. The technology includes monitors in both the remote location and the courtroom so that the defendant retains his Sixth Amendment right to confront his accuser, and his lawyer may still cross-examine the child. At the time it was being campaigned for, it was touted as a major advance. But the law does not appear to have been invoked very often. And to the surprise of some of its proponents, not all defense lawyers are against it.

Michael Frost, a Seattle defense attorney, said he is all for technology that allows children to avoid the trauma of testifying in the courtroom. "I have yet to meet a 4-year-old child who isn't scared shitless of the courtroom," he said. "Most *adults* are frightened." He favors not only closed circuit television but also allowing the videotaped testimony of the child to be admitted into evidence. Videotaped statements may be used in a number of states as evidence presented to grand juries or in pretrial hearings, and in rare instances may be admitted into evidence if the child is ruled to be "psychologically unavailable" to testify in court (although it is unclear if such testimony can withstand objections on appeal).

Although Frost guessed that most defense lawyers probably do not favor videotaped testimony, since it would prevent them from cross-examining the child, he said he favored it because "the most potentially prejudicial part of these trials is when the child testifies." With videotape, "the child is not put through an emotional wringer and the jury is not put through an emotional wringer."[3]

California has a law permitting testimony by closed circuit television that is opposed by defense lawyer Michael Sands, who is a frequent adversary of Jan Hansen's in Sacramento. Although the technology has never been used in a case of his, Sands said he believes if and when it is, it will help the defense rather than the prosecution.

"In my opinion," he said, "the best thing the prosecution has going for it, absolutely the best thing, is the time the jury is seated in the box, [the prosecutors] call their first witness, and . . . in comes a darling little kid who you know has been dressed in the best Sunday school clothes they have. Every kid I've ever had in these cases looks like they're entering a Shirley Temple look-alike contest. I mean, your heart goes out. Even the defense attorney looks there and says, 'Oh jeez. What have I got here?' And what the prosecution is saying is now the jury won't ever see that. The jury will look at a little boob tube."

That will be to his advantage, Sands said, because his clients are generally successful and wealthy—otherwise they could not afford to hire him. "In my cases," he said, "because they have money, you know that the defendant is always going to be well dressed, well shaved, neat looking. He is going to look like your neighbor. And every juror is going to sit there and look at that guy and say, 'Gee, he could be my son, he could be my husband, he could be my next-door neighbor. He doesn't look like a molester.' For the whole trial they are going to look at him, and in my cases I cannot conceive of a case where he will not get on the witness stand, and he will turn and look at that jury and he will talk to them and they will see him as a human being. And if they only see that kid as a vision on a television screen, I personally—and I have not had any personal experience with it yet—but it's my gut reaction that it will help my case."[4]

It remains to be seen how important this technological revolution in the courts proves to be. But it is worth noting that just a few years ago, such innovations were ideas on legal drawing boards. One could not have predicted that they would be on the books and in use so quickly.

Although the momentum for change seems to have slowed, there are still reform proposals circulating. Several seem important and potentially controversial. Heading the list is the regulation of expert testimony. It seems clear that some structure is needed to prevent recurrences of the travesty described in the last chapter. Although a number of prosecutors and others interviewed found the Vachss proposal outlined in chapter 8 intriguing when it was described to them, it remains to be seen whether the courts themselves are sufficiently alarmed by "battles of the experts" to consider innovation. Such battles, after all, are neither new nor limited to sexual abuse cases, and courts may be loath to touch them.

Some commentators who are not enamored of change for its own sake still see the need for reform in two key areas. In a book published by the U.S. Department of Justice, the authors preface their recommendations with this observation:

> Our research leads us to conclude that too much attention is presently directed to legislative reforms permitting innovative practices that benefit only a handful of the growing number of children enmeshed in the criminal justice system. A large portion of the effort now devoted to statutory reforms might be more productively focused toward alternative techniques that are less dramatic, yet equally—or even more—effective. In other words, creative exploitation of resources that are already available might achieve many of the same goals.[5]

With that caveat, they go on to recommend two statutory reforms: adopting special hearsay exceptions permitting certain out-of-court statements by children to be admitted into evidence, and abolishing competency requirements for child witnesses.[6] First, it should be noted that these recommendations were aimed at criminal rather than family court. Many family courts already allow special hearsay exceptions, and frequently children do not have to testify at all in such forums.

But the situation is different in criminal courts. There is rarely much, if any, corroborating evidence in sexual abuse cases, and prosecution often rests on the testimony of the child. When the child is young—under 10, for example—questions may be raised concerning the child's ability to understand what it means to tell the truth. Without that ability, some say, the child cannot be relied on to testify truthfully. Others have argued, however, that adults who are psychopathic liars testify in court regularly and that it is up to the judge or the jury to decide whether the witness is credible. They argue that the trier of fact can do likewise with child witnesses, no matter how young. In support, they point to the federal rules of evidence, which contain no competency requirement. There, the trier of fact decides what weight to give a child's testimony.

VOCAL stands adamantly against this position. The standard arguments are that children lack the mental or moral or mnemonic capacity to be competent witnesses and cannot distinguish between fantasy and fact. People like Lee Coleman have argued further that children who have been subjected to repeated questioning by parents and investigators are often psychologically incompetent, since they are no longer capable of distinguishing what they actually remember from what they have been told by parents, by other children, and by investigators who reveal subtly (and not so subtly) what they want to hear. And the example to which Coleman and VOCAL regularly return is Jordan (see chapter 6).

The hearsay issue, while more complex, is no less controversial. Hearsay is an out-of-court statement offered for its truth. It is not usually admitted into evidence because its truth is considered un-reliable, since there is no opportunity to cross-examine the speaker in court and the statement itself was not made under oath. If an abused child is not deemed to be a competent witness or is psycho-logically too fragile to testify, however, the hearsay testimony of a parent or therapist may be the only means by which the court may learn what the child has said about the abuse. Videotaped testimony is another example of hearsay evidence, and where it is allowed, it can only be admitted under a special hearsay exception. The theory under which it is allowed is modeled after the reasoning that has permitted witnesses too ill to testify in court to videotape statements from their hospital beds, for example. In those cases, the court deems witnesses "unavailable" to testify in person, and thus permits a hear-say exception. In the case of children whose mental and emotional state is delicate (as certified, for example, by a therapist who has evaluated or treated the child), the court may deem the child "psy-chologically unavailable" to testify and admit videotaped testimony in the child's stead.[7]

The analogy used here is similar to other efforts that have been made to introduce children's statements under other hearsay exceptions. But in recent years, several states have enacted special hearsay exceptions for sexually abused children. New York's Family Court Act has a provision for child protective proceedings that allows the admission of "previous statements made by the child relating to any allegations of abuse or neglect." Such statements, however, must be corroborated before a finding of abuse or neglect is made. A recent amendment to the law specifies that "any other evidence tending to support the reliability" of the child's statement "shall be sufficient corroboration," and that "the testimony of the child shall not be necessary to make a fact-finding of abuse or neglect."[8]

According to the American Bar Association's National Legal Resource Center for Child Advocacy and Protection, at least a score of states admit hearsay statements into evidence in criminal or civil proceedings or both.[9] An example is Washington's statute, which applies to both criminal and civil cases:

9A.44.120. Admissibility of child's statement—Conditions

A statement made by a child when under the age of ten describing any act of sexual contact performed with or on the child by another, not otherwise admissible by statute or court rule, is admissible in evidence in dependency [civil] proceedings . . . and criminal proceedings in the courts of the state of Washington if:

(1) The court finds, in a hearing conducted outside the presence of the jury, that the time, content, and circumstances of the statement provide sufficient indicia of reliability; and

(2) The child either:

(a) Testifies at the proceedings; or

(b) Is unavailable as a witness: *Provided*, That when the child is unavailable as a witness, such statement may be admitted only if there is corroborative evidence of the act.

A statement may not be admitted under this section unless the proponent of the statement makes known to the adverse party his intention to offer the statement and the particulars of the statement sufficiently in advance of the proceedings to provide the adverse party with a fair opportunity to prepare to meet the statement. (Emphasis in original)

The gravamen of the controversy such laws are sure to raise is twofold. First, defense lawyers argue that it is important that they be permitted to cross-examine children. As defense lawyer Sands argued (chapter 4), if investigators are not willing to challenge children, feeling their jobs are rather to "support the child," then the defense lawyer in court may be the first and only person to do so. To allow in the child's out-of-court statements is to deprive the defense of the ability to challenge the child's story. And second, the witnesses likely to testify most frequently as to what the child said will probably be social workers, police officers, and therapists who have discussed the abuse at length with the child. These are the very professionals defense lawyers and VOCAL supporters have accused of bias. In their view, granting these professionals the authority first to ask children leading questions then to testify in court what the children said would be a travesty.

Sands, for example. recounted a case in which he claimed the police officer led a child victim. "One of the last cases I had," he said, "a cop says, 'This is my system. This is the way I ask questions.' And he says, 'My practice is not to tape-record,' but out of twenty-some-odd kids, he recorded three of them, two of whom had nothing to do with our case whatever. But we listened to the tapes and we listened to his technique. Suggesting. Suggesting the name of the person who did it, suggesting what he may have done, just putting all sorts of ideas in the—and then he gets on the witness stand and says, 'I never say that. I never do that.' Frankly, we won that case probably as much because the jury had no confidence in the investigating officer."[10]

Clearly, Sands is not likely to agree that the officer's testimony of what the child said—and what he said to the child—is acceptable under a hearsay exception. But what he does want is a requirement that all interviews with a child by investigators be video- or audio-taped, so that he can review the process that preceded the child's statement.

The demand for the recording of investigative techniques has become a rallying cry of VOCAL and, especially, of Lee Coleman and others whose involvement in these cases is largely made possible by videotape, without which they would be hard-pressed to evaluate such techniques. And so what began as an innovation sought by prosecutors primarily to reduce the number of times a child had to repeat his or her story to investigators (who could share a single tape), and then was seen as a possible alternative to a child's live testimony, has now been seized by the adversary.

The response from the other side has been unclear but appears mixed. Some child advocates are concerned that taped statements may weaken cases, since children's early denials, which are common, will be recorded along with their disclosures. Recantations, which are also common, will be recorded as well and may be used to impeach the child's credibility. But others acknowledge that VO-CAL has expressed legitimate concerns, that the defendant has a right to accurate information about the investigation, and that investigators must be held accountable for their techniques. Although enthusiasm for introducing videotapes in court seems to have waned, prosecutors and police departments continue to purchase equipment and to remodel special rooms where children can be videotaped comfortably and unobtrusively.

The universal adoption of videotape as an investigative tool seems inevitable. It is a valuable means of preserving evidence, of reducing the number of (often traumatic) interviews a child must submit to, and of sharing information among investigators, lawyers, therapists, and parents. Furthermore, it provides a means not only of evaluating but also of refining techniques. Tapes can be reviewed by those who made them and can also be used to train beginning investigators in proper and improper interviewing methods.[11]

Recycled Innovations: The Child Advocate

Some of the most important innovations are not new. Although that sounds like a contradiction, it is not. These are ideas that have been around a while but have not yet been implemented in many jurisdictions, so in that sense they are still new. Furthermore, they are being used in new ways and are still quite controversial.

One is the child advocate. This is an individual who either supports or represents a child in a criminal or civil proceeding or both. Programs that provide for such advocates vary widely. In some jurisdictions private organizations provide volunteer lay persons to explain court procedures to a child and to see that the court, in turn, is kept apprised of the child's needs. In other places, support is provided by victim witness assistance programs. Many family courts and some criminal courts appoint independent counsel to represent the best interests of the child. These law guardians (a name we prefer to guardians *ad litem*, for reasons explained earlier) may function in the dual role of lawyer and support person, or they may work jointly with others who provide support.

They are most commonly found in family courts, where the child's welfare is the focus of the trial and the appointment of independent counsel for the child is mandated under the Child Abuse Prevention and Treatment Act of 1974 for states wishing to receive federal funds.[12] In criminal courts, support persons have been more common than independent counsel, but there has been a (thus far) limited trend toward legal representation in those proceedings as well.

Traditionally, in criminal courts the defendant is represented by a lawyer, and the victim is presumed to be represented by the prosecutor. But in reality the prosecutor represents the state, not the victim, and the interests of the two may be quite different. An interview with several parents whose children testified in the McMartin pretrial hearing (and who asked for anonymity to protect the privacy of their children) revealed how disparate those interests can be.[13]

The parents were angry at the treatment of their children in court. They complained about the length of cross-examinations (one child was on the stand for sixteen days), the types of questions children were asked, and the manner in which they were addressed by one of the defense lawyers. Although they were angry with the lawyer, they were furious with the prosecutors, who they felt did not protect the children from what they considered legal abuse. They felt their children were in need of independent representation, but it was not available to them.

One parent offered a specific example. Children's medical records were subpoenaed in the McMartin case, and several parents did not want the information released, fearing it would embarrass their children. But a prosecutor told them they would have to hire their own attorneys to attempt to quash the subpoenas. "So your kid's victimized once," complained the parent, "your kid gets victimized on the stand again, then they subpoena records, and you're paying money out. How many people are going to be able to afford that?

"The prosecutor has a conflict of interest," the parent continued. "I don't care what they say. They may love that child, but they want a conviction, and if that means that kid's going to break down, or that kid's going to get asked questions that are probably objectionable, they're going to let them go because they want to hear what the answer's going to be . . . I don't blame the prosecutor. He wants a conviction, and their objective is to ensure that this defendant is put behind bars. But the kid's going to get lost in the shuffle, and that's why you need somebody in there representing the child."

Polk County, Iowa, has had law guardians in family court for years. And a 1985 statute allowed unpaid victim assistants (who could be lawyers but did not have to be) to represent children in criminal court as well. A number of professionals familiar with both courts said it was too early to tell what effect the law would have.[14] They were concerned that the volunteers might be "do-gooders who know nothing about the issues." On the other hand, they worried that when child advocates are lawyers, they may come into conflict with the prosecutor or may be objected to as "second prosecutors" by the defense. They were eager to see how the program worked, they said, but were disappointed that the statute made the appointments discretionary, and in many cases they were not being made.

A more established program (and one touted as a national model) is Philadelphia's Support Center for Child Advocates.[15] A private, not-for-profit agency that receives funding from a number of sources, the center was incorporated in 1977, and its advocates are all full-time lawyers elsewhere who donate time to the center. Many are employed by large firms that allow them to include the hours spent working on these cases toward the minimum billable hours the firm requires of its employees. Although the lawyers begin their work for the center without experience in this area, they are trained and supervised by the center's staff, according to Naomi Post, until recently the center's executive director and a lawyer herself who frequently represents children.

Their training consists of a day-long seminar, along with a manual explaining the relevant laws and procedures in civil and criminal courts, and follow-up lectures as needed. Post acknowledged that such training barely skims the surface but added that the attorneys work closely with one of three experienced, full-time social workers on the center's staff.[16] She emphasized the importance of these social workers, who are experienced in conducting independent investigations that the lawyer can rely on instead of being forced to conduct his own (for which he is not trained), or to accept the findings of Social Services workers, whom Post described as "incompetent, they're overworked, they have a lack of skills." In addition, she said, new lawyers are supervised by more experienced lawyers. Post estimated that there were about five hundred lawyers who had an average of two years' experience working for the organization. In addition, about three hundred paralegals volunteer time.

The center has focused almost exclusively on sexual abuse cases, Post said, and frequently takes on the most difficult ones. Most children in family court cases are represented by lawyers from a special unit in the Public Defender's Office. Lawyers there have huge caseloads, she said, and do not become involved in criminal proceedings. The center tries to choose cases that may involve both criminal and civil cases. Its lawyers are usually appointed at the outset of a court case, but sometimes the center requests a court appointment even before a case is pending.

"I think that's important because a lot of cases never make it to court," Post explained. When the center learns of a case where advocacy is required but court intervention is unlikely, it petitions the court for appointment and then conducts an independent investigation. If, for example, the victim were nonverbal and Social Services did not indicate the case because of a lack of evidence or lack of cooperation from the family, the center would investigate, develop a plan for the child and family in cooperation with Social Services, and then monitor the situation, she said. If the lawyer decided the child should be removed from the home and Social Services was unwilling to file a petition, the center would do so.

Post cited a recent example of the center's intervention on behalf of a 3-year-old who had gonorrhea. The center was informed of the case by a local hospital, and learned that both parents had admitted having gonorrhea and that the Social Services caseworker had said he was not going to indicate the case because he believed the disease could be transmitted via bathwater. The center got the court to appoint one of its lawyers. After consulting with his supervising attorney, the law guardian had a physician call the caseworker to set him straight. The case was now indicated, but still no petition had been filed. The family had agreed voluntarily to accept services—including the removal of the perpetrator from the home. But the law guardian was skeptical and monitored the home closely. Within a few weeks the perpetrator was caught there with the children. The lawyer told Social Services, "If you don't file a petition, I will." A petition was filed. The lawyer also tried to have the case prosecuted in criminal court, but the District Attorney's Office balked because of the child's age.

The program may be criticized for its reliance on volunteers, a practice that can be seen as minimizing the system's obligation to children as opposed to adult defendants who are, by law, guaranteed a paid attorney. Post acknowledged as much. In an ideal system the lawyers would all be paid, she said. But in the real world—the world in which Post spent more than half her time raising funds just to keep the center afloat (and which contributed to her decision to leave)—she believed the program was the best available in the country. What elevated it, she said, was the training and the supervision. Those ingredients made the center's lawyers better than the private lawyers who were sometimes appointed in criminal court when the center was backlogged, Post said.

"That private attorney has no training and no support," she argued. "The private attorney shows up in court never having met the child, never having evaluated the safety of the child. . . . They don't have a clue as to how to work with that child." She was bitterly opposed to programs that provided children only lay advocates. "I really resent [them]," she said. "I think it's nice to provide a companion for children, a support person, but you need an attorney who's involved. You need someone who, when you're in that criminal court proceeding, if there's a problem they can file a petition in [family court] for relief that's not available in criminal court.

"I think the justification," Post continued, "is that although the child is a complainant in the criminal court proceeding and is not, by law, entitled to counsel, and the defendant is entitled to counsel because he or she may be incarcerated or subjected to another type of penalty, what people fail to realize is that children can be subjected to a lifetime of sexual abuse or physical abuse if that proceeding does not go well and if that child is not provided with adequate representation."

Such appointments are not always made even in family court, however, as Judy Coletti (chapter 5) found out when the Illinois judge who heard her daughter's case refused to appoint a lawyer for the child despite Coletti's specific request. One reason is that cases may begin as divorce proceedings without abuse allegations, as Judy's did—although a strong case can be made that children under such circumstances are in need of representation as well.[17] But, as Post pointed out, the appointment of a lawyer does not guarantee adequate representation. A study of New York law guardians referred to earlier, for example, revealed that in 45 percent of the cases studied the representation was "seriously inadequate or marginally adequate," and in only 4 percent of the cases were the lawyers judged "effective."[18]

Although the quality of representation is of indisputable importance, from the court bureaucracy's perspective probably the two most attractive selling points of Post's program are the price and the ability of the lawyers not only to cover two courts but to assist in coordinating their activities. The frequent lack of coordination—or even simple communication—seems to be a source of increasing concern.

Kee MacFarlane spoke of the frequent battles in Los Angeles over the release of records between courts. A few years ago, she recalled, "I was involved in a case where [an assistant district attorney] had this child in a criminal case and had interviewed her and whatnot, and the dependency [family court] hearing was going on at the same time, and the A.D.A. went to dependency court, into the courtroom, and he was thrown out by the judge—I mean bodily removed from the courtroom. It's that bad."[19]

In cases where it is not that bad, there is simply no liaison between the courts. King County, Washington, has attempted to solve the problem by requiring lawyers to file papers with all courts.[20] But that does not always happen. Clearly, having a lawyer representing a child in all courts would obviate the problem, but not all those who would be affected by such a program are enthusiastic. Becky Roe, who supervises the Prosecuting Attorney's Sexual Assault Unit in King County, saw a problem coordinating family court and criminal proceedings,[21] and sometimes looked longingly at jurisdictions where the prosecutors who handle criminal cases handle the civil cases as well (although she added that she was not entirely sold on the idea). But she did not support the idea of law guardians in criminal court. There are support people provided by the victim/witness assistance program who advocate for the child, she said. But where prosecutors were concerned, her attitude was essentially, one is company, two is a crowd. "Any two lawyers are going to disagree," she said, "and so you end up, to my way of thinking, encouraging a disruption of any sort of a proper relationship between the prosecutor and a child."

Roe was not alone. Several other prosecutors interviewed were also unenthusiastic, believing that a dedicated prosecutor was the only legal advocate a child needed. The authors of the U.S. Department of Justice book cited earlier found that "[v]ery few of the judges we interviewed objected to the concept of independent representation for a child victim in criminal proceedings." However, "the prosecutors were more likely than judges or defense attorneys to object to a child having independent representation."[22]

But the issue may be moot if no funds are available. Although Post said lawyers volunteered $1 million of their time each year to the Support Center for Child Advocates, she still had to scramble to raise her $250,000 annual budget. At a time of increased competition for limited funds, it may be a hard sell for an agency looking to replicate the model—especially when some people within the system suggest it is unnecessary.

The role of an independent counsel may take on increasing importance,[23] on the other hand, as the battles between the various interested parties, including prosecutors, defense attorneys, advocacy groups, and the growing number of "experts," expand and grow ever more vitriolic. Panels of trained law guardians assigned to cases on a rotating basis, as is the theory at least in New York,[24] may represent the best hope to inject objectivity into a process in which cries of "foul" may be as difficult to assess as they are inevitable. It seems clear as well that unless someone is specifically assigned the task of representing the best interests of the child and only the child, it is far from certain anyone will.

Pretrial Diversion

Another program that is not new but in some ways is as controversial today as ever is the pretrial diversion of incest offenders. Like child advocate programs, pretrial diversion is set up differently in different jurisdictions. What diversion programs have in common is that incest offenders are permitted to avoid prosecution that could result in a jail or prison term in exchange for either an informal admission or a formal confession of guilt and a commitment to attend a treatment program. In some places the offender has a criminal record, in some places he does not, after having satisfied this commitment.

Supporters of the concept argue that it is both humane and practical. The child is validated, while spared both the trauma of having to testify against a parent and the guilt feelings that often accompany that testimony. The offender is allowed to get help—something that in all likelihood will not happen if he goes to jail. At the same time, supporters say, it forces the offender to face the reality of his crime. Often the rest of the family enters treatment as well, with the idea that the family may be reunited at the conclusion. The environment to which they return, however, will be safer because, through treatment, they all will have learned how to prevent further abuse.

Critics contend that this approach minimizes the crime, treating it as if it were just a "problem" like drinking or drugs. Some particularly resent offenders' admitting guilt but then having no criminal records to show for it—as if it had never happened. And, detractors add, no program should begin with the goal of reuniting the family. The sole goal should be the safety of the child, whatever that requires. Finally, many question whether treatment works.[25] Are they really getting better, some wonder, or are they just manipulating the system to their advantage—these men who often are able to abuse children for years because they are master manipulators.

The diversion concept grew out of a treatment approach pioneered by Henry Giarretto in the early 1970s. His Child Sexual Abuse Treatment Program of Santa Clara County, California, championed a "humanistic" approach to incest treatment, as opposed to the more traditional punitive approaches that relied heavily, if not exclusively, on incarceration. Giarretto believed it was important to recognize that the offender is a human being who would not be offending if he were not "hurting," and that if he were taught other ways to meet his needs and build his self-esteem, he would no longer need to offend. As Giarretto wrote: "The father-offender (or any offender) will stop being an offender when he is taught to become aware of all his needs for self-realization and to become personally responsible for meeting them.

"The same evolutionary rule that applies to offenders holds true for the officials who handle their cases," he continued. "They, too, behave the way they know best . . . Criminal justice system personnel, whose actions are vital to the success of the CSATP, will continue to use traditional methods until they are shown better ones."[26]

What Giarretto tried to show them was that most incest offenders were not "mentally disordered sex offenders," as defined by California law, and that they could better be treated by humanistic therapy and a self-help group guided by Giarretto and his colleagues than by incarceration or commitment to a mental institution. He succeeded beyond anything he could have imagined when he began in 1971. By 1975, the program had been designated a state demonstration and training center and a model for other programs in California and nationwide. The program has been widely replicated in this country and abroad, and countless therapists, administrators, and others with an interest in the field have sought training there— including a number who are now well known in their own right. The primary self-help component, Parents United, has well over one hundred chapters.

But Giarretto has by no means convinced everyone. Alan Nudelman, Santa Clara's assistant district attorney who supervises the Sexual Assault Unit, is a severe critic of Giarretto's philosophy. He is skeptical of the efficacy of treatment and disgusted at the prospect of returning a child to an abusive parent. "If you think I'm an angry man, I'm very angry," he said. "I'm angry that we have a system that perpetuates a revolving door policy that puts pedophiles back on the street after receiving ostensible 'treatment,' only to victimize children again." He blames the system for "trying to deal so humanely with the most perverse individuals in our society that it betrays the security of the citizenry at large."

Speaking of reuniting a child with a man who has molested her, Nudelman added, "To a degree, that is putting the imprimatur of society on the conduct of the defendant. To put the victim in the hands of the assailant is unconscionable in many cases—perhaps most cases. I think in some cases it is appropriate because we're not talking about courses of conduct; we're talking about individual acts."[27]

While tension between those who seek to treat offenders and those who wish to see them punished is not uncommon, neither is it universal. And not all programs are the same. Where Giarretto's program is seen by some in the District Attorney's Office and in the San Jose Police Department as soft on offenders,[28] a Sacramento program modeled after it has been widely praised by prosecutors and police officials alike.

Sandi Baker, executive director and founder of the Sacramento Child Sexual Abuse Treatment Program, said that when she began working in the field as a child protective worker, she too believed in removing children forever from abusive homes.[29] But then she found that it did not work. Incest victims were being referred for treatment, but the incest was not being addressed. And no one was working with the families, she said. Baker began treating the children, dealing directly with the incest. But of the family, she believed at that time: "What should happen is that those rotten, no-good parents—a mother who could let this happen, a father who did it— should just be expunged from [the children's] lives. That was my initial treatment philosophy, thinking me on my white horse, I would protect all these kids from these evil, horrible parents. And you put them in foster homes, and they would repeat the cycle by setting up the situation of seducing the [foster] parents, for one thing. But in addition to that, they'd run back to the parent who you had rescued them from.

"So it finally dawned on me. Well, if they keep running back, maybe we ought to work with the family. Brilliant deduction there. And so we started the group for mothers as well as kids." At that point, the offenders themselves were still excluded, she said. They were the "enemy." "But then we found out that all of them still loved him and were still tied into that, so then it occurred to me, maybe we ought to add the fathers into this. . . . We realized it's not just the identified victim that's the victim, but the whole family is, so we became a whole family treatment program."

In order to establish the program, Baker (like Giarretto before her) had to convince various agencies that her approach would be more effective than the alternatives. She succeeded, several officials at those agencies said, because her approach has been firm and even confrontational as well as humane. Said Jan Hansen, the deputy district attorney who supervises the Sexual Assault and Child Abuse Unit, "I think we have a pretty good, tough program that's pretty demanding. Our pretrial (or in lieu of prosecution) diversion is a lot tougher than [prosecution where] people get on probation after a conviction and have a probation officer and are supposed to get counseling but don't necessarily have to follow through."[30]

One of the strengths of the program, Hansen said, is that offenders must make a formal confession and waive the statute of limitations and their speedy trial rights. That way they know, "if you screw up you will be prosecuted and we've got a dead bang case because you confessed," Hansen said. On the other hand, she added, "as a prosecutor, I think there should be a price to pay, and I think [diversion] is an escape. I think there should be some consequence to doing that, whether it's just a conviction on your record and probation, or whatever."

Prosecutor Becky Roe takes a hard-line approach in Seattle, where there is no diversion program. "Our recommendation is almost always some combination of jail and treatment," she said. There are provisions for prisoners to be released for treatment, so that offenders may be treated the entire time, she added. Her colleague, Lucy Berliner, explained the difference in philosophies.[31] "I've talked to Sandi Baker many times. I think she runs a very tight ship and has an excellent program," Berliner said, adding in reference to her disagreement with that approach, "It's just a philosophical thing.

"I don't see any reason why a person who commits as serious a crime as sexual assault of a child deserves a special deal, why they don't have to be legally accountable for their behavior like every other person who breaks the laws in a serious way," Berliner said. "I think it's completely bogus for moral reasons . . . and second, I think it's completely unnecessary. I think programs like ours demonstrate you don't need to give them a special deal. You can get convictions, and then let the decision making about what happens to them take place following the conviction, or the guilty plea."

As to what that should be, she said, "Frankly, I think you should give them, every one of them, some amount of jail time. I think none of them should have no jail time. . . . And I think in every single case where it's possible it should be work release, not straight time, because work release gives you exactly what you need." Work release in effect makes them pay to go to jail, and it requires them to take financial responsibility for their families, she said. Incarceration, she added, sends a clear message to the child and society.

The foundation of Seattle's philosophy is confidence that the system works. The key is their belief that, in Berliner's word, diversion is "unnecessary." But others who were once inclined to take a hard line have grown disillusioned with the results. Kee MacFarlane is one.

"We get better and better at getting children to talk," MacFarlane said.[32] "I know so much more than I did ten years ago about the techniques. I know how to do that, I think, with abused kids—get them over the hump of the secret and the fear and the threats. For what? To drop kick them into a system that turns them into hamburger?"

MacFarlane worked with Parents United groups for years and was the project officer in Washington, D.C., who oversaw about a hundred federal grants awarded to programs that included a panoply of diversion approaches. She has tried to work with prosecutors and has come to the conclusion that "the goal of these cases should not be prosecution—meaning prosecution with the goal of conviction in the traditional sense—because to do it, you have to get your evidence out of the back of the child and you've got to prove it with a credible adult's word against that of a little kid.

"I don't come at that strictly from a point of view that child sexual abuse is a sickness and nobody should go to jail and all that," she continued. "It comes from the fact that it doesn't work and in the majority of cases in this country, most of them never see a courtroom anyway. In L.A.—I have never seen this number published, but I was told this by a member of the D.A.'s Office—of the cases that are presented by law enforcement to the D.A. for prosecution, 85 percent of them are dropped. They don't even file."

Her faith now is in programs like Baker's. "Given the way our system is set up and the way society feels about this problem, you've got to have something to offer these guys besides the loss of everything they ever had in life—their freedom, their family, their homes, their jobs . . . " But the something they are offered, MacFarlane added, "does not have to be free lunch." That is why she likes the Sacramento program, which, she said, "has more control over those guys than any other program I have seen in this country . . . But what that program, and many others like it, has discovered is a very magical kind of thing in this field. The threat is greater than the actuality in our system. The threat of the criminal conviction, the threat of all the other things that can happen is a powerful weapon. It has to, in my opinion, be associated with the criminal justice system."

And what is perhaps the bottom line, MacFarlane believes offenders are amenable to treatment. She has treated offenders herself, she said, and "for anybody who's worked with child sexual abusers, they are, for the most part, a population of people who are real vulnerable to clinical intervention because by and large, they do hate themselves, it's not something they've chosen, it's not something they want." On the other hand, she added, "they generally need some kind of real strong legal incentive [to accept treatment], because it's very painful therapy."

Berliner's bottom line, on the other hand, completes their philosophical differences. "I don't know if those guys wouldn't be as free from future offenses if they spent one or two years in jail as they would by being in a community treatment program," she said. "We just simply don't have the data, because those type of guys have never gone to jail or prison. . . . The teacher, the community leader, the 'nice guy' incest offender are never being sent to prison . . . I would like to believe that the treatment programs are in themselves effective, but I'm not persuaded."

One thing seems clear. The diversion programs that have the best chance of success are those that have a reputation as "tough" and have the support of the various community agencies such a program comes into contact with. Without that cooperation, a program will not have clients, and without continued cooperation, it will have a hard time succeeding. That is why pretrial diversion—and Henry Giarretto—are closely linked with the concept of the multidisciplinary team, which Giarretto, among others, also pioneered.

The Multidisciplinary Team

The concept of a multidisciplinary team of social workers, prosecutors, police officers, and therapists working together and meeting regularly to discuss issues and resolve differences is not new and is not a legal reform, although it may still be a trend. Far from being innovative, it is as close as this field has to a truism. When written out, the truism goes something like this: in order for sexual abuse cases to be handled successfully, individuals from different agencies with disparate goals and philosophies must work together. And in order to facilitate such cooperation, those individuals should meet regularly. It has been discussed for years and done for years, in some places. But not everywhere. For that reason alone it is worth looking at. It is also one of the most important concepts in the field.

There are certain components that seem to be generally accepted requirements for such teams.[33] First, the team must have regular players. Normally this means members of specialized units in the various agencies that deal exclusively or mainly with child sexual abuse. This is not essential, however. The police in Polk County, Iowa, have only recently begun to specialize, but they have participated in team meetings for years. The minimum requirement, however, is that participation must be regular in order to build relationships. Next, there must be a leader (although formal designation is not required), a regular schedule, and an agenda. A protocol among the various agencies is a goal of most multidisciplinary teams and may be negotiated by the team or in another forum. (Without a protocol that spells out the responsibilities of the various agencies, and the procedures they are to follow in fulfilling them and communicating with each other, meetings are more likely to resemble tag-team wrestling matches than professional discussions.) Within this basic context, the groups can vary tremendously, as the three meetings described below illustrate.

The Polk County, Iowa, Intra-Family Sexual Abuse Program (IFSAP) was first formed by a county attorney who heard about Giarretto's program in Santa Clara County, took an assistant county attorney and a social worker out to a training with him, and when they returned they were "Giarretto junkies" (as they were affectionately called back in Iowa). Most IFSAP cases are processed through a diversion program that has reportedly grown "more hard-nosed" than Giarretto's. The county is small enough (with a population of 300,000) to permit discussions of virtually all cases that require attention in the weekly IFSAP meetings. The program's coordinator, who is employed by the Social Services Department, reviews the previous week's minutes and advises the group of new developments—court orders needed, interviews scheduled, recantations reported. Then the discussion begins: a social worker describes her efforts to monitor a home; a policeman talks about the lack of manpower that makes it difficult for him to interview both children and suspects in a timely fashion. The assistant county attorney shares his first impressions of an alleged perpetrator with offender therapist Paul Hanna (see appendix): "You should take a look at him," he tells Hanna, "but from everything we're hearing, you probably won't like what you see."[34]

Philadelphia's Law Enforcement Pilot Project holds very different meetings, which are monthly, not weekly. Although the composition of the group is similar to IFSAP's (minus the offender treatment component), group members could never discuss even a fraction of their cases at their meetings (given the city's 1.7 million population). They discuss problems instead. The meetings began in 1978, and despite the group's name there are no plans to end them. Although they are only monthly, there is homework. Committees meet and report back to the large group. Naomi Post, formerly of the Support Center for Child Advocates (but still a member of the group), plays an active role, discussing an upcoming seminar organized for judges. The group discusses a new family court judge who is said to have issued "bizarre" decisions, sending children home to "high-risk, dangerous situations." The judge does not understand the dynamics of incest cases, someone notes. Post suggests that she be encouraged to attend the seminar, and someone else suggests that a women's group that supported her election be asked to have a talk with her.

Plans to begin joint interviews of children by police and social workers—long discussed and often delayed—are discussed once more. An assistant district attorney mentions a hearsay bill that needs to be lobbied in the legislature. And then there is a presentation. Usually these are case studies by group members illustrating problems the group then endeavors to solve, but today there is a guest lecturer. He is employed by the City Health Department's Division of Disease Control. The Pilot Project wants to know what records are available for use in court, and how they may be obtained. They ask about chlamydia and are told it is not reportable in Philadelphia and is neither tested for nor tracked. Why? The tests are expensive and not entirely reliable, he says. Are labs mandated reporters of sexual abuse? No, he says. They frown. Why not? Because the department's primary role is to stop the spread of sexually transmitted diseases; reporting could inhibit that.[35]

Seattle also has monthly "network meetings," and in many ways they resemble Philadelphia's. They originated in the mid-1970s as part of a grant, and the first participants were actually paid to attend. When the grant ran out, they still came. They too discuss problems rather than cases (the county's population is 1.3 million), try to work out disagreements, kick around ideas. They talk about the possibility of prosecuting mandated reporters who fail to report abuse. Policeman Larry Daly (see appendix) complains about the difficulty he has getting through to CPS caseworkers on the phone and about the repeated failure of hospital employees to report cases to the police as well as to Social Services. A guest announces a new "consultation network" that consists of three physicians and a caseworker who may be telephoned by social workers, doctors, lawyers, and other professionals who wish free consultation on child abuse cases. They will also review medical records and may be available to provide expert testimony in court. Finally, Becky Roe leads a discussion of proposed sex crime revisions. They brainstorm possible name changes: child rape? sex with a child?[36]

Later, in her office, Roe offered advice to those considering launching a multidisciplinary team: "I guess my greatest advice is not to look for fancy gimmicks and fancy systems—to pick up the damn phone and call whoever it is you need to try to work out a system with, and meet with them, and do it. And don't spend a lot of time talking about it, and come out to Seattle, or have people from Seattle come out to you to tell you how to do it. You know, the bottom line of it is in sitting down and talking to people. Magically enough, you will get ideas on how to make the system better."

The Wave of the Future: Civil Lawsuits

It is only appropriate that this chapter end by discussing an area that is genuinely new and innovative. Of all the possibilities, none seems more important than civil lawsuits.

A variation of Murphy's law is proving true in this emerging area. Everyone who can sue will sue. And everyone who can be sued will be sued. Parents who claim they were falsely accused have sued social workers, police officers, and prosecutors. Parents, acting on behalf of abused children, have sued doctors, social workers, and various child care facilities and government agencies. This is not to say, of course, that the suits will be successful. Given the speed with which cases move through the civil courts, the juries will probably be out for years.

We have already seen one example in the suit charging the Fresh Air Fund with negligence in its screening of caretakers (chapter 3), and there have been and will be many lawsuits charging organizations with negligence when children in their care are abused. Among the more interesting cases are those that attempt to hold liable government agents charged with licensing and monitoring child care facilities in which children were abused. Some of the other questions courts may answer in pending and future cases are:

Under what circumstances, if any: (1) is it malpractice for a doctor to fail to report abuse? (2) can a doctor be held liable for failure to report abuse? (3) is a public official liable for failure to investigate properly an abuse report? (4) is a public official liable for the emergency removal of a child from the home? (5) is a public official liable for failure to select or monitor properly a child's placement outside the home? (6) is a parent liable for failure to protect a child from abuse? (7) is a person who files a "bad faith" report of abuse liable? (8) can a court-appointed lawyer in an abuse and neglect proceeding be found to have provided ineffective assistance of counsel?[37]

Civil court decisions may well have profound effects on the field. And there is at least one area in which results are already emerging. In the past few years there has been a growing number of lawsuits brought by children charging parents with damages resulting from incest. And there have been at least a handful of clear successes. Some observers believe that, given the odds against offenders' incurring substantial punishment at the hands of the criminal justice system, lawsuits may be the most potent deterrent of all. But the obstacles remain formidable.

Undoubtedly the largest obstacle is the statute of limitations. There has a been a trend for states to extend the statute of limitations in sexual abuse cases in the criminal courts. Current laws range from Alaska's requirement that charges be filed within a year following the time the abuse is first reported or following the child's 16th birthday (whichever comes first), to ten years following the report of a nonmisdemeanor offense in Colorado.[38]

But the big battles are those yet to come in civil courts, where precedents will be set and large verdicts could result. And where the term "delayed discovery," referring to the time the victim first perceives a means of redress, is heard often and has so far spelled defeat.

The case study that follows is the story of one lawsuit brought by a woman against her father. It is also a study of the successes and failures, of the emotional roller coaster that those who have worked with incest survivors—and would-be survivors—know too well.

11

Case Study: Angela "Doe"

S HE seems to have everything going for her. She is young and pretty, she has a steady job she likes, and she lives in an affluent suburb of New York City. She does not look injured. In fact, that was the very argument used against her in court; she appears absolutely normal.

But she does not *feel* normal. And the reason is that her family, which also appeared normal, was not. Angela was sexually abused by her father for a period of four years, beginning when she was 12.

Her case, unfortunately, is not unique. It is not even unique in her own family; her two sisters were also abused. But what *is* unique is that Angela sued her father and in 1986, when she was 22, was awarded more than $350,000 in damages. Her lawyers believe it was the first successful case of its kind in New York State and at the time one of only a handful nationwide.

Nobody knows how many incest victims have sued their abusers—nor how many have won—but the number of cases is growing, according to Judith Musick, director of the Institute for the Study of Sexual Assault, in San Francisco. She knows the numbers are increasing, Musick said, by the number of successful case summaries included in the annual compendium the institute publishes.[1] And the volume of calls she receives has risen, even though the organization is known to the lawyers who provide her with information mainly by word of mouth.

The largest award Musick was aware of was in a 1985 case in which the jury awarded a Texas woman $10 million. The woman's father filed for bankruptcy, however, and she has yet to collect any of the judgment. There have been several other very high verdicts, Musick said, but these seem to have been largely symbolic gestures by juries when there appeared to be little chance the money would be collected, either because the defendant did not have it or because he had fled the jurisdiction. A great many of the cases are settled, she said, and many more are thrown out of court (often on statute of limitations issues) or are dropped by plaintiffs who succumb to the pressures of litigation—and the pain of reliving the past. And some of the most intense pressures may never appear in court (as we will see).

Although the barriers to winning such cases are still daunting, it is easier to bring one today than it was a few years ago, said Musick, who was trained as a sociologist. "You're not likely to walk into an attorney's office and have him turn you away because he's never heard of anything like this before," she said, adding: "Victims and parents of victims are more likely to react with anger than with shame," as they were until recently.

And cases like Angela's have made future litigation easier by establishing important legal precedents. Although Angela has previously shunned publicity, she granted an interview in order to discuss the importance of her case—and the lessons it presents.[2] She asked only that her name be changed (as it has in court papers, filed under Angela "Doe").

The Family

When Angela decided to sue she knew the move would not be popular, but she expected at least *some* support from her family. If from no one else, then from her sisters.

She was wrong.

Angela described the relentless pressure to which she was subjected during an interview at a restaurant across from Grand Central Station. (Her therapist later explained that she and Angela meet there regularly because although Angela has no problem riding the train from Westchester, she is afraid to take the subway to the therapist's Greenwich Village office—one of many fears caused by the abuse.)

"I've had negatives from grandparents, aunts and uncles, cousins, sisters—I've had it all round," said Angela. She and her paternal grandfather have rarely spoken since the case began, and her relationship with her grandmother has also been strained.

"My grandmother," she continued, "I mean she wants me to get what I deserve, and I think she's finally realizing that what he did was wrong, so that's fine, but she still doesn't want—it's her son and she doesn't want to see him . . . " She did not finish the sentence.

"But she still calls me up on the phone," she said after a pause, "and she's crying to me and I'm trying to explain it to her. I say that I just can't, you know, this is my decision and she's just going to have to live by it. I'm tired of living under people's planning."

She was particularly disappointed by the lack of support from her sisters "because I figured, you know, it happened to them, too, why aren't they supporting me? But I don't make it bother me because if I worried about everybody, I think I wouldn't be here today."

How she got "here today" is the story of a child who was exploited by her only surviving parent and who slowly, painfully, learned to fight back. In order to understand her fight, we have to go back to another struggle—this one fought by Angela's younger sister—on a night in late October 1981. At a time when her friends were busy preparing scary Halloween costumes, the horror for Angela's sister was all too real. The child, then just 13, was sexually assaulted that night by her father.

It was not the first time. Her father had first raped her a month earlier. But this time the youngster managed to fight him off and run from the house. When she reported the assault to the authorities, the family secret at last unraveled.

Frank Stern[3] had been living alone with his three daughters since the death of his wife eight years earlier. Angela and her older sister were abused repeatedly during at least half that time. Stern admitted as much in a Westchester County Family Court hearing following the disclosure of the abuse,[4] and at the conclusion of the hearing the two younger children, who were still minors, were placed in the custody of relatives.

Three months later, Stern pleaded guilty to a criminal charge of second-degree rape in Westchester County Court. In addition to five years' probation, he was ordered to see a psychiatrist and to avoid unsupervised visits with his daughters.

The Genesis of a Lawsuit

And there the story might have ended, had Angela not kept in touch with her family court–appointed attorney—Andrew Vachss (see chapter 3).

When Angela called him in late 1984, however, it was not with the idea of filing a lawsuit; it was with a problem. She wanted to go to college but could not afford it. She believed that her mother had intended to pay for her education but was told by relatives that everything had been left to her father.

"Her father was approached through an intermediary and asked for money for the child to go to school," said Vachss.[5] "She was refused in such a way that upset her very much, and she was in great despair because her mother was dead, her father was going to do nothing for her, and she felt truly abandoned and without resources. She wanted to know if anything could be done, and it's then that we began to discuss the possibility of bringing a legal action to make him pay for what he did.

"The idea of making a perpetrator responsible for his crime has a particular attractiveness when the criminal justice system hasn't done so," Vachss continued. "Probation had no impact on this guy's life whatsoever. So, in effect, he was able to rape his daughter on a continuing basis and not suffer any disruption—indeed, he may have even economically benefited because, as far as I know, he stopped paying child support once the children were removed from his home."

Vachss brought in Melvin Borowka, who specialized in personal injury cases. The two had collaborated successfully on a number of occasions in addition to the Fresh Air Fund lawsuits (chapter 3), and they said in interviews that they were working on another half-dozen suits involving children allegedly abused in schools, camps, churches, day care centers, and foster homes.

Borowka had no particular interest in or knowledge about child abuse before Vachss first called him. The association has been successful, according to Borowka, because it brings together their different backgrounds, disciplines, and legal skills.[6] Vachss's strengths are in investigating, formulating strategy, framing appellate issues, and providing support and services for clients. Borowka's expertise is in torts and the mechanics of personal injury actions.

Despite the satisfaction of trying cases "on the cutting edge of the law" and of "creating a remedy where one has not always been available," and despite the personal reward derived from "standing up for the right side," Borowka doubted lawyers will soon be lining up for these cases. "It's a difficult, difficult area—one that's very gut-wrenching from an emotional level . . . and it's not a standard situation where you look at a case and you know what the value of the case will be."

But such cases can be lucrative, he acknowledged. "I don't think anyone goes into battle without thinking that there's going to be a victory," he said. "If we were able to do everything that we could, I believed that we could obtain a sizable judgment. . . . Judgments are only that which would adequately compensate the victim for the loss sustained. Unfortunately for the victims in these cases, the loss is large—that's why it justifies large verdicts. This is not something that's just for sympathy or for inflaming the passions of the jury. These are young people whose lives have been destroyed, in many cases."

Victory and a large verdict were a long way off, however, when Vachss and Borowka filed their first brief in February 1985. They charged that Stern had physically, sexually, and psychologically abused Angela, had neglected to perform "the minimal duty of care required of a parent," and, as a result, Angela had sustained severe and permanent physical and psychological injuries. They asked for $10 million.

Stern was represented at the time by Thomas Altieri, who has a general practice with no particular interest in sexual abuse cases. In fact, Stern was the first client he had defended on such charges, representing him in the criminal and family court proceedings before the lawsuit. Altieri insisted, however, that inexperience in this area was no disadvantage and that he achieved the best possible results for his client—particularly in getting him probation in the criminal case.

In responding to the complaint, Altieri denied all charges—despite the fact that he had been standing next to his client in family court when Stern admitted he had repeatedly raped his daughter. Angela's lawyers moved for summary judgment, claiming that the facts were indisputable and that Angela had been "abused enough by defendant. She should not now have to recount the unfortunate experiences of her childhood because of [Stern's] deceit."[7]

Altieri said in an interview that he knew he had a weak case and that the only question was, How much money is she going to get?[8] Vachss and Borowka were also convinced Angela would be awarded summary judgment. In fact, Angela herself is the only one who said she had doubts. ("I never made myself believe I was winning," she explained. "I didn't want to get my hopes up just in case I did lose.") As it turned out, Angela's pessimism was well founded.

Defeat

In a one-sentence decision, Justice Joseph Jiudice denied summary judgment: "Issues of fact are present which preclude this Court from holding this plaintiff is entitled to relief as a matter of law."[9] Reached in his chambers, Justice Jiudice said he had no recollection of the case.[10] Asked to speculate on the reasons for the judge's decision, even Altieri confessed that he was mystified.

But it was that very defeat that made the case so important. Without it, there would have been no appeal. And had Vachss and Borowka not appealed, there would have been no appellate decision establishing a precedent and, in effect, an incest tort in New York State.

"I'm glad that we didn't get summary judgment," Vachss said. "That would have been one judge doing the right thing. Now all judges in the [state] supreme court will do the right thing. That issue is now laid to rest by an Appellate Division that made a decision that was both legally and morally correct. I'm always glad to 'lose' like that. Make my day."

When the appellate court awarded Angela summary judgment, they sent the case back to the trial court for the sole purpose of assessing her damages. But the appellate decision was not a total victory for Angela; it was a victory on only one of the causes of action: for assault and the intentional infliction of emotional distress. The court dismissed the negligence cause of action. As it turned out, the ruling did not affect the final result. But had the defense prepared a stronger case, the ruling might have been pivotal.

The statute of limitations for negligence is three years. Angela filed the suit within three years of having reached majority (when the statute starts running). But the negligence complaint was dismissed, leaving only the charge of assault, which carries a statute of limitations of only one year. Angela did not come close to filing within a year of majority.

But Altieri never argued that the statute of limitations had expired on either cause of action. The omission was particularly surprising because statute of limitations arguments are routinely raised by defense attorneys trying these cases—and often successfully.

Altieri said he believed the suit was brought within the prescribed time. Vachss called the statute of limitations "a bogus issue," insisting that the clock should not necessarily begin running when an incest victim reaches her majority. "Incest certainly can traumatize you into a kind of 'psychiatric coma' where you walk and you talk, so you appear to be 'normal,' but you are severely impaired," he said. "During that period of impairment, I don't believe a person should have the statute of limitations running against him—especially where the original trauma took place while they were a child."

Another argument he advanced is that the statute should not begin until a victim perceives she has been victimized and also perceives a remedy. Under that theory, Angela's clock started "when she realized that there is a way of seeking redress"—shortly before the suit was filed. Although it did not affect Angela's case, the issue is one that is likely to be contested again and again in courtrooms around the country.

Likewise, the negligence issue is sure to be relitigated. Vachss said that although he disagreed with the dismissal of the action, since the court simultaneously awarded summary judgment, he had no grounds on which to appeal. He still believes a negligence tort "could, should, and eventually will be made, if not by me, by someone else." He explained his reasoning: "The law says if you're a mother and your husband is abusing your child and you know about it but don't do anything, you're guilty of child neglect. If the law imposes that duty on a person who is not the perpetrator, how could it impose a lesser duty on the person who is?"

Even though the appellate decision meant Angela had won, neither she nor her lawyers viewed what remained as a victory lap. From the outset, all three had anticipated that the highest hurdles would never appear in court or in legal briefs. And looking back they said that, if anything, they underestimated the power of family pressure.

Concerned about Angela's ability to withstand such pressure, her lawyers had her evaluated by Flora Colao shortly after they filed the suit. Colao had previously worked with the lawyers' clients in the three Fresh Air Fund suits (see chapter 3)—all under an unusual arrangement. She evaluates and treats the clients with the understanding that her fee will come out of the judgment, if the clients win (or settle), and that if they do not, Vachss and Borowka will pay her themselves.

"I told them that I thought that it was very important that she undertake [the lawsuit]," Colao said.[11] "I felt that it was a real act of strength on her part to be doing that and that yes, it was going to be difficult, but I really felt she could handle it." It was nearly a year before Angela began seeing the therapist, however. The reason, Colao said, is that "she saw going to therapy as a sign of weakness and going to therapy also made her have to deal with the reality of the aftereffects [of the incest]. . . . She was very busily running away from her feelings. When she found she couldn't run anymore and [the trial] was getting closer and her anxiety built up, she came to me to relieve the anxiety."

The Trial

As the trial approached, Angela's lawyers anticipated two main problems: they did not know how their client would hold up—both in and out of court—and they did not know how their evidence would be received. It can be difficult establishing damages that cannot be seen, explained Vachss, adding, "Lawyers would rather have a broken finger than a cluster [migraine] headache because they can prove the break . . . They want to know: 'Where's the medicals? Where's the X rays?' Even the concept of psychiatric damages, unaccompanied by physical trauma, is difficult."

The lawyers decided to waive a jury and let the judge try the case in order to expedite the trial and avoid forcing Angela to testify before a group of strangers. The move also made it easier to avoid unwanted publicity. And finally, the lawyers were wary of problems that a jury might create, such as confusing the question of damages with Stern's responsibility for causing them (which had already been decided by the appellate court), or coming in with a verdict so outlandish that it might be altered on appeal.

As it turned out Altieri was also looking to waive a jury, fearing their emotions might lead to a very large verdict. "Plus," Altieri added, "this particular judge, when he was a private practitioner, spent his career in the personal injury field . . . I felt that he, the judge, would turn to plaintiff's counsel and say, in effect, 'Yes, you're entitled to damages. Let's not get emotional about this case. I mean the facts are horrendous, but what the hell are her damages here? What has she sustained? Now you haven't brought me a doctor, you haven't brought me a psychiatrist, you haven't shown a series of medical treatment . . .' " Without any corroborating evidence from an M.D., he did not even think the judge would allow in Colao's testimony.

The speculation ended July 28, 1986. Seventeen months after the suit was filed and nearly five years after the abuse was first disclosed, the trial itself lasted less than three hours.

Colao was qualified as an expert witness and testified about Angela's fears and anxieties, her low self-esteem, her inability to trust others, and her sense of having been betrayed. She spoke of Angela's feeling "that part of her died when this happened and that it's a part of her that she'll never get back—that she lost her childhood . . ." Angela attempts to block out unpleasant memories by working extremely hard in school, at her job, and in the gym so as to avoid having to think about them, Colao added.

Finally it was Angela's turn. Her anxiety had been building as the day approached—much of it centered on the impending confrontation with her father. "I was mostly afraid of him," she said, "having to face him, say things about him in court." Although she was nervous at first, she said the judge's reassurances helped calm her. Borowka asked her very few questions—basically, when the events occurred, how she felt about the situation, and how she felt generally. "Our position," he explained, "is that she would not really be competent to testify as to her damage, and the framework for that was established by the testimony of the certified social worker, who said that the plaintiff blocked all of this out."

The cross-examination was conducted by Rocco Cardillo, Jr., whom Altieri brought in to handle the trial (he was out of town). It too was very brief. "As I recall," said Cardillo, "I only asked her basic things: whether or not she was working, where she was residing, trying to elicit that she has a fairly normal life-style. I mean she's not confined to a bed, she's working, she went to school, she went to college . . . she's gainfully employed, she has a good work record, that was basically what I was trying to show."[12] Cardillo acknowledged that the main reason he did not cross-examine Angela more extensively was to avoid creating sympathy for her.

Plaintiff rested, and that was it for the testimony. There was no rebuttal evidence at all. "This [case] is all on the testimony of the social worker," Altieri explained. "Looking back in hindsight is very easy, but at the time, when this person is testifying, you have to conclude that this was an extremely weak case as far as damages were concerned. . . . Let's drop it all here and let the judge decide."

And that was what they did. Cardillo said he could not recall his summation well enough to synopsize. According to Borowka, Cardillo argued for no damages whatsoever, asserting that nothing was wrong with Angela, that she was perfectly normal, as evidenced by her employment and scholastic records. If anything was wrong with her, however, it was attributable to her mother's death. Furthermore, he claimed that Stern gave his daughter money from time to time and that she sent him a Father's Day card, indicating that the relationship was not as bad as described.

In his own summation, Borowka basically reviewed Colao's testimony, emphasizing the trauma and its severe and permanent effects, such as her loss of childhood, her inability to cultivate intimate relationships with members of either sex, her feelings that she is "different" and is a "bad person."

Altieri said he expected a verdict of "under $50,000." Cardillo would not say what he expected. Vachss and Borowka said only that they expected considerably more than the $100,000 they were willing to settle for at the pretrial conference. The judge did not disappoint them. He announced his verdict from the bench: $350,000 general damages, $11,700 special damages (to pay for therapy), and $255 court costs, totaling $361,955.

Cardillo was "surprised," Altieri "taken aback" by the size of the verdict. In an interview, Justice Vincent Gurahian said it would be "inappropriate" to discuss how he arrived at the figure.[13] He acknowledged that "it's probably a little more difficult to set [damages] on psychological [injuries] because it's something less tangible" but added that it was not an especially difficult case to decide. "I mean it was not an easy case to decide in the sense of how you arrive at the figure," he continued, "but there's nothing peculiar about the case itself other than the peculiar set of facts from which it emanates."

The judge said he was unaware that the suit was apparently the first of its kind in the state. "I never made any assumption one way or another," he said. "To me, it's another lawsuit. Someone claims a wrongful act and they claim they were damaged as a result of the wrongful act. There was no defense issued. There was no testimony to rebut any of the testimony produced by the plaintiff's case. Strictly—it almost came down to an inquest."

Angela was both "relieved" and "shocked" by the result. "I didn't expect that much," she said. But "I didn't feel sorry for my father," she added firmly. "I just felt he was stupid enough taking me all this way thinking he could win—I guess he was misadvised by his own lawyers—but I didn't feel sorry for him."

Nor did she believe her father had learned anything from the lawsuit. "He's still the same way," she said, "he still doesn't think he did anything wrong . . . If he would have come and said he's sorry to me or said something, then I would have maybe, you know— but he never said anything."

Angela's therapist saw the suit as the first step in her patient's struggle to change "from victim to survivor." Asked what the victory means to her, Angela said: "Freedom. It means to me that he can't— there's no way anymore that he could manipulate me, knowing that if he tried, I wouldn't stand still and just take his abuse."

She hoped that the money, too, would buy her freedom. "I would like to move out [of her aunt and uncle's house] and find a place of my own, get my life together, do some things I've never done," like travel, she said.

Beyond what the victory meant to his client, Vachss believed its implications for other victims and potential victims may be vast. Most experts believe few incest offenders are prosecuted, fewer are convicted, and fewer still are punished significantly. "Most incest offenders operate under the assumption that their child will grow up and they will get away with what they did, that there will never be retribution," said Vachss. "Taking financial resources from a perpetrator may do more to deter other such activity than the very remote threat of criminal prosecution."

In July 1987, the judgment was satisfied in full. Angela agreed to accept a cash payment of $150,000 along with an interest in property owned by her father, Borowka said.

Yet according to Angela the family pressure, far from diminishing, actually increased following the verdict. Early in the case, her relatives did not consider it likely she would win. When she not only won but was awarded a large sum, the response from virtually all her relatives was identical. "Their feeling was, 'Take what you deserve, but don't throw him out in the street,' " she said. They wanted her to settle for less, despite the verdict.

Although she seemed weary—battle-worn—from the long succession of confrontations, Angela clearly relished the validation she found in victory.

"Finally," she said, "I won this one."

12

The State of the Art

Objectivity and Responsibility

WHEN you blow away all the smoke, most people say they want two things: objectivity and responsibility. Boosters and critics of the system alike say they want objective investigations conducted by responsible investigators. They want professionals to approach their tasks without bias and to perform them in a manner that elicits the truth without influencing the result. And they want these professionals held responsible for their actions. At least that is what the most responsible and objective advocates on both sides say.

It looks straightforward on paper. Unfortunately, that is not where it counts. Contrary to popular opinion, a trial is not a search for the truth. A trial is an adversarial proceeding in which each side seeks a desired result (and each side's advocates should not be expected to be objective observers of the system—or criticized when they are not). A defendant charged with sexual abuse does not enter a courtroom to learn the truth, nor does a child who says she was abused. "You don't need a judge or a jury to tell you what happened," Lucy Berliner tells her child clients. "You know what happened. You were there."

But as we said at the outset of this book, not much in the world of child sexual abuse is clear-cut, and for every statement one expert makes you will find many more who will dispute it. Take Berliner's statement. Lee Coleman would argue that in many cases children do not know what happened, cannot distinguish what they remember from what they were told. And if you looked long enough, you could undoubtedly find an "expert" to tell you that many offenders do not know what happened either.

Despite the realities, despite the convolutions and imperfections of the system, we can still hope the result of a trial reflects the truth. We can still strive for objective, responsible investigations. We can still struggle to learn from the system's failures and mistakes and try to correct them. And anybody with knowledge of the system who is unwilling to admit that there are many failures and mistakes—of omission and commission—is either biased or irresponsible or both.

Few topics elicit as emotional a response as child sexual abuse. Even people with only a casual interest in the subject quickly become animated when discussing it. People with a serious interest grow more than animated. And those who are personally involved may be more than emotional. In discussing the reactions of parents who believe their children have been sexually abused, Kee MacFarlane remembered receiving a telephone call from social workers in the Midwest who wanted her to help them investigate allegations of mass molestation in a preschool. "Look," they said, "we don't know whether what we have on our hands is the real thing and a lot of teachers are molesting kids, or whether we have a bunch of hysterical parents."

"What makes you think that those two things are incompatible?" MacFarlane replied.

In fact, unfeigned hysteria might allay suspicions that parents have coached the children. Hysteria is hardly an abnormal reaction to such circumstances. But it does not say anything about the abuse—only about the parents' beliefs. Conversely, when a man learns he has been accused of raping a child, he too may react with hysteria. But unfortunately that tells you nothing about the truth of the allegation.

It is all too easy to assign undue significance to these emotional reactions. The Grays were openly angry at West Point (see chapter 5) and were rumored to be pursuing a personal vendetta. Judy Coletti testified in as composed a manner as she could during her Illinois hearings and was criticized as cold and aloof. When she made an emotional plea to the judge to protect her child, she was viewed as hysterical. It is just as easy to impute character disorders to the accused, and it must happen all the time.

What does all this prove? Nothing about guilt or innocence. It proves how difficult it is to separate emotion from fact, and how easy it is to get caught up in emotion. There are crusaders who believe all children all the time, and there are others who believe all the accused all the time. Some are reacting to personal experiences in which the system truly failed them. Through their courage and perseverance, they may become committed and constructive lobbyists. But when their minds are closed to cases that do not conform to their own beliefs, they may damage their own credibility and that of their cause. And when they embrace others who are disingenuous or just plain dishonest, they may do more damage still. It is time for ombudsmen—whether hired, elected, or self-proclaimed—to investigate before they speak.

And it is time for straight talk. It is time for tough questions. It is time for those on the "same side" to challenge false and misleading information. When treatment programs claim less than 10 percent recidivism rates, they should be challenged. When prosecutors claim to have evidence they fail to produce, some hard questions should be asked. When researchers base conclusions on a half-dozen cases, objections should be raised. And when an "expert" says that most fathers accused of incest are jailed, there should be demands for data.

Straight talk means that it is time for all parties to acknowledge that child sexual abuse is a large problem (although how large is as yet unclear), and that few of the perpetrators are caught and fewer still suffer serious punishment, even when prosecution occurs and is successful. Of those perpetrators who are confronted, the vast majority neither confess nor desist voluntarily, and those who stop usually do so only when forced. Sexual abuse cases pose extraordinary challenges for the entire system, from social worker to defense attorney, and they probably always will, despite the best efforts of legislatures, courts, and the various participants. Though inherently imperfect, the process should be made as professional and objective as possible. Following are some recommendations proposed to do just that.

Recommendations

1. *Panels of expert validators should be chosen by courts to interview children alleged to have been sexually abused.*[1]

Without doubt, validation is the most controversial area in the field. Even if it is done well, it will continue to be subject to heated disputes because, as prosecutor Barbara Egenhauser observed (in chapter 4), it is the center of the case against the accused and the logical target of defense attack. So attacks themselves should not be seen as proof that there is a problem. But interviews are not always done well.

The purpose of the panel is, at a minimum, to provide courts with a list of true experts from which to choose when one is needed. Used another way, it can provide a structure through which all children alleged to have been sexually abused may be interviewed.

The key is a selection process free from financial or political influence. A court (or district) could select a panel from a list of nominees presented by a court-appointed committee. Such a committee might consist of criminal and family court judges, prosecutors, defense attorneys, police officers, social workers, and law guardians. The validators themselves would not be restricted to any one profession, such as psychologists or social workers. Physicians, for example, might also be nominated. The committee would promulgate qualifications for the position, giving due consideration to appropriate education, training, and experience in interviewing children and in testifying in court. Candidates should also have a track record demonstrating that every child interviewed was not found to have been abused. (One should not simply compare the percentages of candidates, however, since a social worker in a hospital emergency room, for example, is likely to see a higher percentage of indicated cases than is a therapist in private practice.)

The panels could be used in a variety of ways. Lawyer Andrew Vachss, whose idea this is (see chapter 8), conceives of validators as forensic specialists comparable to ballistics experts and medical examiners, although admittedly their skill is more of an art than a science (as opposed to the others). He would like to see the use of validators become just as routine in sexual abuse cases (whether they are destined for family court, criminal court, or neither) as the use of those other specialists is in cases where the evidence falls in their domain.

In cases where a court's involvement precedes the allegations, as in a custody case during which an allegation arises, all parties would agree in advance to accept the court's appointment of a validator. (This is not to say that they agree to accept the validator's opinion, which they are welcome to contest; only that they agree that the validator appointed by the court will be the one and only expert to interview the child.) Then three experts could be chosen randomly from the panel, and each side could have the power to veto one. In all other cases, the validator would be chosen randomly on a rotating basis.

It is also possible to conceive of a system in which the panel is relied on only for cases that present special problems, such as custody cases and the like.

However it is used, the system should be clearly defined. A clear provision should be that only one validation will be conducted, although that does not mean that it has to be done in one session. In addition, validators who are therapists should not be permitted to treat the children they interview, so as not to appear to have a financial interest in the result.

The court-appointed committee should establish a protocol outlining the proper method of conducting a validation. This should spell out what information a validator should review prior to and following the interview, where the interview should take place, and what methods the court deems admissible (anatomically correct dolls? drawings?). Arrangements for videotaping all validations should also be made. The panel should be subject to regular recertification, which could include peer review, to ensure quality and objectivity.

2. Panels of doctors should be designated by courts to conduct expert medical examinations of children who have allegedly been abused. They should be chosen along the same lines as the validators discussed above. All doctors should have the legal option of referring cases of suspected abuse to such panels rather than reporting them to their states' central registries.[2]

There has not yet been a great deal of publicity on the growing medical controversy in this area, but it is probably only a matter of time before it explodes in the same way that the battle of the mental health experts has.[3] And some of the same players will be involved; in fact, they already are.

Lee Coleman was the keynote speaker at VOCAL's Second National Conference, held, ironically, in Torrance, California, where archadversary Roland Summit is based. A brief description of his presentation at the October 1986 conference appeared in a VOCAL newsletter:

Dr. Coleman, psychiatrist and author, launched one segment of a two part presentation with the caveat, *"Doctors are not any smarter than anybody else . . . and in some cases they aren't even that."* This being so, he cautions us to not let ourselves be intimidated by the fact that some prosecution experts are medical doctors. In fact, he stated that, "You can become more knowledgeable in a particular area that is of interest to you than the people who are up there with the M.D. after their names."

The objective of the defense attaining this new mind set, he held, was to hammer home to the judge or jury that *medical fraud* is being foisted on the judicial system and on all concerned with child sexual abuse allegations. In this regard, Dr. Coleman referred to the absence of <u>any</u> "blind" studies which can establish scientifically the "normal" size of vaginal and anal openings in children of a range of ages. Further, he pointed out that those who claim to be able to determine abuse by referring to "abnormal" sized openings, themselves admit that there is no scientifically determined "normal" opening that has been established. He also criticized as being fraudulent, use of the term "consistent with." This term, he states, is intended to confuse the court into believing something significant is being said, when in fact nothing is.[4] (All emphasis in original.)

Clearly, Coleman has further expanded the issues he has chosen to address, as he acknowledged in an interview.[5] He said he has testified in courts as a medical expert on the "methods, conclusions, treatments, and writings" of doctors performing examinations in sexual abuse cases. "While I'm not qualified to do physical examinations myself," he said, "and would never agree to do it, I can still, as a doctor, study the state of the art. I can study what they're doing and see whether they even agree with each other. What's going on," he added, "is a medical fraud, in a high percentage of these cases . . . There's just as much unscientific claims being made there as in the interviews."

Coleman is not alone in broaching this subject. There have already been if not full-scale battles, at least skirmishes between medical experts in court. Walter Urban was prepared to raise the issue in the McMartin trial, had charges against his client not been dropped (see appendix). Dr. Jeffrey Gilbert has seen some of it firsthand.

Gilbert, an internist who heads the child sexual abuse unit at the New York City Health Department's Bureau of Sexually Transmitted Diseases (see chapter 2), has testified for the prosecution and he has testified for the defense. He starts with the presumption that children have not been abused, he said, "and I have to show myself that there's evidence that they were."[6] He argues for the importance of objectivity and asserts his own. "There's no pressure on me to find yes or no. This a patient who's in front of me . . . I have no personal gain to prove that children are being molested. I would much rather examine these kids and find they weren't molested.

"It's fine to testify for the defense," Gilbert said. "But testify to medical facts. When I'm called by the defense in a case, I will review the medical facts and I will say, 'Yes, this is consistent with the history,' or 'No, this is not,' and why." However, he has had occasion to observe doctors testify that gonorrhea was acquired through bedsheets and towels, that chlamydia can be contracted by a child from breathing it in the air, and to other "medical facts" he finds outrageous: "There are doctors now who are going to go out there and testify for what the defense wants to hear, and I know them and I see them, and I can tell you that they prostitute the truth, and they misrepresent the truth."

It was as a result of these experiences that Gilbert decided courts should appoint expert panels of doctors to ensure competent, objective medical examinations. When performed by an expert, such examinations need not be, and generally are not, traumatic (despite misconceptions to the contrary), Gilbert said. And he sees a further value in such a panel. As a realist, Gilbert recognizes that many doctors do not report sexual abuse because they do not want to be subjected to the anxiety and possible humiliation of cross-examination, or because they do not wish to lose the business that days of testimony may require, or for a variety of other reasons, including their own lack of expertise. He does not condone these reasons, but he recognizes them, he said, and he also recognizes that doctors are not being prosecuted for failure to report—and probably will not be soon.

The solution Gilbert proposes is that doctors be given the option of reporting suspected sexual abuse in the normal way—to the central registry, or the police, or Social Services—or by referring the case to the expert panel (but only the expert panel, rather than to another doctor who may be no more willing or qualified to examine the child than the doctor making the referral—as we saw all too clearly in chapter 9). If such an alternative increased reporting, thousands of children might benefit, Gilbert said.

3. *Just as there is a need for standardized protocols for validation interviews and medical examinations, there is a need for standardized protocols for child sexual abuse investigations, whether conducted by social workers, police, prosecutors, or others.*

This is not to say that protocols could or should be precisely the same in Alaska and Florida (and everywhere in between). But there should at least be recommended national standards that all professionals are aware of, even if all do not employ them. Some basic protocols are already virtually universal. For example: an alleged child victim in a sexual abuse case should not be interviewed in the presence of the alleged perpetrator. Where possible, the child should be interviewed alone in a neutral setting. Almost every protocol currently in use probably says something similar.

In fact, a comprehensive review of protocols would probably reveal many standard components. Radical differences in approaches are probably attributable more to inexperience and lack of training than to philosophical differences between competent agencies. But there is no reason why all jurisdictions should do things in precisely the same way. During criminal investigations in Seattle, prosecutors interview children while police officers take notes. Westchester County, New York, has a special police unit that conducts such interviews. There is no single way, and to try to impose one would probably be counterproductive for two reasons.

First, it is important for agencies that work together to solve problems in ways that suit their strengths and weaknesses. If there is no specialized police unit but there are highly skilled child protective workers in a county, then why should the police interview children just because that is the way it is done elsewhere? And second, the state of the art is not such that it can be said with anything approaching confidence that a particular protocol works best. There is room for experimentation. A national protocol is still worth having, however, because it *is* possible to say with some confidence what does *not* work best.

At this writing, a project is just under way to produce a "consensus" protocol in the handling of child sexual abuse cases recommended for the medical field. Joyce Thomas, formerly of Children's

Hospital in Washington, D.C., and now executive director of the newly founded Center for Child Protection and Family Support there, is spearheading the effort, in collaboration with the Surgeon General's Office.[7]

4. *There should be a reassessment of the value, if any, of psychological evaluations of an allegedly abusive parent and an accusing parent (when there is one) following an incest allegation—whether or not the allegation is related to a divorce and custody proceeding.*

It is one thing to interview a child in order to elicit information about what may or may not have happened to her. It may be difficult to do, and the results may be questionable or inconclusive. But it is quite another to evaluate someone for the purpose of determining whether he has a personality compatible with someone who molests children.

First, there is no psychological profile of the child molester to measure someone against. According to the best information currently available, all that can be said is that different types of people molest children for different reasons and under different circumstances. And there does not seem to be any more information about what kind of a person would falsely accuse a spouse of such a crime.

Second, even standardized psychological tests can yield different results at different times and when administered by different people. When an individual is under the intense pressure of a court case, knowing that the results of an evaluation can have a material effect on his future, the circumstances themselves can have a profound effect on the results, as almost all of the professionals involved in evaluating the Fahrnhorsts (see chapter 9) freely admitted.

Gregory Lehne's testimony in the Timberlake trial (also cited in chapter 9) illustrated the way such testimony can obfuscate rather than clarify the issues. Testifying without the jury present, Lehne described the personality of the pedophile, despite the fact that most people in the field, including his own collaborator in the Fahrnhorst case,[8] believe there is no such thing. He then explained why Timberlake did not fit the mold. Even if there were a reliable way for Lehne to make such a determination, Timberlake was not charged with being a pedophile; he was charged with having molested his patient. The distinction is likely to be lost on a jury, however, and for that reason its prejudicial effect would far outweigh its probative value. To his credit, Judge Whiting struck Lehne's testimony in the Timberlake trial, ruling that the field was not "sufficiently advanced."

In calling for a "reassessment," two things are proposed. Judges should carefully consider the value of such testimony before admitting it into evidence. As one professor of psychiatry wrote: "Testimony involving psychiatric or psychologic study of the parents is irrelevant and should not be admitted. I submit that such study adds nothing but innuendo and prejudice. As Newberger and Daniel have said, 'Investigating the parents to determine culpability in child abuse cases has been characterized as "clinically unhelpful, ethically absurd and intellectually unsound . . . " The clinician may find himself playing a detective game for which he is professionally unprepared.' "[9]

Lee Coleman agreed with this sentiment wholeheartedly, suggesting that it was one of the few areas on which he and his critics would likely agree.[10]

In cases where such testimony is required by a court, it should be conducted by psychologists and psychiatrists who are chosen from a panel on a rotating basis in a manner similar to the way other experts are selected in the proposals described earlier. Without regulation, the Fahrnhorst fiasco will be repeated ad infinitum. The Baby M trial presented another example of the inevitable confusion that results when a court makes no effort to winnow the experts to a manageable and objective group.[11] The surrogate mother in that case was evaluated by a parade of therapists chosen by the prosecution, the defense, and the baby's law guardian, inundating the judge with a mass of contradictory analysis and recommendations.

In an article on the questions the Baby M case raised, Dr. Richard Gardner, a clinical professor of child psychiatry at the College of Physicians and Surgeons of Columbia University, was quoted as saying, "I would not make a custody evaluation for either side, but only if I were court-appointed. The best evaluation is impartial, rather than an advocate for either side."[12] Gardner, author of *Family Evaluation in Child Custody Litigation*, added, "A psychiatric diagnosis does not tell you much about a person's parental capacity, unless the problem is debilitating."

In the same article, Dr. William Hodges, a clinical psychologist at the University of Colorado, said, "There is no empirical evidence to show that a parent's behavior during a custody evaluation is a true predictor of how fit that parent might be as the child grows.

One problem is that you are seeing people when they are upset, angry, hurt or frightened, and you are trying to guess what they would be like when not under stress. It's small wonder that experts can disagree."

It is worth recalling that the surrogate mother in that case once threatened to accuse the biological father of having sexually abused her 10-year-old daughter.[13] She never did, but one cannot help but wonder how such an accusation would have affected the psychologists' and psychiatrists' evaluations. And would the lawyers have called on the same experts, a separate team of sexual abuse experts, or both?

5. Independently funded evaluations of offender treatment programs should be undertaken immediately by professionals who are both experienced in the field and committed to objective research.

Several therapists who work at treatment facilities considered highly reputable within the profession spoke of the importance of this kind of review. Sandi Baker, executive director of the Sacramento Child Sexual Abuse Treatment program, said she believed research would prove her program effective, "but if it proves something different, then we need to know that for the field also and change and modify what we're doing to be more effective.

"I would welcome it. I would love to see it happen. And I wouldn't want it to come out of my treatment budget," she added.[14] Not only would research prove financially debilitating to some programs, but true independence would be impossible without independent funding. The need for independent researchers was also emphasized by Baker. Her program has regular internal "post mortems," Baker said, at which the staff looks at problems. One thing they discovered was that therapists were unconsciously colluding with clients who asserted they were cured.

"They wanted to be successful therapists," Baker said, "so when they'd say, 'Do you still have a desire to molest your kid or have fantasies?' and the client would say no, we wanted to hear that, so we weren't pushing it. . . . We were not helping them deal with it. Everybody was in a collusion to be successful, instead of knowing dynamically that that wouldn't happen that simply."

There is no way to be sure, but it would not be surprising if the problem were widespread in these programs. And the same phenomenon undoubtedly occurs among therapists dealing with victims, as well. Kee MacFarlane noted an example. "I know a woman who has become fascinated with these satanic cases," she said. "She hasn't been involved with any of these preschools, but she's done charts of all the different things that kids have said and is trying to do sort of an analysis of it, and she has like four or five different points. And she has grown the largest practice I've ever seen of ritualistic satanic abuse cases. Now, I wouldn't trust her anymore because she's starting to get it in every kid."[15]

The importance of evaluators who are knowledgeable in the field cannot be overemphasized. The "evaluation" Jerome Kroth conducted of Giarretto's program was counterproductive in that it validated an absurd statistic,[16] the existence of which calls into question all recidivism rates in the field. Kroth accepted statistics (from a variety of sources) that no one with knowledge of the field would take seriously—incuding Giarretto himself. It demonstrated once again that any research is not necesssarily better than none at all.

Offender treatment programs are by no means the only ones that could benefit from independent evaluation (although they do seem to be in greatest need). Philadelphia's Support Center for Child Advocates and the Polk County (Iowa) Intra-Family Sexual Abuse Program both were subjected to what was described as independent evaluation.[17] The Iowa evaluation seemed particularly valuable and might well serve as a model for others. The report that resulted is over one hundred pages, includes specific recommendations, and describes broad systemic and logistical problems alike. It manages to convey a sense not only of the strengths and weaknesses of the program as a whole, but also of some specific problems the individuals involved must contend with.[18]

6. Polygraph examinations should not be relied on as a source of information about sexual abuse.

The results of polygraphs are not admitted in court, but they are still widely used in the field and may be influential. For example, Gerald Fahrnhorst (see chapter 9) took two polygraphs, one at the request of Social Services, while Sarah refused the agency's request. The agency had no legal right to make this demand on either parent, but it seemed influenced by the parents' choices.

Although polygraphs cannot be admitted into evidence because they have not been proved scientifically reliable, Judge Whiting allowed testimony on Gerald's tests, adding that he could not consider them in his decision. Why, then, did he allow the testimony in the first place?

In the West Point case, the FBI made decisions during the crucial early weeks of its investigation on the basis of polygraphs. There is no way of knowing how often the tests are administered in sexual abuse investigations and with what results. Sometimes there may be utility in doing so. Undoubtedly confessions are coaxed from some abusers who fear facing the machine. And others confess after "failing the test." But the danger lies in what happens when a suspect "passes." Some of them are ultimately convicted in court. But that is less likely when investigators treat a polygraph as dispositive and follow it with some cursory questions before summarily closing the case.

Some men pay private practitioners to administer the tests (as Gerald did for his first exam). This obviously raises additional questions of reliability, but polygraphs can never be viewed as definitive no matter who administers the test and who pays. An unusual and troubling precedent may have been set when *The Sacramento Bee*, as part of its investigation into a highly publicized sexual abuse case, paid for a suspect's polygraph test—which he "passed." The paper duly reported this information, along with the flaws it said had undermined the police investigation.[19]

Asked whether use of the test was an implicit endorsement of its validity, the paper's executive editor said he did not think it was, adding, "I have no problems with the ethics of it."[20]

A more conventional use of the polygraph is by offender treatment programs, seeking to extract honest answers from clients. Northwest Treatment Associates in Seattle uses them to see whether men are following the treatment program, according to therapist Tim Smith. But Smith acknowledged the dangers of giving the test credence—especially in this field in which offenders frequently use them to bolster cases—and he added that the results were viewed with some skepticism and that no client was expelled following a failure.

Polygraphs in child sexual abuse cases should be used judiciously, and skepticism of the results is not just healthy—it is essential.

7. Education must be expanded, training must be provided, and licensing must be initiated for professionals working in the child sexual abuse field.

At present, doctors receive little or no training on this topic in medical schools. One sure way to change that would be for the National Board of Medical Examiners to include a number of relevant questions on the examinations students must pass for their medical licenses. Medical schools would magically find time for a subject currently ignored. Alternatively, if doctors were going to jail for their failure to report, medical schools might well add a few lectures—at their students' insistence.

The education of medical residents, psychologists, teachers, and social workers should also be greatly expanded. It would be particularly useful for those who are likely to have contact with the courts (such as pediatricians and child protective workers) to receive specific instruction in testifying. Without it, they are often forced to learn "on the job"—to the detriment of the case and, sometimes, at the expense of the child.

The issue of professional credentials has so far remained on the back burner; it has been raised only occasionally, when a witness's qualification as an expert is challenged in court, for example. But it is a troubling subject that is likely to be the center of future controversy. One problem is that there are no degrees in child sexual abuse. To assume that a child psychiatrist or a psychologist or a social worker has special expertise, by sole virtue of a degree, is ludicrous. Coleman was certainly right when he told the VOCAL convention that a medical degree does not necesssarily make an individual more knowledgeable on this subject than a layperson. But there is no shortage of people—with and without degrees—who claim to be experts. And neither the courts nor the general public should be forced to be true experts themselves merely to identify one.

Those who are considered most knowledgeable within the field have for the most part learned through experience. They have also read extensively, written on the subject, and exchanged views with colleagues at conferences. Some began their work when the profession was in its infancy and have grown as the field has grown. But as the profession enters adolescence, there is a need for a more efficient means of education than trial and error. Teachers, curricula, and specialized degree programs are needed, as are licenses to ensure that those who claim expertise meet certain minimal standards of knowledge.

Coleman and Ralph Underwager, a Minneapolis psychologist who has also been active testifying for the defense, have along with others claimed that their expertise is in mental health, and that has been their standing to speak on this subject. But they have become spokesmen on child sexual abuse in general and are frequently quoted as experts on the subject (a characterization they do not seem to have resisted). They have a right to speak out, and their criticism may ultimately prove salutary. But if they are going to speak as experts, they have a responsibility to make themselves knowledgeable. That knowledge should even include—should especially include—the work of those with whom they have publicly disagreed. Yet both men admitted in depositions taken in the Country Walk case that they had read but one or two of the authors recognized as leaders within the field. (Coleman said that the deposition did not reflect his true knowledge and that he has since read much more.)[21]

Not speaking about specific individuals but about professional responsibility in general, Lucy Berliner said, "I think you have no business in a field where there is a body of knowledge, deciding that you don't have to know that . . . To me, the essence about being a professional is that you know something that other people don't know. Ten years ago, that wasn't really the case . . . there wasn't a specialized field. There wasn't a huge body of knowledge, there weren't national conferences and seminars and workshops, so ten years ago I think it was perfectly legitimate that people started fumbling around and trying what they thought worked. There's no excuse for that now . . . I think there are plenty of people in the field who consider themselves to be quite knowledgeable, who have chosen just not to read, or make known to them certain parts of the information because it conflicts with ideas that they hold dear."[22]

Required course reading should include the backlash as it has appeared in the popular media, as well as the accommodation syndrome. Although it is unprofessional for critics to be ignorant of the vast body of literature in the field, it is not unprofessional but it seems a mistake for someone like David Finkelhor, an important author and researcher who is among the most knowledgeable and respected professionals in the field, to ignore Coleman, whose articles he admitted he had not read (though he expressed an interest in doing so).[23] Kee MacFarlane also admitted never having read the man who has been one of her most severe critics, explaining that she had avoided doing so mainly "out of self-protection."[24]

The issue of licenses, however, is likely to take on a more concrete meaning than individual definitions of professional responsibility. Washington State's Department of Licensing and its Examining Board of Psychology have been sued for permitting Northwest Treatment Associates to practice in the field of psychology without licenses (potentially a misdemeanor offense). In a separate action by the same plaintiff, Northwest and three of its therapists were sued for malpractice.[25] Founded in 1977, Northwest has a reputation as being one of the best programs of its kind. The therapists named in the suit all have degrees, although none in psychology. Two have Master's degrees in counseling (M.Ed.) and the third, a psychiatrist, holds an M.D. Their education and, more important, experience in the field would seem to make them far more qualified to evaluate and treat offenders than a freshly licensed psychologist—or any other therapists in the area. At this writing, it is unclear what the results of the suits will be, but whether successful or not, they do seem to point up the inadequacies of current licensing practices.

8. Multidisciplinary teams should be organized in all jurisdictions to facilitate handling of child sexual abuse cases. Particular emphasis should be placed on improving communication and coordination between criminal court and family court.

A rationale for this recommendation was offered in chapter 10. We should note in addition the importance of establishing a system that can survive the loss of individuals from the team. Such losses are inevitable. There will always be a high burnout rate in this field because it is hard, low-paying, and largely thankless work. If a system depends on a personal relationship between a prosecutor and a police chief for its smooth functioning, sooner or later it is going to be in trouble—unless they and the team surrounding them have the foresight to build a structure around the relationship. That is the great value of written protocols—of having interagency agreements signed off by representatives of each agency. They will not eliminate disputes—nothing can—but they provide a structure within which arguments may be settled, with the help of the entire team. And they can help the team survive the loss of key players.

9. *Publicly funded therapy for child victims should be available whether or not a court finds a child has been abused. Therapy for their parents and siblings should also be available for free or, if funds do not allow, on a sliding fee basis. Where successful prosecution occurs, sentences should include restitution to the family in an amount that will at least cover the cost of therapy for all.*

Consider the following scenario: the prosecutor says a child has been abused by a day care provider. Lee Coleman (testifying for the defense) claims the child has been abused not by the defendant but by the unethical techniques of investigators, adding that the child's parents have also been abused by officials who "brainwashed" them into believing the child was abused. It is a scenario that has already been staged,[26] and no matter whom you believe, it leaves a child and parents in need of therapy.

If a perpetrator is identified and convicted, then the sentence should require that the offender pay restitution of his victim's therapy as long as it is needed, even if that includes several years' hiatus before therapy is resumed, at puberty, for instance. But if he is unable or refuses to, public funds should be available. Ideally, the provider of the therapy should seek reimbursement from the offender, so that a child is not deprived of treatment if the offender, who has already abdicated his deepest obligations to the victim, does so again by failing to pay. That arrangement would also prevent a situation from occurring in which parents or the victim herself seeks to avoid therapy by using finances as an excuse (a problem described by therapist Flora Colao as frequent).

Such avoidance is not uncommon, as we saw in earlier chapters. In some cases parents actively deny reality, but in others they may not understand the importance of treatment or the avenues available. The grandchildren Don Tynan assaulted (see chapter 3), for example, saw a therapist for a few months following their disclosure, after which their parents were told the children were okay. The parents said later in an interview, however, that the girls (then 7 and 9) still wet their beds and masturbated frequently. The parents were troubled by the behavior, but when asked why they did not seek therapy for the children at Tynan's expense—an obligation imposed by the court's sentence—they said they were not aware that they could.

In such cases social workers and law guardians may be instrumental in a family's recovery—if they continue to monitor the family, as they should. Sexual abuse affects children in different ways, but early intervention is critical in at least some cases. And the more contact families have with knowledgeable professionals, the better the chances that their needs will be met.

The frontline workers may be even more important if the abuser is not identified or is not taken to court. In these cases the child may easily slip between the cracks. And these are the children who will be at risk of further abuse, and worse. The litany of destruction is by now familiar; all too often it includes drug abuse, alcoholism, prostitution, crime, and mental and emotional illness. Sometimes former victims grow up to abuse children themselves—physically or sexually or both. Other children never reach adulthood at all, succumbing to the teenage suicide epidemic that has been widely publicized of late.

Ironically, it may be easier in some cases to get help for a child who has already traveled down this self-destructive path than for one who is simply at risk. As Kee MacFarlane noted with dismay, "If you have a kid who's an alcoholic, you don't have to go to court to prove he's an alcoholic. And there's various substance abuse programs that are subsidized by the state and federal government. And we don't have to go, 'Well, gee, maybe he's really not an alcoholic.' I mean, you've got people who have diagnosed him as an alcoholic and you treat him." The same should be true of children believed to have been sexually abused, she said. And if others believe a child was not abused but "brainwashed," then the child may be no less in need.

But sometimes a therapist's assessment of what a child needs conflicts with a prosecutor's judgment of what may damage a case. In Jordan, the defense in the Bentz case argued that contact between the children and investigators, children and therapists, and among the children themselves had tainted their testimony. Since then, prosecutors have been increasingly nervous about the potential impact of such contact. There seems to be an as yet unpublicized debate as to whether a child should be treated before prosecution, and if so, whether group therapy is appropriate. Some professionals say individual therapy is best before the case comes to court; others say it is better to avoid treatment entirely. And in the McMartin case, several parents said in an interview that not only were their children kept apart, but even the parents were told by prosecutors to avoid contact with each other.

"We're in a community of two square miles, all our kids are the same age, and we're not supposed to talk to each other," said one exasperated mother. It was futile, another explained: "We finally realized that we were going to be accused of talking to each other anyway."[27]

As for their children, "we kept all the McMartin witnesses out of group therapy to the detriment of some of those kids," MacFarlane said. "In Jordan, one of the things they hung the D.A. on was the fact that they were housed in the same motel, never mind sitting around in a room talking about who touched their 'peepees.' And yet, without a doubt, if there's one thing we've learned in the history of this field, it's that group therapy is one of the most healing, confirming processes that can happen to children. If you can't do another thing for them, that's the treatment of choice, and so we're up against these terrible dilemmas around what should you do with a kid if he may end up being a witness."

Barbara Egenhauser, who prosecuted the Mount Vernon day care case, said that a certain amount of contact between children is inevitable and that juries are capable of understanding that.[28] "The children do not love to talk about their experiences," Egenhauser said. "Little girls don't get together and say, 'Well, what did he do to you?' I think it occurred to the jury that these little girls—you can't get them to say what happened in a courtroom. They're not going to a birthday party together to sit around and talk about child sexual abuse."

There are no easy answers, but ultimately there will probably have to be compromises in order to get help for the child (as opposed to putting therapy on hold for what may be years waiting for a trial that may never come) without unduly jeopardizing the prosecution (as group therapy may well do). The solution may be individual therapy until after the trial.

But the parents are another matter. Parents can affect a case in a variety of ways. Sarah Fahrnhorst (see chapter 9) probably hurt her own by fleeing with her children and by failing to prevent her relatives' letter-writing campaign. But had it not been for her persistence, there would have been no case to hurt. The power of a group of parents in a mass molestation case, on the other hand, can be global. The Country Walk parents effectively lobbied for legislation that seemed to have little or no chance of passing.[29]

Their combination of power and anger can make parents unnerving to prosecutors. "They're afraid of us," one parent said of the McMartin prosecutors. "They're afraid of us because they've seen our anger. They're afraid of us when something happens like they drop [charges against] the five [defendants]." The power of the parents is in their single-mindedness, their knowledge (many read voraciously on the subject and become extremely knowledgeable), and their access to the media. Prosecutors may be legitimately fearful that the parents will turn public opinion against the case, or they may be afraid that their own (mis)handling of it will be exposed.

But it is important to remember what Flora Colao said about parents (chapter 5): they are secondary victims of the abuse. To ignore that is to ignore their needs. They feel a loss of control similar to what their children feel and frequently need help regaining it. Not only is it difficult for them to accept what has happened, but they must project strength for their children at a time when they feel anything but strong. Their emotions pull them in all directions. They are angry at their children "for letting it happen" even while they know that it is not their children's fault. Their rage at the abuser is almost uncontrollable (many fantasize about killing him)—equaled only by their anger at themselves, coupled with a profound sense of guilt, for having failed to protect what they hold most dear. Yet all they can do is watch as their children's childhood slips away. Those children, however, are not necessarily what outsiders imagine when they think of child victims. All too often in the aftermath of the abuse they act out. And then devastated parents, unwilling to play the strict disciplinarian, are also unable to cope with the resulting chaos. What they are left with is a crying need for therapy.

A model for what can be done occurred in Westchester County, New York, following the exposure of abuse at the Martin Day Care Center in Mount Vernon. A vital role was played by the county's Social Services Department, which arranged for therapy for the children and hired therapists from a private agency specializing in crisis intervention to work with the parents. They organized a series of Wednesday night meetings that were also attended at first by the child protective services workers who investigated the case.

"The first meeting was pretty chaotic," recalled therapist Ann Kliman, who led it.[30] "There was a lot of free-floating rage, denial and disbelief," Kliman said, noting that these were typical initial reactions. At the second meeting, she said, the parents began coming to terms with the abuse and expressing support for each other. It was at the end of that meeting that the parents made a key decision. They decided to hold additional meetings on their own on Saturday afternoons.

"Once a week wasn't enough," one parent explained. "At home we could let out our anger the way we wanted," added another. And there was no two-hour time limit, as there was on Wednesdays. They organized barbecues and birthday parties, they watched videotapes of the news coverage and shared articles they had clippd from newspapers and magazines. They discussed the difficulties they had handling their children. And they shared their rage and grief.

"I might be feeling bad," said parent Ed Clark.[31] "I might go over to someone's house just to be there, to have someone to be with. And I might not even bring up the abuse. But I feel better because I know they're available to me."

The parents said they never had friendships that developed so quickly or intensely. It is not unusual for crisis victims to pull together, Kliman said. "When utilized appropriately, tragedy and disaster and horror and outrage can facilitate bonding and competence," she said. "I was struck at how these dissimilar people came together as hurting, angry individuals and formed a group that became a power in the community.

"And the reason it's so important," Kliman continued, "is not just for the parents' comfort, but in order to provide a safe environment for the children. That's really the first step in therapy for the children: to work with the parents."

Not only did the parents learn the importance of controlling their anger in front of their children, Kliman said, but they learned that there was strength in the group. There was great pressure to drop the matter applied by supporters of Mrs. Martin, the widely respected leader of a church choir. But the parents pressed for the prosecution that led to Mrs. Martin's conviction of child endangerment and the multiple rape conviction of one of her employees. And they have led a drive to educate the community on this issue.

"Even though we're going through a lot of pain and hurt, I'm pretty sure we're going to be blessed," said one father near the end of a Saturday meeting. "We're getting help, and our children are getting help. And we have a message that people can learn from."

The meetings had the full support of prosecutor Egenhauser. "People draw support from other people who are similarly situated, and they're entitled and they need that support. I'm not going to deprive them of that because it's going to make my job more difficult at trial." During the trial, Egenhauser continued, "every parent was asked about the group meetings. Every parent answered about the group meetings, and I don't think it harmed the case one bit.

"The same arguments used to be made about civil lawsuits," Egenhauser said. "There are those who believe you would always advise the victim against filing a civil lawsuit—at least prior to the trial—because, you know, at the trial they're going to be asked about it. That's a lot of garbage. You have a civil remedy and you have a criminal remedy every time you're injured. File your civil lawsuit, and when you're asked the questions at the criminal trial, answer truthfully and honestly."

A Profession under Fire

If the Martin case presented a child protective agency in the best light, it is a light such agencies have basked in only rarely in recent years. More often they have been scrutinized in the hot glare of interrogation lights—the kind that draw sweat from the brow.

As Howard Davidson, longtime director of the American Bar Association's National Legal Resource Center for Child Advocacy and Protection, noted, "[T]he legal child protection system is now under serious attack from the political Right and Left, as well as the populist Center (by Center, I mean the parents who are affected by CPS agency actions). . . . If we do not listen to what these critics are saying, and fail to work on difficult but necessary systemic legal reforms, I honestly believe that our ability to protect children, and to maintain public confidence in that effort, will be severely eroded."[32]

An example of the unity such criticism has created is that a longstanding VOCAL recommendation now finds supporters among the opposition. Proposed is the creation of independent review boards to monitor Social Services Departments. The proposed boards would either investigate complaints or randomly evaluate casework or both. It is a proposal that Sandi Baker is pushing in Sacramento. Herself a former social worker, Baker explained why: "When you have agencies that exist totally separately without any accountability to anybody else, which unfortunately is the way our local child protective services system has worked for a long time—I know because I came out of it—they don't like to be questioned or overseen."

Although the Sacramento agency regularly sends representatives to meet with other agencies, those representatives have no authority, according to Baker. "What they do," she said, "is send people so they can say they send people. But if a kid dies in foster care, there's no outside review process that says what happened." The very existence of a review board would be salutary, she said, adding that the Sacramento Child Abuse Council has joined her efforts.

"It's the principle that counts," Baker said. "The idea that CPS even knows their cases are subject to review externally makes the whole internal system work differently." One percent random review of cases might be as good as any other method, she added, "because nobody knows for sure which one it's going to be."

What makes such efforts seem likely to succeed—as they already have elsewhere[33]—is the sustained attacks on Social Services Departments. And if anything, they have redoubled since Davidson made his remarks. Given these circumstances, protective agencies may come to see review boards not as a threat but as a means of self-protection. Without them, all errors can be cast by critics as systemic, a charge to which an agency will be hard-pressed to respond. The shield of confidentiality behind which many agencies have sought protection may deflect criticism, but it will not foster confidence. This is not to say it is unimportant to protect the privacy of children and families, but the press has demonstrated a willingness to conceal identities while examining the system. Without the accountability of public review—whether by a board or in the media—the public will have no means of controlling these public agencies. And such a system is not only open to criticism, it is open to abuse.

But before endorsing the concept, one question should be considered: Does it attack the root problem or the symptom? Let us say that the review board finds that CPS is doing a terrible job in a given county. The chances are excellent that the information will come as no surprise to anyone familiar with its operations. What then? Will the review board tell the agency what the problem is and how to solve it? Probably. But in many cases the problems are obvious and so are the solutions. The real solutions, however, will take more than a review board to put in place.

When there is a 50 percent or more turnover of child protective workers within a year or two, it does not take a review board to descern a problem. There are child protective agencies across the country with turnover rates as high or higher. For critics to suggest that the core problem is that workers are indoctrinated at workshops where experts teach them that children never lie is to miss the point. Most child protective workers do not stick around long enough to learn the basics, much less the dogma. Besharov suggests that they practice "defensive social work" by removing children from homes.[34] When in doubt, pull the kid out. Defensive social work, as social workers will attest, is not pulling the kid out; it is staying in the office. There is nothing defensive about going out in the field to what may be a dangerous and unfamiliar neighborhood in order to accost strangers who may be violent and disturbed and tell them they must relinquish their children because they are child abusers.

Do social workers worry that they will be sued if they improperly unfound cases? If they do, it is hard to understand why the unfounded rate is as high as Besharov and company complain it is. Are they motivated by greed? Allen McMahon, a defense lawyer active in VOCAL, was quoted as arguing,

> The federal government is pumping these obscenely huge amounts of money into the state and local children's protective service agencies. And the amount of money they get is dependent on the number of cases they have filed! So even if this is never actually spoken, if you're that social worker, imagine the pressure on you to open as many new cases as you can. And this is the answer to why these social workers are trying to open so many new cases, when most of them are clearly bullshit, and they have as many as a hundred and sixty cases in their caseload already.[35]

This argument is worth quoting only because it is repeated often and has formed the basis of VOCAL's assertion that child abuse is a "growth industry." No one has yet been able to document the charge that agencies are paid by cases filed, and all such agencies interviewed denied it. Why a social worker who is overworked, underpaid, and overwhelmed would seek to increase his caseload is difficult to fathom, unless it is because he knows he is leaving next week anyway and it is easier to open a case than to investigate one.

Even if their agencies were getting rich (and most complain they are understaffed), social workers and their supervisors are not. Child protective workers in many instances are not even paid more than social workers with far less stressful jobs that involve no more danger than driving to work and nothing more hostile than a file cabinet full of forms. It does not require a review board to discover that, and such issues probably have much to do with the turnover rate. And the turnover rate has much to do with the lack of training.

Our society is dissatisfied with the quality of social work, and in many cases justifiably so. There is also general dissatisfaction with the quality of our public schools, and again with good reason. Why are we unable to attract better social workers and better teachers? Because the jobs are difficult, low-paying, stressful, and unappreciated. There is no argument that the best and the brightest are not attracted to these professions. Nor is it difficult to understand why. Yet loud complaints are raised that teachers are not competent, that social workers do not have advanced degrees—or any degrees—in social work. What is truly remarkable is that anyone goes into these fields at all, and that some are dedicated professionals who are committed enough to stay.

A review board may be helpful in some places. Accountability *is* important. But a review board will not attract qualified people and it will not train them to become competent social workers. The parallel situations of teachers and social workers is no coincidence. This country's commitment to children has been highly verbal and woefully inactive. In short, money and mouth seldom meet.

But against all odds, there are good social workers. They must be thick-skinned, however, to survive these days. Said a social worker in Sacramento: "We learn to live with the criticism. There's always controversy and has been since I came here twenty years ago. It just shifts from program to program. It's good, too, because we get changes in the system from controversy."[36]

Speaking of the problems created by the McMartin case, the coordinator of a hospital-based social work department said, "All that stuff could have happened here very easily. I think we've been informed by that practice. Like we were informed by being sued. You know, it challenges you."[37]

The parents whose children were abused at the Martin center in New York had nothing but praise for the social workers who investigated.[38] But it did not start out that way.

"We worked against them because we knew Mr. Martin and we thought we knew Mrs. Martin," said one father. "But [the social workers] didn't stop behind closed doors. My son didn't open up to me. He didn't talk about it until he told them, and they convinced him that he shouldn't be afraid to tell us.

"If not for CPS, I wouldn't have been aware of what was going on with my child. It was their persistence." He was not the only parent who initially resisted the social workers' efforts. And these are not the only social workers who won the respect and, ultimately, gratitude of parents. But it is rare when they hear praise and rarer still when it is repeated publicly.

Recognition of the importance of their work is essential if the image—and reality—of the profession is to change. There must be specialized units that are accorded prestige and commensurate salaries. Training and supervision must be provided, minimum performance standards promulgated, and workers must be encouraged to advance their skills. Scholarships for advanced training, including Master's degrees, should be available to workers who demonstrate special aptitude and dedication.

Beyond that, there must be a realization that child protective workers are frequently required to make difficult decisions that are, esssentially, judgment calls. Their jobs can be made easier if they are no longer saddled with the impossible task of simultaneously judging what is best for the family and what is best for the child, and then doing what is best for both. That may be possible in some instances, but a potential for conflict is always present. The solution is to assign one social worker to the family and another to the child. But there is no way to eliminate the subjective judgment of the worker from the job. Workers still have to analyze often conflicting information and decide whether a child is safe. Unfortunately, no amount of preparation, dedication, and training can ensure a correct decision, and in many cases adults who do not like the result will complain long and loud, whether justifiably or not.

Social work will probably always be a profession under fire; that comes with the territory. But even valid criticism can inspire improvement only if the means are there. To date, only the means of destruction seem aligned. In warning of the coming backlash against the profession, Besharov wrote, "In Arizona, VOCAL members were temporarily able to sidetrack a \$5.4 million budget supplement that would have added seventy-seven investigators to local child protective agencies."[39] In follow-up interviews, Besharov said he had reason to believe this information was inaccurate, and the head of Arizona's child abuse program denied that the measure was ever delayed.[40] But the state's VOCAL coordinator disagreed, insisting that the organization's efforts to block the additional staffing had at least slowed the process. The rationale, she explained, was that "the more workers there are, the more cases there are. If we didn't have the workers, we wouldn't have the cases."[41] Whether the funds were delayed or not, it is clearly the view of some that the best way to improve child protective agencies is to dismantle them.

If they succeed, it will not be the profession for which we will mourn but the children it can no longer protect.

Time Will Tell

Following is a news item about a case—hardly a headline-maker— that appeared next to the obits:

> A 74-year-old Las Vegas man was arrested for sexual assault and lewdness with a minor after his step-daughter's English teacher was alerted by the child's paper on sexual abuse.
>
> The teacher believed the assignment, written in the third person, had more information than it should, and arranged a meeting between her pupil and a school counselor. The counselor then reported the girl's accusations to the Nevada State Welfare Department.
>
> After their investigation, the family was interviewed by officers from Metro. The young girl said the attacks would take place at night and have been occurring for several years. The girl's mother

said she was made aware of the incidents by her daughter and last November put a lock on the girl's bedroom. Both the mother and daughter reported to police the abuse stopped after the lock was installed.

The step-father was informed of his rights and he agreed to make a statement, claiming he did not want to cause the family any trouble. He admitted to the crimes and informed police he also engaged in sexual activity with two other step-daughters, who have since moved out.[42]

As brief as this item is, a lot can be read between the lines. Here was a case that almost fell between the cracks, as the two others that preceded it (involving the other stepdaughters) apparently did. How many other children did this man abuse before he was caught? It is hard to believe that he molested his first child as a septuagenarian.

It was only fortuitous that he was ever reported. It took an English teacher who was alert enough and who cared enough to pick up the cue. But even she did not report it, as required by law. Would she have if the counselor had not? There is no way to know, but many cases are not reported because one professional passes the buck to a second and assumes his responsibility is ended. Fortunately, it worked in this case. The counselor, who was at a minimum the sixth person to know about the abuse, was the first to report it. And the police followed up. Sometimes under these circumstances everyone decides to let it drop (as the mother apparently did). The attitude is: it's over, it's done with, let's just forget about it. It may not be nearly over for the victim, though. It was not for this girl, or she would not have written about it.

The most unusual aspect of the story is that the stepfather confessed. And he not only confessed to the crime under investigation, he confessed to previous crimes, although he does not seem to have been charged with those. Without his confession, however, the two previous victims probably would never have been identified.

In a way, this is an encouraging story. Children are talking about sexual abuse, writing about it in school, and when they report it there is a greater chance than there once was that they will be believed. Society's attitudes have changed—sexual abuse is no longer a forbidden subject. It no longer seems strange to read stories like this in family newspapers. And the reporters who write them have demonstrated a respect for the privacy of victims.

But what happens to the victims? The child in the story was abused for years before she was helped, and the first assistance she received was clearly inadequate. She will not have to testify, at least, but will she get the help she needs? And what about her sisters? What help is available for them? Would they have been better off had the authorities intervened on their behalf, as they did for their sister?

A county attorney who works with the Polk County (Iowa) IFSAP program (chapter 10) said he has often wondered whether the children he sees are more often helped or hurt by the program.[43] He has video- or audiotapes of all victims and offenders who have come through the system, and now he would like to follow up, to interview the children whose fathers were prosecuted, whose families attended treatment, and ask them, Was the intervention a positive or negative thing? Initially, he guessed, a lot of the children would talk about the "hassles," but he predicted their answers would change as they got older. He also wanted to ask them how they would change the program.

There are so many unanswered questions. And so many of them are so basic. Perhaps the largest is this: Is time working for us or against us? As children grow up, they may be able to provide the answers the Iowa county attorney and others like him are asking. What actually happened in Jordan, at the McMartin school, and in other cases that have been fiercely debated? It is possible that the children involved may eventually give us more complete answers.

But it is far from certain. Children who have been traumatized (whether by sexual abuse or by intrusive investigations) do not necessarily gain insight into the origin of the trauma. And while they may repress what happened, others are only too eager to deny or forget. Or they already "know" what happened and are uninterested in the facts.

Will time unlock secrets, or will it encourage us to forget? What effect will it have on our society? And what effect will it have on children who have been sexually exploited and have not been treated? Some warn that these children are walking "time bombs" and that what we do not face today, we will pay for dearly tomorrow. It is a dark picture they paint, a nightmarish reversal of the Sixties' antiwar chant, "Don't shoot; we are your children." In this new picture, it is the parents who will plead for their lives, although the pleas will not necessarily come from abusive parents. When badly damaged children grow up and lash out, we are all potential targets.

It has been suggested that, given the vast array of crime and violence that can be traced to those who were sexually abused as children, child sexual abuse represents a greater threat to this country's future than cancer or nuclear war. Hyperbole? Time will tell. For now, as with so many questions in this complex and troubling field, we can only work to advance what is known and speculate about the rest.

Appendix:
Excerpts from Interviews

1. EILEEN WOLFE, incest survivor.
Interviewed December 14, 1986.

Wolfe, who was 34 at the time of the interview, is employed as a sales coordinator at a drug company. She has spoken about her experiences on television and radio and in lectures, and has been featured in newspaper articles as well. She lives in the suburbs of New York City.

Q: Let me start out by asking you if the *Newsday* article ["The Incest Nightmare," February 8, 1984, in which Wolfe is featured] is accurate.

A: No.

Q: Can you tell me what is inaccurate?

A: [Reporter] David Behrens apparently had a difficult time dealing with somebody having full intercourse at the age of 5, and he called me and we went back and forth on this, and no matter what I told him—I told him, "If you cannot deal with that, then I would hope that you would not print anything, just leave it alone." And he put it in a quote here somewhere—here it is: "partial penetration," and he put it as if I said it, but that's not so, okay? He did not understand how long molesters really work before they have intercourse. They could go as many as two years—and that's what my father did —for two years' preparation, and [Behrens] had a very difficult time with that.

Q: So it was full intercourse, and he for some reason couldn't say that.

A: No, he didn't feel comfortable saying that. He had spoken to some—I think it was a female doctor who said, "It's not possible because she would have been ripped apart." That would have been true if it was a normal child at the age of 5 that was raped. That would be so. But it's not true of people who've been molested in their homes.

Q: Everything else in the article is accurate?

A: I think so.

Q: Do you feel you have recovered from your experiences?

A: You know, it's funny when you use the word "recover." In incestuous homes, I don't think you can say that because the psychology is there from infancy. When you recover you're normal, then you're traumatized, then you recover. People have the tendency of thinking that incest begins when there's sexual intercourse. But the psychology is there long before that, so

I couldn't really say recover because there was nothing to recover from. Let's say I'm leading as close to a normal life as possible, and that's important.

Q: To what do you attribute your survival and ability now to lead as normal a life as you are?

A: That's a good question and one that comes up often. There were three of us in our family, so I think the thing that helped me survive when my brother and sister did not was I was never really aware—I was aware of what was going on, but I had a great imagination, and because of my ability to mother myself, more or less—because that was what was necessary—I did not really see things as they were. Almost like a Cinderella, looking at things that were positive rather than things that were negative, where my sister and brother saw everything as it was happening, and had to deal with that. I didn't have to deal with it. If my mother said one thing had happened, I'd believe her and push away the thing that had actually happened, until I reached adulthood.

Q: How old are your brother and sister?

A: My brother now is 35 and my sister is 32—she'll be 33 this month.

Q: And you intimated that they have not survived. What do you mean?

A: No, both my sister and my brother were—my sister more particularly— was put in a school for severely disturbed children. My brother, they had been trying to put him into one of these programs and he resisted, but by the time he was about 12, or in the sixth grade, they really couldn't do anything more with him. He was very disturbed. Right now he is an alcoholic and he also takes drugs. He's never had a driver's license for that reason. He can't stay sober long enough to do anything. He can't hold down a job. My sister is a prostitute, and she had three children, and two of them are dead, and nobody really knows why. Or I don't know why. It could be something—she's been reported to CPS many times because she forgets to feed her child, her one and only child. He's needed surgery, which she's neglected to give him, and he's been thrown out of the house in the snow by her boyfriends or whatever, and he's living quite a sad life.

Q: How old is the kid?

A: I think he'd be about 10 now. I haven't seen him. I've never met him.

Q: All three of you were sexually abused?

A: No, just me.

Q: To what do you attribute the problems that your siblings have had?

A: Dealing with that. It's funny, but my father was sadistic, which is very, very rare. It happens with rape maybe 4 percent of the time. My father was aroused by inflicting pain. And for me, that was the way he inflicted pain. To my sister, he would just beat her till death's door, and my brother he would humiliate with words.

Q: So your father was abusive to all three of you in different ways, somehow in keeping with his perceptions of your personalities? How do you think he chose his—

A: Me? I was much more pliable. I was much more accommodating. And I was much more fearful of him. My brother and sister were not fearful of him. I was and I didn't want to get on the bad side of him, so I think he found our weakest point. For me, the thing I could not tolerate was the sexual abuse, so that was how he'd get at me. For my brother and sister, daily he would do something to them, so it was just a matter of—he had been able to figure out the absolute point that we were most vulnerable and go after it.

Q: What did he do to your mother?

A: I think at first it was that abusing us would upset her. But after a while that was not the case. He sexually abused her, though.

Q: By which you mean what?

A: Mainly the same thing he did to me he would do to my mother. He would inflict pain during intercourse, or whatever, because I could hear her through the door.

Q: Are you as angry at your mother as you are at your father?

A: Much more angry at my mother than I am at my father. I think while the sexual abuse was going on, I got to direct a great deal of my anger at him. I have never been able to do that with the anger at my mother, never.

Q: So you've never been able to express it to her?

A: No. Oh, I've had the opportunity to express it, but she's not an approachable person, and she thinks she did everything perfectly right, and she thinks I seduced him. And basically, that's where her reality is. The reality for me is something totally different and there doesn't seem to be a compromise between the two, so I no longer see her.

Q: In the article, the reporter specifically says that you refuse to name your mother and father on the record. I don't have any particular interest in knowing who they are, but I am interested in what feelings you have about the idea of naming your mother and father publicly.

A: I have great feelings for that. I wouldn't do it simply because—I know it's really strange to want to protect my parents, but I really do. I feel that they were victims. My father was definitely a victim of sexual abuse as a child, and I think my mother may have been, so they're acting out their victimization. They're just as much a victim as I am. They're unable to deal with it. So I don't want to punish them any further.

Q: How do you know your father was sexually abused as a child?

A: Because he continued to have intercourse with his mother way into his married life, and my mother doesn't know that.

Q: How do you know it?

A: I was there.

Q: You saw him?

A: It wasn't until I was about 5 years old that I recognized the bed banging against the wall for what it was, and if it hadn't happened to me, I would never have known what that was. But my father used to take me to my grandmother's house all the time and then they'd disappear, and it wasn't until I was 5, and it was quite a shock to me when, you know, the headboard banging into the wall registered. And when it did, it was one of the most frightening experiences I've ever had.

Q: Children who are abused from an early age—it may take a while for them to understand what's happening, and to understand what's right and what's wrong.

A: I'm glad you brought that up. My feeling is that children instinctively know what's right and what's wrong, because they would be much more free talking about it. I hear this all the time. They don't know it's wrong? Yeah, we know it's wrong, because we don't talk about it at all. And you know kids cannot keep secrets, but that's a secret they will keep. So I don't really believe that children don't know what's right from what's wrong. Instinctively we know it's wrong, we know it hurts. It hurts emotionally, and it hurts physically and once that happens, once that intercourse or that molestation takes place, that's the end of childhood. We know that.

Q: Did your father impress upon you the need for secrecy?

A: Yes.

Q: And how did he do that?

A: When I was very young, he didn't really take much to threaten me. I was really humiliated. It was something I couldn't discuss because I didn't know what was happening. I just knew that it hurt. And I don't remember what he did to make me keep the secret when I was very young. But as I got older he did. And you know something really strange happened the first time. First he promised me something. You can have this bicycle, this tricycle, whatever, all to yourself. But the strangest part of it was, see we were kept in the basement—until I was 5 years old we were in a basement.

Q: What do you mean?

A: In the basement, that's where we were kept.

Q: You mean the kids lived in the basement?

A: For the day, yeah, we would be locked—because my parents worked. My mother worked in the city and my father worked in Jamaica [New York], and they would lock the door and lock us down there. I was 2, my sister was 1, and my brother was 3 when it first started.

Q: No supervision? Just . . .

A: No. We were locked in a basement. There was no light, no heat, no floor, and that was that. And of course we weren't fed. So when my father got home every day, he would beat us because we were all wet and dirty. Nobody had ever taken the time to housebreak us, but it would just upset him tremendously. So he'd beat us up and throw us into bed until my mother came home. Nobody ever fed us. That's the life. For three years we went through this. And on the third year, we were fighting over a tricycle, so my father pulled me aside and he said, "You want that tricycle?" and I said, "Yeah, yeah," and he said, "Well, you come with me and then you can have it for the rest of the day." But the thing that scared me more than anything was that he was suddenly generous, he was suddenly kind, and this was nothing that I had ever dealt with. And I was very frightened, very frightened, because it was not the norm for him, and I didn't know what was coming. And afterwards it hurt really bad, so when I went to sit on that tricycle it really hurt, and I can just remember going in circles, just taking the tricycle and going in circles, and I was crying and I was on there for a really long time. When my mother came home—now you know parents do this all the time. If I would stick my hand in the cookie jar, my mother would say, she'd be cooking and she'd say, "Get your hand out of that cookie jar," and I'd say, "How'd you know?" and she'd say, "I have eyes in the back of my head; I know everything." That was a big mistake, because when my mother came home, I expected that she would know and she would do something, and I was really angry with her that she didn't. But it wasn't her fault, she really didn't know. I think that's when the anger started coming. And then I became fearful of telling her simply because the more I let it go on, the more I felt responsible for it.

Q: What makes you believe your mother was abused as a child?

A: A couple of things. I remember my grandparents' apartment—I think they called this a railroad [flat]: the kitchen is here, and the hall was where the beds were and there were like four people to a bed, more or less, and my grandparents lived down here, and there were eighteen kids. How could you have intercourse without everybody knowing? There was no real way. I have a feeling that that's what was going on. The other thing was when I was very little, I went to my grandfather's house. My grandmother was dead and my father put me into a bed, he took all my clothes off, and he put me into my grandfather's bed, and my grandfather was masturbating in front of me and laughing. So I get the feeling that it's quite possible that that had happened to her also. Maybe she saw too much or something, but she certainly had no respect for men—or she didn't trust them. And I just have this sneaking hunch. She's never said anything about it.

Q: Were you hesitant to have children yourself?

A: It's really strange, I didn't think I had a choice. I just had children. Now I recognize I had a choice. If I knew I had a choice, no, I wouldn't have children.

Q: Why?

A: Because I think it's really very, very difficult for someone who suffered that kind of a life to be able to deal with children, because they can't deal with themselves. I face feelings in my children, or dealing with my children, that I have not figured out for myself. And it's very difficult.

Q: How many kids do you have?

A: I have two. My son and a daughter.

Q: How old?

A: My son is 7 and my daughter is 13.

Q: How do you think it's affected the way you have raised them?

A: I think it's affected them greatly. The one thing that I pick up from both of them is that they don't get attached to toys like other kids do. When I was a kid, I couldn't get attached to a toy because my father would rip it to shreds. And I see that in them, it's the strangest thing. I know that psychologically I'm passing down much of the fears that I have, I'm passing down much of the distrust that I have, and I'm passing down the inability to become—not intimately involved with somebody, but certainly emotionally involved with anyone, and my pushing people away. And my children seem to be overcompensating, because they are very demonstrative. I know it has a lot to do with it.

Q: Do you feel that that same pushing away, as you described it, affects your relationship with your children? Afraid to get too emotionally close to them?

A: Yes, definitely.

Q: How about your husband?

A: I don't push him away.

Q: Does he—is there some way that he attempts to balance?

A: Yes, I would say so.

Q: One statistic that's bandied about, I don't know with what validity, is that women who were sexually abused as children are more likely to physically abuse their own children. You've heard the same thing. Do you believe it?

A: Yes.

Q: Did you have children before or after you heard that?

A: Before.

Q: So you had children already and then you heard it. How did that hit you?

A: There was a group out in West Hampton Beach. They were abusers, child abusers, they were parents, mainly they abused their own children. And it just casually came up one day that one of the women had been sexually abused by her parents, and slowly each one of them disclosed the same thing, and that to me was absolutely shocking.

Q: So this is a self-help group of physically abusive women?

A: Yeah. I believe it to be true. As far as my kids are concerned, I find punishment very difficult. If I get angry enough I will spank, but it's rare. My husband usually does that, but I don't believe that you teach a child anything by spanking her. I really don't. You certainly don't teach them to be kind to one another by proving you're powerful and they're not. I really think there's very little, other than expressing total frustration, and if you have total frustration you don't deal with it by spanking a child. That's not going to help. It's better to punch a bag or punch a pillow or go away, but there's nothing to be gained by that.

Q: Why do you think that women who were sexually abused as children have a greater propensity to physically abuse their own children? I mean, can you explain that psychology?

A: No, I'm not really sure. I would say that it's total frustration and total anger and many times their children appear as *they* did—very vulnerable—and they don't want that child to be vulnerable, so they're going to take away that vulnerability, and maybe toughen them up or something. That would be the only way I would imagine it to be, but I really don't know why for sure.

Q: Or maybe self-hatred. Like hitting the—

A: Yeah, or maybe it's feelings that come up that this person cannot deal with. You know, children constantly have emotional needs and because we have not been able to satisfy our own emotional needs, it's very frustrating to have to deal with a child, so that anger comes in, pushing the child aside more or less.

Q: I have heard people say—not incest survivors, these people—that the way child sexual abuse cases are handled by the various agencies that intervene, when there is intervention, is more traumatic than the abuse. What do you think of that?

A: I think that's true, and I think the reason for that is that there's a hidden message that these adults give to a child when they handle the child, and I think that most of it is that the way children view intervention is very unrealistic, and I think that people don't really know how to deal with it, and have a tendency to be very cold because they don't want to be hurt, and they don't want this to hurt them. It's difficult for a person to deal with a child's expectations, and I think that people who work in this area have to be cold, but they project that on the child, and then the child feels vulnerable, the child feels responsible. I think also that the person, the perpetrator, says to the child, this is going to happen, that's going to happen, this is going to happen. "I'm going to go to jail, you're going to do detention, your family's going to stop." And all those things really do happen. So once they begin to happen, the child wants to take everything back and stop it. But really, initially, the child only wants to make the abuse stop. But that doesn't happen, it really doesn't happen.

Q: Are you basing your assessment on your own experience?

A: Mainly yes, and on others'.

Q: Do you think that some of this has changed over the last twenty years?

A: No. I would have liked to. I spoke at a convention one time and all I heard afterwards, because that was my feeling—this is twenty years ago, we have new insight, we have new information, there are new special teams that work with these children. It's really sad; it's still happening. Twenty years later and it's still happening the same way. And it's pretty frightening for me.

Q: In that case, what would you recommend a child do?

A: I wouldn't recommend anything. I would never make that assessment. I think that the child knows, instinctively, how far they can go. I think they test the waters. I know I did for years before I attempted to tell anybody. I wouldn't recommend anything, because I think the child really is adult enough, believe it or not, to know when it's safe and to know when it's not.

Q: I've heard people say—again, not incest survivors—that while some limited treatment may be beneficial, the best thing to do for child victims is to let them forget about what happened and get on with their lives.

A: No, that's totally wrong.

Q: Why?

A: Because a child really has to deal with the matters at hand, has to deal with the anger, has to deal with the frustration, has to deal with the self-hate that they feel, and the blame, and if you don't deal with it immediately, the child will continue to blame themselves all the way into adulthood. Children cannot forget it. They'll never forget. The best thing to do is to deal with it immediately and then they can get on with their lives. But you can't ignore it.

Q: Some of these people would say, "Yeah, okay, I can see a kid getting treatment for a few months, six months, but what's the point of going over and over and over it for a year or two or three?"

A: First of all, I want to take that word *treatment* out of there. It's not treatment. A perpetrator needs treatment, a child needs solutions, needs options, needs an ear to listen, a caring person. The molester is the one who needs the treatment; the child never does.

Q: What do you object to in the word *treatment*?

A: It brings to light people's feeling that there's something wrong with the victim, and that that's why it needs to be treated. There's an illness. It says right out in the open: mentally disturbed person, and the mentally disturbed person is the perpetrator, not the child. As far as the services that a child would need or the psychological help, or whatever, I think it's great for a child to really get out into the open and deal with something very early. We have statistics that show that children who get services while it's just taking place, or just afterward, integrate into society much more easily than a child that isn't.

Q: What kind of counseling have you sought, if any?.

A: I see a psychiatrist regularly, and I've had some work with a psychologist.

Q: [*Interview resumes after tape is changed.*] To review what you were just saying, when you were 25 you were trying to lose weight, engaging in self-hypnosis, and your mind kind of went out of control and you had all of these intrusive flashbacks, and you responded by . . .

A: Moving.

Q: Moving. By trying to run away. You quit your job and got another job and then you left your husband then you moved three times in a year and it didn't work. You still had these intrusive flashbacks. Then when you were 29 you started attending New York Women Against Rape meetings. And the problem that you felt with that is that the other women would distance themselves from you because they felt more responsible for what happened to them since there had been violence associated with your sexual assaults, and you had been pregnant when you were twelve, so it was a different situation. And also meeting once a year was not adequate.

A: Right.

Q: But when you were 31 things changed because this *Newsday* article was written, and the article revealed things to you that you hadn't even known. For example, the reporter dug up the court records, and you didn't even know they existed.

A: When this happened, I appeared before a grand jury. They questioned me. That was another thing that happened. My mother told me to say, when she called the police, she said, "You tell them it happened once, and that's it." But you know, they never asked. They never asked me. When my father was convicted, I was not aware of it. So as the rapes continued afterwards, I had a recourse that I didn't know was available to me. No one ever came to the house to check on me, nobody ever asked me any questions, and when they were doing questioning even for the case itself, they only asked me about the one particular night. What told me things were very strange was I read the doctor's report, and he mentioned vaginal tears, and he mentioned physical signs, and it didn't dawn on them that the experience had happened three months ago. We went in June. The experience my mother told me to tell them was April 18th, about that time. And the doctor found physical signs. It never dawned on him that that was continuing to happen? It's very appalling to me. I find it very difficult to deal with. When I saw the reality, I kept it in my mind—a dream— that if somebody knew that this was happening, they'd stop it. But, what really frightened me was everybody knew and they didn't stop it. Which made me really feel much more responsible for the things that had happened. When I was about 7 years old, or a little older, my mother said to me, "You can make it stop if you want it to," which said to me: "And if you don't, you really want it." What it said to me also, was: "You are responsible for the behavior of an adult." The child is never responsible for the behavior of an adult. But I felt responsible. And when this court case happened, it really validated that. See, every time, as I was growing up, before my mother was involved, I would look to her, and I would say to myself, "If she knew, she would stop it." From there, after she did become involved, that if anybody outside knew—uncles, aunts, or relatives—they would stop it. Well, I told a cousin, and she then abused me sexually for four years, so that didn't work. By the time I was 12, I said, "Well, if the law finds out, they're going to stop it." At that point I gave up. At the age of 12, I recognized that nobody could make it stop.

Q: Can we go back to the cousin? What happened?

A: I guess I was about 8 years old when I told her what was happening. And it seemed to excite her tremendously. She thought it was great. She thought it was a great experiment. From that point on whenever I stayed over, she would sexually—we would have a sexual interchange or whatever. And the feeling that I got from her—because she always brought up the experience before anything happened—the feeling that I got from her was, "If you don't do what I want, I'm going to tell," and that was one of my biggest fears, that somebody would tell.

Q: Why did you tell her in the first place?

A: Because I . . .

Q: Was she somebody that you especially trusted?

A: Yeah.

Q: And she took advantage of that trust.

A: Yeah.

Q: So you said that if you would have known that there was a court record, you would have had recourse. Tell me what kind of recourse.

A: All I had to do was tell anybody. He was on probation.

Q: Tell anybody like a policeman?

A: Anyone: a schoolteacher. A relative.

Q: And you think what would have happened?

A: Since he was sentenced to three years at Sing Sing, but he was given five years' probation, anybody knowing it could send him to jail.

Q: It was a suspended sentence?

A: Yes.

Q: When you were pregnant at age 12, did you have an abortion?

A: That depends on how you want to say that. My father did it in the bathroom.

Q: Your mother was aware of that?

A: Yes. It was the night he got out of jail.

Q: Did the doctor know you were pregnant?

A: He had done some tests. One came out positive and one came out negative.

Q: You had a follow-up?

A: Yes.

Q: And?

A: By the time he got around to the second test, I wasn't pregnant.

Q: They didn't ask any questions? Is there a way to talk about the trauma of that experience?

A: When we went in to have the physical examination, the whole experience was really very strange to me. When my mother reported it, I can see that they had a preconceived notion about me, because they came into the room. I was crying the whole time, "Oh, oh, oh, I've been so wronged!" And to me, they handled me as a prostitute. And nobody ever approached me in any way, nor were they eager to deal with my feelings. And when they didn't, I felt very responsible. When they took me to the doctor, it was with two detectives and my mother and myself, and apparently the doctor interviewed my mother, and spoke to her. He never interviewed me. And then I was told to take off all my clothes. That was great, you know. Here I am disclosing sexual abuse, and the doctor wants me to take off all my clothes. So I took off all my clothes, and I come out in this gown that was hanging onto the floor because it was meant for an adult, and the doctor looks at me and he says, "So, I heard you've been touched," and I look at him, and I don't know what he's saying. He said, "You know, down there." And I just nodded. He said, "Get up on the table." I get up on the table, which was huge to me, because I was very small, and he does an examination that really hurt. And I didn't know why it really hurt, because it shouldn't have. Now I know why—when I read the review. He did a rectal examination, not a vaginal examination, and that hurt a lot. "Okay, get dressed," but his dealing with me said to me that I was really spoiled, and that I was the only one responsible. My father wasn't responsible, my mother wasn't responsible, I was responsible. They always kept me, you know, two paces behind them. They all walked together and I was way behind them. I found that very hard to deal with. My father went to jail at that point, and all the relatives came over. My mother sat on the couch and she was crying, and one by one the relatives passed me, and during that time they were saying just terrible things. "How could you do this to your mother?" I did this to my mother? I thought it was done to me! But I felt very responsible. and my father was in jail for five days. On the fifth night, when he got out, it was in the evening and he came home. The bathroom was connected to the kitchen—not directly, but there was a wall, and because of the tile, the way it was, you could hear so clearly between the walls. You could hear what was going on in the bathroom, or if you were in the bathroom, you could hear what was going on in the kitchen. I have this very bad habit. When I'm frightened, I hold my breath. So as soon as my father walked in, I held my breath, because I heard him and he hadn't been home in five days. I didn't know what was going on. Nobody told us what was going on. So he came home, and my mother tells him I'm pregnant. And my father came up to the bathroom, and made no bones about it, no whispering, no nothing. Opens the bathroom door, puts his hand on his hips and says, "So! Your mother tells me you're pregnant!" And I was really frightened because he was talking so loud! And that frightened me, because I was always used to the whispering, and the hiding, and all that stuff. Whenever he changed, it always frightened me. So, he closed the bathroom door, and he got this syringe out, a douche thing, with a bulb attached. He turned on the hot water and he waited and he waited. And when the steam started coming out, he filled the bulb up with water and he inserted it, and then he couldn't insert it anymore, so he gave one big shove, and of course it went through the cervix, and he entered the bulb in my body. And then he left. And I remember pulling my legs very tightly because I hurt, but the one thing you never showed was fear, and you never showed emotion because if you showed any emotion, you'd be physically abused. I remember closing my legs very tightly, trying to conceal the pain, and I tried to get out of the tub, and as I did, the blood started just to fly. And I was really scared. I was afraid they were going to find out. And that there's all this blood and the mess. What if I make a mess in the bathroom, then I have to clean it up, and the whole bit. So I tried getting out of the tub without unclosing my legs, and that didn't work. So I didn't tell anybody, and when I opened the door my mother said, "Eileen, is that you?" That's a stupid question. My first thought was, That's really dumb, and my other thought was, Where are you when I need you? And I went to bed that night, and when I woke up there was blood everywhere. And my feeling was, I'm going to get in trouble because look at all this mess on the sheets, and I remember my mother going into the bathroom in the morning, and I just stood behind the door and I waited for her to come out, and then I whispered, "Mommy, there's blood all over my sheets." And she said, "Good." In other words: the task is completed. And again I was so startled because the reaction that she gave me was not one that I had perceived, and that was very important to me because I always looked ahead at how somebody would deal with this, how somebody would deal with that, and I always felt that I was one step ahead of them. So when she didn't react the way I had expected, she knocked me off my feet, emotionally, because I thought I was really going to get it. And I was shocked when it didn't happen.

Q: Whew. [*Pause.*] So, at 31, you recognized all this, and then what?

A: Not recognizing all of this per se. I recognized my inability to deal with it. And this was so shocking to me, and to read it from somebody else, when I didn't know it myself, was a shock to me. Then to read all the [court] papers, and to see how many people really knew what was going on when I thought, it was kind of—nobody knew, and then to know nothing was happening really threw me for a loop, and that's when I started seeing a psychologist. Then what began to happen was I started remembering everything all at one time. Everything I *could* remember I started to re-member, and I couldn't deal with that because no matter how hard I tried to keep things back, because I didn't want to remember, they were very anxious to come forward apparently, and that was a terrible year for me.

Q: What happened after that?

A: I had one seriously very bad year, and then I was okay for a few years, then it started coming back. That's what seems to happen: you go through all this psychological growth or whatever, and then you can live a normal life up to a point, but then something else comes in, because your mind is ready to deal with it, and it's still happening. And I'm apprehensive about the future, because I don't want to remember anymore. I want to just put it aside because I don't want to be hurt anymore. And that's how I deal with it—I guess I feel hurt.

Q: When did you start seeing a psychiatrist?

A: This year in October—no, in September.

Q: What made you decide to make that move?

A: I was suffering from severe depression. Normally it hits just about November and it lasts until the spingtime, and I didn't realize this but this is the way depression goes. It has a cycle, and most everybody has the same cycle. I thought, Oh, I'm so unique. But I am not. This is the way it is, and it starts out with insomnia, it starts out with confusion and an inability to deal with anything, and having very quick thought patterns—so quick that nobody can keep up with it, but you can't concentrate on any task at hand and you can't complete anything because you're always ten steps ahead of it. And I recognized that this was going to be a bad year, if it's starting in September. So I mentioned it to my boss, and I said, "Would you know anything about it?" because he's very knowledgeable about a lot of things. And it just so happened that he did. . . . I finally got a telephone number of a psychiatrist and he takes insurance, so that's been beneficial. See he treats it with drugs, which is the normal thing. Apparently my body manufactures a lot of adrenaline, because as a child I had to have all this adrenaline to survive. But the body doesn't know when to stop; it just keeps doing it. So this is what happened.

Q: So you thought that a psychiatrist would be better able to help to deal with this?

A: No. I had hoped never to have to deal with it again. I had contacted a psychiatrist and I hoped that all he would do was prescribe the drugs that I needed and just leave me alone. (In order to prescribe drugs, he has to be a psychiatrist.) Unfortunately, that's not working. He's trying to get into it, and I'm trying not to get into it. We always seem to be locking horns. We don't really get along, that's one thing, and he seems insensitive. He's probably ignorant to this extent. He asked me, on more than one occasion, did I like it? He said, "In sixteen years, you didn't like it? Not even once?" That's a dumb question. You should never, no matter who, you should never ask a question like that. If a man was mugged, would they ask him what he was wearing? If he was mugged twice, would they ask him if he enjoyed it? No. They would perceive him as a victim of crime, but here for some reason they have to make it light, and I don't like that. Another thing he asked me was, did I ever receive favors, or did I ever want favors in exchange for sex? And that was another stupid question. I never had the opportunity, but it's not wise to ask questions like that. It's not wise to make a victim responsible for the actions of somebody else. And they only seem to do this with women.

Q: I've certainly read accounts by women who have gone through incestuous experiences where they talk about how they feel greater complicity because at times they did enjoy it, and at times they did exchange favors for certain rewards, so I don't have any desire to defend this guy, but . . .

A: What you're saying is true, but in no way should a child be placed in a position of being responsible. The women I have met who have had these experiences where they did receive some pleasure have a tremendous amount of guilt, much more than I would, because I wasn't, there was no enjoyment.

Q: That's my point. Is it possible that the psychiatrist, far from attempting to further victimize you, was attempting to get at associated guilt that you may feel, et cetera?

A: Okay, but blatantly he should come right out and say that.

Q: Why do you continue to see this guy?

A: Because he's a pharmacologist and I need one.

Q: What has been your experience with counseling personally, and what's your view of it generally?

A: It depends on the person doing the counseling, and I think that you really need somebody who is a good mother, more than anything, because this is what is required—and [someone who] isn't fearful of that kind of dependency, because it takes a long time for a person to come from [being] a victim, to become stronger.

Q: You mean the therapist has to be someone who's good at—

A: Mothering, because that's what's missing.

Q: And [he must] not [be] afraid that you—or the client—will become dependent for a long period of time before you're ready to—

A: Graduate into adulthood.

Q: How important has the counseling you've received been to your survival?

A: I think paramount. I don't really think I could have progressed at all without good counseling.

Q: Is it the single most important factor in your ability to—

A: It's one of the most important. The other one is having a family that really can support that kind of emotional need also.

Q: What would you recommend for others who have gone through experiences like yours, who are looking for answers?

A: I would say that the self-help groups are one of the best ways for them to get the validation they need. And they are the most successful way of getting it. Actually, I would not prescribe anything for any one person. I think that deep down we all know what we need, and that you have to progress to a point where you can deal with what you need. But that's much more difficult than it sounds, because you deny your feelings for so long, you don't even know what your feelings are anymore. I wouldn't prescribe any set thing for anyone, but I would hope that they get the strength that they need to deal with what they have to deal with. And to progress how exactly they need to do, not me or somebody else, because we all have different ways of dealing with things, and for me to say, "You should do this, and you should do that," means I'm not listening to that person. I would hope that there's somebody who can listen to them, and who can empower them to do what needs to be done themselves.

Q: What about people who have limited financial resources? What are the options?

A: That's one of my biggest problems, and I feel so angry sometimes. I feel that my parents are getting away with all this and I'm the one who's financially responsible. We constantly have to pay for this ourselves, and that's a high bill. To see a psychiatrist is $100 a week, and they usually want to see you more than once a week. And I feel really angry with [my parents], because the statute of limitations has prevented me from suing my parents—or anybody else—[to force] them to carry the burden of emotional support. There's really a lack of good services that survivors can turn to and some of them are very expensive.

Q: So you've considered suing your parents.

A: Oh yes, I did.

Q: When?

A: About five years ago. I had an attorney look at it for me and he found out that the statute of limitations had expired. Because there was so much physical damage to me and emotional damage, they thought that they could have a strong case in trying to overturn that statute of limitations [if the statute] read three years after the point that a person realizes that they're being troubled because of it. It doesn't read that way now.

Q: How can we ever know that counseling or self-help groups or any of the services or treatments that may be available have beneficial effects, since it's impossible to know what would have happened in their absence?

A: The best thing that you can do is wait about ten years and then take a survey, and find out those who did some treatment, or services and those that did not. And I think that's the only way you're going to know.

Q: What should the survey ask them?

A: How quickly, how much more quickly the child reentered childhood, because once a child is victimized in this way, childhood ends. Those people who return to childhood, those are the really successful people. Those that didn't were not successful.

Q: One thing that occurred to me is that we could look at people who went through periods with and without [counseling]. You're one. You went through a period where you did not seek any special help, correct?

A: Right.

Q: And then at a certain point in your life, fairly recently really, you decided that you did need help. It's not exactly the same as comparing someone who did and didn't. If you had gotten help earlier, you might not have been ready for it, too.

A: Definitely. Definitely. That was my point of dealing with it. It was the only way I could, with that distance. But I can also safely say I wouldn't be alive unless I did.

Q: Why?

A: The suicide rate for people that have had my background is very high.

Q: Have you ever attempted suicide?

A: No, but I have certainly thought about it quite a bit.

Q: What concrete—if you can answer this in concrete terms—what concrete changes have you seen in yourself and in your life since you sought help?

A: I think I'm a better mother now than I was before. I think I am much calmer than I've ever been before. I've been able to set a goal for myself and attain it.

Q: Can you give me some examples of the ways in which you feel you're a better mother?

A: Before this I had little knowledge about what a child deals with and what these children are going through, and I had no patience for them. I had unrealistic expectations of what the child should be doing at a certain age. I knew nothing about children. My 2-year-old, I'd tell him, "Get up and help yourself, get up and have breakfast, or get up and do this." That was unrealistic, very unrealistic, and I think now I have a better understanding of what the child is supposed to be capable of at a certain age.

Q: From groups? I mean how, where did you get this?

A: From counseling. From counseling period. It made me much more aware that what was done to me seems to be repeating itself. As my parents were very unrealistic in the way they dealt with me, this was my frame of reference.

Q: So you would talk to your counselor about the problems you were having as a mother, and you recognized that some of the problems were directly related to the fact that you didn't have proper models when you were growing up and you were repeating the models, however inappropriate they were, that you had experienced.

A: Exactly.

Q: You say you're calmer. Can you give me some—

A: I was off the wall a few years ago, absolutely. I was hysterical constantly, I cried constantly. I hid. I moved in order to get away from something. I would not deal with whatever feeling was at hand. I just wanted to run away. I wanted to be numb or I wanted to be dead, because I just didn't want to deal with it anymore. All I had dealt with was I was not successfully handling this, and I was very hard on myself for that. I think counseling helped me recognize that I was punishing myself when it was my parents I had been angry with, or upset with, instead of myself.

Q: What are some of the goals you've set and now attained?

A: There are normal goals that people would set for themselves [like] in ten years I want to own a house, in five years I want to do this. My thing is being home when I'm upset. Believe it or not, that's a goal because whenever I'm upset I run away from home, never run to it, because I felt the most threatened in the house, or more confined, and I couldn't deal with those feelings so I would constantly run away. Now I can do it. I can be home and be upset and deal with it fine. I also can tell somebody that you're responsible for your feelings. And if you're upset with something, I shouldn't be responsible for your feelings. I shouldn't placate you because you're angry. That's what I did to my father. I knew how angry he was, and I always placated him because otherwise I'd be beaten. That was something else that changed. Whenever somebody was very angry, not only did I feel responsible, I felt the fear of death. This person is really upset, he's going to kill me.

Q: Even when it didn't have to do with you.

A: Exactly. Anything that went wrong, I was somehow to blame or my life was at stake.

Q: You said that your goal at one time was to be numb. When people feel that way they often turn to drugs or alcohol. Did you?

A: No.

Q: Why not?

A: Because my father was an alcoholic and I hated it.

Q: What are the most positive changes that you've seen in the area of child sexual abuse over recent years?

A: The acknowledgment that it's wrong. Plain and simple. Somebody is now saying, "It's wrong." That's something we've never done before.

Q: Let me ask you a couple of quick questions that refer to things that you said. One is something you said just a little while ago—that for the child's sake, the child should be told that your father loves you, he's a nice person, but he needs help. In some cases, does that not simply perpetuate the fantasy that is not true, has never been true, and never will be true? In other words, there are cases in which the father is neither a nice person nor loves the child, and through all these experiences the child has tried desperately to believe that [the father is nice and loves her], and in fact, it's the last illusion the child cannot give up. Her family has never been and will never be a real family and she cannot change that.

A: You know what? You're one of the first people that I have ever heard that recognized that. That's true. In most incestuous homes, there'll never be a family. So I don't understand why all the state programs deal with keeping the family intact. What family? What are you talking about?

Q: If you had sued your father, there would have been publicity. Would that have been of concern to you?

A: Yeah. I don't know why I feel very protective of my parents.

Q: That's what I'm trying to get at. On the one hand, you're angry at them and you're willing to—you were actively considering suing them, which would have brought them publicity, and forced them to be financially accountable, as well as publicly accountable, in a way that they probably hadn't been. On the other hand, you are protective of them.

A: I recognize how this is a conflict, but it is a conflict that I face all the time. On the other hand, I have to recognize that they are also victims. It's a conflict that I have in myself that I have not been able to deal with appropriately.

Q: You don't harbor any illusions that [your parents] will ever come knocking at your door and apologize, or do you?

A: It's a dream.

Q: But you know it's a dream now.

A: Yeah, I know it's a dream now.

Q: When did you first know it was a dream that wouldn't come true?

A: I think when I was in counseling.

Q: Just a few years ago?

A: Yeah. I had to face the fact that it was my mother who was trying to kill me and not my father, and that was hard to deal with.

Q: How could they ever repay you?

A: I don't think they ever could. There's so much damage that was done. When abuse happens from infancy on, it really impedes psychological growth. There's nothing they can do, there's no way to repay. I'll never have parents. I miss that more than anything. I'll never have parents. There's no way to repay me, because there's no way to undo all this damage.

Q: How do you feel during, like, Mother's Day and Father's Day?

A: My parents used to—my mother would always ring my phone and hang up on Mothers Day. She would never do it on Fathers Day. Her birthday, her anniversary, my birthday, my anniversary, she used to ring the phone. I feel a great sense of loss—almost a mourning. It's really funny, but I feel like I'm mourning for my parents constantly. If they would die, I think I'd be more happy simply because it would be over with. But to mourn them for thirty years—it's just devastating.

Q: Does that really make you feel like a freak when—

A: Yeah, and people do it all the time. When people get together, they always talk about their childhoods and what they did, and I have to sit and say nothing because if they found out what my childhood was like . . . You know what happened that was really strange? I was a member of the PTA and I went into Albany because they had a big convention, and I was always pushing for personal safety curriculums, and there was a man there who taught at a college, and he said more than anything he would like to get a person who had been victimized to talk to his kids because he felt that that's the person who could make a greater impact on them. I said, "Oh, I'm a victim of sexual abuse and I would love to!" He backed away, and I never saw him again. He was talking to me all during the whole thing because he [also] came from Suffolk County. He never spoke to me again. He took two steps back and said, "Oh, that would be fine," and that's it. And I feel like that happens all the time. I feel like a freak, I really do.

Q: Why do you think that happens?

A: When you talk about child sexual abuse it really raises some very strong issues with people, and they have preconceived notions that all victims are in psychiatric wards someplace, and are falling apart and could never have survived it, and all perpetrators are in jail, drooling, you know? It's hard to deal with a person who's a real person, is tangible, and is close to you.

2. ROBERT RHODES,
NAMBLA spokesman.
Interviewed May 1, 1986.

The North American Man/Boy Love Association, better known as NAMBLA, was founded in December 1978. According to Rhodes, there are three active chapters—in New York City, Los Angeles, and San Francisco. About 350 members subscribe to the organization's newsletter, Rhodes said, while 80 more receive complimentary subscriptions in prison. Rhodes joined in March 1979 and has appeared as a spokesman in a variety of settings, including radio and television talk shows, gay groups, and college classes—about thirty to forty appearances in all, he estimated. At the time of the interview, Rhodes was 40 years old. Although he is a lawyer admitted to the Massachusetts bar, he lives and works in New York City. He declined to say where he is employed other than to say he is "a bureaucrat."

Q: Do you believe NAMBLA to be aligned with any other gay groups now?

A: What do you mean by aligned?

Q: Do you believe that all other factions of the gay rights/gay liberation movement have divorced themselves from NAMBLA, or is there an alignment?

A: Oh, I see. Basically I think NAMBLA is highly controversial in the gay movement. The groups that tend to emphasize the gay liberationist approach tend to support NAMBLA, although they themselves may not be particularly interested in this issue. Some of the ones that are seeking to be accommodationists have denounced us. Certainly as an organization, NAMBLA has been active in the gay movement. NAMBLA is a member of the International Gay Association and last year at the International Gay Association Conference [in Toronto], we were the only voting gay organization from the United States.

Q: Do you see yourselves as advocates for children?

A: Yes. Considering the legitimacy of sexual relationships with children, there's two main theories that you can work from. One was the classical Greek theory—that is to say that the older partner in a sexual relationship served as initiator and tutor of the younger partner. You can also take a children's liberationist's viewpoint—that is to say that children insofar as is possible—and it's far more possible than the current structure allows—

should be given liberty to run their own lives as they choose, including the ability to determine how and with whom they should have sex. Again, that's spelled out in great detail in our position papers.

Q: Let's talk about the age of consent. Do you think there should be any age of consent law on the books?

A: No.

Q: Do you think that all children can handle sex?

A: At some level, probably. Certainly they can handle the idea of sex. The actual content of their sexual experience, if any, would probably vary absolutely enormously from none to quite torrid affairs. But if they were allowed to determine their own conduct, their own level of involvement, and proceed from there and to withdraw from it if they found it painful and so on, yes, I think they could handle it.

Q: How about incest?

A: NAMBLA's never taken a position on incest. I personally view incest as the most problematic of that sort of relationships simply because any relationship where you're so involved with the other person that you can't get out of it—certainly it's almost impossible for an external observer to tell whether it's truly consensual or not. The dynamic of most incestuous relationships is extraordinarily different from the dynamic of man/boy love things. We're talking here about the stereotype form of the father/stepfather-daughter incest. The dynamic in those sorts of situations is actually solidification of the family structure—that is to say, normally you have a mother figure who is withdrawing from the sexual arena for various and sundry reasons and somewhat acquiesces in the thing frequently and the result of the thing is actually to make the nuclear family more introverted and tightly involved. Normally where the damage comes in is where the daughter realizes that this is an atypical sort of situation and she feels extraordinarily betrayed that the father or mother did not explain how this situation would be viewed externally. Now man/boy relationships are most frequently, I would say, the result of the boy's exploration of his sexuality and encountering an adult male and developing a relationship from that. Usually it follows and doesn't precede sexual exploration with age peers.

Q: The situation you described as common in incest relationships—could it not be duplicated in a relationship between a man and a boy in that the boy may not understand how this is going to be viewed externally in the same way that the daughter may not in an incestuous relationship?

A: Yeah, well, if you assume that both partners are relatively strangers—at least they aren't living in the same place—the boy certainly has a choice of getting involved, which is different from the incestuous relationship. Now the degrees of knowledge about it vary a lot. I don't think anyone that hasn't been through it realizes exactly how horrible police involvement is in these cases—for everybody concerned except, perhaps, the police. But certainly most boys are aware that sex is in some sense considered bad or wrong or is a forbidden area and that they are deliberately exploring what they know to be a somewhat forbidden area. If the adult partner was wise, if he in fact knows himself—some people are extraordinarily naive about legal implications—they would certainly explain to the younger partners exactly what's involved.

Q: Are you saying that that's what adult partners should do?

A: Yes. **Right now the situation of man/boy love in America is quite analogous to the situation of Jews in Nazi Germany before it crystallized.** That is to say, they're not rounding us up and throwing us in concentration camps merely for existing, but certainly if they have any excuse they're certainly doing horrible things. And in among that you have the horrible situation of the younger partners who are brutalized by the police to extract confessions frequently; psychologically traumatized by what they view as their betrayal of their adult lover, and plus dealing with their relations with their families and friends, depending on how much publicity the thing receives. And of course the adult's career is usually destroyed even if he's not convicted in a legal proceeding.

Q: Do you consider a 3-year-old boy capable of consent?

A: By and large I would say probably a 3-year-old would not be interested in sexual relationships. They'd possibly be interested in playing doctor, but probably nothing beyond that. And certainly I think any sort of genital relationship involving penetration would be utterly inappropriate.

Q: Let's talk about fondling. Would it be in any sense inappropriate or wrong for an adult to fondle a 3-year-old boy?

A: If he objected to it, certainly. Now you've got to realize that the United States' cultural prejudice against fondling is again relatively new, historically speaking, that there are a lot of cultures including southern European ones—Italians—that believe in masturbating infants as a way of quieting them down and letting them sleep. Also infants masturbate a lot themselves if they're not suppressed by their parents. That was one of the reasons that circumcision became popular in the nineteenth century. And in memoirs of Louis XIV, his court physician was telling how the young prince went around displaying his genitals and various people fondled them without thinking it a sexual act with particular implications.

Q: So the answer is a 3-year-old—

A: If it causes him any sort of anxiety or problems, yes, it should not be done.

Q: But if it doesn't—if he seems to enjoy it, then it's okay.

A: Yes.

Q: Now the argument that's often on the other side is a 3-year-old, 4-year-old, 5-year-old, and indeed even a 10-, 12-, 14-year-old is not capable of understanding the implications that the activity is going to have on the individual's life.

A: We can separate this into two things: those sort of reactions that are intrinsic to the act itself, and secondly the sort of societal reactions that will become related if in fact the act becomes known. And certainly I don't see that the act itself has any particular major league implications. In other words, I don't see whether or not a boy masturbates or is fondled has any particular implications to his psycho-sexual-social development of itself— absent legal interference.

Q: Given the world we live in, is it not reasonable for a person to predict that engaging in sex with a child has a reasonable likelihood of causing unhappiness to that child at some point?

A: Actually, if anyone were to ask me, "Should I have a relationship with a boy?" I would probably say, "In the present environment, no, don't." However, the question is seldom if ever presented to me in that fashion.

Q: Why?

A: Because these are people who are already involved in relationships. What you're speaking of is a very broad, very abstracted, denatured sort of consideration. Normally, as these situations present themselves to individuals, they are a particular boy and a particular situation.

Q: Would you say that these relationships are emotionally bonding relationships?

A: In many cases, yes. Like any other human relationships, they run a whole gamut between very unpleasant sorts of things and highly desirable sorts of things.

Q: But if someone were to say, "If these men cared—really cared—about these boys, they would restrain themselves because of what is likely to result from this relationship," what would you say to that?

A: I would say that that shows a highly abstracted and unreal view of the way people behave. You can make an argument that everyone ought to restrain themselves sexually before a legal marriage after having attained a sufficient income to support oneself, one's wife, and one's prospective 2.3 offspring. People very seldom behave in that fashion, and to expect them to is to just not be real.

Q: Is NAMBLA involved in any activities designed to change the laws?

A: Specific lobbying? No. About the closest we've gotten is we were consulted and our declaration on youth liberation was used as part of the basis for the Green party in Germany's platform on children. That's about as close as we've ever gotten to actual politics. The question right now is so far out of the mainstream that basically what we're attempting to do is simply survive as a group disseminating a distinctly nonmajoritarian opinion on the subject, and basically present a rational alternative. There's no reasonable expectation at this time of that becoming even a sufficiently large minority position to be acceptable within the political arena.

Q: What would have to happen for the laws to change in accordance with your philosophy? Can you imagine anything happening in your lifetime that would—

A: I don't know. Changes in sexual mores are always unpredictable. The thing I find most difficult in discussing with people is the tremendous fear and terror that the whole idea of sex generates. These irrational fears are by far the most difficult things to deal with. We need to get to a point where people are in fact capable of dealing with sex rationally. Now what it takes to get to that point, I don't know. Right now, of course, we've had for a number of years—though it's weakening after overreaching somewhat but probably has a few last spasms—is an antisexual movement which seeks to arouse by fear and hatred and demagogy all sorts of primordial passions on the subjects of pornography, homosexuality, what's labeled child sexual abuse, and all of those things.

Q: Do you avoid saying things in [your newsletter] so as to avoid prosecution or harassment?

A: No. We do avoid certain things. For example, in certain respects it would be desirable to have a pen pal service in the bulletin. We've avoided doing that simply because of the potential for misuse by law enforcement agencies.

Q: Or classified ads or something. You don't do them.

A: No way.

Q: Is that one of the reasons?

A: Yeah. That's one of the reasons.

Q: Are there laws currently on the books concerning children, adults, and sex that you agree with?

A: Ones that we would agree with totally? No. Certainly we would support laws relating to harassment and assault.

Q: You said you support sex education for children as young as 5 and the concept that you have control over your own body?

A: And you have the right to say no, but we'd go beyond that to say, "You also have the right to say yes." Our whole problem with the current system of laws is that they don't work very well when they depend on outside intervention. The best way they work is when the child perceives a problem and can go and do something about that problem himself.

Q: What could a child do?

A: In an appropriate situation, he could leave home, go to a shelter, and then not be required to go back until the situation had been adjusted to his satisfaction or not at all. Any adult who notices a situation should attempt to deal with it. The more people can do on their own, the more likely it is to get done correctly. Once you start involving any layers of bureaucracy, you start getting their agendas entangled with it and this does things very badly in most cases.

Q: You don't break the law?

A: No. And indeed we can be seen not to break the law because I think it would be intuitively obvious that we are under considerable scrutiny. Not only do we say we don't break the law, it can be fairly well seen that we don't. If in fact one were considering criminal conspiracy, one of the less intelligent things to do would be to announce yourself, attempt to publicize yourself, go on speaking engagements, conduct interviews, write books, et cetera.

Q: Do the relationships that NAMBLA members engage in with children break laws?

A: If in fact NAMBLA members—well, it depends. If in fact their relationships are such that one of the two partners is underneath the age of consent in the relevant state, yes. As to how many members of NAMBLA might be violative of laws, I have no idea and certainly do not wish to know. Certainly among NAMBLA activists I would suspect the number to be extraordinarily small—again, because of the level of scrutiny. In many cases they choose between being activists in NAMBLA and having any sort of sex lives. In other cases their partners happen to fall above the relevant age of consent.

Q: What about "kiddie porn"—does NAMBLA have a position on that?

A: We do not believe that sex is a bad thing, therefore we don't believe that visual depictions of sex is a bad thing. We are opposed to any form of exploitation and wish that the privacy rights of individuals involved be respected.

Q: What price have you paid to be a member of NAMBLA?

A: The only problem I've had is incipient paranoia and the fact that my apartment was raided by the FBI in December of '82. That's been my only personal price, and I think it's been more than compensated by the privilege of associating with some people I regard as truly outstanding.

Q: What if you found out that one of your members had used force in a relationship with a child? Would that in some way violate a rule and lead to the expulsion of a member?

A: This situation is not the sort of situation that is likely to come about simply because there would be no point in discussing sex lives as part of NAMBLA and a great deal of reason not to. This is one of the reasons why I find Mr. [David] Techter [of the Lewis Carroll Collectors' Guild] to be something of a sleazoid. In his appearance on [the NBC broadcast] "Silent Shame," he was telling about having relationships with two young girls and how he had coerced them into remaining silent by attempting to play on their own guilt feelings. I regard that as despicable and I would not wish to be associated with Mr. Techter in any sort of fashion whatsoever.

Q: Would he be denied membership in NAMBLA if he applied?

A: Yes, I would certainly hope so. Again, I'm not on the steering committee this year so I wouldn't be the person making the judgment, but I certainly would hope the steering committee would make that decision.

3. PAUL HANNA, therapist and clinical coordinator for the Intra-Family Sexual Abuse Program of Polk County (Iowa).
Interviewed May 30, 1986.

Hanna, who was 35 years old at the time of the interview, has a Master's degree in counseling and has been employed by the Department of Psychiatry at Broadlawns Medical Center in Des Moines since 1977. In 1980, when the IFSAP pretrial diversion program was initiated, Hanna was asked to treat offenders. "I had no idea what I was getting into, but I agreed," he said. He has been doing it ever since.

Q: How has the program changed over the years?

A: It's totally different now than it used to be. When we started, the emphasis was on individual therapy, because that's what we mainly do here, and with some marital therapy and some family therapy at the end and with the idea that we were going to change the family systems, and that's what we were trying to do. We have since changed that whole philosophy a great deal in that we now emphasize working with the offenders and we put them in groups and we do a lot of really intensive confrontation and work at changing their—we're working with their sexual fantasies, their sexual autobiographies, their sexual preference, how they see women as objects and we're really trying to change some significant things in their personality. As an adjunct to that, we also work with the families, but we feel we have to do a lot of changing with these men in order to feel safe with them outside. And I think that's really made a big change in the product we're coming out with—with the people as they leave therapy. They seem to have changed more. I feel pretty good about that. We have a lot of problems with the mothers. The men we have less problems with because we have so much hanging over them in terms of they can't go back to live with their families until they've made changes, they have criminal proceedings going on, which means they could go to prison if they don't do well—that kind of stuff. But mothers: the most we have is juvenile court and some of the mothers don't care if they lose their kids. They'll fight every inch of the way, but that isn't that big a deal to them. So we have a lot of problems with the mothers and we're trying to do our best to tighten up that part.

Q: How comfortable do you feel when most of the men walk out of here?

A: We can tell you when they leave how comfortable we are. There are some men who do real well and we feel for a fairly extended period of time they ought to be pretty safe because they've done a lot of changing and we've done a lot of changing in the family so that there's all these other safeguards built into the system they're in. Other men don't do much— either they're limited in terms of intellectually or their defenses were so strong that they could only make limited changes. Then we don't feel as comfortable. Then we try to build in as many safeguards as we can in terms of extending the aftercare or putting some things in their probation that will give us further assurance—that sort of thing. So it varies from man to man and you can't even tell when you first see them which men are going to be the toughest or which ones are going to work the best. In terms of follow-up and knowing whether they are going to remolest, I really can't say that anybody in the country could really give you an idea of how many would because the only way you're going to find out is if they get caught again. So being real honest, I don't think any—unless you could get maybe some sort of data from psychological tests, I don't think that you could really demonstrate that these people are safe and I don't think that the data exists on psychological tests. I don't think that there's testing instruments to prove that they are safe again.

Q: Some of them walk out of here and you gulp and knock on wood?

A: Yup.

Q: How do you feel about that?

A: Well, we've done the best we can. Undoubtedly they've gained stuff, but they're still a risk. You hope that they don't get associated with a— say that they're divorced from their wife and you hope that they don't go find another woman that they can dominate and get into another situation where they have access to kids.

Q: Is that good enough? Not for you, but the system?

A: It has to be for us. We just can't do any more.

Q: Is there a problem with a system that leaves you gulping and knocking on wood when these guys walk out the door?

A: Well, I don't know how else you could do it. I suppose you could say that's a problem and it's something we just kind of live with, but in our whole area of therapy, that's the way it always is—with every population we deal with, so it's not unusual for us. I treat somebody for depression. They're suicidal. I don't know if they're going to commit suicide. I try to guess when they're most likely to do it and get them in the hospital in a safe environment, but it's kind of like I've got to live with the idea that they might go out and do it. Or the physical abusers—the same thing. Abuse their wives or kids.

Q: Do you subscribe to the belief that these guys are like alcoholics: they will never be cured, they can only learn to control their behavior?

A: Definitely. Definitely. And that there are certain factors that can throw them back into old behavior.

Q: Do you have a sense of a percentage of men who return to the family situation intact—that is, a reunited family as a result of the IFSAP program?

A: Of the people referred to us, I would say about 50 percent end up, after treatment's over and, say, give a few more months for kind of a settling out, I'd say 50 percent do go back. Occasionally there might be one of the children that doesn't go back for one reason or another—it may be because the child is 17 and has elected to do something else—they're almost an adult anyway. We won't allow the man to go back if we think it's going to hurt the kid.

Q: Do you feel better when they leave here not going back?

A: There's two ways of looking at that. If we've done significant work with the family and they go back to the family, the family might be a safer place for them to be because we have all these safeguards built into the system. If they start acting funny or doing funny things, then the daughter or the mother might confront them or let us know or do something about it. If they're divorced, sometimes that's easier for the kids—if there's a lot of damage done and the kids aren't that close to the father anyway (that's the other side of the coin)—maybe it's easier for the kids sometimes if the divorce occurs, but where does that offender go? These guys don't go and live alone and not meet other people, and so they're likely to go meet someone else and who knows what's going to happen there. So we don't feel like we have as much control over that. So there's two ways of looking at that.

Q: If the mother calls up and says, "My daughter told me something's happening again," what would you do?

A: Well, beyond reporting it, they probably wouldn't get back into treatment. It would be investigated. If it was something really blatantly sexual, like if there was fondling or some sort of approaching the daughter and saying, "Let's go to bed," or if it was actual sexual intercourse with penetration or any of those kind of things after they've been in the program, they go to prison. Period. If it was like, "Daddy kissed me funny," or "Dad opened the door on me when I was taking a shower," we would probably pull him in and start doing some more family therapy.

Q: Because all of the family members are undoubtedly acutely aware of the potential for prison, the likelihood of those controls leading to a report is quite slim, wouldn't you say?

A: I understand what you're saying. That could reduce the possibility that they would report, but at the same time hopefully we've changed this mother so that she's much more supportive and so she puts her kids first and she's real clear with the offender that "hey, you don't get away with this and if you do this, I'm going to somebody who's going to do something about it." With mothers who haven't done much change, who haven't done much work, who are still on that old system where they're saying, "My husband comes first, my kids come second," then you're really dealing with some problems there in what you're saying. I agree with that.

Q: Wouldn't it be more likely that women who have really come to believe and act on the belief that their kids come first and their husbands come second will be divorced at this point?

A: No. Not necessarily. They might divorce after this action, though. Many times the kids want them back and the mom might even be fighting the kids when she divorces the husband, so it isn't quite that cut and dried.

Q: Doesn't, additionally, the fact of jail looming over everyone's head make statistics all the more suspect?

A: Yeah. I can see your point. The problem is, if you don't have that leverage on these people—and we've had people who didn't have the criminal charges against them—without that, they just don't change or they don't change as much. Sometimes you can get some change, in terms of them admitting to what they did and saying they're remorseful for it and accepting responsibility for it, but then they don't go out and change all these other behaviors that surround it—like the alcoholism. They have a whole set of attitudes and behaviors that go along and reinforce this alcoholism. They call it a "dry drunk" when an alcoholic stops drinking but he still has all these attitudes that reinforce his drinking so sometime in the future he's likely to start drinking again, or he still keeps the family in the same system that it was before. And so, as with the dry drunk, we feel we also have to change these attitudes that surround the abuse. Just stopping them and getting them to accept responsibility is only the first step. It's very important for the victim to see that—very, very important—but it doesn't change the system that the victim lives in.

Q: What do you think about Giarretto saying that there's a 1 percent recidivism rate among his population?

A: I don't see how he could say that. I mean that's wishful thinking. The individuals you're treating vary so much that I don't see how you could say that, taken as a whole, they're not going to reabuse. Some are more likely to reabuse than others—that's as clear as day if you've spent a lot of time with them and are realistic about what you see. Some just have so many more strengths than others, or their family is stronger and they can work together so much better, and others have nothing. We have people who live in missions that come here and as long as they're in a mission atmosphere, they're certainly more likely to reabuse than somebody who has a strong family that's going to help him change and keep those changes in place.

Q: Maybe it's also political thinking—for funding?

A: True.

Q: Is funding also an issue for you, like: "See what a great job we do? Look at our stats!"

A: No it isn't—in that sense. In terms of respect, in terms of working together as a team, getting other people to work with us and to feel good about referring to us and accepting our recommendations, that's very important; but in terms of funding, it isn't. We don't have much for statistics— it's not really built into our program because we don't have the staff time to devote toward it. We're a county hospital, which is probably a really unique situation. There may not be very many of them in the nation. We're the hospital that treats the indigent people in Polk County, where the people don't have the money to pay, who don't have insurance, who the county more or less foots the bill on. We also will treat other people who have insurance or who are paying themselves, so we have kind of a tier system. Depending on how much money you earn, they charge you a certain rate. So I think our system's real different from other systems. But one thing that that does is we have to go to the board of supervisors or to people in the county government and get our funding, so every staff member we have has to be clearly needed and they have to pay their way. Now that's not that unusual, maybe, for other organizations, but we don't have much leeway and I, as coordinator, do a lot of treatment. I do coordination kind of on my own on the side, so there really isn't time for me to do much statistic gathering. I think it would be a useful thing to do if I could do it, but they don't feel like that's the critical item right now so I do what I need to do.

Q: I understand that you initiated a pretty thorough screening process in the last two years. Can you describe what the process is and how it has changed what you do?

A: We were getting people who maybe fit the minimum criteria, but then came in and didn't work—didn't do anything, were people who just weren't motivated to do any work in treatment and so we faced the problem of what to do with them. Once they're in the program, it's hard to send them to prison. They may not know that, but it is hard. It's hard to identify how they fail. Someone attends all the appointments, they answer your questions in one or two words—when the court asks, "Well, are they attending regularly?" They don't ask you how well they're doing in terms of how they're working, and it's so hard to describe that in some sort of objective way—to quantify their participation. So what we wanted to do was screen up front, so we see them for approximately three to five hours. We'll sit down and go through what they did and get all kinds of information in terms of social history—that kind of thing. We have them do a sexual autobiography. They start that right at that point. So they're bringing in all this information to us so that we can get a handle on what degree of sexual attraction to kids they have, what kind of personality pattern we're dealing with, is this somebody who's extremely rigid, obsessive, that sort of thing. Are they showing remorse? Are they denying a lot of stuff? Are they minimizing a lot? They all minimize a certain amount. They all deny a certain amount. They all probably have some type of personality disorder, but are they too much for us to be able to treat on an outpatient basis? So we're looking for their attitude towards what they've done and towards treatment as a whole. And we're also giving them assignments so they're going to have to already show us that they're willing to go home and do some work. Basically, we're also trying to screen out people who are going to be a risk. So if they're going to be a significant risk to remolest while they're in treatment, or to be dangerous either to therapists or to their family or to someone else, then we don't want them in our program.

Q: So what personalities are you screening out?

A: We're not necessarily screening out whole personalities; what we're doing is the extremes of them. The antisocial who doesn't care about anything but himself—we treat antisocials, but they have to be willing to work. We aren't saying we won't treat them, because I have a couple who have done really good work. But others who are only concerned about themselves, they're not concerned about what happened to the victim—they may have had anal sex with their son and not really cared or understood the pain they inflicted on the child. It's important for them to get a handle on that because they've got to come out with feelings, they've got to understand how they hurt somebody; they've got to open up their feelings to people in the group and in individual [therapy] and that sort of thing. You won't see it all, but you've got to be able to see a capacity for that. So, some of the antisocials, we get some narcissistic people, but it's really hard for me to say which ones won't make it. We clearly won't take somebody who's mentally retarded at too low a functioning—maybe [an I.Q. of] sixty-five or less we wouldn't take them. Organic [brain damage]—that can be a problem. We will take some organic people because we get a lot of substance abusers and a lot of them have some organic damage from all the drinking they've done. But if it's too extensive, they're probably not treatable, so we do a lot of psychological testing if we think that's the case. If they're schizophrenic, we probably wouldn't take them. If they're having all kinds of delusions and they're psychotic, we probably wouldn't want to take them, even if they get to the point where they weren't psychotic anymore. But then again they might not have to face charges. They might be able to get by. We get a number of passive-aggressive personality disorders, the schizoid personality where they're really away from people, distant from people—that's a frequent one.

Q: Do you ever take people who have victimized children other than their own (that come through the IFSAP program)?

A: Yeah. We'll take a few of those.

Q: Would that be a reason not to take someone? If it looked like it was an out-and-out pedophile who was not simply regressive but chronic, repetitive, compulsive—

A: Okay, we don't use those words anymore. *Regressive*—we don't use that. We see sexual attraction to kids as being in degree. We don't see it as being fixated or regressed. We don't use that because we don't feel that those categories actually exist in any kind of pure form at all. And we don't use the word *pedophile* much, either, because we see them as—all our men are sexually attracted to kids, all of them period. Even the men who are very physically aggressive when they are sexually abusive. The theory was they do it out of power. We say they're still attracted sexually to kids. We find with every one of them that they are. When they're in treatment they all admit that they had fantasies about it. It varies a great deal in degree and it varies in what age you're looking at. Some offenders are attracted to kids from 10 to 13, some are 2 to 8; it varies a lot in that. But when you start using the word *pedophile*, I see you start separating out the ones who are interested in kids that are out there and the incest population that are interested in the kids that are in the home. We don't see that much of a difference. We just think that it's more available, that it's easier for those people to molest inside the home. If they ended up staying somewhere and there were kids there, they might be a danger there, too, even though those aren't their kids. We don't see that sharp a distinction, although people who have a high degree of sexual attraction to kids are more likely probably to go get a neighbor kid and do it to them and to go hunting, cruising, that sort of thing. So I guess that would be more of what other people would call the pedophile. At that extreme range, we would feel uncomfortable with their coming into our program because they don't have the controls necessary to come into an outpatient program and be safe. We can't have them come into our program and molesting out there, so that's why we would want to exclude those—not because of how they think, how they act, or what we're treating, because we feel it's pretty close to the same thing, especially the group work and the individual work we do.

Q: But you don't feel confident that you can say, "This is a guy who has molested his kids and is really not much of a danger to other children?"

A: No. If he was in a situation where he had access to someone who developed a trusting relationship with him, or he could develop a trusting relationship, we would be afraid of that, too.

Q: Isn't it valid to draw a distinction between men who are a risk to all children and men who are a risk only to their own?

A: I think we're fooling ourselves if we do. It's kind of like these are worse than these. And we don't see them as being worse, so much. Because when you go out and talk to people, they either have in their minds that incest is worse or pedophiles are worse, and I don't know which—depending on who you're talking to. And in terms of whether they're treatable, we don't see that so clearly that way. Right now the program is set up so that we treat intra-family, and that's how we make a distinction. I think it's mainly a way for us to limit our numbers so that we have reasonable numbers and for us to have some controls over these people, but not so much because of treatability.

Q: Would there be any difference in the way you treat an incest offender from a man who chronically abuses children indiscriminately and compulsively?

A: The difference would be in terms of control. This person who is doing it with all these people obviously has very poor control over his sexual behavior, whereas the other one has some control over his behavior, so we would differentiate on the basis of control. It probably would be harder to treat number two, who has had all those experiences. This guy may be a sexual addict. We divide it up into three categories. We don't have a clear distinction, but we see the kind of passive/dependent people, we see power and control people, and then we see the sexual addicts. There's a mixture in there sometimes, but the sexual addicts are very, very close to the alcoholic who just wants that sexual high and just is looking for more and more and more wherever he can get it. I think the sexual addict is the highest risk because then you're really dealing with somebody who's like the alcoholic—it's so easy for him to slip back.

Q: Do you screen them out?

A: No.

Q: Are those the guys you gulp and knock on wood when they leave?

A: Well, yeah. Actually all three of them will have some people in them that we will gulp and knock on wood. The power controlling—I just had one leave who I think did a lot of work in treatment and did a lot of changing but he's so aggressive still—we couldn't take that out of him—and he was abused repeatedly as a kid and you can talk about that and work on that, but at some point it's still part of him and that anger is always in there and he's so much better at dealing with people and he's so much more gentle and he deals with his kids so much better—he ended up divorced, but nonetheless he still sees his kids—but he is somebody who is so aggressive that at some point you could see him again slipping back into old behavior and becoming sexual in terms of how he's dominating other people. It's very possible, so he's kind of a gulper, although he did a lot of work and he changed a ton of stuff.

Q: What percentage of your patients have been abused as children themselves?

A: Oh, close to 50 percent, I'd say.

Q: Any follow-up on the men who have completed your program?

A: Of our earlier groups of men that went through, seven of them remolested between 1980 and the middle of 1985 [out of a total of about one hundred twenty to one hundred forty] and none have remolested since that time that have successfully completed the program—that we know of. We have had approximately two hundred to two hundred twenty offenders go through treatment since 1980. We have fifty-one in treatment now. [Screening began in 1984.]

Q: What happened to the seven who remolested?

A: They were brought back on charges. From what I remember, I think they were sent to prison—I think all seven were.

Q: How many didn't successfully complete the program?

A: I don't know. [No way to get statistics, he said.] And it's changed so much. It's really hard. You know, statistics back then of what is successful completion and what is successful completion now is totally different. I mean they go through so much more now than they used to.

Q: What do you think of the Giarretto IFSAP model?

A: Well, it's a place to start, I suppose. I think it might be pretty good for aftercare—the Parents United model for somebody who went through treatment and they want to stay thinking about sexual abuse and stay in tune with all that they've learned. I'm not all that sold on it. I think it may be a little too soft [on offenders].

Q: What effect does that have?

A: Being too soft on offenders? They aren't going to change enough because they're going to avoid that in every way they can all the way through. You have to push them every inch of the way. Only maybe 5 or 10 percent of them are really going to go in here and do the work and all you have to do is guide them.

Q: Think more of them should be in jail? I mean a long time in jail.

A: [*Pause.*] Yeah. They get off pretty easy sometimes. I don't know if the jail system is adequate to handle all the people that we could send there.

4. LAWRENCE DALY, detective, King County (Washington) Department of Public Safety.
Interviewed August 7, 1986.

Daly, 32, had been a police officer in Seattle for ten years at the time of the interview. He was assigned to the Special Assault Unit (handling adult and juvenile cases) in 1984 and began specializing in cases involving child victims in 1986.

Q: When you initially got into Special Assault, what made you decide you wanted to do it?

A: I think it was the curiosity of not knowing a lot about it. Secondly, I knew that they were complicated cases, and I knew that it would be good experience because eventually I want to go to homicide.

Q: It seems that among all the agencies that get involved in child sexual abuse cases, the two that perhaps have the hardest time getting along are CPS [child protective services] and the police.

A: That's true, and I can tell you why if that was going to be your next question. The ideologies of CPS people and law enforcement are different, they're distinct. CPS is not concerned with prosecution; they're concerned with making sure that the child is safe. We on the other hand are interested in securing the safeness of the child by prosecuting. What happens is CPS is doing what they think is right, we're doing what we think is right, and what eventually happens is conflict. They're social workers. They're educated for that. The other thing is, everyone's guilty. If they get a report, he must have done it. They don't reason the facts as well as we do. We are just fact takers. I mean, we go out and we look at a case. The first objective is—in any investigation—is to always to keep an open mind because the suspect is innocent before he is guilty. Vice versa with CPS. I argue with them daily. This guy did not commit this act. Yes he did. No he did not. Bullshit. That's what it turns into, and then that's where the conflict comes in, because they instantly believe the child. That's bullshit. If anybody instantly believes a kid, right there they've already focused in: he is guilty, the kid is right. That doesn't work all the time. I'm not saying that we shouldn't believe what the kid's saying, but if you instantly take that and move on, I mean—and that's where the problems are.

Q: What do you think the solutions are? These conflicts are everywhere.

A: The solution is to keep an open mind. That's so important. There are so many allegations. A perfect example are the divorce cases, where you have Mom and Dad conflicting over the child, family court's becoming involved, because now they're going to have to decide about custody. It's common for us to get a case where the child has spent the weekend with the dad and all of a sudden, she's been molested. And then you bring the kid in and the kid says, "Well, he was giving me a bath and he did touch my vaginal area." Oh. Now everyone overreacts. You've got CPS saying, "Oh, he's a pervert!" you know? And then I say to them, "Well, wait a minute! I gave my daughter a bath and she's 3 years old; am I a pervert?" Be open, do not lead, and listen, because a lot of people don't listen. A lot of the people don't listen to the witnesses, they don't listen to the suspect, but there's a lot of circumstances when you're talking to suspects that you have to look at. I mean I usually know, 99.9 percent of the time. A suspect comes in, is he appropriate or inappropriate? I mean, they don't fool you too much. They have a classic personality.

Q: Describe that personality.

A: The personality of a child molester is a person who, I believe, is insecure, is insecure with his feelings with adult people. A child molester—see there's a difference. There is no such thing as pedophiles. *Pedophile* is clinical/psychological terminology for a person who relates better to younger children. A child molester is a person who is basically a pedophile in that he relates to younger children, but he desires them, so the characteristics would—there's your individual characteristics where you have a man who is married, but he marries because he wants to be close to children. It's an access route. He has a sexual relationship with his wife, but he enjoys the children, and you've heard this before. So the thing is, his characteristics are going to be pretty obvious when he comes into the room. He's going to have conflict in his marriage. His children are going to be deadly afraid of him. His behavior in the office is going to be nervous. He won't look at me exactly in the eye when I talk to him. He will be evasive about answers, or he will place blame on the wife. I mean those are most of the things. They always place blame. But if you can eliminate the blame, and allow them an escape route, meaning giving them an alternative on how to confess, what do you call it, an easy way out? Like the alcoholic who comes in and says, "God, you know, I was intoxicated and I don't remember what happened." But the 9-year-old girl—you touched her? Is it possible? "God, it is a possibility." So what you do is you attack the alcoholism and not the individual, and then you allow him to admit to it finally. Those are key things. Each person's going to have an individual trait, and when you see that trait, you have two minutes, I figure two minutes when a suspect comes in on a child molestation case, to evaluate him. If you evaluate him wrong, you've screwed your interview. So what happens is when you evaluate him, you've got to take advantage of it and lead him down a path of confession, I call it. I know my suspects. I teach profiling at school, I teach interview techniques at our academy here in the state of Washington. I mean, that's my specialty, is interviewing, and I explain to them that you've got ninety seconds. How are you going to interview me? Establishing a rapport with the suspect is the most important thing you can do in an interview. You just can't sit down and say, "You have the right to remain silent," because I don't do that. I don't advise rights until I want to talk with them about the crime. Some people say that's dangerous because the guy could yell, "I did it!" I'm still going to advise him of his rights. If he doesn't say, "I did it," I can't use it.

Q: In your criminal investigations, who interviews the child?

A: The prosecutor. The problem with that is that they have different techniques in interviewing than we do. They are not trained interviewers. It's really hard to clarify it, but the prosecutor has a way of interviewing somebody on the stand. We have a way of interviewing in the field which is totally different. I've never been able to put my finger on it, but I go into interviews with these prosecutors and there are some up in our prosecutor's office that are great interviewers, but then on the other hand there are some that are just terrible. So what happens is you wait until they get done and then you ask the questions that they missed. I mean like Becky [Roe] and those people, they're excellent in what they do because they've interviewed so many kids. I mean, you've got to get good. Practice will make perfect. But I think that their system is appropriate, I think that it is least harmful to the victim. Sometimes, in a case like I just recently had where a stranger raped a girl, they wanted to set up a joint interview and my comment to them was, "If you want the interview, you call the victim, and you set it up. I've already talked to her. I've already taken her statement. I don't need to be present during the interview." That really made them mad. That's okay though. It won't be the last time they're mad at me.

Q: Now, I understand that there's considerable turnover among prosecutors who handle these cases. They don't stick with these kinds of prosecutions for that long a time. Is that true?

A: That's true.

Q: Maybe about a year?

A: Not even that. Six months to a year—and justifiably so. They work their asses off. I mean, I don't know how they do it.

Q: That means that the people that you have in this joint interview doing the interview with the child in most cases do not have a great deal of experience interviewing children.

A: That's right. They come from district court, juvenile court, they're given one training lesson, then they go, and that's the problem. See, that's where we, as the police, have to teach them how to interview.

Q: How do you do that?

A: After they've watched a couple of interviews, they'll come in and—like let's say this is their first interview by themselves. And they'll go through A through Z from what they've learned from the two interviews. Now—

Q: They watch a couple of interviews that you do? Is that how it works?

A: They go with a prosecutor who's experienced. And whoever the officer is, they watch. Then you come in and you say, "Who's my prosecutor?" And they say, "Pat." And you say, "Okay, who's Pat?" Because now they've made a change and you go, "Oh, great. Here we go." So you go in there and you let Pat lead the—usually they're appropriate, do everything right, but they miss key things that are so important. They miss—and this is where the prosecutors have to be careful. I had several rape cases when I was working the adult side where the victim was lying. No doubt in my mind she was lying, and they wouldn't confront her. So it was my turn, and I just turned around and said, "You're lying!" And they just—I mean the prosecutor, [and King County] Rape Relief [were shocked]. "How dare you challenge a rape victim!" That's crapola. If I didn't ask that question, who's going to ask that question? The defense attorney is going to get her on the stand and make her look like an idiot. Now how do we alleviate that? We have to confront the victim with the inconsistencies. A new prosecutor who's never tried a rape case, because they've just come to the unit, doesn't know those kind of things that they're going to get surprised with. Me, who's been to several trials, who's been through several interviews, who's been through da-da-da-da-da, knows that those questions have to be asked. So some people get a little shocked when you say, "I ain't buying it. I ain't buying this story." Especially with teenage girls. We have a lot of problems with veracity, and that's what the defense attorneys attack.

Q: So you think that that protocol works reasonably well?

A: I think it's great, I really do.

Q: How long does it take you on this unit to get good at investigating child sexual abuse cases?

A: Well, I've got to clarify it in two ways. If you come like I did—I had a year and a half experience as a burglary detective, so coming into the unit was not difficult at all. It took maybe a month to understand the mode. For a person that comes out of patrol, I would say six months to a year, depending on your previous experience. Like we had a female detective who never had any detective experience, so her empathy towards the victim— I mean because a detective has a different empathy than a patrol officer. Patrol, it's a quick one: you're here, "Sorry this happened," and then you leave. A detective always has to remain in contact with the victim. It's a consistency of empathy. She had difficulty with that because she didn't know when to show the empathy, she didn't know when to turn it off, and it really became a problem. In fact she got a couple of complaints on it from victims. But it took experience. Now she doesn't have that problem. So it matters on the background.

Q: But it doesn't take that long to get reasonably competent in investigating these cases?

A: I'd say six months. But we have a training phase here. You usually train with somebody, and if they don't know, like—I seem for unfortunate reasons, I don't know why, but I seem to be the leader of our group. So if they have a question, they come to me, and they say, "Let me throw this at you." And if they don't feel comfortable with that, they go to the sergeant, or they go up and talk to the prosecutor. So you always have resources you can move to.

Q: What kind of training is involved?

A: None at first. Myself, I read every handout I could get upstairs [in the prosecutor's office], I went to profile schools on rapists, I went to several training courses they've had on victims of rape and advocacy. I've attended many [network] meetings. The department doesn't do it. The department does not provide specific training, and to ask this department for any specific training is like pulling teeth because of the money allocation. It's another government problem. There's a school back in Chicago that's going on this week, I think—$1800. But boy would it have been beneficial to go to. The department doesn't have that kind of money.

Q: Would you like to see training formalized at the beginning and, you know, along the way?

A: I think so. I really do. I think you have to know—well, let me explain this to you. Physical evidence is a big thing in a lot of these cases. I was an evidence specialist on this department. I've done many homicides, et cetera, et cetera, and I've done some rapes before I became a burglary detective, and then I dealt with specific evidence in burglary—fingerprints, and body fluids mostly. And then you come into this unit, and people start talking about Pap smears, pubic hairs, sperm, and if you don't know anything about that, you have no idea of how to correlate it to the crime. When you get a report from the hospital, what does it mean when they say there was a laceration, or there was something on the vaginal tract, or what does it mean when on the anus there's a scar at the twelve o'clock high? You know, those types of things. You ain't just gonna pick it up. So there should be some formal training.

Q: Are all kids taken for medicals?

A: Only if the circumstances indicate that evidence may be possible. We do not want to put them through medical examinations because it's so traumatic. So if it indicates that there possibly was some type of penetration, some type of continuous abuse where there was penetration, then we would have them examined.

Q: Many people say that CPS should err on the side of safety—that is, take the kid out for a while, if they need to, to be sure that they have a safe environment before returning the kid. They're not in the same position as the prosecutor, where if they don't have a case that they can prove, they can't file. But then there are other people who say, well, although that may sound somewhat reasonable, when you look at what happens to people who are accused—they get stigmatized, they lose custody of children for longer periods of time than one might think, because this is a bureaucracy and because there may be antagonism between the social worker and the family—there are a lot of families that are being abused by the intrusion and intervention of child protection services. Those are the two sides. Which side do you take?

A: If there's any doubt or any question in my mind that leaving the child in the home—if there's a possibility that the child could be in danger in any manner, I would remove the child. Not because I question Dad or Mom, because when there's a question, safety does become the importance. I mean, what if we're wrong? I think that we have a duty to a child to remove them until we know for sure that the actions of the parents are appropriate. That's the side I take.

Q: Okay, but that flies in the face of what you were just saying about innocence, when you were looking at the criminal side.

A: I think that criminally speaking, you have more—if you want to use the word—defamation to somebody, such as the thing you saw on TV [the local news] last night—the basketball coach. Hell, he's guilty already. I mean, they've got him on every charge in the United States.

Q: What's he been charged with?

A: Molesting his basketball players. So the thing is, like his attorney said on TV, he's defamed. But let's say one of the basketball players was in his home, and it's a question if he was being abused or not, physically, let's just say physically, and CPS found out and said, "Hey look, Coach, we're just going to remove him for a couple days until we get things straightened out." The media's not going to pick up on that. Nobody's going to pick up on that.

Q: I'm looking at sexual abuse, though, and the media will pick up on sexual abuse.

A: That's right. And they will defame. That's the problem with the media, but we have a right in the community to know who we should be careful with, who's a threat to our children, you know? I'm glad they're there. I guess you're damned if you do and damned if you don't, because I believe that the safety of the child is the most important and if the parents get upset—I'd be mad. I look at it that way. I'd be mad if somebody came out and told me they were removing my 9-month-old child, and I have a 3½-year-old too, from my home, because they heard something that was bullshit. I think I'd be contacting a lawyer and suing some people. I think I'd be quite upset, unless they could substantiate that to me why. Why this has to be done. I'd be real upset, and I guarantee you I wouldn't be working here anymore. I'd be owning this place. So I understand what you're saying, but the safety of the child is the most important.

Q: According to your protocol, CPS never does full investigations [in criminal cases]?

A: They have to do the same things we do, but they don't do it in the context of how we do our investigations. I mean, they want to get the facts against these people if they've done something wrong. They get the medical reports, they take photographs of the injuries if they're the first person out there. They take terrible photographs, they're not trained in evidence, they're not—see it's a difference in the training. They're there to make sure the child's safe. We're there to make sure that we can collect all the evidence and prosecute the suspect—and make sure the child is safe. They have one goal, we have numerous. Recently we attacked CPS and we had a right to. They weren't reporting properly, they were making big errors and we wanted them to know. I got tired of it. I got tired of getting a fractured skull on a 9-month-old three months after the incident occurred! Who am I going to interview, the sink? I mean that's crap. Getting a report that I've got a kid half dead up at the hospital when it should've been reported on the night of the incident? That's crap. And that's what they were doing.

They became the investigators. They wanted to do the job, but they're not investigators! We're the investigators. We're the ones that are going to make sure that this did, or didn't, occur. CPS is there to make sure the child is safe.

Q: Do they agree?

A: Oh to a point. I think they agree to the point that they would like to believe that they are investigators. I think the problem is that they're frustrated police officers, and we're frustrated social workers. I really do.

Q: What's the solution to that?

A: The solution is training, education, more meetings with law enforcement to show that it is a cooperative effort, but to understand their lines of responsibility and to understand our lines of responsibility.

Q: If they get more training in evidence, isn't it more likely that they will see themselves as police?

A: We hope that that isn't what the education is for. We hope that the education is for them to understand that if they see evidence, they notify us and tell us that it's available, that it's there. That's the reason.

Q: I talked to Teri Perry [a child protective supervisor], and she said that there had been these breakfasts set up for CPS and the police.

A: We've had some breakfasts with them, yes.

Q: Have those been productive?

A: Yes, they have. We have an investigation to do. We have to contact so many people. We have to do this, we have to do that. I mean, you can't really screw that up unless you're an idiot. CPS, on the other hand, has certain responsibilities to lead us to that investigation. If they fail, we can't do anything. So what we were explaining to them at that meeting is that your referrals are not coming in on time, you're not calling us and asking us this. You are doing this, this, this, this. And when the meeting was over it was over. There wasn't one complaint ever lodged against us, except please keep us informed. And they're right; we were not keeping them informed. The Seattle Police Department wouldn't talk to those people. The Seattle Police Department [not to be confused with the Department of Public Safety, for which Daly works] wouldn't talk to Rape Relief because of the breakdown. I see them as a useful tool in that goal towards protecting the child and prosecuting the suspect. If we don't utilize them as a resource, we're defeating the purpose.

Q: The statement that there's not much we can do wrong—I don't know. There are a lot of mistakes made by policemen in a lot of cases. I'm not talking about Seattle, necessarily, but I mean, what can be done wrong? Well—

A: You name it.

Q: Yeah. I can rattle off a whole bunch of things that police officers have done wrong in specific cases.

A: Oh, I understand that. Well, look at the one in California. But anyway, I know what they did wrong there. But that wouldn't happen here, because we learn from our mistakes. And I just did a case just like that, and the thing is even when I talked to my sergeant, even though it wasn't important, I wrote it in my log—because of the McMartin case. You learn from it.

Q: What did you learn from the McMartin case? And what happened in this case that you just had?

A: I learned that if you're going to do a major investigation, that it is so important that everything you do is listed. What comes out of the effort is listed. Meaning that if you went out and talked to Sue Smith, what did Sue Smith have to add to that investigation? The investigation I had, as I'm sure you're going to read in *The New York Times*, I'm investigating a church that is sexually repressed, and now they are coming out of their shells. Unfortunately they're molesting children, they're molesting each other, divorce rate's, suicide rate's high. You're writing a book on this— you could write another book on that. And I learned how to be methodical— you have to be in an investigation like that. If you're not, you're real stupid, and that's what happened in the McMartin case. I think that they got too much too fast, not enough organization. But what I was saying, back to your point there about police officers making mistakes, is that we don't make mistakes reference to CPS when we talked about, like, sometimes we might not refer a case back to them, okay? It's really hard to make a mistake in reference to them, but if they don't give us an investigation, what can we do? We don't know about it. That's where the big error comes in. That was the big concern. But the thing you have to understand is that I don't believe that I should be calling CPS and telling them every move of my investigation. That's not my responsibility. I don't have any responsibility to them. I have a responsibility to the victim, and that was where the concern came. And our protocol, and I missed it—you know, things have to be pointed out to you sometimes, you have to be slapped a few times in the face. It does say that we will notify them for the joint interview. So every time, now, I notify them for the joint interview. It was a result out of the breakfast meeting.

Q: Leading questions. This is raised a lot.

A: And it's true and it drives me crazy.

Q: Who asks them, how?

A: Frustration causes leading questions. I won't say that in the two years I've been doing this job that I've never led a kid. I'll never say that because I think we have a tendency to get frustrated and lead, but because of the leading nature of an interview, we decline to prosecute. I'll say that much. But what concerns me, and it's kind of a personal thing, is you've got a victim who's 3½ years old, there's a custody battle going on, and Mom says, "Dad abused my daughter." So we say, "Okay, take him to the hospital." No medical evidence. So they say, "We better put this kid in counseling." Eight months goes by. Not a disclosure, nothing. Then out of the blue: "Daddy touched me." Now you're telling me that after eight months of asking if Daddy touched me that that isn't leading? For eight months you're telling this kid? And then they call someone and make a report. And I say bullshit. That's—you've got tainted evidence there. First of all, was the kid traumatized? There's nothing to indicate the kid was traumatized. The kid is acting out behavior that he's been told for the last eight months every time he's being interviewed by this counselor! Did your daddy ever do this? Did your daddy ever do that? If the questions were never asked, they'd never come out. That's leading to me. That's crapola. Another thing is the CPS caseworkers' not being good interviewers. Leading, and then it's a conjecture. I mean, I've had [CPS] reports that have come in and say, "Victim said this and this and this." The kid's interviewed [by the police] and the kid doesn't say anything. So you call the CPS worker and say, "Did you have to lead this kid?" "Well, we don't do that!" Right! I think—and this is what really makes prosecutors mad—I think they ought to be required to videotape every interview, and I think that that interview should speak for itself.

Q: You mean they being CPS? Or—

A: No, what I'm saying is anytime—that's not a bad idea—anytime a child is interviewed by anybody, that child should be put on tape, because then you eliminate suggestiveness, leading, any type of—I don't care, sometimes you have to pull teeth to get [information] out of kids. But you can do that without being leading. You don't take out a doll and say, did your dad touch you there? Because that's leading, and now what happens in the focus of that child is the child says, "Yeah, Daddy touched me there." What if Daddy didn't touch her there?! Now, you can pick up the doll and say, "Does Daddy ever touch you?" "Well, hey, he touches me here." Okay great. But if you've got that on video, it shows integrity, it shows honesty, it shows that you've got nothing to hide. They will not do it because of the leading natures of the interviews. They're never going to do that. There's a lot of guilty people that might get away with it, but there's a lot of innocent people that are getting hammered that don't deserve to be hammered. See that's why it's so important to keep an open mind in this job. You have to keep an open mind. They don't play fair! Counselors don't play fair, CPS don't play fair, prosecutors don't play fair, even the cops. But I do, and that's what's important. And I don't put up with leading crapola questions, because I'll put it right in the statement: CPS caseworker asked—we interviewed the child, and CPS finally decided to talk to the child and had to lead the child into saying these things. Leading. I put it right in there.

Q: Now, I talked to Judge [Robert] Dixon. He said when you've got a young child, sometimes to get a story, just to get an account in a case, you have to ask some leading questions.

A: You do. But I'm talking about where you pick up the doll, an anatomically correct doll, and you say, "Did your Daddy touch you here? Did your Daddy touch you here?" That's crap. You can talk to the child and say, "Are these your feet? Is this your nose? What do you call this? What do you call this? Do you call this anything?" But as soon as you suggest, the child responds because they think that you want that answer. I mean, I remember being 10 years old and Dad saying, "Come on, son, let's go play baseball. Did you clean up your room?" And you think to yourself, "If I say no, then he's not going to be happy with me." It's a suggestive type thing, so you have to be careful. But you can lead the kid a little bit. "Were you in the bedroom with your Daddy?" Well, if Daddy didn't do anything wrong in the bedroom, the next question's going to be, "Did anything happen in the bedroom?" That way you can lead, but you don't say, "Did Daddy touch you there in the bedroom?" But they do that, and that's bull.

Q: What about cases where the allegations involve threats, very serious threats, and children are very, very fearful. Is it okay for an interviewer—I'm thinking like a McMartin type case. If we believed everything that has been alleged in McMartin, we've got kids who saw animals killed before their eyes, et cetera, right? And this has been going on for a long time and they're very scared and they're very young. Is it okay for an interviewer to say something like, "It's okay to tell us if anything happened." Something like that?

A: Yes.

Q: How supportive can an interviewer be?

A: I'll tell you—and I really appreciate the prosecutors up here, don't get me wrong. There comes a time when they need to lead. The prosecutors up here explain to the child why they're there. Let's take an infant 6 years old. We explain to that 6-year-old why they're there, who I am. Sometimes I give them my badge and let them play with it.

Q: What would explaining why they're there include?

A: What we tell them is we say, "We heard something bad happened to you and we'd like to talk about that, but first we want to find out about you." That's how you interview. I mean it isn't, "We heard daddy touched you." No way, no way. Because what happens is one thing leads to another, such as you say, "Well, who do you live with?" "I live with my mommy, my daddy, my brother." "Well, do you like your brother?" "Yeah." "Do you like your mommy?" "Yeah." "Do you like your daddy?" "No." "Why don't you like your daddy?" "He touches me in places." Great interview right there. "Where does he touch you?" Okay? See, that's where you develop. But there's some guys who'll say, "You don't like your daddy? Why?" Here we go! "Does he do things that bother you?" And we get it, then comes the leading. And you try, and really those prosecutors really try. They really do a great job.

Q: Have you seen prosecutors starting to do that when you were there?

A: Oh yeah.

Q: What have you done?

A: What have I done? Just told them at the end of the interview, "We don't got nothing." And they agree. But the thing is, though, I'm not always there. When my cases come, I tell the parents, I tell CPS, "Nobody—nobody—is to talk to this child until the joint interview. After the joint interview, you can counsel him, whatever." It is not uncommon for me to get a call back from CPS saying, "She disclosed something on the way home to me." I could give a shit, because I know what the CPS worker did. "Are you sure your daddy didn't stick his finger in your vagina?" "Yeah." The CPS worker calls and says, "She told me that daddy stuck his finger up her vagina." That's a sore subject with me.

Q: Have you seen CPS workers in court get called to testify?

A: Yeah.

Q: And what happened?

A: See, we haven't been hit with one of those cases yet. But it's going to come, because not everyone's going to follow guidelines. There are some CPS caseworkers that I've found inappropriate. But see, we don't—I would say that there are some law enforcement people that do it, but we don't interview them. I mean, CPS and the prosecutors do. We sit there and just take the statement, follow the guidelines.

Q: Now what about in a case where there are alleged to be multiple victims. Would it be okay to say, "We've talked to other kids, and they told us bad things happened to them, and we wanted to talk to you."

A: That's right. That's okay. There's nothing leading about that. You're not suggesting that they should say, "Henry touched me on the vagina." What you're trying to do is ease them into a conversation.

Q: What about if you say, we already know about X, Y, Z, A, B, D?

A: Wrong. That's leading. I wouldn't allow that, and if they did it I would jump all over the prosecutor for doing it, because then you have tainted evidence.

Q: What about, "Johnny told us that this happened to you, did it?"

A: No, that's not right.

Q: Do you have any suggestions to make to other police agencies elsewhere, or any other components of the system dealing with these cases?

A: A couple things. One, if the money is available, then the training should be allowed. I mean you should have that training available: evidence specifically dealing with child abuse, psychological things. Also, you should establish a rapport with the people who you work with: CPS. And don't be afraid to tell them that they're full of shit. I don't know how you do that—see, I have a personality that's very open, candid, and sometimes arrogant. But those people know when I call on the phone I mean business. I'm not here to play games. I'll joke with them, but goddamn it, this is serious, we've got a child here who's suffering and we're going to take care of this kid. And I am not going to play your stupid games. Did you lead the interview? What did you really find out? I see here what you've got here in black and white, what the hell's going on here? Don't feel that there is a reason not to ask the appropriate question. If you feel a victim is lying, tell the victim you think they're lying, but tell them the reasons why. A lot of prosecutors and cops won't do that because they feel that Rape Relief or they feel CPS or somebody is going to say, "You can't question the victim." If you don't, the defense attorney will and you will look like an idiot, and I don't care what anybody says. The other thing is to keep an open mind. Don't make a judgment against the offender until you have all the facts, because what appears to be something might be something else. And always show empathy towards that victim, even though sometimes it's hard.

5. WALTER URBAN, defense attorney.
Interviewed July 29, 1986.

Urban, 41, is a Los Angeles attorney who has practiced law for twelve years. He represented one of the defendants in the McMartin case through the pretrial hearing, following which charges against her were dropped. He hired Lee Coleman to review the videotaped interviews in that case, and he spoke at VOCAL's First National Conference in Minneapolis.

Q: Why don't I start out by asking you when you became involved in the McMartin case, how you became involved, and to briefly describe what your involvement was throughout.

A: I was retained on the day that the seven defendants were brought into court after they were arrested. The family retained me. I went down to talk to her in jail—my client's name is Betty Raidor—and then made my first court appearance the following Tuesday trying to get her released on bail. The publicity had already begun and I knew that the case was unusual, the way it was being handled in the press, and then from that point on I was virtually in court every day for the next eighteen months until the case was finally dismissed.

Q: Why did Mrs. Raidor hire you? What's your background?

A: I'm a criminal defense attorney, former public defender, trial lawyer. I deal exclusively—well, essentially criminal defense work.

Q: Had you had experience defending people charged in sexual abuse cases before?

A: Yes.

Q: A lot of experience? Can you guess how many cases over how many years?

A: Oh, it's hard to say. If you're asking me if that's my specialty, no. It became—that case became my specialty, as it did for every lawyer involved, because it was just all-consuming.

Q: Would you say defending someone in a child sexual abuse case is very different from other sex cases?

A: You know what happened—when the McMartin case broke, it was the first time that this new kind of so-called therapy was used and the first time we saw this medical evidence, this so-called medical evidence, so that was new, novel. It was the first time it was directly attacked also by the defense. It had been used in other cases. Are you familiar with dependency cases? Do you know what they are? Okay, I've done tons of those too.

Q: You mean juvenile court proceedings—the kid is declared a dependent of the court and protective action can be taken.

A: Yeah, right. You have trials in those courts too, but they're all done in front of a judge with a real low standard of proof. The only issue is did something happen and usually they're believed. So, the medical evidence that was used in the McMartin case has been used in those courts earlier and had never really been addressed, had kind of been accepted. So we for the first time had to address that.

Q: Is this colposcope evidence?

A: Yeah, and Dr. Woodling and his crew of doctors who see things that other doctors don't see. And of course the interview techniques of the Children's [Institute] International, Kee MacFarlane and crew—they had been used extensively in the dependency courts, but never in a large sex abuse case before. That was new. But if you're asking, Is a child sexual abuse case different or more difficult to handle, we never had preschool mass molestation cases before. There weren't any. There was no precedent. There were a lot of new issues being addressed in this case, coupled with political overtones, a lot of people's careers on the line professionally—the therapists, the medical people, certain D.A.s. It was a real unusual combination.

Q: Was it exciting to be involved in?

A: Oh yeah, extremely exciting for a while. But then after a while, it just became extremely grinding. The case—I think anybody involved in the case would say it's too bad we didn't do this, it's too bad we didn't do that. Some of the early decisions made by the prosecutor were bad, were just a classic case of bad lawyering.

Q: For example?

A: Well, the size of the case, for example. The only reason the case was that big, in my opinion, is that they wanted to make sure those people stayed in jail. The original indictment wasn't that big of a case. When they later filed the second case, and made it in excess of two hundred counts, that's just not manageable. It's unnecessary. What they should have done is they should have selected, after doing an investigation, what we call the strongest counts and proceeded that way. They should have gone after one defendant or two defendants first, and then, doing whatever they could do in those cases, proceed later. But taking all of the counts, all of the children against all of the possible defendants at one time was just outrageous.

Q: Define the word *outrageous*.

A: Well, unmanageable, let's say that. When you go into court and you have three or four defendants, each of them have an attorney, just on a one-count case it's longer than average. Now you figure two hundred and some counts, figure seven defendants, seven different attorneys, and the press there—every time you turn around you've got a camera in your face—it just wasn't going to be handled at all. Everybody was posturing. The whole thing kind of broke down. It would have been nicer to have had more experience on the prosecutor's side, more experience for the judges involved. By that I mean, our judge was relatively new, never handled a case of this magnitude. It would have been nice to have someone a little more experienced. She was constantly under the glare of the camera, and I think she was pressured, so it would have been nice to have had separate cases, had defendants treated separately in different courts. But they had a program that they decided on. I think the D.A.s were really, really under—well, they still are—under a lot of pressure from the parents, who had become convinced early on that the molest occurred. And I've seen the evidence—been on the case a long time. Those molests did not occur. It's really tragic.

Q: You're convinced that nothing ever happened to any kid there?

A: Yeah. You see, that's my opinion, sure. And that's not because I'm just a defense attorney. If you say molest occurred, you have to believe all of the evidence, and to believe the stuff that came down just in court is just impossible. And then if you—

Q: I just don't follow that statement.

A: Let's back up. The use of so-called medical evidence—you referred to as a colposcope, all right? Is that reliable, number one? Legally it's not reliable. At some point that will be addressed in some other court. It already has been addressed in other cases in other courts. I think you'll see more of that in the future—where the medical evidence will be addressed, what it really is. Right now we have doctors who are aware of leading medical evidence, who will say that, at the very least they'll testify that sure, that's consistent with sexual abuse, but it's also consistent with a parade of things, all of which are innocuous type of injuries that we're talking about, can be sustained many different ways. That's the evidence. The other is the so-called disclosure interviews where the children are seen on videotapes. Those, if you see them and really spend some time with them, you'll see that there weren't any disclosures made. Disclosures were put into the minds of the various children.

Q: With all the interviews you say?

A: Yeah.

Q: How many interviews did you have access to?

A: Well we had access to forty-one. I don't know how many else there were.

Q: The question that's got to linger on everybody's mind is, If nothing ever happened, how could this story be told by so many children?

A: What story?

Q: The story of being molested.

A: Is that what your understanding has told you?

Q: My understanding is that a number of children said they were molested.

A: Well, do you understand the process of how that was reached? How it got to that point?

Q: Different people could probably give me different explanations of what that process was.

A: Generally, the case began when one parent accused a teacher, Raymond, of molesting her child. He was arrested. He posted bond, was released, then this big investigation begins. Manhattan Beach sent out a letter to parents, and the kids start being grilled: "Have you been molested, have you been molested?" Graphic details. Most of the parents respond in writing that nothing happened. Somehow or other Children's Institute International gets involved and kids start getting referred there. A lot. They went through four hundred to five hundred kids, past, previous, whatever. McMartin students. And they had a little routine that they sent them through, and one of the things they did was they had the parents fill out a long questionnaire about the kid. They did that and again, for the most part, there's nothing in there, no disclosures. Then when they get them into the video-taped interview, they have a certain script which they followed, and the script is ultimately the so-called disclosures. They were taken out of context. The parents were going to be shown—usually, that's how the thing went. The parents were then brought in. The therapist tells the parents, "Your kid's been molested. And we have it on tape. Now we'll go to the tape." Fast forward to various segments where people say something, fast forward it further, "See we've got the proof now. Would you please take this list

of referral counselors, therapists, and then have your kid go in there." And
that's what they did. They got into group sessions of parents and abused
kids. Certain people encouraged them to file lawsuits, and form organizations, and pass laws, and on and on and on. It just got completely out of
control. By the time it got into court, you've got a kid that has been to
counseling for something that may not have occurred and is used to discussing it, because he's going on a weekly or biweekly basis in which they
were encouraged to talk about the molest. So by the time you get a kid
into court, you don't know what you have in terms of what the testimony
is, what the kid says, or how reliable it is. But they're not telling all the
same story, to answer your question. And the story they do relate is, for
the most part, just too fantastic. Remember, there's no confessions by the
people accused, no adult witnesses to any of these acts. There's also a large
segment of kids who went to the McMartin Preschool who said nothing
happened. You don't use the number. Understandably.

Q: How do you explain—you sort of imply what your explanation is, but
why don't you go ahead and state it further—how the children who did
say they were molested and did claim that other things happened to them
came to tell those accounts?

A: I'm saying quite simply you could send any kid in there and he would
have come out saying he was molested—because of the process.

Q: In that case, why didn't every kid who went in there say the same thing?
Or say that they were molested?

A: Okay, your problem is that you haven't seen the tapes [access to the
tapes could not be obtained by the author].

Q: And that's something that I'm willing to do anything I can to—

A: I know, I know. And you haven't seen the transcripts of the interviews.

Q: It's true, is it not, that not every child who was videotaped and interviewed by MacFarlane, for example, said he or she had been abused?

A: We only had access to forty-one of the videotapes, and there were some
four hundred who went through the system. I don't know what the others
said. The ones that I was exposed to, in my opinion, any kid who went
through would say something that they could construe to be that they've
been molested.

Q: How did you handle cross-examination during the pretrial hearing?

A: First of all, the D.A. objected to nearly every one of our questions.
You've got to remember there's seven, okay? That means each one of them

has the right to cross-examine each child. That's routine. They insisted that we were harassing the children, and that our method to win the case was to scare the parents and the kids out of the case and all that kind of stuff. So they objected and we would have to argue the objections. It was unbelievably time consuming, painstaking. One of the defense attorneys kept a child on the stand for a long time. Didn't make the rest of us look too good.

Q: Which attorney was that?

A: I'm not going to mention names. Everybody knows who that is [Daniel Davis]. There was disagreement among the defense attorneys.

Q: What were the areas of disagreement?

A: I didn't think it was necessary to continue to question the children. I didn't think it was getting us anywhere. I wanted to speed the case up. I felt that the best thing that could happen for anybody and everybody involved was to get the thing to trial right away, get it in front of a jury once and for all. That's what's fortunate—those people in the Scott [County] case [better known as the Jordan, Minnesota, case] were very fortunate that it got to trial right away. They separated two of them out, they tried two: acquittal. I'm sure the prosecution was shocked by the acquittal. They reevaluated their position and then wound up dismissing all the rest. That's the way a case is normally handled. In our case, they created this monster and it developed a life of its own. There was no one in control.

Q: Were there strategies where there was disagreement?

A: Generally, when you have a client when there's a lot of evidence against them, shall we say a guilty party, the common tactic for a defense attorney is to try every possible procedural effort to hopefully win on a technicality—delays, that kind of thing. The posture is, "I'm going down fighting." That's generally the posture because you know that once the trial begins, then it's kind of all over. I'm talking about a case where we have a signed confession, or a videotaped confession, eight eyeball witnesses, finger-prints—that kind of case. Well, then you might luck out and get some procedural victory for the guy. In our case, these people are innocent—factually and legally. There's no reason to delay. That's my point. I say, let's get the thing rolling. Let's move it right now in front of a jury, and it'll answer a lot of questions, because other cases similar in nature in the South Bay that went to trial, once they went to trial, the community would live with it. Whatever the jury decides, the court decides, fine. They had a lot of cases with hung juries, later dismissed, that kind of thing. Once a jury decides, it's in the courts, people can live with it. Now, when you delay like the McMartin case, no one knows. It's in a state of limbo. And when the D.A. is dismissing, that's still in a state of limbo. It leaves too many unanswered questions.

Q: Would you have preferred it if the D.A. had not dismissed the charges against your client?

A: Oh, heck no. I can't say that. I'm still representing my client. I'll take a dismissal any day. Any attorney would. However, it would have been nice to go to a jury a year and a half ago, say, and show the public through the jury trial what evidence there really is.

Q: How could the protracted pretrial hearing have been avoided?

A: The D.A. could simply have said, "Go ahead and have a trial." The preliminary hearing is supposed to function as a screening process, after a complaint has been filed in a municipal court. It's an opportunity also to get discovery. Okay, that means we can cross-examine. You see a bare bones kind of a case put on, just enough to "bind them over." Did a crime occur, and is there a reasonable suspicion that this guy sitting over here did it? That's all they have to prove. You can waive the preliminary. You don't have to have one. If both sides agree, you don't have to have it. Five of the seven [defendants] kept saying, "We don't want a prelim, we want to go to trial," and [the prosecutors] said, "Sit down, you're going to ride along," because they made a strategic decision, the D.A.s, to keep everybody together, because then the children would only have to testify one time. And they would only have to testify and be videotaped at the preliminary hearing, and then at the trial level, the plan was that they would introduce the videotaped testimony, so the children would be exposed to the courtroom only once, one time only.

Q: If it had gone to a trial for the seven—well, even for the two remaining defendants, are they going to be able to introduce videotaped testimony in lieu of the appearance of the children?

A: We'll see. I don't know what they're going to do. I'm sure they're going to try to do that. Who knows what they're going to do. In a way, the videotapes are good evidence for the defense because the kids say all sorts of inconsistencies. It's not really good prosecution kind of evidence, and for them to introduce the tapes, some of those kids were on the stand seven days, eight days. One was at it for fourteen days, so how can you expect the jury to pay attention to that kind of thing—a videotape that long? They probably will wind up with live witnesses.

Q: If they had severed [the cases], then they could have had preliminary hearings with two, and they could have gone straight to trial with five.

A: Yes.

Q: And they chose not to do that?

A: Yes.

Q: And you think that was a mistake for everybody?

A: Yes. They should have severed, they shouldn't have filed that many counts, they shouldn't have tried to keep everybody together. They should have been a little more selective. And they should have done their investigation before they filed, also. That would have been nice. They filed two hundred and eight counts and then went out and did their investigation. They formed the Child Abuse Task Force during the preliminary hearing to run down the leads that developed after the case was filed. In other words, the filing act itself occurred and they hadn't done what they normally—what's expected to do before they file. They'd done a real cursory job. You figure a case of that nature, it would be real nice if the prosecutor was a little more careful in filing.

Q: Which prosecutors, according to you, made mistakes? And what is the explanation?

A: Hard to say.

Q: Do you think it was inexperience in handling something like this?

A: I can only speculate, you know. I know the experience level of the three D.A.s and they're not, at the time that the case began, they certainly weren't the most experienced trial lawyers in the D.A.s office.

Q: What was the experience level of the three when the case started?

A: They averaged about seven years, maybe—seven or six years, something like that.

Q: There are more experienced people?

A: There are more experienced people, certainly.

Q: Do you know the other people in the office, either by reputation or personally, from experience?

A: What other people?

Q: The other D.A.s in the office.

A: Sure. I deal with them on a daily basis.

Q: Were there others who would have seemed to you more appropriate to handle this case?

A: Yes.

Q: Why would they have been more appropriate, in your opinion?

A: Experience.

Q: Anyone have particularly a lot of experience in this area, however?

A: What area, in child abuse?

Q: Yeah.

A: You know, a child abuse case is no big deal as far as a criminal prosecutor or defense attorney. It's just another type of case. It doesn't require a special knowledge. It's not a special—a real specialty. Some lawyers specialize and do nothing but these kinds of things, but really, in terms of being a prosecutor, I think anybody, any D.A. with say, ten, fifteen years in the office could certainly handle the case. I keep repeating myself, but the basic rule is if you make your case too big, you're creating too many areas of potential problems. They decided to go "no bail." That was a new law they were testing. So my client was—they said, "You're staying in. You're not going to be allowed to have bail." She was 64 years old and never even had a traffic ticket. All of a sudden she got a no bail hold like she's a master criminal. And then they said, "You have to have a preliminary hearing," and we said, "Well, fine, we're not going to waive our rights to a speedy trial." And they said, "Yes you are." You're not supposed to be able to do that. They can't force you to do that. It's one of the fundamental constitutional laws. So we had to take that up on appeal, and it resulted in my client being released early on, which then they turned around and filed another complaint, forcing her to stay in, and we filed other writs. It was just—a case that large is going to have a lot more problems than a real simple bare bones kind of case.

Q: What could the judge have done to prevent—or what did the judge do to create—chaos?

A: I don't feel real comfortable blaming her, or blaming anybody in particular. I think that the organism that they spawned out of the D.A.'s Office, no matter where it would have gone, it would have been problematic. I mean you can say maybe she should have controlled the attorneys a little bit more, or maybe she should have done this or that but, you know, we were sitting in court, we never knew whether they were going to add more counts or whether they were going to arrest more people. It was a real bad climate for at least a year, real bad. I mean the tide was definitely against us. We were stuck.

Q: Are you talking about the public opinion tide?

A: Yeah.

Q: And how did that affect you in court?

A: How did it affect us in court? Well, we had the public there all the time—we had the media there all the time. We averaged about fifteen, twenty members of the media there most of the time, okay? And when you have that kind of scrutiny, people don't act normal. Cameras on them a lot. They turn the cameras on in the courtroom, all of a sudden posture improves, speeches are longer. The first fight we had, one of the first fights we had was access to the tapes, which [the judge] granted us, and then she withdrew it, and then she granted it, and it was back and forth. Every time there was a ruling there was an opinion, immediately. So is she, or are we, pressured by all the publicity? You know you can't just ignore it. It certainly has a lot of effect. Cases are traditionally handled, not necessarily quietly, but supposedly in the courtroom, so that things will be as objective as possible. When you've got the media commenting—it was the lead story every night, for weeks and weeks and weeks: another twist in the McMartin case kind of thing. The D.A. stood up one day and said, "Aha! We've discovered corroborating evidence to the children's stories." They had no physical corroborating evidence to any of these charges, okay? They discovered corroborating evidence to the satanism stories. They've got a witch's cape, they've got rabbit ears, the kids said that they were mutilating animals and they said they found it. They announced it. Of course, boom: headlines, big story. D.A.'s got the evidence. We said the same day we'd like to see the evidence. Discovery again, please. It took us a week to force them. It took us a week to get the damn evidence into court. They brought it into court and it turns out it wasn't what they said it was: it was a toy cape, it was a hare's ears, clearly the victim of a buckshot, they weren't hacked off, and the candles, which were supposedly part of the ritual, were just ordinary candles. They then begrudgingly admitted no, they are not corroborating evidence. But by then, of course, the story was out and talk to John Q. Public: well, they've got corroborating evidence, don't they? The impression that's conveyed is that they've got evidence. And that's the kind of thing we were fighting all the time. They said they've got tapes, they said they've got photos. We found out two months later there's nothing.

Q: What kind of responsibility do you fix on the media for all this? What should the media do, what shouldn't the media do, and how do you assess what they did?

A: That's a long question, requiring a longer answer. I think careers were on the line in the media, too. I got the impression that certain members were benefiting professionally in covering the story, at the beginning at least. The new Manson kind of case, horror story: animals being mutilated and kids being sold into prostitution. You know the media reporting on stuff, they just take whatever the D.A. says. Now, okay, so they're supposedly naive. If we can't believe the D.A., who can we believe? Well, when you start hearing the stuff that they're talking about and then, number one, there's no evidence to support this stuff—they didn't question that. They would then accept the next explanation, and report that. And then the D.A. would be found to be misrepresenting that, and then they'd accept the next version. See that "Believe the Children" thing there [*pointing to a small sign in his office*]? That question mark I put on [so that it reads "Believe the Children?"]. That's a bumper sticker which parents of the children involved and a number of other people put on their cars in the South Bay area. The reason for that is because the kids' versions, or the kids' stories, became impossible to be believed. Such as: "I was molested." Where did it occur? "In a hot air balloon over the desert." "In a ski boat, where sharks were all around, and they told us that we were going to be thrown to the sharks if we didn't agree to be molested." That kind of stuff. And you think, *what*? Where did this occur? "Well, it occurred in a tunnel." Where's the tunnel? "Underneath the school." So they dig underneath the school. There's no tunnel there. There's no nothing. So, the therapy group said, "Well, okay, that's true. Those are fantasy stories, and the reason is because they're children testifying. But what you have to do is whittle away at that kind of material, and believe the core, and the core is they're disclosing that they've been molested." So what you do is you believe the kid whatever they say. And some members of the media would be accepting that kind of thing and reporting it. So you think, "What could the media have done?" Well, they've got resources. They should have conducted an investigation on their own, instead of just accepting everything. You could see them down there every day. They'd be down there, the D.A. would be asked a question, we would be asked a question, and then zingo, it would be on the news that night. I mean, just editing, just nothing. They didn't know what they were doing. There had never been a case that big where there was no evidence. Never been a case that big of falsely accused people. The system of media, as a system, in reporting crime stories and criminal cases didn't know how to handle it. Slowly, over time, certain members became skeptical. Sort of a chipping-away process. I allowed my client to be interviewed right from the very beginning. She was on television all the time. My position was we had nothing to hide, she's innocent, but because of the preliminary hearing it's going to be a year and a half before we put in defense evidence. Since the case is being tried in the media anyway, we might as well put our case on the media too. And once she was exposed to the so-called hard-hitting journalists, they would say privately, "No way.

She can't be guilty. No way." Those kind of doubts evolved among certain members of the media, and then you started seeing the coverage change. What could they have done differently? They should have done their own investigation.

Q: Are you involved with any of the civil lawsuits?

A: Yes. I'm defending my client because she is being sued by a number of parents. I'm also—my associate has filed plaintiff's action against the city, the county, the state, Children's Institute, ABC, Mr. [Robert] Philibosian [the D.A. at the time the case was filed], and a number of other people.

Q: Do you feel the system here is fair to defendants?

A: When? Where?

Q: Let me ask the question this way: Is the McMartin case representative enough of how the system works to judge the system on·the basis of that case?

A: No.

Q: Why not?

A: First of all, the scale. I don't think there's ever been a case with that kind of press coverage over that long a period of time. Other cases get publicity, but they have a beginning and an end. This one never seemed to end. It was an unfortunately unique group of people involved, the principals involved, which caused problems. Another group of lawyers—just a few changes in the lawyering involved—and it would have been a different case entirely.

Q: On both sides?

A: Yeah.

Q: All right, you've tried these cases before and since, you're involved in a trial right now. Do you think that the system in general treats defendants in these cases fairly?

A: If you're talking about do they get a fair trial, they can. It varies from judge to judge, it varies from lawyer to lawyer, that kind of thing. It's certainly possible in the system. But I think what you're really getting at is, Will the McMartin remaining defendants get a fair trial?

Q: No. You answered that part. You said you can't judge the system on the basis of the McMartin case, so let's just look at the system, then.

A: Okay, well, I'm getting at whether the system can ensure a defendant charged in this kind of case a fair trial, and the answer is, yes, it can.

Q: How about child victims—and I'll use that word without saying *alleged* victims; let's talk about a case in which there really is a victim. Does the system adequately protect a child victim—the mental health of a child victim?

A: See, we went through a lot of that in the McMartin case. We heard from a lot of so-called experts about the trauma of testifying in court, and they were trying to get closed circuit testimony—we had closed circuit testimony, and all the justification for that. Who knows whether it's good or bad for a child to testify in court? There's no one really, in my mind, that knows the answer to that question.

Q: And they can't get the same answer for every child, either.

A: Certainly not, so there's no real hard and fast rule. I would say that most—the person in charge is the judge, and most judges treat children—they protect them quite well. If a kid breaks down and cries, everything stops. If it becomes obvious that the child can't testify, then fine, it stops. To justify closed circuit TV, they tried to introduce all these studies show-ing the children suffer irreparable damage if they have to repeat in public court the nature of the abuse. Well, maybe there are cases like that. But I think generally it's also therapeutic, other experts will say, for a child to testify in court, knowing that they're in court and this is the judge, and the judge is going to—you tell this, and the bad man, or whatever, will be punished. This is the way the system works, so maybe it instills some values in the kid at an early age when he sees that his testimony will be respected and will result in what is appropriate. And what about the cases where the kid testifies and the guy's acquitted? Well, fine. I don't know. I don't know the answer. I generally do not believe that the system abuses anybody—witnesses and whatnot.

Q: A whole lot has been said—it seems like there's less said now than there was at one time—but a whole lot has been said about cross-examination by defense attorneys. You have seen other defense attorneys cross-examine and you've already made some criticisms of some that you've seen. What do you try and do when you cross-examine a child? And I'd like you to answer the question [as it relates to] preliminary hearings and whether there's any difference in preliminary hearings and [trials] in front of a jury.

A: It varies from case to case, but there are some attorneys who say that we've got to destroy the kid, okay? We've got to grind that kid and really get him terrified and confused, and all that kind of stuff. And they do it by being forceful. I personally never do that. I will be cross-examining that kid just like any other witness and I'm not about to get that kid pissed off at me. Because it's not necessary. If you have any experience with kids, you don't have to give a hardened look to get whatever information you want out of them. You don't have to be tricky. It's best to be as straightforward and simple as possible. If you're going to do it in front of the jury, I mean what's the value of attacking the child in front of the jury? You're going to run the risk of angering some jurors.

Q: How about when there is no jury [as during a preliminary hearing]?

A: Well, when there's no jury, the judge is going to stop you, in most cases. Attorneys aren't allowed to just tear into kids routinely. That's nonsense. That's just propaganda from the prosecutor's office. It just doesn't happen. In those cases, in the rare case when it does happen, I would say I'm sure it backfires.

Q: Aren't there cases that one can imagine where it would be useful to scare a child, or to intimidate a child?

A: To scare them? Into what?

Q: Inconsistencies, saying wrong things.

A: You mean trick them into being inconsistent? Let's say that you've got a kid on the stand who says that she was molested in the bedroom of her apartment. You get an investigator to go to the apartment, and you have a photo of the room and you start asking questions about the room. And you get the kid to say that the window's here, the window's there, whatever the facts are, and you know that that's not true. Then if you confront the child: "Is this a picture of the room—the one you just told me about?" "Yeah." "Well, where's the window?" Is that scaring a kid? I don't think it's necessary to scare. I think it's much more effective to just not let the kid know what you're getting at or where you're going. That's true about cross-examination of any witness. You just ask questions, and they don't know what you want or where you're going and you don't tell them. You never let them know, and you stop when you think it's appropriate. I don't know if you've ever testified. I have. It can be unnerving. I didn't know what was going on. I felt—you're up there in the chair, all these people looking at you, and all of a sudden, the simple question becomes, "My God, wait a minute!" You're asking a question of style in cross-examination. Each lawyer has his own style, but, there's no reason to intimidate children.

Q: Is there any ethical consideration that leads you to adopt this style with children?

A: My style?

Q: Yeah.

A: No. I've discovered that that's an effective style.

Q: Is there anything unethical about adopting another style?

A: Unethical in what sense? For me to do what?

Q: Is it unethical for a defense attorney to intimidate a child?

A: See, I don't know what you mean by intimidate. I'm not trying to be a lawyer with you. It's—I mean if you're talking about sitting in court and the kid walks in and you stand up and say, "I'm going to get you, you little so-and-so, as soon as you hit the stand," or let the parents know, "Boy, you're not going to have the same kid again."

Q: To raise one's voice, to ask questions in an accusatory tone and phrasing in an accusatory manner. Let's take the stereotype. Whatever his name is—Berger, Perry Mason's opponent [in the TV series]? You know, to play the archvillain type of attorney. Is there anything unethical about that?

A: I don't know if *unethical* is the right word.

Q: Are there any ethics that should govern the way a defense attorney cross-examines a child in a sexual abuse case?

A: None—the ethics are the same for any witness. You're asking whether kid witnesses should be given special treatment, or held to a standard, or there should be special ethics rules? No. The law says that a witness is just that, a witness. Once a judge rules that they qualify to act as a witness, that's it. Same rules apply to everybody.

Q: What has been the personal cost to you, the personal benefits and personal costs to you, of having been involved in the McMartin case?

A: Who knows, it's not over with. It was a grueling experience, personally.

Q: Is the media largely responsible for that? Or do you have other contact with people outside that made it difficult?

A: No, just being in court every day with the same case, and getting nowhere on the case is exhausting. It would have been nice to be proceeding at a snail's pace. I would have liked that, but it was almost going backwards in time on a daily basis. With no end in sight.

Q: How did your friends and aquaintances and other contacts you had with the general public—how did that go?

A: By the end of the case, especially when the dismissals were rendered, everybody's mind changed—public opinion and mood drastically shifted. They were all guilty before that. They had been tried and convicted in the media, and, you know, I'd hear, "You? How could you represent those guilty people? They're the worst scum of the earth," that kind of stuff. I'd say, "Well, they could very well be innocent." "Oh yeah, yeah. Well, you're the lawyer. You're paid to say that."

Q: Close friends would say this?

A: Sure. Everybody is exposed to the media, every day.

Q: Did it have an effect on some of those relationships?

A: No. My professional life doesn't necessarily affect my social life. If there's someone who would choose to disassociate themselves with me because of a case I'm handling, well, fine. I don't need to be around that person anyway.

Q: What changes, if any, would you like to see in the system?

A: You know, these kind of questions, they irritate me in a way—I don't mean personally.

Q: Too broad?

A: It isn't that. System. The word itself: what we really have is sort of an agreement among all parties. It's like a game: here are the rules, let's play by the rules. The rules change from time to time. You know it's like in any sports. Look at pro football. Rules change as we discover that there's too many points being scored by this and whatever. There's a lot of so-called experts in judicial procedures and judicial administration who are saying, "Well let's do this, let's do that." There's always pressure to change because there's people involved, so there will be changes. Are there any changes which are really, really overdue? I'd say, no, I don't see them. If you're referring to the changes as we dealt with the McMartin case—should the system have handled the McMartin case differently? Oh yeah, yeah, a lot differently.

Q: How?

A: Well, I already told you that number one, they shouldn't have filed that big a case with that many people; number two, they should not have tried to keep everybody in jail; number three, they should have done their investigation before they filed. You know, those are basics. I hope the D.A.'s Office is aware of this. There'll never be another McMartin case. I hope they learned their lesson as lawyers that they should never do that type of case in that type of fashion. They were flying by the seat of their pants, okay?

Q: The changes that you just suggested strike me as not so much changes in any system as decisions that were made by individuals.

A: Well, the system is made up of individuals.

Q: Right.

A: And you talk about, like, the role of the judge. I mean a judge has a wide area of discretion. You can take one case in front of one judge and get one ruling, and the same exact case next door and get a different ruling. I mean you know that. That's just the way our system is. The bottom line is people.

Q: I could conceive of changes in rules, or procedures, that one could advocate.

A: Such as?

Q: Well—

A: Remember that I'm in the system, okay? I don't think it makes any sense for me to advocate a change in the system, because from case to case it varies. In one case I want a speedy trial, in this case I don't want a speedy trial. In this case I want to do this, this case I don't want that. This case I want them to turn over discovery, and this one I don't want them to. I mean, remember as an advocate, I'm sort of—

Q: Maybe that answers the whole question. You don't have any problems with the system as long as the system adequately protects your interests, and you feel it does.

A: My client's interest.

Q: Yeah.

A: And I think that system provides an opportunity for an individual to have his rights protected, yes. Okay? The McMartin case, for example, did result in dismissals eventually. That was done by the system. That was done after a judge had found evidence, was done bravely by the District Attorney's Office, who said, "Hey, wait, we really don't have a case. We better get out of this thing now." That's the system. Of course the system created the thing, too. As long as the system remains flexible, then I think we're in good shape.

Q: What do you think about VOCAL?

A: I don't know, it's a grass roots, kind of typically American organization. It's apparently still going on. They had a convention last year. I was at it—the national convention.

Q: What did you think of it?

A: I spoke at it. It was impressive to see that many people. It's a good opportunity to show the common threads among all these cases. We have to get organized. The need for organization is pretty clear, and I'm sure it will continue.

Q: Think it's going to have a positive effect on—

A: I think it already has. You figure that any legislator that's approached by a group of—child molesters are getting organized these days? I mean, it's like robbers or burglars forming a group, and saying, "Hey, we're the burglars, and we don't think we're getting a fair shake." But they're saying, "Hey, we're accused, we're falsely accused."

Q: Any misgivings you have about the organization?

A: Such as?

Q: Some people say that there is no way to know who is falsely accused and who has been properly convicted in that organization.

A: I don't know. You mean are there real pedophiles in the group?

Q: That's a misgiving that some people have about—

A: There's pedophiles in the D.A.'s Office, there's pedophiles who are policemen! There's pedophiles who are parish priests and this stuff. You can't really be that harsh about VOCAL.

Q: Maybe a difference that could be drawn between a D.A.'s Office and VOCAL is that—actually, what I was going to say I can see some holes in, but I'll say it anyway. VOCAL is set up to support people who are falsely accused, and give them at least information and assistance in that respect. If they are providing the same thing for people who are properly accused, who are really guilty, they could be getting criminals off.

A: Nah. I think that's remote. First of all, they don't have the resources. It's really usually educational more than anything else.

Q: But isn't part of the education giving the person information that could be used to get an acquittal when one shouldn't come down?

A: You're entitled to whatever resources you can get to provide a defense for your case. There's nothing wrong with that. The same information could be obtained elsewhere—other sources.

Q: Do you think there are legitimate reasons for people to be concerned about child sexual abuse in this country today?

A: Well, there's always been legitimate reasons for that.

Q: Do you believe child abuse is on the rise?

A: No. My understanding of the statistics, whatever they are—I don't know how valuable they are—but there's a guy (what's his name?) who says that apparently the reports of child abuse have gone way the heck up—dramatically increased. At the same time, the unfounded, or unsubstantiated complaints—

Q: Douglas Besharov.

A: There you go. Since you know who he is, you know about what I'm saying.

Q: Yeah. How about comments about [Dr. Lee] Coleman and [Dr. Ralph] Underwager. What do you think about them?

A: I know them both. They're both excellent professionals. At the very least their opinions—they're both respectable opinion givers in terms of evidence—that's what we're talking about. You mentioned Dr. Summit in the beginning of this conversation. Dr. Summit has his opinion, and that's the way our system works—that he's rendering an opinion. Okay, let's hear another opinion.

Q: What do you think of Summit?

A: I've known him, known of him, for a number of years. What do I think of his syndrome, you mean? It's opinion, let's put it that way. Does it have scientific validity? No, I don't think so.

Q: Do you have respect for him as a professional in this field?

A: No more than any other doctor.

Q: Do you have respect for any professionals who are on that side?

A: What do you mean by do I have respect for them? Well, I respect them as human beings, you know. I wouldn't be screaming at them.

Q: Do you consider anyone like Summit, who testifies as an expert in court and who is considered by others in that profession an expert, do you consider him an expert?

A: Well, you know, if enough people call you an expert, all of a sudden you're an expert.

Q: Do you consider Coleman an expert?

A: He's as much an expert as Dr. Summit. He's a child psychiatrist and has been in practice. He's testified as an expert on psychiatric issues in other cases, unrelated to child molesting. So he's got the credentials, yeah.

Q: How about Underwager?

A: I've never had him on the stand. I've met him a couple of times. Apparently he's testified. He's got a doctorate. His credentials qualify as an expert witness, yes.

Q: So you don't have a personal opinion about the—

A: My personal opinion about whether they're good experts or bad experts—it really doesn't make much sense. If you're asking me how would they testify in court as an expert witness, I think I'd definitely use Coleman. And I would definitely use Underwager. That's routine. And if you're trying a liability case involving, you know, a glass bottle that breaks up, you're going to get an expert. You're going to find out the other side that you're suing or you're defending or whatever, that they have experts who say that your side, you're full of hot air.

Q: One of Coleman's long-standing arguments is that there should not be mental health experts used in this kind of fashion, and he includes child sexual abuse cases. What's you opinion about that?

A: That's why I like Coleman, basically. I think that adds to his credibility. One of the things you've asked about is the change that they try to advocate in the experts who come to court and testify that abuse occurred, so that the child never has to take the stand. The expert will just be rendering an opinion, and they wanted to have the case presented in that fashion. I think that's really, really bad. It's fundamentally wrong. There's a real abuse of the mental health professionals who are used in court. That's one of the things they've tried to push for a long time.

Q: What's your objection to that?

A: Well, basically, you know, we're supposed to have trials with live witnesses so that we can confront and cross-examine the accuser in this. If you're going to stick somebody in jail for a number of years, you might as well let them have a trial too. That's the American way—Anglo-Saxon jurisprudence—and it's worked for a number of years.

Notes

Introduction

1. Author's interview with Tim Smith, a therapist who treats sexual abuse offenders at Northwest Treatment Associates in Seattle, Aug. 6, 1986.
2. Hollingsworth, J., *Unspeakable Acts* (New York: Congdon & Weed, 1986); about the Country Walk case in Florida. (Copyright © 1986 by Jan Hollingsworth. Reprinted by permission of Congdon & Weed, Inc.)

Chapter 1

1. Tulsky, F.N., Judge is taken off cases: he's probe target, Harris tells court. *Philadelphia Inquirer*, Nov. 15, 1986.
2. Author's interview with Toni Seidl, Child Abuse/Child Sexual Abuse Coordinator, Social Work Department, Children's Hospital of Philadelphia, Nov. 20, 1986.
3. Hannah, S., A judge's remarks: a look at the case. *The Milwaukee Journal*, Jan. 17, 1982.

Chapter 2

1. Author's interview with a confidential source.
2. Child sexual abuse: what your children should know, produced by WTTW, Chicago. Broadcast in New York City on Sept. 17, 1984.
3. Peck, J., Members of clergy support Grady by raising $27,000 in defense funds. *Reporter Dispatch* (Gannett Westchester/Rockland [N.Y.] Newspapers), Nov. 23, 1985; and David, W., Grady to congregation: 'I'm innocent.' *Reporter Dispatch*, Jan. 24, 1986 (articles covered trial and conviction of the Rev. Nathaniel T. Grady).
4. Clark has allowed his name to be used to ensure the credibility of the parents' group that was formed shortly after the abuse was disclosed.
5. Hechler, D., Day care center owner named in $280 million lawsuit. *The City Sun* (Brooklyn, N.Y.), Aug. 28–Sept. 3, 1985.

6. Mount Vernon case information based on author's interviews with parents whose children were abused at the Martin center.

7. Hollingsworth, J., *Unspeakable Acts* (New York: Congdon & Weed, 1986), p. 243.

8. Author's interview with confidential source.

9. Colao, F., and Hosansky, T., *Your Children Should Know* (New York: Bobbs-Merrill, 1983), pp. 25–26.

10. Summit, R.C., The child sexual abuse accommodation syndrome. *Child Abuse & Neglect* 7 (1983):177–93. (Copyright 1983. Reprinted by permission of Pergamon Journals, Ltd.) This article in particular and Summit in general have been bitterly attacked by VOCAL and its most prominent proponent, Dr. Lee Coleman. The controversy will be aired in chapter 6, but suffice it to say here that Coleman's main disagreement with Summit's thesis centers on its application to cases other than incest in intact families.

11. Ibid., p. 186.

12. A number of psychiatrists and others have written critically of psychiatry's attitudes over the years to child sexual abuse. The reader is referred to Masson, J., *The Assault on Truth* (New York: Penguin Books, 1985); Peters, J., Children who are victims of sexual assault and the psychology of offenders *American Journal of Psychotherapy* 30 3 (1976):398–432; Rush, F., *The Best Kept Secret: Sexual Abuse of Children* (chapter 7: "A Freudian Coverup") (Englewood Cliffs, N.J.: Prentice-Hall, 1980); and Miller, A., *Thou Shalt Not Be Aware: Society's Betrayal of the Child* (New York: Farrar, Straus & Giroux, 1984).

13. Summit, The child sexual abuse accommodation syndrome, p. 186.

14. Ibid., p. 188.

15. *National Catholic Reporter*, June 7, 1985, articles by Jones, A. and Berry, J. (Reprinted by permission of the National Catholic Reporter, P.O. Box 419281, Kansas City, MO 64141.)

16. Ibid., Jones, A., Legal actions against pedophile priests grow.

17. Hill-Holtzman, N., Bernstein guilty of not reporting molest charge. *Los Angeles Herald*, July 25, 1986.

18. Author's interview, Oct. 17, 1986.

19. Dobbs, D., Legal responsibilities and liabilities when treating child abuse. *Pediatric Emergency Care* (Mar. 1986):40.

20. Sanderson, B., Doctor charged with failing to report child abuse; and Mother wants charges pressed against doctor. *Concord Monitor*, Sept. 22, 1984, and Dec. 1, 1984.

21. James, J., Womack, W.M., and Stauss, F., Physician reporting of sexual abuse of children. *Journal of the American Medical Assocation* 11 (1978):1145–46. (Copyright 1978, American Medical Association.)

22. Saulsbury, F.T., and Hayden, G.F., Child abuse reporting by physicians. *Southern Medical Journal* 5 (1986):585–87; Saulsbury, F.T., and Campbell, R.E., Evaluation of child abuse reporting by physicians. *American Journal of Diseases of Children* 139 (1985):393–95.

23. Kim, D.S., Most doctors don't tell. *Justice for Children* (Spring 1985):17. (Reprinted with permission from Justice for Children, P.O. Box 42266, Washington, D.C. 20015.)

24. Helfer, R.E., Why most physicians don't get involved in child abuse cases and what to do about it. *Children Today* (May–June 1975): 30–31.

25. Author's interview, July 30, 1986.

26. Sgroi, S.M., et al., *Sexual Assault of Children and Adolescents* (Lexington, Mass.: Lexington Books, 1978), p. xvi.

27. Author's interview, Dec. 16, 1986.

28. "The McMartin Pre-School" produced by L. Bergman, "60 Minutes," Nov. 2, 1986. (© CBS Inc., all rights reserved.) The exchange quoted was by no means the only—or even the most egregious—flaw in the program. The lead-in probably was. The camera panned across a couch on which were seated the five defendants against whom all charges were dropped. Wallace: "Do these women look like child molesters?" As a viewer who wrote a letter aired the following week noted, a child molester does not necessarily look any different from anyone else. There were also gaping holes in the story. For example, why were no police or D.A.'s investigators interviewed or even mentioned during the broadcast? Why all the blame on the therapists from Children's Institute International? If they were not trained investigators (and they do not claim to be), why did those who *were* require their assistance? And if D.A. Ira Reiner believed the evidence was so weak against the five defendants, why did he wait until the eighteen-month preliminary hearing was completed before dropping the charges? These questions were never asked.

29. The unwillingness of doctors in private practice to report as frequently as those in public facilities also skews the meager statistics in this field. Public facilities are more likely to see people from the lower socioeconomic groups, and consequently these groups are overrepresented in the statistics, providing fodder for those who prefer to view sexual abuse as a problem of the lower classes.

Chapter 3

1. Author's interview, Apr. 16, 1987.

2. Author's interview, Apr. 1, 1985.

3. C. Stephen Heard, Jr., said in the interview that he was responsible for the decision to request a gag order and that it was designed to protect the charity at a time it looked to be under severe attack. It was also in keeping with the plaintiff's decision to use a fictitious name and to seal the court file in the case, he added.

4. Murphy, F.T., Who speaks for the abused child? *New York Law Journal*, Mar. 29, 1985.

5. Their names were changed in court papers to protect their privacy, their lawyers said.

6. Information from bankruptcy court file, referred to later in the chapter.

7. Author's interviews with several confidential sources, including a parent who claimed her son was abused in a Friendly Town. Additional examples were cited in the author's earlier investigation: Fresh air can be dangerous. *The City Sun* (Brooklyn, N.Y.), July 11, 1984. The assertion that abuse, even when disclosed, may not be publicized is further substantiated by the Fund officials' revelation (during the interview) that they have successfully handled a half-dozen emergencies over the past couple of years. Those cases have certainly never appeared in the New York City media.

8. Author's interviews with Johnson, Oct. 26, 1984, and Apr. 5, 1985. Interview with Attorney General Stephen Merrill, Apr. 24, 1985.

9. Author's interview with Tom Karger and Fund lawyer Robert Gaynor, Apr. 22, 1987.

10. Davis, H., 'Friendly town' was torture city, says girl, 5. *New York Post*, Mar. 26, 1981; Hawtin, G., The scent of scandal fouls fresh air fund. *New York Post*, Oct. 16, 1981.

11. Fresh air fund hosts recall city children's 'firsts.' (Unsigned.) *The New York Times*, May 12, 1985. (Copyright © 1985 by The New York Times Company. Reprinted by permission.)

12. *Marion Gaskin* v. *The Fresh Air Fund*, filed in State Supreme Court in Manhattan.

13. Author's interviews with New Hampshire volunteers were conducted in October 1984, and March and April 1985. There were multiple interviews with several individuals.

14. Author's interview, Apr. 1, 1985.

15. Author's interview, Apr. 4, 1985.

16. Author's interview, Apr. 22, 1985.

17. Author's interview, Apr. 5, 1985.

18. In the interview, the Fund confirmed that Walton was the chairperson in 1981, although it did not say whether she was also in charge the following year.

19. A fuller explanation of the arrangement between therapist Colao and Vachss and Borowka can be found in chapter 11.

20. The Fund lawyers acknowledged that they did not learn of Tynan's record from Johnson.

21. Author's interview, Apr. 30, 1987.

22. An "infant's compromise order" allows courts to set the percentage of a lawyer's fee in a civil case involving a child plaintiff.

23. The Fund had no way of knowing, of course, that the author had interviewed the New Hampshire attorney general eighteen months earlier and found him sympathetic to Jane's case.

24. Author's interview, Apr. 24, 1987.

25. One value of computerized records is that if an abusive host moves (as Tynan moved from New Hampshire to Massachusetts before moving to Arizona), he can be checked on the computer and will show up as unacceptable before he is given another child.

Chapter 4

1. For convenience's sake, we will call all such agencies Social Services Departments throughout this book, even though they have different names in different states—Human Resources Administration, Division of Youth and Family Services, and so forth.

2. Author's interview with Diane Soares, Debra Travers, and Gary Winn, June 4, 1986.

3. This position has been argued most persuasively by attorney Andrew Vachss, who wrote in the Oct. 13, 1985, *Parade Magazine* (p. 19): "The current system of using the same social workers to simultaneously protect the child and rehabilitate the parent must be replaced by separate teams. If a lawyer tried to represent both the abuser and the abused, the cries of "conflict of interest" would echo throughout the courthouse. Yet when a social worker routinely does the same thing, we call it "family therapy" and accept it. Current laws require child-protective workers to "work with the total family unit" and too many caseworkers find the dual role impossible to perform. In a choice between an adult who can express (and excuse) himself and a child who may not be able to speak at all, some deadly mistakes are inevitable. It is up to society to bring about the needed legislative changes. Children cannot vote."

4. Quoted from *Federal Standards for Child Abuse and Neglect Prevention and Treatment Programs and Projects* (draft), National Center on Child Abuse and Neglect, Department of Health, Education, and Welfare, Mar. 1978, in *Child Abuse and Neglect Litigation: A Manual for Judges*, National Center on Child Abuse and Neglect, Department of Health and Human Services, Mar. 1981, p. 22.

5. Hechler, D., Lawyers for children: no experience necessary. *Justice for Children* 1 (1985):14–15. (Reprinted with permission from Justice for Children, P.O. Box 42266, Washington, D.C. 20015.)

6. Gratteau, H., Abuse-case guardian lawyers accused of neglect. *Chicago Tribune*, Aug. 12, 1986. The article detailed complaints that law guardians in Cook County, Illinois, were guilty of "incompetence and chronic neglect."

7. In many states they are called guardians *ad litem*, but that term has a broader meaning: a person—not necessarily a lawyer—appointed by a court to protect the interests of a ward in a legal proceeding. For lack of a better name, we will call them law guardians, a term which may not be widely used but at least has one clear meaning where it is.

8. Author's interview with Andrew Vachss, Aug. 27, 1986. An example of the situation described here occurred in the much-publicized case of a 13-year-old girl who was raped first by her adoptive father, then by fellow residents in two successive group homes in which she was placed by family court. When she returned to court following the third attack, her law guardian recommended she be returned to the adoptive mother in the home where she was first raped, even though the original rape occurred with the mother's knowledge. The law guardian's supervisor later explained that the child had told them that she wanted to go back there. It was later reported, however, that the girl had an

IQ of seventy and, following news accounts of the case, she was finally placed in a home for children with limited intellectual abilities. It was reported in the same article that she did not want to go back to the adoptive mother. The story was broken by columnist Bob Herbert, New York *Daily News*, Feb. 5, 10, 24, 1987; and followed up by Barron, J., Girl attacked in city centers was 'trusting'. *The New York Times*, Feb. 7, 1986.

9. Former New York State Family Court Judge Sondra Miller (now sitting in state supreme court), quoted in Hechler, D., Redefining 'corroboration' in child sex abuse cases. *Justice for Children* 4 (1986):10–11.

10. Four examples among many articles of this type are: Joyner, G., False accusation of child abuse: could it happen to you? *Woman's Day*, May 6, 1986, pp. 30–42; Black, E., and Sharkey, M., Child abuse: are we too quick to accuse? *Woman's World*, July 8, 1986, pp. 6–7; Wexler, R., Invasion of the child savers: no one is safe in the war against abuse. *The Progressive*, Sept. 1985, pp. 19–22; and Elshtain, J., Invasion of the child savers: how we succumb to hype and hysteria. *The Progressive*, Sept. 1985, pp. 23–26.

11. Carlson, A.C., Family abuse. *Reason* (May 1986): 34–41. (Reprinted, with permission, from the May 1986 issue of *Reason* magazine. Copyright © 1986 by the Reason Foundation, 2716 Ocean Park Blvd., Suite 1062, Santa Monica, CA 90405.)

12. Author's interviews with confidential sources revealed several examples.

13. Eberle, P., and Eberle, S., *The Politics of Child Abuse* (Secaucus, N.J.: Lyle Stuart, 1986), p. 284.

14. Author's interview with Jeanine Ferris Pirro, an assistant district attorney and chief of the Domestic Violence and Child Abuse Bureau, Apr. 20, 1987.

15. Two newspaper articles cited this statistic. Both appeared in the *Reporter Dispatch* (Gannett Westchester/Rockland [N.Y.] Newspapers), May 27, 1986. The page-one account ("O'Rourke picks county lawyer as running mate," by Joel Benenson) had the subhead "Jeanine Pirro is undefeated as local prosecutor" and repeated the record along with the fifty trials in the body of the article. The second article ("Who's Jeanine Pirro?" by Michael Slackman) contained this sentence: "Of the roughly 50 cases she has prosecuted, she says she never lost one." In her interview with the author, however, Pirro said she did not remember saying that, adding only, "Most of the cases I've handled I've won." She said she did not remember whether she had ever lost a case during her twelve years in the D.A.'s Office.

16. Author's interview with Gary Winn—see note 2.

17. Author's interviews with Angela Baris and Dottie Morea, Apr. 17, 1987. Judge Sondra Miller and defense lawyer (and former Bronx prosecutor) Roger Milch also said Pirro's office was less than aggressive prosecuting child sexual abuse cases. Author's interviews, Apr. 20, 1987.

18. Author's interview with Jan Hansen, assistant district attorney, Sacramento, California, July 15, 1986.

19. Author's interview with Nan Horvat, assistant county counsel, Polk County, Iowa, May 30, 1986.

20. Gary Winn—see note 2.

21. Author's interviews with Susan Mason, Ray Blase, Candice Bennett, Marti Anderson, Paul Hanna, and Linda Rae Hardwick of the Polk County Intra-Family Child Sexual Abuse Program (IFSAP), May 29–30, 1986, and attendance of IFSAP weekly meeting May 29, 1986.
22. King County Network Meeting, Aug. 6, 1986. We will take a closer look at these meetings, and multidisciplinary teams in general, in chapter 10.
23. Author's interview, Apr. 14, 1987.
24. Author's interview, July 15, 1986.
25. Author's interview, Aug. 4, 1986.
26. Author's interview, Dec. 14, 1986.

Chapter 5
West Point

1. The Grays have appeared in articles and on television using their real name, but they have asked that their name be changed here because, they said, books last longer than articles or television broadcasts and they wish to protect their daughter's privacy.
2. Author's interview, Apr. 21, 1987, and follow-up Apr. 22.
3. Michaels, J., "The teacher hurt me, mommy": the sex abuse scandal at West Point. *Redbook*, Jan. 1986, p. 142.
4. Author's interview, June 13, 1986.
5. It is common for soldiers to be transferred after four or five years at one base. Although the Grays are suspicious of some of the transfers, there is no evidence that any were part of a concerted effort to "make the problem go away."
6. Not her real name.
7. Thompson, P., and Meehan, A., Army sergeant charged in infant's murder. *Times Herald Record* (Middletown, N.Y.), Mar. 18, 1983; Meehan, A., Hard labor sentence given sergeant in infant's death. *Times Herald Record*, May 10, 1983.
8. The mother, Gray said, was a single parent and dependent on the Army for her livelihood. She did not pursue the matter, as far as Gray has been able to learn, and has since been transferred to Germany.
9. See note 7.
10. The Praca day care case, which resulted in three convictions.
11. Apr. 22, 1987.
12. Not her real name.
13. Author's interview, Apr. 27, 1987.
14. Meltzer added that since the West Point case, she has videotaped about two or three interviews with children for courts. Although none of the tapes figured in the court cases, she has not heard complaints that they were leading or suggestive, she said.
15. Asked if she would prefer to answer questions about the videotapes after she had had an opportunity to review them, Meltzer said she did not believe she had copies and declined.

16. Author's interview with James DeVita, Apr. 24, 1987.

17. Author's interview, June 17, 1986.

18. There have been a number of mass molestation cases in which children have reported being forced to perform sex acts with other children. The Mount Vernon day care case is one example.

19. Author's interview Aug. 22, 1985, on the general subject, not specifically about West Point.

20. One of the problems in prosecuting these cases is that young children's use of language at times seems incoherent and may be idiosyncratic. An investigator who has little experience interviewing children may thus discard as gibberish what turns out to be vital information. A number of Donna's statements to her mother are prime illustrations of language that at first seemed nonsensical.

21. Army officer charged with endangering child. (Unsigned.) *Times Herald Record*, Sept. 25, 1984.

22. Letter of Oct. 20, 1986, to Walter [Gray] from Col. Richard Singleton, inspector general; chief, Assistance Division.

23. In addition to news broadcasts, the Grays were quoted in dozens of newspaper and magazine articles, and Walt appeared on "The Phil Donahue Show."

24. The Grays put the total amount they have spent on the case to date at more than twice this figure.

Judy Coletti

25. Not her real name. At Judy's request, her ex-husband's and her daughter's names have also been changed—mainly to protect her daughter's privacy.

26. *In Re the Matter of the Welfare of [Lisa Coletti]*, hearing of Apr. 25, 1984, Hennepin County Juvenile Court, Judge H. Peter Albrecht presiding. The court decision makes specific reference to the Illinois and Minneapolis investigations. Hereafter *Albrecht*.

27. There are no statistics to prove that an increasing number of sexual abuse cases involve more than one state, just as there are none to support the suggestion that the number of sexual abuse allegations arising out of divorce and custody litigation is increasing. Both observations are based on anecdotal evidence. The increase emanating from divorce cases has been widely noted and nowhere disputed, although there has certainly been argument over how big an increase it has been. Interstate jurisdictional disputes are harder to document, but the author's contact with a number of sources around the country suggests that it is at least a growing problem.

28. *Albrecht*, p. 2.

29. *In Re the Marriage of [Judy and Tom Coletti]*, hearing of May 28, 1981, Lake County, Illinois Circuit Court, Judge Alphonse Witt presiding and quoted on p. 2. Although Judy originally filed for divorce, Tom became the petitioner after she had moved to Minnesota. Hereafter *Witt*.

30. Ibid., p. 5.

31. Author's interview, Mar. 15, 1987.

32. *In Re the Matter of the Welfare of [Lisa Coletti]*, Hennepin County Juvenile Court, Deposition of [Tom Coletti] dated Jan. 25, 1984.

33. Ibid., p. 102.
34. *Witt*, p. 6.
35. Several Illinois judges heard the case. This was the decision of Judge Terrance Brady. He preceded Judge Alphonse Witt, who presided over many of the Illinois hearings and later ruled that Judy must move and that Tom had the right to weekend visits.
36. *Albrecht*, pp. 3–5.
37. To be precise, it was a battle between a family court and a circuit court.
38. *Albrecht*, p. 5.
39. Ibid., pp. 5–6.
40. *In Re the Marriage of [Judy and Tom Coletti]*, hearing of June 10, 1982, testimony of Francis B. Petrauskas, pp. 11–12. Hereafter *Petrauskas*.
41. The Szondi and Rorschach tests are projective tests that allow the psychologist to evaluate the subject's true personality by analyzing his answers to questions about a series of photographs of psychiatric patients in the Szondi test, and about a series of ink blots in the Rorschach test.
42. *Petrauskas*, p. 18.
43. Ibid., p. 20.
44. Ibid., pp. 25–26.
45. Ibid., p. 26.
46. Ibid., p. 29.
47. In one of its more strenuous enforcement efforts, on Jan. 13, 1983, the court ordered Judy to post a $5,000 bond, to be forfeited if she did not produce Lisa for visitation on the appointed day. She did not comply, however.
48. Actually a guardian *ad litem* in Minnesota's jargon, but for reasons explained earlier, we will use law guardian throughout this book as the preferred term for a lawyer representing a child in court.
49. *In the Matter of the Welfare of [Lisa Coletti]*, Hennepin County Juvenile Court, Dec. 23, 1982, hearing, Judge Allen Oleisky presiding, pp. 13–14.
50. *Albrecht*, p. 8 and "Memorandum."
51. There was one additional legal action in this complex, serpentine case. In Oct. 1982, a lawsuit was filed in Hennepin County District Court on Lisa's behalf charging that Tom had caused his daughter severe and permanent physical and emotional harm as a result of his sexual assault. In June 1985, Lisa won a verdict of $325,000. Judy said she doubts the money will ever be collected, however, since it will be difficult to enforce the Minnesota judgment in Illinois. (See chapter 11 for a case study of another such lawsuit.)

Chapter 6

1. Shipp, E.R., Children testify against parents over abuse. *The New York Times*, Sept. 3, 1984.
2. *Report on Scott County Investigations*, Minnesota Attorney General Hubert H. Humphrey III, Feb. 12, 1985. Hereafter *Attorney General*.
3. Ibid., pp. 12–13.
4. Ibid., p. 17.

5. The three commissioners were Special Commissioner Lynn C. Olson, an Anoka County judge, and assistant commissioners Julius E. Gernes, the Winona County Attorney, and Irene F. Scott, a lawyer in Bloomington.

6. *Report to Governor Rudy Perpich, Commission Established by Executive Order No. 85-10 Concerning Kathleen Morris, Scott County Attorney*, p. 4. Hereafter *Commission*.

7. Shipp, E.R., Prosecutor in sex case to stay in office. *The New York Times*, Oct. 11, 1985; (AP) Newcomer beats prosecutor of abuse cases in Minnesota. *The New York Times*, Nov. 6, 1986.

8. *Commission*, pp. 52–53.

9. Ibid., p. 53.

10. Ibid., p. 54.

11. *Attorney General*, p. 5.

12. A series of articles in the *San Francisco Examiner*, Sept. 28–29, 1986, included brief descriptions of many of the publicized cases around the country along with quotes from prosecutors and a variety of experts. The similarities among cases are clear; the explanations, of course, vary dramatically.

13. One problem with the theory that investigators coach children to tell satanic stories is that it implies they are looking for these allegations. The evidence is to the contrary. As noted in this chapter, there is evidence that the Jordan investigators were skeptical of the ritualistic stories. A number of prosecutors have acknowledged in articles and in interviews with the author that such allegations make prosecution much more difficult. If it was not clear at the time of Jordan, it is clear now that abuse cases with satanic elements are generally harder to win. Consider the following from the *Examiner* series (see note 12): "Prosecutors [from the Country Walk case] told The Examiner that even more bizarre and grotesque allegations were kept out of the trial for fear of jeopardizing the case" (Ross, A.S., Child-abuse cults: how real? Sept. 29); "In the 1985 Concord case, in which jurors deadlocked 6–6, Deputy District Attorney Hal Jewett said jurors who voted for acquittal told him they did not believe the girl's allegations of devil worship and murder. 'I wanted the jury to focus on child sexual abuse. I wanted to de-emphasize the satanic aspect as much as possible,' Jewett said. 'But it was something you either had to swallow whole or reject whole. I had absolutely nothing to corroborate the girl's stories of satanic worship. I have no doubt that if she hadn't talked about that, they would have believed she was a victim of molestation.' " (Ross, A.S., Satanism or mass hysteria? Sept. 28. Reprinted by permission of the San Francisco Examiner.)

14. Barbara Egenhauser, who prosecuted the Mount Vernon day care case, suggested that molesters may consciously incorporate bizarre, ritualistic elements in order preemptively to reduce a child's credibility, should the child ever disclose. "The more bizarre the allegations," Egenhauser said, "the less likely the child is to be believed. If a perpetrator . . . puts a mask on his face, commits the crime, says, 'I'm the Lone Ranger,' and the kid comes in saying, 'The Lone Ranger . . . did it to me,' no one is going to believe the kid." (Author's interview, Apr. 14, 1987.)

15. Children were allegedly drugged in a number of cases, raising the possibility that the blurring of fantasy and reality might have been drug-induced, in some instances.

16. Rigert, J., Peterson, D., and Marcotty, J., The Scott County case/how it grew; why it died. *Minneapolis Star and Tribune*, May 26, 1985.

17. Shipp, E.R., The jeopardy of children on the stand. *The New York Times*, Sept. 23, 1984.

18. Morris had already announced that because she had become an issue in the cases, the second trial would be prosecuted by one of her assistants.

19. Se also *Commission*, pp. 38–42.

20. "VOCAL Introduction," undated paper provided to author by VOCAL national headquarters, Minneapolis, Minnesota.

21. Author's interview with Andrew Vachss.

22. Wimberly, L., VOCAL: speaking out against child abuse legislation. *Voir Dire* (Lincoln Law School, Sacramento, Calif.) (Winter 1986):7–15.

23. Hansen, J., Another perspective to child abuse legislation and criminal prosecution. *Voir Dire* (Spring 1986):8.

24. Wimberly, VOCAL, p. 8.

25. Author's interview, July 11, 1986.

26. Author's interview, July 21, 1986.

27. This impression is perhaps reinforced by the fact that VOCAL sends "courtesy newsletters" to prisoners. *VOCAL National Newsletter*, Sept.–Oct. 1986, p. 11.

28. Author's interview, July 15, 1986.

29. Author's interview, Aug. 7, 1986.

30. Author's interviews, Aug. 7–8, 1986.

31. The first was held in St. Paul, Minnesota, Nov. 14–16, 1985; the second in Torrance, California, Oct. 25–26, 1986.

32. Schultz, L.G., Child sexual abuse in historical perspective. *Journal of Social Work and Human Sexuality* 1 & 2 (1982):28–29.

33. Ibid., p. 30.

34. Ibid., p. 31.

35. Joyner, G.P., False accusation of child abuse: could it happen to you? *Woman's Day*, May 6, 1986, pp. 30–42.

36. Hollingsworth, J., *Unspeakable Acts* (New York: Congdon & Weed, 1986), p. 496.

Chapter 7

1. Russell, D.E.H., *The Secret Trauma* (New York: Basic Books, 1986). Victim statistics have not been discussed here largely because they have already been written about so extensively, and the other statistics in this chapter seemed more central to the current controversies.

2. Besharov, D.J., 'Doing something' about child abuse: the need to narrow the grounds for state intervention. *Harvard Journal of Law and Public Policy* 3 (Summer 1985): 539–89.

3. Ibid., p. 556.

4. Karlson, K.J., Child protection system said out of control. *St. Paul Pioneer Press*, Nov. 15, 1985. (Reprinted by permission of St. Paul Pioneer Press Dispatch.)

5. Besharov, D.J., An overdose of concern: child abuse and the overreporting problem. *Regulation: American Enterprise Institute Journal on Government and Society* (Nov.–Dec. 1985):27. (© American Enterprise Institute, 1985.)

6. One way Besharov's figures have been misused is that they are cited in discussions of false allegations of child *sexual* abuse, when his unfounded rate clearly applies to all forms of maltreatment (which most studies agree is higher than that for sexual abuse alone). See, for example, the opening two paragraphs of Coleman, L., Therapists are the real culprits in many child sexual abuse cases. *Oakland Tribune* Apr. 24, 1986.

7. Besharov, Doing Something, p. 557.

8. Besharov interviewed by Maria Shriver on NBC-TV's "1986," Dec. 9, 1986. The segment on which he appeared was "A Terrible Shadow," produced by K. McCleery, on the case of Dr. Lawrence Spiegel, a psychologist who was eventually acquitted of sexual abuse charges and wrote a book about his experience. During the broadcast, Besharov also said, "If there is any reason— the slightest reason—to believe the child might have been sexually abused, courts switch custody." This sweeping statement is simply untrue. For a clear counterexample, see chapter 9.

9. Karlson, Child protection system.

10. Wexler, R., No one is safe in the war against abuse. *The Progressive*, Sept. 1985, p. 20.

11. Besharov, Doing Something, p. 556.

12. Besharov, Overdose, p. 26.

13. Ibid., p. 26.

14. Ibid., p. 26.

15. The Child Welfare League of America (CWLA), Too young to run: the status of child abuse in America. 1986, p. 12. (With permission of The Child Welfare League of America, 400 First Street NW, Washington, D.C. 20001.)

16. Penal Code, §11169, quoted in *Child Abuse Prevention Handbook*, California State Attorney General's Office, rev. 1985, p. 20.

17. Author's interview with Betty Suzuki, July 15, 1986.

18. Golubski, S., Abuse stats lie, docs say. New York *Daily News*, Nov. 1, 1985. One of the sources of the story, Dr. Jeffrey Gilbert, confirmed the practice in an interview and said that it is still true.

19. Author's interview with Susan Mason, coordinator, Polk County Intra-Family Sexual Abuse Program, Apr. 30, 1987.

20. Suski, L.B., Child sexual abuse—an increasingly important part of child protective service practice. *Protecting Children* (Spring 1986):7.

21. CWLA, Too young, pp. 3, 6. These statistics have not prevented others from going even further than Besharov, inflating the unfounded rate beyond belief for sexual abuse cases, and then claiming that everyone agrees with statistics not even attributed to any database. For example: "Meanwhile, the number of victims steadily mounts. The volume of reported cases of child sexual abuse

has tripled since 1981, to 250,000. *Even the child-savers admit that 80 percent of these reports are unfounded,* up from 40 percent only five years before. The sky-rocketing number of parents and teachers *falsely* accused of child abuse who consequently suffer from permanently damaged reputations has finally drawn the attention of the mainstream media." (Emphasis added.) Carlson, A.C., Family abuse. *Reason* (May 1986):41.

22. Hechler, D., Rotation of caseworkers is criticized. *The New York Times*, Oct. 14, 1984. New York social workers were quoted in this article. The author has also interviewed social workers in California, Iowa, New Hampshire, and Washington State.

23. Besharov, Doing Something, p. 561.

24. Author's interview, Feb. 25, 1987.

25. Author's interview, Apr. 30, 1987.

26. Some misuse of statistics results from inadvertent error. There is no effort here to impugn the motives of all who have ever misused a statistic. If one uses them long enough, one is sure to do so.

27. Benedek, E., and Schetky, D., Allegations of sexual abuse in child custody and visitation disputes, in Benedek and Schetky (eds.), *Emerging Issues in Child Psychiatry and the Law* (New York: Brunner/Mazel, 1985), pp. 145–56.

28. To cite but one example: "In another case of brainwashing, Kate, age 11, gave a credible and consistent story of her stepfather tickling her private parts but, under pressure from her mother and stepfather's attorney, retracted her story saying she'd been mistaken and that his hand must have 'slipped' " (p. 149). What do the authors mean by *brainwashing*? (The term is never defined.) What was Kate brainwashed to say, and by whom? Was the "credible story" caused by brainwashing, or was the retraction? Do the authors believe brainwashing is the same as "pressuring?" Many of their capsule descriptions raise similarly troubling questions.

29. Gordon, C.L., False allegations of abuse in child custody disputes. *Minnesota Family Law Journal* (July—Aug. 1985): 225–28.

30. Pollack, K., Flawed guardian of young. *The Sacramento Bee*, Aug. 4, 1986. Although the article did not mention the Benedek/Schetky study by name, the study cited was completed in 1984 and Pollack informed the author in a tele-phone conversation that it was the one he was referring to.

31. Speech at the Fourth National Conference on the Sexual Victimization of Children, New Orleans, May 15, 1986.

32. Chapman, J.R., Smith, B., and Brennan, N., *Child Sexual Abuse: An Analysis of Case Processing*. Criminal Justice Section, American Bar Association, Mar. 27, 1987, p. 70.

33. Jones, D.P.H., and McGraw, J.M., Reliable and fictitious accounts of sexual abuse to children. *Journal of Interpersonal Violence* (Mar. 1987): 38. Briefly, two samples were studied: all cases of sexual abuse—both founded and unfounded—reported to the Denver Social Services Department in 1983; and twenty-one fictitious cases culled from several hundred cases seen at the Kempe Center between 1983 and 1985. Jones determined that 8 percent of the Denver cases

were fictitious, and that more than half the cases in the small sample involved custody or visitation disputes.

34. Author's interview, Jan. 9, 1987.
35. Renshaw, D.C., When sex abuse is falsely charged. *Medical Aspects of Human Sexuality* (July 1985):121.
36. Schultz, L.G., Fifty cases of wrongfully charged child sexual abuse: a survey and recommendations. Unpublished paper, 1986, p. 2.
37. Benedek and Schetky, Allegations of sexual abuse, p. 147.
38. Thoennes, N., and Person, J., Summary of findings from the sexual abuse allegations project, to be published in a forthcoming American Bar Association manual.
39. Author's interview with Nancy Thoennes, Apr. 29, 1987.
40. Author's interview, Apr. 25, 1985.
41. Finkelhor, D., et al., *A Sourcebook on Child Sexual Abuse* (Beverly Hills, Calif.: Sage, 1986), p. 119.
42. Ibid., p. 130.
43. Ibid., p. 132.
44. Ibid., p. 133.
45. Author's interview, Aug. 6, 1986.
46. *The Denver Post* first broke the story of the inflated missing children statistics in May 1985 and followed up with a series of articles that earned it a 1986 Pulitzer Prize in public service. The story was eventually picked up by newspapers around the country.
47. Author's interview, July 15, 1986.
48. Kroth, J., *Child Sexual Abuse: Analysis of a Family Therapy Approach* (Springfield, Ill.: Charles C. Thomas, 1979).
49. Author's interview, July 22, 1986. Carroll also confirmed that when Giarretto says 90 percent of the families in his program are "reunified" following treatment, this means only that the child is back in the home with the mother, not necessarily with the father as well. This statistic, then, is also misleading.
50. Author's interview, July 21, 1986.
51. Kroth, *Child Sexual Abuse*, pp. 123–24.
52. Finkelhor, *Sourcebook*, p. 142.
53. Ibid., p. 16. Finkelhor coauthored this chapter with Stefanie Doyle Peters and Gail Elizabeth Wyatt.
54. See note 31.

Chapter 8

1. Vachss, A., article scheduled for publication in a forthcoming issue of *Justice for Children*.
2. *VOCAL National Newsletter*, Sept.–Oct. 1986, p. 10.
3. Ibid., back cover.
4. Fiore, F., Lawyer: delays in reporting abuse hurt case. *The Daily Breeze* (Torrance, Calif.), July 26, 1986 (quoting Daniel Davis, Lawyer for Raymond Buckley).

5. Coleman, L., *The Reign of Error: Psychiatry, Authority & Law* (Boston: Beacon Press, 1984).

6. Author's interview, July 18, 1986.

7. *State of Florida* v. *Francisco Fuster*, Circuit Court of the 11th Judicial Circuit, Dade County, Florida, Sept. 24, 1985, pp. 27–28. Hereafter *Fuster*.

8. Coleman, L., False allegations of child sexual abuse: have the experts been caught with their pants down? *Forum* (published by California Attorneys for Criminal Justice) (Jan.–Feb. 1986):12. (© 1986, California Attorneys for Criminal Justice.)

9. Ibid., p. 12.

10. Author's interview, July 28, 1986.

11. Coleman, L., Has a child been molested? *California Lawyer* (July 1986): 15.

12. Author's interview, July 28, 1986.

13. Author's interview, Aug. 5, 1986.

14. *State of Iowa* v. *Duane Myers*, Supreme Court of Iowa, decision filed Feb. 19, 1986, pp. 3–4.

15. Ibid., p. 14. The case is *People* v. *Bledscoe*, 681 P. 2d 291, 301 (Cal. 1984).

16. Ibid., pp. 15–17.

17. Sgroi, S.M., *Handbook of Clinical Intervention in Child Sexual Abuse* (Lexington, Mass.: Lexington Books, 1982).

18. Miller, S., *New York Law Journal*, Oct. 19, 1984.

19. Vachss, A., memorandum of law, *In the Matter of Tara H.*, Aug. 27, 1984, pp. 2–3.

20. Ibid., p. 24.

21. Ibid., p. 10.

22. Ibid., p. 21.

23. Ibid., p. 22.

24. Ibid., p. 6.

25. Ibid., p. 33.

26. Author's interview, May 10, 1986.

27. Jones, D.P.H., and McGraw, J.M., Reliable and fictitious accounts of sexual abuse to children. *Journal of Interpersonal Violence* (Mar. 1987): 42.

28. *Fuster*, p. 230.

29. Author's interview, May 1, 1987.

30. Coleman expressed his concern that children had been told Fuster was in jail in his testimony at the Country Walk trial: "The interviewers didn't seem to be concerned that maybe the child's statements were in any way influenced by those outside contacts. For example, some children would come in and talk about so and so in jail. The child wouldn't . . . have any way to know that." *Fuster*, pp. 49–50.

31. Author's interview, July 22, 1986.

32. Author's interview, July 22, 1986.

33. MacFarlane, K., et al., *Sexual Abuse of Young Children* (New York: Guilford, 1986).

34. Author's interview, Jan. 14, 1987.

Chapter 9

1. Judge Henry Whiting, Circuit Court of Warren County, Virginia. What is referred to as Judge Whiting's decision is technically a "letter . . . in explanation of my ruling of Oct. 28, 1985." The letter is dated Nov. 12, 1985.
2. Ibid., p. 2.
3. These include transcripts, depositions, a social worker's notes, medical records, and psychologists' evaluations, among other documents.
4. Some identifying characteristics have also been changed.
5. Rossiter's transcription of interview with [Sarah Fahrnhorst] dated Feb. 27, 1985, p. 1.
6. Ibid., p. 15.
7. Ibid., p. 13.
8. Dengel testimony at court hearing of Feb. 18, 1985, p. 9.
9. Ibid., p. 9.
10. Ibid., p. 10.
11. Rossiter, p. 3.
12. Dengel testimony, p. 22.
13. Green testimony at court hearing of Feb. 18, 1985, p. 90.
14. Kiczales deposition taken Feb. 17, 1985.
15. Green deposition taken Feb. 17, 1985, p. 15.
16. Dengel testimony, p. 18.
17. Ibid., p. 27.
18. Rossiter, p. 1.
19. Webb report dated Nov. 29, 1984, pp. 1–2.
20. Webb deposition taken Aug. 13, 1985, p. 69.
21. Whiting, p. 5.
22. Pate testimony at court hearing of Feb. 18, 1985, p. 18.
23. Ibid., p. 19.
24. The gynecologist was Gwen Steeley.
25. Chronological listing of events prepared by the Warren County Department of Social Services and corrected by Sarah Fahrnhorst, dated June 26, 1985; entry for hospital visit dated Jan. 13, 1985. Hereafter *Chronology*.
26. As Judge Whiting pointed out in his decision, it was false in that it said that on Jan. 10 Gerald threatened to come to Massachusetts and harm Sarah, even though she did not leave Virginia until Jan. 13, Gerald had no contact with her after she did, and she never testified that he threatened her.
27. Whiting, p. 10.
28. The term used in Virginia is guardian *ad litem*, which, for reasons explained in the notes to chapter 4, has been changed.
29. Carter report to Judge Whiting dated Mar. 15, 1985, p. 2.
30. The pediatrician was R. Winston Lutz.
31. *Chronology*, entry for Mar. 31, 1985.
32. Rossiter letter to Judge Whiting dated May 20, 1985, p. 3.
33. Lehne report to Warren County Department of Social Services dated Aug. 15, 1985.

34. Lehne deposition taken Sept. 12, 1985, p. 61.
35. Ibid., pp. 59–60.
36. Ibid., p. 63. M.M.P.I. stands for Minnesota Multiphasic Personality Inventory, a widely used self-reporting test designed to allow the examiner to determine the subject's personality profile as well as any tendency to lie or fake.
37. Josselson deposition taken Sept. 12, 1985, p. 8.
38. Higham deposition taken Sept. 13, 1985, p. 5.
39. Ibid., pp. 5–6.
40. Ibid., pp. 6–7.
41. Ibid., p. 3.
42. Zuckerman testimony at court hearing of Sept. 14, 1985, p. 290.
43. Ibid., p. 295.
44. Ibid., p. 297.
45. Ibid., p. 320.
46. Josselson, p. 32.
47. Whiting, p. 11.
48. In most cases and places child protective workers are supposed to be advocates for the best interests of the child, as the job title implies. But as was discussed in chapter 4, they sometimes see themselves as "family advocates." The point is, they *should* be advocates. Those who claim to be disinterested may mean uninterested.
49. Court hearing of Sept. 30, 1985, pp. 29–30.
50. Sharp's "Report of the Guardian Ad Litem" dated Oct. 4, 1985, pp. 7–8.
51. Rossiter's transcription of interview with [Gerald Fahrnhorst] dated Mar. 22, 1985. Although Rossiter wrote notes explaining the strategy of the session following the transcript of the interview (the only time she ever did so), her claim that she was manipulating Gerald in order to encourage his cooperation and goad him into "slipping" is beyond credibility and, even if true, no justification for her actions.
52. Ibid., p. 3.
53. Ibid., p. 5.
54. Ibid., p. 5.
55. Ibid., pp. 2–3.
56. Lehne deposition taken Sept. 12, 1985, p. 30.
57. Fordney, C., Timberlake found not guilty. *The Winchester Star*, June 6, 1984. Although he was acquitted, Timberlake was later found guilty of unprofessional conduct by the Virginia State Board of Medicine and his license was placed on indefinite probation (under the terms of which he was not permitted to treat males under 18 years old). Lazazzera, T., Timberlake censured by state board. *The Winchester Star*, Sept. 3, 1985.
58. *Commonwealth of Virginia* v. *Byron Timberlake*, Winchester Circuit Court, trial transcript dated June 5, 1984, p. 111.
59. Ibid., p. 118.
60. Ibid., p. 119.
61. Ibid., p. 131.
62. Ibid., p. 131.

63. Ibid., p. 133.
64. Whiting, p. 11.
65. Carter deposition taken Aug. 22, 1985, pp. 37–38.
66. Douglas Napier letter to Carter dated Apr. 2, 1985.
67. Lehne report dated Aug. 15, 1985, appendix.
68. Sharp, p. 20.
69. Ibid., p.20.

Chapter 10

1. The disillusionment described here is not unique to the legal profession. Many people have idealized—or at least highly abstract—views of professions with which they have had little or no personal contact. Certainly many people find their first contact with journalists disappointing, and often describe journalists in the same terms—insensitive and arrogant. The same words have been used to describe politicians, doctors, entertainers, and many other professionals as well.

2. Author's interview, July 15, 1986.
3. Author's interview, Aug. 4, 1986.
4. Author's interview, July 15, 1986.
5. Whitcomb, D., Shapiro, E.R., and Stellwagen, L.D., *When the Victim Is a Child: Issues for Judges and Prosecutors*, U.S. Department of Justice, National Institute of Justice, Office of Development, Testing, and Dissemination (Washington, D.C., 1985), p. 111.
6. The proposed competency reform was also included in *Victims of Crime: Proposed Model Legislation*, published by the U.S. Department of Justice's Office for Victims of Crime, in cooperation with the National Association of Attorneys General and the American Bar Association, May 1986.
7. Parker, J.Y., Rights of child witnesses: is the court a protector or perpetrator? *New England Law Review* (1981–82): 643–717.
8. New York Family Court Act, §1046 (vi).
9. Hechler, D., Redefining 'corroboration' in child sex abuse cases. *Justice for Children* (Winter 1985): 10.
10. Author's interview, July 15, 1986.
11. This may prove particularly valuable, since Coleman has said he has never seen a "good interview." Nor has he ever seen interviews that resulted in charges' being dropped, since there would be no case for him to review. When asked in court what a proper interview would look like, he and others hired to testify on this subject usually answer in vague abstractions. It might be enlightening if he were to join a panel of experts, including police investigators, prosecutors, and social workers, to view and discuss a number of actual tapes (electronically altered to retain confidentiality). Although such a session might not achieve a consensus, it might help define disagreements in concrete terms.
12. Whitcomb, Shapiro, and Stellwagen, *When the Victim Is a Child*, p. 91.
13. Author's interview, July 29, 1986.
14. Author's interview, May 29, 1986.

15. A chapter about the center, "Criminal and Civil Court Coordination" by Naomi Post, was included in *Papers from a National Policy Conference on Legal Reforms in Child Sexual Abuse Cases*, published by the American Bar Association's National Legal Resource Center for Child Advocacy and Protection, 1985.

16. Author's interview, Oct. 22, 1986.

17. The so-called Baby M case in which a surrogate mother and the couple that hired her engaged in a bitter contest for custody of the child is an example of the need for independent counsel to represent the child (as there was in that case). The case is also relevant in its demonstration of the need for regulation of expert testimony, and in the fact—almost lost in the massive publicity— that the surrogate mother admitted that she had threatened to charge the father with having sexually abused her 10-year-old daughter if he continued to seek custody.

18. Hechler, D., Lawyers for children: no experience necessary. *Justice for Children* (Spring 1985): 14.

19. Author's interview, July 28, 1986.

20. Author's interview with Robert Dixon, who at the time was presiding judge, Criminal Department, King County Superior Court, Aug. 4, 1986.

21. One of the problems, Roe explained, is that her office is not entitled to CPS records. Confidentiality statutes are designed to protect the privacy of families, and they restrict access by the District Attorney's Office in order to prevent such records from landing in the hands of the defense, which would have a right to demand them on criminal discovery. The defense cannot demand them from the Attorney General's Office, however, which represent the Social Services Department in family court. Lawyers at the Attorney General's Office have been cooperative, Roe said, but the problem is that poorly trained CPS workers who are questioned orally by her assistant district attorneys frequently do not understand what information is important to them.

22. Whitcomb, Shapiro, and Stellwagen, *When the Victim Is a Child*, p. 95.

23. A recent case that has received national publicity, including a story on "60 Minutes" (Mar. 8, 1987), may have set a troubling precedent that could undermine the independence of children's counsel. The law guardian in the case took a position opposed to that of Social Services. The agency objected, and the lawyer was removed from the case. Other factors were also involved, the lawyer, Jane Harlan, acknowledged (author's interview, May 1, 1987). Harlan has appealed her removal and it is at least a case worth watching.

24. There is no panel of law guardians in New York City, where children are represented by Legal Aid lawyers.

25. The question of whether offender treatment works may be argued in the not too distant future in an Iowa court. Recently, a large health maintenance organization there that had previously paid for such treatment under its coverage plan refused to do so on the grounds that the treatment was ineffective. So said Susan Mason (author's interview, Apr. 30, 1987), coordinator of the Intra-Family Sexual Abuse Program of Polk County, a pretrial diversion program that now has on its hands offenders who have opted for the program but are not sure where the money will come from. Although Mason said she had not

yet heard of any legal challenges to the action, it is hard to believe there will not be.

26. Giarretto, H., *Integrated Treatment of Child Sexual Abuse: A Treatment and Training Manual* (Palo Alto, Calif.: Science and Behavior Books, 1982), p. 18.
27. Author's interview, July 22, 1986.
28. Author's interview with Patricia Alvarez, an investigator on the San Jose Police Department's Sexual Assault Unit, July 22, 1986.
29. Author's interview, July 15, 1986.
30. Author's interview, July 15, 1986.
31. Author's interview, Aug. 7, 1986.
32. Author's interview, July 28, 1986.
33. This description is based on the author's readings, observations of three multidisciplinary team meetings, and follow-up interviews with the various participants. For the interested reader, there are many books on the subject. A good one to start with might be Suzanne Sgroi's *Handbook of Clinical Intervention in Child Sexual Abuse* (Lexington, Mass.: Lexington Books, 1982).
34. Author attended meeting of May 29, 1986.
35. Author attended meeting of Oct. 22, 1986.
36. Author attended meeting of Aug. 6, 1986.
37. Many of these questions are based on information found in Bross, D.C., Professional and agency liability for negligence in child protection. *Law, Medicine & Health Care* (Apr. 1983): 71–75.
38. *Victims of Crime: Proposed Model Legislation*, published by the U.S. Department of Justice's Office for Victims of Crime, in cooperation with the National Association of Attorneys General and the American Bar Association, May 1986, p. VI–3. The legislation proposed here suggests that states extend statute of limitations in criminal cases of child sexual assault without specifying a length.

Chapter 11

1. Author's interview, Apr. 30, 1987. The compendiums include judgments and settlements of cases involving both child and adult victims, Musick said, and are published as close to annually as the institute can manage. To obtain information, or provide it, contact: The Institute for the Study of Sexual Assault, 403 Ashbury, San Francisco, CA 94117; Telephone: (415) 861–2048.
2. Author's interview, Nov. 1, 1986.
3. Not his real name. Her father's name has been changed to protect Angela's privacy.
4. Quoted in plaintiff's appeal from denial of summary judgment, submitted by Melvin Borowka, July 11, 1985.
5. Author's interview, Oct. 21, 1986.
6. Author's interview, Oct. 24, 1986.
7. Borowka's notice of motion dated Mar. 26, 1985, p. 3.
8. Author's interview, Nov. 6, 1986.
9. Court order dated Apr. 26, 1985.
10. Author's interview, Nov. 12, 1986.

11. Author's interview, Nov. 11, 1986.
12. Author's interview, Nov. 7, 1986.
13. Author's interview, Nov. 5, 1986.

Chapter 12

1. Based on a memorandum of law by Andrew Vachss (see chapter 8).
2. Based on a proposal by Dr. Jeffrey Gilbert during the interview quoted from in this chapter.
3. Two new methods of obtaining medical findings using techniques that are not new but were only recently adapted to use in this field have already drawn controversy. The colposcope is nothing more than a large microscope that can be used for vaginal examinations. The latest models permit the addition of 35 mm or video cameras. There has already been some controversy over its use, especially in California, where Dr. Bruce Woodling has come under attack. And a "new" dye test that has reportedly been in use for nearly a century by obstetricians for the detection of cervical cancer has been adapted for the detection of sexual abuse. When it is painted outside of the vaginal tissue of children within forty-eight hours of an incident of abuse, it is said to triple detection of breaks in the skin. It is unclear whether the technique will have a significant impact (since most abuse is not reported within forty-eight hours of an incident) and how it will be received by the courts, but it is safe to guess there will be objections. For more information, see McCauley, J., Gorman, R.L., and Guzinski, G., Toluidine blue in the detection of perineal lacerations in pediatric and adolescent sexual abuse victims. *Pediatrics* (Dec. 1986): 1039–43.
4. *VOCAL National Newsletter*, Sept.–Oct. 1986, p. 6.
5. Author's interview, May 1, 1987.
6. Author's interview, Dec. 16, 1986.
7. Author's interview, May 4, 1987.
8. Ruthellen Josselson, as quoted in chapter 9.
9. Bursten, B., Detecting child abuse by studying the parents. *Bulletin of the American Academy of Psychiatry and the Law* 3 (1985): 280.
10. Author's interview, May 1, 1987.
11. The 1987 New Jersey case in which a couple was awarded custody of the child the surrogate mother they had contracted with sought to keep.
12. Goleman, D., Why experts differ in custody cases. *The New York Times*, March 10, 1987. (Copyright © 1987 by The New York Times Company. Reprinted by permission.)
13. Diamond, R., and Mustain, G., Surrogate mom accused father. New York *Daily News*, Sept. 13, 1986.
14. Author's interview, July 15, 1986.
15. Author's interview, July 28, 1986.
16. See chapter 7.
17. Both programs are described in chapter 10.

18. Project Evaluation, Polk County Intra-Family Sexual Abuse of Children Program, August 1984. The evaluation, which also includes samples of the questionnaires used, is available from the National Criminal Justice Service (Rockville, Md.) through interlibrary loan or its photocopying service (which charges a fee). For further information, call (800) 851–3420. Refer to the title above and identification number NCJ 95598.

19. Wilson, W., 'Snuff film' accusations 'fell apart at the seams.' *The Sacramento Bee*, Oct. 27, 1985.

20. Author's interview with Gregory Favre, Apr. 28, 1987.

21. Author's interview, May 1, 1987.

22. Author's interview, Aug. 7, 1986.

23. Author's interview, Jan. 9, 1987.

24. Author's interview, May 1, 1987.

25. *William D. Seaman* v. *Northwest Treatment Associates, et al.* Seaman said in an interview (Sept. 14, 1986) that he was evaluated by Northwest at the direction of a school he was employed by as part of its recertification process, and that he has never been accused of or charged with a sex offense.

26. In the Country Walk case.

27. Author's interview, July 29, 1986.

28. Author's interview, Apr. 14, 1987.

29. Hollingsworth, J., *Unspeakable Acts* (New York: Congdon & Weed, 1986), p. 310.

30. Hechler, D., Parents of abused children find help in support group. *The New York Times*, Sept. 15, 1985. (Copyright © 1985 by The New York Times Company. Reprinted by permission.) Therapist Kliman cofounded the Center for Preventive Psychiatry, the agency hired by the Social Services Department to intervene.

31. Clark, a Mount Vernon police officer whose daughter was abused, has allowed his name to be used to ensure the group's credibility (see chapter 2, note 4).

32. Davidson, H., testimony before the National Advisory Board on Child Abuse and Neglect at the Seventh National Conference on Child Abuse and Neglect, Chicago, Ill., Nov. 12, 1985, pp. 3–4.

33. Arizona, for example, has state and county foster care review boards mandated to monitor periodically all children who have been placed in foster care by Social Services. (Author's interview with Darwin Cox, who administers the state's child abuse program, June 29, 1987.)

34. Besharov, D., 'Doing something' about child abuse: the need to narrow the grounds for state intervention. *Harvard Journal of Law and Public Policy* (Summer 1985):577.

35. Eberle, P., and Eberle, S., *The Politics of Child Abuse* (Secaucus, N.J.: Lyle Stuart, 1986), pp. 140–41.

36. Author's interview with Betty Wright, chief of Foster Care, Adoptions, Licensing, and Guardianship, Sacramento County Department of Social Welfare, July 9, 1986.

37. Author's interview with Toni Seidl, Child Abuse/Child Sexual Abuse Coordinator, Social Work Department, Children's Hospital of Philadelphia, Oct. 17, 1986.
38. The principal investigators were caseworkers Gary Winn, Diane Soares, Debra Travers, and Iris Davis of the Westchester County Department of Social Services. Their supervisor was Carol Hardesty.
39. Besharov, D., An overdose of concern: child abuse and the overreporting problem. *Regulation: American Enterprise Institute Journal on Government and Society* (Nov.–Dec. 1985):27.
40. Author's interview with Darwin Cox, May 1, 1987.
41. Author's interview with Mary Margaret Chapman, May 28, 1987.
42. Man arrested in sex abuse. (Unsigned.) *Las Vegas Sun*, Dec. 7, 1986.
43. Assistant County Attorney Ray Blase.

Index

Page numbers followed by t indicate tabular material.

About the Author

D AVID HECHLER is an investigative reporter whose work has appeared in *The New York Times*, the *Village Voice*, and the New York *Daily News*, among other publications. Before beginning his career in journalism, he was a secondary school teacher. He holds Master's degrees in teaching (Brown University) and journalism (Columbia). He lives in New York City.